# ACKNOWLEDGMENTS

How can I thank the many who have been a part of this effort? In my mind's eye, I see individuals and audiences in India, Korea, Singapore, Moldova, the UK, Germany, Luxembourg, Australia, USA, and Canada—various ages, multiple backgrounds—people listening keenly as I have delivered the lectures that form the backbone of this book. Often after a seminar, there have been those who offered comments or asked questions, and such feedback has guided future sessions. To them all, I owe a great debt.

This book is an adaptation of THE STRANGER ON THE ROAD TO EMMAUS—it "stands on the shoulders" of that product. All those who helped me with THE STRANGER are really part of BY THIS NAME—the artists: Matthew Almy, Adah Biggs, Don Dolton and Ian Mastin; the staff at GOODSEED and many, many more. Once again, thanks so much. In addition, I want to express my appreciation to Mitch Kary, Jim McCulley and Scott McGhee for their part in creating the cover.

The following are those who gave significant time or talent to the making of BY THIS NAME. To them I extend my sincere thanks.

*Ann Abeysekera, Bev Alfred, Rachel Bader, Baripaul, Christine Berwick, Corrie Bramsen, Paul Bramsen, Derek & Chantal Chen, Charles & Carol Clough, John Cook, Andrew Cross, David Cross, Paul & Kathleen Humphreys, Dr. Jayakumar, Troy & Naomi Johnstone, Jon Junkers, Richard & Ann Knowles, John Krajec, Keith Krell, Roger & Renee Laws, Tom Leger, Julie Lundy, A. Paul Martin, Chuck & Connie Mathias, Dr. Mark McDonough, Scott McGhee, Richard & Keri Nakamura, Gaetan & Ivy Pilon, Stephen C. T. & Antoinette Premkumar, Ponniah. D. Premnath, Captain Al Raithel Jr., R. Sarma Rakesh, Mohit Ramamoorthy, Lloyd Roedel, David & Miriam Schartz, R. Birlla Ravi Shanker, Akilan Sivanathan, Russ Smyth, William Tsui, T. Vithiyanandan, Kristi Whiteford, Dr. Wayne Whitbourne, Dr. Carl Wieland, Ken Woodbridge*

Last, but not least, I wish to thank my wife, my faithful companion for more than three decades. She has worked tirelessly, a full member of the team. Her support and understanding have been limitless.

To my wife, Janice E. Cross, I dedicate this book.

# CONTENTS

*by this*

# NAME

John R. Cross

Published by GoodSeed® International

# By this Name
Edition 1a

Copyright © 2007 by GOODSEED® International

All rights reserved. No portion of this book may be reproduced in any form without the written permission of the copyright holder. GOODSEED, www.goodseed.com, The Emmaus Road Message and logo design marks, are trademarks of GOODSEED International.

Published by GOODSEED® International
P.O. Box 3704, Olds, Alberta, Canada
Email: info@goodseed.com

**Library and Archives Canada Cataloguing in Publication**
Cross, John R
By this name / John R. Cross.
Includes bibliographical references and index.
ISBN 978-1-890082-03-1
1. Bible—Introductions. I. Title.
BS475.3.C756 2007          220.6'1          C2007-900937-9

Printed in Canada

To maintain ease in reading and to remain consistent with the Bible text chosen, in most cases I have used small initial letters for pronouns and certain nouns that relate to God. In areas where there might be confusion about who is being referred to, I have used capital letters consistent with traditional grammar rules.

All Bible portions are italicized and indented. Where Scripture text is boldfaced, an emphasis has been added. Square brackets in the Scripture text indicate additions for explanatory purposes.

BY THIS NAME introduces the reader to nine different translations of the Bible. None of the translations differ in content communicated or affect the accompanying commentary.

# PREFACE

We live in a world of many different belief systems. Whether you call them *religions, faiths, or cults,* what people believe cannot be ignored. History is strewn with wars and scrapping over religion. In the past these battles were fought on a local level. Now, with the advent of the global village, people of very different beliefs are being pressed up against each other, and the potential for major conflict is enormous.

It is important to know what our neighbours believe and why they believe it. Though we may never agree with them, when we know what others believe, we can disagree without being disagreeable.

By THIS NAME is about "The Holy Bible." If you are one of those who seriously wants to understand the central message of the Bible, then this book is for you.

In communicating the Bible's message, I've tried to be as objective as possible. That is not easy. By its very nature, the Bible demands a response. Nonetheless, I've sought to explain the Bible clearly, allowing it to speak for itself, but letting you draw your own conclusions. What you believe is up to you.

Some may accuse me of losing objectivity because I've communicated the Bible as fact. I've felt that it was a risk I must take as the Bible presents itself that way. To do otherwise would not be true to the text. The Bible is quite direct in what it has to say, and I was determined to avoid watering down its message or resorting to vagueness.

So read on. There is a reason for the Bible being the all-time best seller. It's a fascinating story, a story you really must know for yourself.

The Holy Bible says:

*… "Come!" And let the one who is thirsty come; let the one who wants it take the water of life free of charge.*

Revelation 22:17 NET

# CHAPTER ONE

# 1 THE UNIQUE BOOK

Over half of the world's population claims to follow all or parts of the most widely distributed and most vehemently disputed book in history. This book is called *The Holy Bible*. An additional percentage would state that it is a good book with many good things to say. These are impressive figures, but very few of the same people could explain even the most basic concepts found in the Bible.

Scholars agree that for centuries the Bible has been a best seller. It's ... *the most quoted, the most published, the most translated and the most influential book in the history of mankind.*[1] Yet, in spite of its distinction, it is a neglected volume, even among literature professors and students. A best seller? Seldom read? It doesn't make sense.

Why read it anyway? That question has many answers, but three are especially significant.

First of all, the Bible speaks about the source of joy and sorrow. It gives counsel on marriage, parenting, children, and employer/employee relationships. It talks about the wise use of money, talents, and time. It is a gold mine of facts about life in general, and much of that advice is couched in interesting stories—stories that have inspired countless books and movies.

Secondly, the Bible has much to say concerning what happens to us after we die. What makes this information so critical is that the Bible says *this life* affects the *next life*—one cannot wait till death to be informed. Then it will be too late.

Now I know there are those who say, *"I believe that when I am dead, I am dead. Nothing more!"* But that sort of thinking is like a fetus in a womb saying, *"I don't believe in life after birth. Life exists only for the here and now, right here in this dark, warm womb."*

It would be foolish for a fetus to say such a thing. No, at the very least, it would seem wise for one to investigate a book that talks about a "life to come," and see what it has to say, whether good or bad.

Thirdly, approximately 27% of the Bible is prophecy and a significant amount of it has been precisely fulfilled. Think of yourself predicting in writing the exact town in which a world-renowned leader would be born—700 years from now! In your prophecy you give the name of the town as well as the region. But at the same time, unknown to you, others have also been making prophecies about that same leader. Hundreds of years before the fact, they have been putting in writing the exact family into which this leader would be born. Still others are predicting in detail the way this leader would live and die. What would be the probability of all these things coming true?

Well, the Bible records such prophecies being fulfilled, and not only once but a multitude of times. It really is astounding! And the Bible says the reason it gave those prophecies is so that we would be "astounded" enough to pay attention to the rest of what it has to say—about life, death, and life after death!

These three areas alone are valid enough reasons to gain a basic knowledge of the book called *The Holy Bible*.

The word *Bible* is derived from the Greek and Latin word for *book*—it has no mystical implications. The word *Bible* doesn't even appear within the Bible's pages! Instead the Bible refers to itself as *Scripture*, which simply means *writings*. That both *Bible* and *Scripture* should be referred to as *holy* has greater significance. The word *holy* means *"that which is set apart, that which is different."* It has the idea of being unique. As I summarize the biblical story in the following pages, we will see just why it is called *The Holy Bible*—literally, *The Unique Book*.

# 2 PRINCIPLES OF LEARNING

Before we begin our overview, we need to establish ground rules for how we are going to proceed. As a starting point, I am going to assume that you have little acquaintance with the Holy Scriptures—perhaps no knowledge of the Bible at all. Now it might encourage you to know that by the time you have finished reading this book, the Bible will make remarkable sense. Nevertheless, read each chapter carefully, making sure you understand the content before moving on.

Many times I will be quoting directly from Scripture. When I do, it will appear as an indented paragraph in italics. At the end of each quotation I will give the *reference* or *"address"* showing its location in the Bible. It will look like this:

> *For whatever was written in earlier times was written for our instruction, so that through perseverance and the encourage-ment of the Scriptures we might have hope.*   Romans 15:4 NASB

## A PUZZLE

As we begin, think of the Bible as a large puzzle with the pieces scattered loosely before you. We will be putting those pieces together one at a time. To ensure that we assemble the biblical puzzle accurately, we will apply four *universal principles of learning* that are used in school and university classrooms every day.

### 1. The Priority Principle

The first principle states that when you study a new subject, *learn the most important information first.* For example, if a builder wants to teach a person how to construct a house, he will stress the importance of laying a firm foundation, erecting solid walls and finishing with a tight roof. He will leave till later such things as choosing furnishings or paint colours.

In the same way, the Bible covers an incredible array of topics, but not all are of equal importance. In this book we will focus on the most significant theme in the Bible. Once you understand it, the Bible will make profound but simple sense.

### 2. The Storytelling Principle

This second principle is intuitive. When one reads a story, one doesn't start in chapter ten, jump to chapter six, read chapter two and conclude in chapter nine. No! We all know that to make sense of a story, one needs to *start at the beginning and move step by step through to the end.* That may seem obvious, but many people tend to read the Bible in bits and pieces, resulting in confusion.

Since much of the Bible is a narrative, we will simply follow its natural chronological progression. At the same time, we will apply the *Priority Principle*, covering the most important stories first, stringing them together in a row, like hanging laundry on a clothesline. Since this overview is far from comprehensive, expect some gaps in the storyline.

The gaps can be filled in later after one has the overall picture. Although this clothesline cannot include every story in the Bible, the events covered will tie together in one continuous narrative.

### 3. The Mathematical Principle

The third principle takes the above progression and adds another dimension to it. *In learning, start with the simple and move to the complex.* For example, children are not taught algebra in kindergarten. Rather, they learn basic arithmetic—equations such as *one apple + one apple = two apples*. Over time they move to complicated mathematics, such as in $E=MC^2$. Teaching algebra in kindergarten would result in confused children.

It's the same way with the Bible. If you skip the basics, your biblical understanding will incorporate unusual ideas, resulting in a muddled message. To avoid that problem, we will progress through the story building on previously gained knowledge.

### 4. The Clarity Principle

The fourth principle addresses two issues. The first area has to do with the *meaning* of certain words. Over centuries word meanings can change, but the Bible has a system that locks the meaning of a word in place. To define a word, the Bible tells a story. Through the story we learn exactly what the word means. It cannot be changed. In this regard, the clarity principle advises us to *let Scripture define its own words.*

The second area has to do with the study of topics. For example, normally we study sciences by subject—such as astronomy, chemistry or biology—without mixing them. For a beginner, listening to a lecture on the solar system and on the structure of the cell at the same time would be confusing. When content is new or unfamiliar, the clarity principle advises a teacher to stick to *one subject at a time.* We will be doing just that.

As we apply these four principles, we will clearly understand the Bible's message—the puzzle will be correctly assembled.

# 3 FORTY WRITERS

Just where did the Bible come from, and how did we get it?

The Bible was written by about 40 men. These men came from every imaginable walk of life—including kings, military generals, statesmen, scholars, peasants, philosophers, shepherds, poets, fishermen, a prime minister, a doctor, a tax collector—to name just a few. Their writing crossed three continents—Asia, Africa, and Europe—with venues as diverse as palaces and dungeons, deserts and cities. They wrote during war and peace, sometimes in anguish, other times in gladness. They wrote in three languages—Hebrew, Aramaic and Greek—two languages from the east and one from the west. In all, they recorded 66 books across a span of 1,500 years. Those books, compiled into one volume, constitute the Bible.

**Although many of these 40 writers never knew each other, and though their subject matter included hundreds of controversial topics, what they recorded spoke with harmony and continuity from beginning to end.**

Now this is quite remarkable. Think about it for a moment. If we had just ten authors—all living today, all from the same generation, all in the same line of work, all coming from the same geographical background, all speaking the same language—what would be the odds of them agreeing if they were given only *one* controversial topic to write on and were unable to consult with each other? The likelihood would be extremely remote. And yet that is what happened with the Bible—not to ten men writing on one topic, but to 40 men writing on many controversial topics. Remarkable indeed! It's one of those things that makes the Bible unique—or holy.

## ONE SOURCE

So how did it happen? Simply put, none of these men claimed to be the *source* of the Bible's information. Instead they claimed a common origin for the thoughts they wrote, a source that spoke as one voice to them all.

**To discover the identity of that one source, we will launch into the biblical text, beginning with the man who wrote the first five books. His name was Moses.** We'll be starting at a point in time about 3,500 years ago, with Moses retelling the events surrounding his own birth.

## A MAN NAMED MOSES

Moses belonged to a group of slaves called *Israelites* or *Hebrews*— numbering about 2½ million—who had been in Egypt for over 350 years. The Egyptian king or *Pharaoh* was worried about their escalating population.

The story picks up with Pharaoh speaking. He said,

> "...the people of Israel are too many and too mighty for us. Come, let us deal shrewdly with them, lest they multiply, and, if war breaks out, they join our enemies and fight against us and escape from the land."
>
> Therefore they set taskmasters over them to afflict them with heavy burdens. ...But the more they were oppressed, the more they multiplied and the more they spread abroad. And the Egyptians were in dread of the people of Israel. So they ruthlessly made the people of Israel work as slaves. *Exodus 1:9-13 ESV*

When forced labor didn't whittle down the number of slaves, Pharaoh revised his plan for population control.

> Then Pharaoh, the king of Egypt, gave this order to the Hebrew midwives..."When you help the Hebrew women as they give birth, watch as they deliver. If the baby is a boy, kill him; if it is a girl, let her live."
>
> Then Pharaoh gave this order to all his people: "Throw every newborn Hebrew boy into the Nile River. But you may let the girls live." *Exodus 1:15-16,22 NLT*

Pharaoh's instructions were horrific, but even under difficult conditions, life goes on. The Scripture says a young Hebrew man took a wife and she...

> ...became pregnant and gave birth to a son. *Exodus 2:2 NLT*

Pharaoh's orders were strict. The infant boy was to be thrown into the Nile River. But the mother...

> ...hid him for three months. But when she could hide him no longer, she got him a wicker basket and covered it over with tar and pitch. Then she put the child into it and set it among the reeds by the bank of the Nile.
>
> His sister stood at a distance to find out what would happen to him. The daughter of Pharaoh came down to bathe at the Nile, with her maidens walking alongside the Nile; and she saw the basket among the reeds and sent her

*maid, and she brought it to her. When she opened it, she saw the child, and behold, the boy was crying. And she had pity on him and said, "This is one of the Hebrews' children."* Exodus 2:2-6 NASB

It's quite possible that Pharaoh's daughter wanted a child but was barren. When the baby came floating along, it was like an instant solution to her predicament. Moses' sister was watching and, when Pharaoh's daughter opened the basket, she slipped out of hiding and approached the princess.

*"Should I go and find one of the Hebrew women to nurse the baby for you?" she asked.* Exodus 2:7 NLT

Moses' sister was offering to find a slave to care for the baby.

*"Yes, do!" the princess replied. So the girl went and called the baby's mother.*

*"Take this baby and nurse him for me," the princess told the baby's mother. "I will pay you for your help." So the woman took her baby home and nursed him.* Exodus 2:8-9 NLT

Moses' mother was paid to care for her own son!

*So the woman took the child and nursed him. When the child grew up, she brought him to Pharaoh's daughter, and he became her son. She named him Moses…* Exodus 2:9-10 ESV

So it was that Moses was raised in Pharaoh's palace.

# 4 AN EDUCATION

The Holy Bible says,

*Moses was educated in all the learning of the Egyptians…*
Acts 7:22 NASB

Even a brief walk through the ruins of ancient Egypt reveals the vast breadth of knowledge Moses received—from architecture to astronomy. Woven throughout every aspect of his schooling would have been the Egyptians' all-encompassing religion.

## NO SACRED BOOK

Though the ancient Egyptians had a well-developed system of beliefs, it would be hard to nail down a unifying theme for their religion. They revered no sacred book or texts; they held no body of teaching as the ultimate test for truth. Individual towns often venerated different gods and goddesses, and even those held in high esteem changed over time.

## One God Versus Many Gods

It is still a matter of debate as to whether they worshipped one Supreme Being who manifested himself as many different gods, or whether they simply worshipped many gods.[2] Perhaps both were true. There is no doubt that the Egyptians were quite broad in their mindset, adopting new gods and adding them to the old, mixing one god's attributes with another, and holding stories as equally authoritative even when they disagreed.[3] All agree that they revered an immense pantheon of deities. Moses would have been well acquainted with all the primary gods and goddesses and probably many of the minor ones.

## The Sun God

The ancient Egyptians worshipped the sun god, *Ra*, as the supreme deity. They believed that *Ra* created himself and subsequently he created all the other gods, goddesses, humans, and animals. *Ra* was sometimes referred to as the *father of gods* or the *god of gods*. He was portrayed as a falcon with a human body and a golden disk (the sun) on his head.

## Very Religious

Although the Egyptians respected their gods, they could also be quite demanding of them at times. But the gods were not ignored. Religion pervaded every facet of life—from the use of charms, magic, and secret incantations to the public celebration of religious holidays. Even their architecture was influenced by the gods.

## Prestige Religion

Four thousand years ago the Egyptian way of life was highly respected. Their beliefs were considered the *prestige religion*.

It was in this world of ancient Egyptian thought that Moses received his esteemed education. But Moses also had the learning of a Hebrew. His true mother had cared for him as a child, and she undoubtedly tutored him in her own faith.[4] The two belief systems contradicted each other, but that made no difference to the Egyptians. They paid no attention to the Hebrew god. After all, a god of the slaves had to be very weak—no one even seemed to know the god's name!

# 5 YAHWEH

In spite of Moses' extensive Egyptian upbringing, he had not forgotten his roots.

> One day, when Moses had grown up, he went out to his people and looked on their burdens, and he saw an Egyptian beating a Hebrew, one of his people. He looked this way and that, and seeing no one, he struck down the Egyptian and hid him in the sand.

> When Pharaoh heard of it, he sought to kill Moses. But Moses fled from Pharaoh and stayed in the land of Midian.　*Exodus 2:11-12,15 ESV*

As a "man on the run," Moses took deep cover. He married a local woman, became a shepherd, and learned to lead sheep.

> Now Moses was tending the flock of Jethro his father-in-law...
> And he led the flock to the back of the desert... *Exodus 3:1 NKJV*

On this particular day he spotted a very unusual sight. Somehow a tree had burst into flames, but as Moses watched, it was evident that the wood was not being consumed. This was odd!

> So Moses thought, "I will turn aside to see this amazing sight. Why does the bush not burn up?"　*Exodus 3:3 NET*

As Moses approached the bush, a voice called out to him from within the fire.

> "Moses! Moses!"　*Exodus 3:4 NET*

You can imagine Moses' fright. Who was speaking to him from inside this burning bush? Was this some sort of god or goddess?

> And Moses said, "Here I am."

> God said, "Do not approach any closer! Take your sandals off your feet, for the place where you are standing is holy ground."
> *Exodus 3:4-5 NET*

Moses must have been bewildered! Why was this ground considered holy—*unique, one-of-a-kind?* If the voice was that of a god, who might it be? Before Moses could say a word, the mysterious voice spoke again.

> *"I am the God of your father, the God of Abraham, the God of Isaac and the God of Jacob."*                      Exodus 3:6 NET

## GOD

The word *god* is a generic word meaning *strong one, mighty leader, deity,* and can be used in reference to any god. It's a broad term. But this god specifically identified himself as the god of Moses' father, and then he mentioned three names: Abraham, Isaac, and Jacob. These three men were long-deceased relatives of Moses—the founding fathers of the Israelite nation, the nation of slaves. Clearly it was the god of the slaves speaking directly from the burning bush—not *Ra* or any of the other Egyptian gods.

Moses had heard stories from his mother about the god who conversed with Abraham, Isaac, and Jacob, but that was long ago. Some wondered if those stories were true. Besides that, an Egyptian scholar would have told you that the gods never stooped to speak to a mere human. They were always distant, silent, or spoke through a temple priest. But now here was the god of the slaves speaking directly to Moses from a burning bush—as one person speaks to another. Truly this god was unique! The Bible says,

> *…Moses hid his face, because he was afraid to look at God.*
> Exodus 3:6 NET

God spoke again.

> *"I have indeed seen the misery of my people in Egypt. I have heard them crying out because of their slave drivers, and I am concerned about their suffering. So I have come down to rescue them from the hand of the Egyptians and to bring them up out of that land into a good and spacious land…*
>
> *So now, go. I am sending you to Pharaoh to bring my people the Israelites out of Egypt."*                      Exodus 3:7-8,10 NIV

Moses was terrified! He had been a fugitive for forty years. His return to Egypt might be tolerated but it was doubtful Pharaoh would welcome his reappearance. How could he ever confront the most powerful man on earth and demand the release of all his slaves? And would his own Hebrew kinsmen accept him as their spokesman?

*Then Moses said to God, "If I come to the people of Israel and say to them, 'The God of your fathers has sent me to you,' and they ask me, 'What is his name?' what shall I say to them?"*

Exodus 3:13 ESV

## POWER?

We don't really know why Moses requested the god's personal name. One possibility relates to the Egyptian beliefs about the source of strength. According to their thinking, each god had a varying degree of power protected by the secret name of the deity. If you knew the god's private name, you also possessed that god's strength and ability.

Since this is what Moses had been taught concerning the Egyptian gods, perhaps he wondered if it also applied to the god of the Hebrew slaves. Conceivably Moses thought that if he could discover the name of the Hebrew god, then he would be better equipped to face a mighty man like Pharaoh. But there was a catch. Moses knew that the Egyptians believed that none of their deities ever disclosed their personal names. But maybe the god of the slaves would be different. What motivated Moses to ask for a name we really don't know, but the reply was certainly clear.

*God said to Moses, "I AM WHO I AM. This is what you are to say to the Israelites: 'I AM has sent me to you.'"*

*God also said to Moses, "Say to the Israelites, '[YAHWEH], the God of your fathers—the God of Abraham, the God of Isaac and the God of Jacob—has sent me to you.' This is my name forever…"*

Exodus 3:14-15 NIV

## THE NAME

In the original language, the phrase *I AM* and the name Y$_{AHWEH}$[5] (yah´way) are essentially synonymous; they both mean: *I AM the one who is*, or *I AM the self-existent one*.

The god of the slaves, by his very name, was claiming to live by his own power. Whereas mankind needed food, water, air, sleep, light, shelter—an endless supply of essential items to live—this god was saying he needed nothing. Apparently this was so true that it was an intrinsic part of his name. He was the *self-existent one*, the *I AM*—Y$_{AHWEH}$. No Egyptian god or goddess claimed this. The god of the slaves was truly unique!

## YAHWEH

The ancient Israelites were in such awe of YAHWEH that in the centuries to come they refused to speak his name. In reading the Scriptures out loud, wherever they came to the word YAHWEH they would simply say "LORD" or "THE NAME" with everyone understanding that it was actually referring to YAHWEH. Even to this day, when you read God's answer to Moses, it is written using the substitute word LORD in place of YAHWEH.

> God also said to Moses, "Say this to the people of Israel, 'The LORD, the God of your fathers, the God of Abraham, the God of Isaac, and the God of Jacob, has sent me to you.' This is my name forever..."
> Exodus 3:15 ESV

So, in the Bible, whenever you see the name LORD, with all the letters capitalized, understand it as the ancients understood it. You are actually reading YAHWEH—the personal name of this unique god. To help us remember that connection I will sometimes refer to this god as LORD YAHWEH. Also, in the Holy Scripture, wherever you see the word god capitalized, as in God, it is referring to YAHWEH.

Some scholars feel Moses was the first person to know this unique God's personal name. He was to tell everyone about him, that he was called YAHWEH. It was a name intended to be on everyone's lips. And unlike the ancient Egyptian gods and goddesses, the LORD God was not threatened by someone stealing his power.

> LORD, there is no one like you! For you are great, and your name is full of power.
> Jeremiah 10:6 NLT

## SUMMARY

1. The generic name **god** means *strong one, mighty leader, deity*. Many other gods and goddesses are mentioned in the Bible. To differentiate between them, when YAHWEH is referred to, god is always spelled with a capital "G" as in God.

2. YAHWEH is often referred to as the *holy* God, meaning *unique, different, one-of-a-kind*.

3. Many centuries after the time of Moses, for purposes of respect, the personal name of YAHWEH was not spoken aloud. Even when written, it was substituted with the word LORD, as indicated by all the letters being capitalized.

4. The phrase *I AM* and the name YAHWEH are synonymous, both meaning *I AM the self-existent one*.

### THE POWER IN A NAME

This story is not found in the Bible—it is from Egyptian mythology.
It illustrates the type of thinking prevalent in the time of Moses.

A story involving "power" is centered on the Egyptian sun god, *Ra* and his granddaughter, *Isis*—a goddess with aspirations to reign over heaven and earth. Jealous of *Ra's* immense power, *Isis* asked him for his secret name. Of course, *Ra* did not divulge it. But that did not end the story. *Isis* privately created a venomous snake and put it in *Ra's* path. As *Ra* took his daily journey across the sky, he "stepped" on the snake only to be bitten severely. As he cried out in pain, other gods and goddesses offered help, but none could relieve his misery.

Finally, *Isis* came forward. She promised to heal *Ra*, but only if he revealed his personal name. Well, of course *Ra* was not willing to do this. He stalled, and then with great reluctance, began to divulge names to her. This did not impress *Isis* who knew that *Ra* was trying to confuse her with fake personal names. She waited and waited. Finally, *Ra*, in deep agony, passed his secret name on to *Isis* and was healed.

As the story goes, *Isis* became a powerful goddess, equal to *Ra*. Often referred to as the *Queen of Heaven, Isis* was adopted by the Greeks and Romans along with many other nations, as the *mother of gods*.

An important distinction between *Ra* and Y*AHWEH* is that the L*ORD* Y*AHWEH* made no attempt to conceal his personal name. Instead, he told Moses to reveal his name to the entire world. Moses did just that when he penned the first five books of the Holy Bible.

# 6 God-Breathed

Moses' encounter with the LORD YAHWEH at the burning bush was just one of many exchanges to come. Moses was the first of the 40 men who recorded the 66 books that constitute the Bible. All of those men except one were Israelites.[6] And it was the LORD YAHWEH who spoke as the one voice—the common source for those 40 men—giving the Scripture its unique continuity and harmony.

## God-Breathed

The LORD did not dictate Scripture to Moses as an executive would to a secretary. Rather, the process was paralleled to *breathing*.

> *All Scripture is God-breathed …*[7]       *2 Timothy 3:16 NIV*

The whole concept of the LORD *breathing out* Scripture is a study in itself. Just as when one exhales his breath, that breath comes from his innermost being, so ultimately all Scripture was to be viewed as coming directly from the LORD YAHWEH himself. God and his words are inseparable, which is one reason the Bible is also referred to as *God's Word*.

> *Your word, O LORD, is eternal; it stands firm…*       *Psalm 119:89 NIV*

In the chapters to come, the story will unfold the foolproof system the LORD used to transfer his *Word* to these 40 writers. You'll be able to judge for yourself whether this system prevented con artists from "fabricating Scripture" and passing it off as coming from God. For now, it is important to understand that all 40 men wrote under the same God-inspired guidance.

## Extreme Accuracy

The LORD's words were first written on a scroll, usually an animal skin called *parchment*, or on paper made from the stem of a plant called *papyrus*. The originals were called *autographs*.

Since the autographs had a limited life span, copies were made of the scrolls. Of course, all of this was done by hand. The writers' awareness that what was being recorded was the LORD's own Word resulted in one of the most remarkable reproduction jobs ever done. In writing the Hebrew text,

*"They used every imaginable safeguard, no matter how cumbersome or laborious, to ensure the accurate transmission of the text. The number of letters in a book was counted and its middle letter was given. Similarly with the words, and again the middle word was noted."*[8]

This was done with both the copy and the original autograph to ensure that they were exactly the same.

These scribes were so accurate in their transcription that when the Dead Sea Scrolls were found (written in 100 BC), and compared with manuscripts resulting from centuries of copying and recopying to a period of time 1,000 years later (900 AD), there were no significant differences in the text.[9]

Dead Sea Scrolls

essentially no change in 1000 years of making copies

Previous Oldest Manuscript

100 BC ————————————————————— 900 AD

Josephus, a descendant of the Hebrew slaves and a historian from the first century AD, summed it up for his people when he stated, "... *how firmly we have given credit to those books of our own nation, is evident by what we do; for during so many ages as have already passed, no one has been so bold as either to add anything to them, to take anything from them, or to make any change in them; but it [is] natural to all [Israelites] ... to esteem those books ... divine."* [10]

These men were absolutely convinced that to meddle with the text was to tamper with the LORD himself. We have ample reason to be assured that what we have today is essentially the same as what the 40 men wrote.

### TRANSLATIONS

Both the autographs and copies were initially transcribed in Hebrew, Aramaic, and Greek. Since many of us do not know these tongues, the Scripture has been translated into many other languages. These translations work from early texts that find their roots in the ancient past. It has been said that the Bible may have been tampered with—changed—so that prophecies would appear to have been fulfilled. But with the finding of the Dead Sea Scrolls and the ability to reach far back in history to see what had been written, reliable scholars agree that no such thing has happened. It is interesting that the ancient writers recorded the LORD himself as saying,

> The grass withers, the flower fades, But the Word of our God stands forever.                    *Isaiah 40:8 NASB*

*…until heaven and earth pass away, not the smallest letter or stroke shall pass from the Law [the five books written by Moses] until all is accomplished.*                    Matthew 5:18 NASB

### FORTY YEARS

We don't know specifically when or where Moses recorded all that the LORD YAHWEH told him, but we do know it would have been written in the last 40 years of his life. We will be following some of his experiences as we continue. As you read, keep in mind that the Bible claims to be the Word of the LORD. We are told that through its pages we can become acquainted with YAHWEH himself. The LORD says,

*"…you will seek Me and find Me, when you search for Me with all your heart."*                    Jeremiah 29:13 NKJV

---

### NAVIGATION AIDS

As we begin to navigate through the 66 books found in the Bible, it is useful to know that each book is divided into chapters, and each chapter into verses. Many Bibles also include historical introductions, footnotes, cross-references, maps, and a concordance. These can be helpful, but we need to be clear in our minds that these "extras" were not part of the Scripture that was given to the 40 writers. They were added by men commenting on the Bible's content.

It is also helpful to understand that the Scriptures are divided into two major sections—the Old and New Testament. Historically, the Old Testament portion was divided into three categories:

1.  The Law of Moses: This section is sometimes referred to as *The Torah, The Books of Moses,* or *The Law.*

2.  The Writings: Sometimes called the *Psalms.*

3.  The Prophets

In the Bible, the phrase, "the Law and the Prophets," is a way of referring to the entire *Old Testament* portion, a part that comprises approximately two-thirds of the Scriptures. The remaining one-third is referred to as the *New Testament.*

# CHAPTER TWO

# 1 IN THE BEGINNING

As Moses wrote the first five books of the Bible, he must have felt like he was back in school again. Certainly he received an education in the process. The Israelites of that day knew very little about their God; so much of what they learned was new.

## FOUR WORDS

The first book was called *Genesis*, which means *beginnings*. Genesis opens with four very profound words.

> In the beginning God...                     Genesis 1:1 NASB

The Bible does not begin with arguments for the existence of YAHWEH—the LORD is just there. He has always existed!

This would have been astonishing news to both Egyptian and Israelite. Even *Ra* had a beginning—the ancients said *Ra* created himself![1] But YAHWEH was saying that he had been there all along. He had always existed, before plants, animals, people—before the earth and the universe. Moses wrote,

> ...from everlasting [past] to everlasting [future] You are God.
>                                             Psalm 90:2 NASB

The gods of the ancient Egyptians were born and grew old with time, but the Bible said the LORD had not only existed from eternity past, but he would live forever.

Since our bodies are finite—living on earth for only a short time—the concept of an eternal God is difficult for us to grasp. But there are illustrations to help our comprehension. For example, we can compare eternity with the cosmos.

Most of us can fathom our solar system—the sun surrounded by orbiting planets. We know it is vast, but space probes have made even the farthest distances seem reachable.

But go a step further and begin to measure the universe. If we were to climb into a spaceship and travel at the speed of light, we would circle the earth seven times in one second! Heading out into space at the same speed, we would pass the moon in two seconds, Mars in four minutes, and Pluto in five hours. From there you are off into our galaxy, the Milky Way.

At the speed of light you circle the earth seven times in one second...

...pass the Moon in two seconds...

...and Pluto in five hours.

Mars in four minutes...

There are 60 seconds in a minute. If you travel at the speed of light you will go 300,000 kilometres or 186,000 miles in just one second. Think how far you would go in a minute, in one hour, in a day, or in a year! At the speed of light, it would take 4.3 years to reach the closest star, which means each second of those years you travel 186,000 miles or 300,000 kilometres—a total distance equivalent to 25,284,000,000,000 miles or 40,682,300,000,000 kilometres!

Our star, the sun, is near the edge of the Milky Way Galaxy. Our entire solar system with its orbiting planets could fit in this box.

# THE MILKY WAY GALAXY [2]

The band of stars you see in the night sky is part of a gigantic family of stars called the Milky Way Galaxy. Travelling at the speed of light, it would take 100,000 years to cross it from one side to the other. There are an estimated 100 billion galaxies in the universe, many comprising billions of stars. Galaxies come in clusters and super-clusters. There are about twenty galaxies in our cluster, and thousands of galaxies in our super-cluster.

**Want a star named after you?** [3]
Based on the present population of the earth, you could have 16 galaxies named after you. That means *billions* of stars could carry your name!

At the speed of light, you will reach the next closest galaxy in 2,000,000 years...

...and the next closest cluster of galaxies in 20,000,000 years.

At this point you have only begun to travel the known universe.

Yes, the thought of eternity is difficult to grasp, but so is the vastness of our universe. Both are mind-boggling, yet both are real. And when it comes to the eternality of the LORD God, the Bible speaks emphatically on this point. It says he is eternal, and his *forever existence* is such an inherent part of his nature that it is used as one of his names.

> *…the name of the LORD, the everlasting God…*   Genesis 21:33 KJV

# 2 A PERSON

One time I was discussing the Bible with a young couple when suddenly the husband stopped me and with a puzzled voice said, *"The way you talk about God is as if he were a person."*

I said, *"Yes, that is correct."* I then asked him what he was thinking.

*"Well,"* he said, *"I've never thought of God that way before. I guess I always thought he was some sort of… some sort of force."*

I assured him that the Scripture defines the LORD YAHWEH as a living being—with character and personality—not as some sort of universal force or divine mind.

## ONE YAHWEH, MANY NAMES

One of the ways the Bible reveals to us the *personality of God* is through his names. Though it is appropriate to say that God has only one *personal name*, he has other names that function as titles, all declaring something about his character. For example, YAHWEH is often called the *Most High.*

> That they may know that You alone, whose name is the LORD
> [YAHWEH], are the Most High over all the earth.  Psalm 83:18 NASB

The name *Most High* emphasizes the LORD's role as a sovereign ruler. Just as ancient empires had absolute leaders or sovereigns who reigned over their domains, so YAHWEH is King of the universe.

We know that the ancient Egyptians believed that *Ra* was the chief god, and that all the other gods and goddesses were created by him. *But was the LORD YAHWEH the chief God in a family of gods? Did he have other gods and goddesses under him? Was the name YAHWEH just another name for the god Ra?*

First of all, it is very important to understand that YAHWEH is *not* another name for *Ra* or for that matter, any other god. Secondly, the Scripture speaks of many gods and goddesses, but they are *not* part of a family of gods with the LORD at the top. As we progress in the story, we will see where the other gods fit in the puzzle, but for now, all we need to know is that…

> … the LORD … is the living God and the everlasting King.
>
> Jeremiah 10:10 NASB

The idea of LORD YAHWEH being king may conjure up an image of an old man seated on a gold throne floating somewhere in the stratosphere. Though the Bible nowhere illustrates the LORD as an old man, it does refer to his throne—not set in a cloud, but rather situated in a perfect place called *Heaven.*

> The LORD is on his heavenly throne. Psalm 11:4 NIV

The Bible tells us that the LORD rules from Heaven. We don't know much about this place, but the little we do know is wonderful. We will discuss Heaven in greater detail later on.

## A SPIRIT

In the Bible the LORD is referred to using the male gender, as in *he* and *him*. This does not mean he has sexual characteristics as do humans. YAHWEH is not like *Ra* or any of the other Egyptian deities—he has no wives or children. The Bible tells us that,

> God is spirit… John 4:24 NASB

The ancients often illustrated their deities as part animal, part human. No such depiction was ever attempted of YAHWEH, since being a spirit he cannot be seen—he doesn't have a body of flesh.

Think of a funeral of a friend who has died. If the casket was open, you may have seen the body, but where was your friend? He was gone; your friend's spirit was no longer present. When we look at someone, we only see their house, the human body; we don't actually see the real person, the spirit. In the same way, YAHWEH cannot be seen because he is a spirit, but he still has all the attributes of a person—having character and personality.

## SUMMARY

We have barely commenced our study, but already we have learned quite a bit about the LORD YAHWEH.

He is an eternal being—not an impersonal force.

He is a spirit—without physical body or bodily functions.

He is the *Most High*, the Sovereign Ruler of all.

And that's the way it was—*In the beginning*…

# 3 Angels and Stars

We now read another word which follows the first four words that Moses wrote.

> In the beginning God **created** …  Genesis 1:1 NASB

The LORD's first creative act is scattered across the pages of Scripture. You can pull together enough information to answer simple questions, but that is where it stops. The Bible was not written to satisfy man's endless curiosity. It gives basic information on some events, but when it comes to further details, the pages fall silent. This is precisely the case with the subject of spirit beings.

## NAMES

The Bible calls spirits by many different names. We often call them *angels*, but the Scripture uses many terms to define them: *cherubim, seraphim, angels, archangels, morning stars*—the list goes on. Collectively they are referred to as *multitudes, hosts,* or *stars.** These spirits are not abstract impersonal forces as one might see in certain movies, but rather they are *persons* or *beings* capable of thought and feeling.

*Not to be confused with stars in the sky.

> The host of heaven worships You [YAHWEH].  Nehemiah 9:6 NKJV

They may all have individual names but only a few are mentioned, such as *Gabriel* and *Michael*.

## INVISIBLE, INNUMERABLE

As with the LORD, spirits are invisible, having no bodies of flesh and blood like you and me. Even though we can't see them, they must be everywhere. The idiom used to number just those surrounding God's throne communicates an unfathomable sum.

> Then I looked, and I heard the voice of many angels around the throne, … and the number of them was ten thousand times ten thousand, and thousands of thousands.  Revelation 5:11 NKJV

Now this leads us to a question. *Since we saw that the LORD's throne is in Heaven, does this mean that Heaven is the angels' dwelling place?* Well, whether angels need a home or not is highly debatable, but taking the body of Scripture as a whole, it would seem that angels are based in Heaven yet can travel anywhere in the universe. The Bible is clear that angels—as spirits—do not live in temples, houses, rocks, trees, or rivers.

## SERVANTS

At this point it would be reasonable to ask ourselves, *"Since the Bible speaks about many different gods, are angels gods or goddesses?"* The simple answer is, no, they are neither. Rather, they are spirit beings created to serve the LORD YAHWEH and do his pleasure. They are called *ministering spirits.*

> *Are not all angels ministering spirits sent to serve…?*
>
> Hebrews 1:14 NIV

The word *angel* is derived from a Greek term meaning *messenger* or *servant*. Because the LORD made them, they belonged to him and did whatever YAHWEH asked them to do.

## CREATOR–OWNER

The concept of the *creator* also being the *owner* has lost its strength in our money-driven economy. I remember walking through a tribal village in Papua New Guinea. Every item I asked about—*"Whose paddle is this?" "Whose canoe is that?"*—elicited a response that designated an owner. When I inquired how they knew who the owner was, they looked at me in disbelief. Apparently I had asked a dumb question. To them it was obvious. *"The owner is the one who made it!"* The creator-owner connection was very strong.

Since the LORD created the angels it was not out of place for them to be considered his possessions. And since they belonged to him, they were to do his bidding—as his servants and messengers. This was not some ancient form of servitude. There are no parallels here to forced bondage. The angels could have had no better Creator-Owner.

## EXTRAORDINARY INTELLECT AND POWER

To carry out his directives, the LORD created the angels with great intellect and power. They were created as perfect beings without any evil. But they weren't robots either; they each had a will which gave them the ability to choose.[4] This is significant.

The Scripture often speaks of the angels praising the LORD as they go about their work. The word *praise* means *to speak of the excellence of a person, to show admiration.*

> *Praise the Lord, you angels, you mighty ones who carry out his plans, listening for each of his commands. Yes, praise the LORD, you armies of angels who serve him and do his will!*
>
> Psalm 103:20-21 NLT

But praise is meaningless if not given freely. Let me illustrate using a different form of human expression—sympathy.

For a while I spent time in a country where it was common to have paid mourners. At a funeral there would be a separate group of people wailing and weeping intensely. It was heart-rending to watch, but they could shut it off instantly, especially if they decided they were not being paid enough. The sympathy they expressed looked real, but it was not genuine. It was empty of meaning.

If the angels had been programmed like robots to praise the LORD, it would have been as empty as the hired sympathy; but since they were created with a free will, any expression of joy, love, or appreciation was genuine. In the Bible the praise of YAHWEH is often connected to the concept of *worship*.

> *You preserve them all, and the angels of heaven worship you.*
>
> Nehemiah 9:6 NLT

## WORSHIP

The word *worship* has the idea of showing someone profound love and admiration because you consider that person *worthy* of esteem. It's a form of praise. In this case the angels worship God.

This is only fitting since the LORD is the Sovereign King and, as such, rightly deserves to be held in high esteem. By way of contrast, if I am boasting about a friend's deeds, someone else could call into question whether my friend deserves as much praise as I'm giving him. But the Bible says the LORD is truly worthy of honour, so the angels are quite right in directing their praise toward YAHWEH—to worship him and him alone.

> *You are worthy, O Lord, to receive glory and honor and power; for You created all things, And by Your will they exist and were created.* Revelation 4:11 NKJV

## SIMILAR BUT DIFFERENT

It should be noted that angels share some similarities with man, though man is not nearly as powerful or intelligent. The Bible says that the LORD YAHWEH made man...

> *...a little lower than the angels...* Psalm 8:5 NKJV

Though similar, angels are distinct from man. They never die.[5] They neither marry nor reproduce.[6] Though normally unseen, on certain assignments they make themselves visible. When they talk to man, the language they use is understandable to the hearer.

Because angels do at times mingle with and talk to people, the Bible states that there are occasions when these spirit beings have been confused with God or gods. But as we saw before, the LORD YAHWEH created them, and they are distinct from him. They are neither gods nor part of the LORD God. Just as a canoe paddle does not fit in the "maker" or "creator" category, angelic beings do not fit in the "God" category. They are distinctly different. One is the Creator, the other is the *created*.

| Role | Category | Personal Name(s) |
|---|---|---|
| Creator | God | YAHWEH |
| created | spirit being (angel) | Gabriel, Michael |

## THE ANOINTED CHERUB

The most powerful, the most intelligent, and the most beautiful spirit ever created was a cherub. Some Bible editions directly translate his name into Latin as *Lucifer*, but the original Hebrew name means *shining one* or *star of the morning*.

> O shining one, son of the dawn! *Isaiah 14:12 YLT*

The *Shining One* was referred to as an *anointed cherub*. The meaning of the word *anointed* has its origins in the ancient rite of pouring oil on *someone* or *something* to set it apart for a special task. The act of anointing was considered sacred and not to be taken lightly.

> "You were an anointed guardian cherub…You were blameless in your ways from the day you were created…"
> *Ezekiel 28:14-15 ESV*

The *Shining One's* job description kept him in the presence of the LORD at all times. We will learn more about this anointed cherub as the story progresses.

## THE ANGELS WATCH

With the creation of the spirit beings, the LORD's creative acts had begun. Now, as all the angelic host watched and rejoiced, the *Most High* embarked on his next great work—the creation of the entire universe.

> "Where were you when I laid the foundations of the earth? Tell me, if you know so much. Who determined its dimensions and stretched out the surveying line? What supports its foundations, and who laid its cornerstone as the morning stars [or spirit beings] sang together and all the angels shouted for joy? *Job 38:4-7 NLT*

# CHAPTER THREE

# 1 JUST BY SPEAKING

The first twelve chapters of Genesis contain critical information for understanding Scripture as a whole. If the Bible were assembly instructions for the puzzle we talked about earlier, then these chapters would be among those labeled, "Read Carefully."

When we say that the LORD instructed Moses to write about the *beginnings*, we mean that quite literally. God had Moses record what occurred on the very first day the earth existed.

### DAY ONE

> *In the beginning God created the heavens and the earth ... God said, "Let there be light." And there was light! God saw that the light was good ... God called the light "day" and the darkness "night." There was evening, and there was morning, marking the first day.* Genesis 1:1,3-5 NET

Notice how God did the creating. The text says that the LORD *spoke* the light into existence. He didn't use hands or tools to create. Rather, the Bible says the whole ...

> *... universe was formed at God's command ...* Hebrews 11:3 NLT

This great person, this great being—YAHWEH—created all we see and don't see, simply by speaking!

Also notice, he made everything out of nothing. We as humans create, but only with pre-existing material. We paint pictures using oils and canvas. We build houses out of wood, mortar, and brick. But when the LORD created, he used nothing. He just spoke!

> *"Let there be light ..."* Genesis 1:3 KJV

... and there was light! And day one was completed.

### DAY TWO

At the conclusion of day one, the earth as created was completely covered with water. Now, on day two,

> *... God said, "Let there be an expanse in the midst of the waters and let it separate water from water." ... God called the expanse "sky." There was evening, and there was morning, a second day.* Genesis 1:6-8 NET

The expanse[1] was probably synonymous with what we call the *atmosphere*. The earth's *atmosphere* and *water* are just two of many features that make life possible on this planet.

On day two we see the first indication that the world as originally created was different than what we now know. It seems it had a different atmosphere and was universally warmer. Later on we will read about the circumstances that may have changed the environment to its present state.

### Day Three

At the beginning of day three, the water under the expanse still constituted one vast ocean with no visible dry land.

> God said, "Let the water under the sky be gathered to one place and let dry ground appear." It was so…God saw that it was good. God said, "Let the land produce vegetation: plants yielding seeds according to their kinds, and trees bearing fruit with seed in it according to their kinds."…God saw that it was good. There was evening, and there was morning, the third day.
>
> *Genesis 1:9-13 NET*

Day three can be divided into two parts. First, we see the dry land appear. Apparently, as the ocean bottom sank forming huge basins for the water, dry ground rose up out of the watery depths. Second, we see the creation of plant life—plants and trees that were already bearing fruit and seeds. The Bible says God created everything in a mature, fully functioning state.

I remember discussing this one time with some children. I asked them to gather as many different seeds as they could find in five minutes. They came trooping back with a whole assortment—seeds with barbs, seeds made to sail on the wind, those that popped when heated; some the size of a speck, others much larger. I explained how each tiny seed contained a massive encyclopedia of instructions stating how that seed should grow—whether its leaves should be broad or narrow, green or red; whether its stem should be delicate as ivy or sturdy as a tree trunk—when it should grow, how fast, how tall, on and on. It also contained instructions on how to manufacture more seeds. When you think about it, the whole process is incredible, something no human has ever come close to duplicating. Yet the Bible says the Lord Yahweh created full-grown plants and trees with all their genetic information, simply by speaking them into existence. Amazing!

> Great are the works of the Lord; They are studied by all who delight in them.
>
> *Psalm 111:2 NASB*

Creation was a solo effort. No other god was involved.

> For thus says the LORD, Who created the heavens, Who is God,
> Who formed the earth and made it, Who has established it,
> Who did not create it in vain, Who formed it to be inhabited:
> "I am the LORD, and there is no other."          Isaiah 45:18 NKJV

Only the LORD was capable of making what we see and don't see.

# 2 THREE ATTRIBUTES

One doesn't have to be a rocket scientist to know that someone who could create this immense universe must also be extraordinarily powerful. The Scripture actually takes it a step further. It tells us that the LORD is **all-powerful**.

> Great is our Lord, and mighty in power...          Psalm 147:5 NKJV

Not only is YAHWEH all-powerful, he is also **all-knowing**. You can see aspects of this knowledge revealed in the complexity of what he created. The Bible says...

> ...his understanding is beyond measure.          Psalm 147:5 ESV

What's more, when one looks at the vastness of creation, one has to conclude that the Creator must have ability to move far and wide, to place the things he has created wherever he wants them. Once again, the Bible takes it beyond what we can observe. It tells us that the LORD YAHWEH is **everywhere present at the same time**.

> "Am I only a God nearby," declares the LORD, "and not a God
> far away? Can anyone hide in secret places so that I cannot
> see him?" declares the LORD. "Do not I fill heaven and earth?"
> declares the LORD.          Jeremiah 23:23-24 NIV

Only YAHWEH possesses this triad of attributes—**all-knowing, all-powerful, and everywhere present at one time**—and only a faultless combination of these three attributes would be able to create the complex realm in which we live.

> He has made the earth by His power; He has established the
> world by His wisdom And stretched out the heaven by His
> understanding.          Jeremiah 51:15 NKJV

In Scripture no other god or goddess is ascribed these characteristics. Neither do the angels possess these abilities, even as powerful and intelligent as they are. And us? We don't even come close to this sort of capability.

For us to construct even the simplest object takes combined human effort. For example, let's say we decide to make a simple chair—the kind you find in a school auditorium.

For starters we need metal. *But where do you find metal?*

In rocks. *But who knows which stones contain the required metal?*

We need a geologist and a prospector who know a great deal about finding the rocks which carry iron ore.

*Assuming we have found the right rocks, what's the next step?*

We need someone with the know-how to manufacture dynamite and assorted mining equipment. We need miners who have the expertise to extract the ore safely from the ground.

*But you still can't build a chair with a mound of iron ore. It needs to be melted down. Can you build a fire hot enough to melt rocks?*

We need those who know the smelting and alloy process. *So we found those fellows, but guess what?*

They just poured for us a glob of steel. At this point we might be willing to sit on the ingot—after it has cooled down, that is! But if we are going to make a chair, it will necessitate having someone who understands how to roll that block into a thin sheet of metal, bend it into a tube and then weld it.

*Welding?* Sounds like we need someone with knowledge in electricity and how to generate it.

As you can see, making a chair is a complicated process. And we haven't even discussed the plastic parts.

*Plastic?* Hmmm. Doesn't that get into petroleum products? Now let me see. Drilling a well to find oil takes…??!!

And all we wanted to do was make a chair. To create even the simplest object takes hundreds of people with combined knowledge and allied skills. No one person knows it all.

No human, no god, no angel, no spirit can be compared in even the smallest way to the LORD, the Creator God, who knows all things, who has all the power to create from nothing, and is present everywhere—so that he can place the objects he has made wherever he chooses. This God stands alone.

> *Ah, Lord GOD! Behold, You have made the heavens and the earth by Your great power and outstretched arm. There is nothing too hard for You.* Jeremiah 32:17 NKJV

## A Person

Not all the attributes of the LORD are equally comprehensible. Somehow it's easier for us to envision God being *all-powerful* and *all-knowing* than to see him being *present in all places at the same time*. But over and over again, the Scripture teaches us that the Creator God is everywhere-present.

In the 10th century BC, a leader of the Israelites wrote these words as he was directed by God:

> Where can I go from your Spirit? Where can I flee from your presence?
>
> If I go up to the heavens, you are there; if I make my bed in the depths, you are there. If I rise on the wings of the dawn, if I settle on the far side of the sea, even there your hand will guide me, your right hand will hold me fast. If I say, "Surely the darkness will hide me and the light become night around me," even the darkness will not be dark to you; the night will shine like the day, for darkness is as light to you.   Psalm 139:7–12 NIV

The fact that the LORD is *everywhere at one time* needs to be differentiated from the concept of *pantheism*.

Pantheism is such a broad concept it is hard to define, but generally speaking, it is the belief that all of nature—from single cell bacteria to the entire cosmos—is somehow part of a god, indeed *is* god. It teaches that this universe-god has a cosmic soul, mind or consciousness with which a person can develop oneness. In pantheism, god is an impersonal force—a universal "all in all."

Moses would have recognized aspects of pantheistic thinking. The ancient Egyptians believed the lines between god, human, animal, bird, insect, wood, and water were quite blurred. Many of their gods had human bodies, but those bodies had the heads of animals, birds or insects. They believed objects could talk, giving them a form of "god-ness." Everything had some sort of life force, so that when corn was harvested and crushed to flour, a farmer was, in essence, cutting the body of the corn god and trampling it to pieces on the threshing floor.

### Creator-Creation Distinction

In contrast, the Bible teaches that the LORD is a *person* or *being* who is separate from his creation. Just as a tribal man is not part of his canoe paddle, so neither is the LORD God part of his creation.

Indeed the paddle could be damaged or destroyed and it would have no effect on the tribal man at all. It's not part of him.

In the same way, the Scripture tells us that Yahweh created the universe and all that is in it, but the universe is not part of God nor is the Lord part of his creation. The Lord God is everywhere, but he is **not in** or **part of** everything. He is above creation and rules over it. The Bible makes a clear distinction between the Creator and his creation, a distinction that it never blurs.

| Role | Category | Name(s) |
|---|---|---|
| Creator | God | Yahweh |
| created | spirit being | Gabriel, Michael |
| created | plant, tree | Fern, Palm, Cedar, etc. |

# 3 Order and Laws

It seems every nation had its own ideas about origins. Moses would have known that the Egyptians had four stories relating to the beginning of the earth, though none of them agreed with the other. Such confusion is common. But now it was as if the Lord was saying, *"Since none of you were around in the beginning, I'm going to tell you how the world began—to stop speculation. This is the way it was done."*

> By the **word** of the Lord the heavens were made, And all the host of them by the breath of His **mouth** … Let all the earth fear the Lord; Let all the inhabitants of the world stand in awe of Him. For **He spoke**, and it was done; **He commanded**, and it stood fast. *Psalm 33:6,8-9 NKJV*

When you really think about it, this is the sort of power you would expect from an all-powerful God.

## Day Four

On the first day of creation, the Lord had drawn back the curtain of darkness when he spoke light into existence. On the fourth day, God created the light-givers.[2] Moses wrote:

> God said, "Let there be lights in the expanse of the sky to separate the day from the night, and let them be signs to indicate seasons and days and years, and let them serve as lights in the expanse of the sky to give light on the earth." It was so.

*God made two great lights—the greater light to rule over the day and the lesser light to rule over the night. He made the stars also.*

*God saw that it was good. There was evening, and there was morning, a fourth day.* Genesis 1:14-16,18-19 NET

We have already learned that the ancient Egyptians worshipped the sun god, *Ra.* They also revered *Thoth,* the moon god.* Back then the people had no way of knowing that the sun and moon were just objects of gas or rock. But now, going solely by what the LORD had Moses write, they could know that the sun and moon were not gods. Rather, they were lifeless *created* objects, distinct from the Creator. The LORD told Moses,

*Though *Thoth* was the moon god, he was illustrated as having a human body with the head of a bird, the *Ibis.*

*"And when you look up into the sky and see the sun, moon, and stars ... don't be seduced into worshiping them."*
Deuteronomy 4:19 NLT

The sun and moon were not to be admired and esteemed as though they were persons. They had no intellect or feelings. They were nothing more than inanimate gas and rock, belonging in the same category as rivers and mountains.

In contrast, the LORD was a living being totally distinct from the sun or moon. The *Maker* was not to be misunderstood as being part of what he *made.*

*I am the LORD, who made everything, who alone stretched out the sky...* Isaiah 44:24 NET

## A GOD OF ORDER

The Bible says that the LORD created the sun and the moon, not only to give light and heat, but to be like huge celestial clocks that would mark off days, seasons, and years.

*He made the moon to mark the months, and the sun sets according to a regular schedule.* Psalm 104:19 NET

The ancients knew that the universe functioned with amazing precision. They could easily see that the LORD was a God of order, that he had *rules* or *laws* to keep the universe functioning properly.[3]

Today we study those physical laws through various sciences such as astronomy, biology, physics, and chemistry. We take these laws so much for granted that we never consider what the world would be like without them. But imagine if, for a few minutes, the law of gravity was suspended. Chaos and death would reign. The law of gravity, as well as all the other laws, are there for a purpose. They keep things safe and secure.

> *He is before all things, and in Him all things hold together.*
> *Colossians 1:17 NASB*

We instinctively treat these laws with great respect. For example, we walk along the edge of a cliff very carefully because we know that to defy the law of gravity has serious repercussions. The reason for this is that *whenever you have a law, you also have a consequence.* Laws define uncompromising boundaries as to how something will function. If you remain within the boundary, you are safe. If you move outside the boundary, you get hurt.

> *Yours is the day, yours also the night; you have established the*
> *heavenly lights and the sun. You have fixed all the boundaries*
> *of the earth ...*      *Psalm 74:16-17 ESV*

These laws—this structure and order—are a reflection of the Lord's nature. The Lord is a God of order, a God who has rules; he is not erratic. A person can count on his consistency and faithfulness.

## Day Five

On the fifth day, God created the whole kaleidoscope of sea life and birds.

> *Then God said, "Let the waters teem with swarms of living*
> *creatures, and let birds fly above the earth in the open expanse*
> *of the heavens."*      *Genesis 1:20 NASB*

This teeming diversity in air and sea was another statement about the Lord's creative ability. And as he had done with the plants, God created full-grown, mature animals. Each animal was fully equipped with a genetic library to determine how it would grow and reproduce.

> *So God created the great sea creatures and every living creature*
> *that moves, with which the waters swarm, according to their*
> *kinds, and every winged bird according to its kind. And God*
> *saw that it was good. And there was evening and there was*
> *morning, the fifth day.*      *Genesis 1:21,23 ESV*

## PERFECT, FLAWLESS, HOLY

As Moses wrote, he would have noted that YAHWEH ended each creation day with the words:

> …*God saw that it was good.*                    Genesis 1:25 NASB

This was possible because in the totality of his being, the LORD is perfect; he is good.

> *As for God, His way is perfect…*                    Psalm 18:30 NKJV

Moses would have known that the gods of the ancient Egyptians were very human in their thoughts, emotions, and actions. They had wives and children, allies and enemies. Quite promiscuous in lifestyle, they plotted, deceived, fought for power, and brutally killed each other. Ultimately, they controlled the other deities through manipulation and magic.

But YAHWEH was different. His character is without blemish—perfect. One of the words used to describe that perfection is the word *righteous*. It means *upright, honest, honourable.*

> *Splendid and majestic is His work, and His righteousness endures forever.*                    Psalm 111:3 NASB

The LORD's purity—his righteousness—is unique to him.

> …*the holy God will show Himself holy in righteousness.*
>                    Isaiah 5:16 NASB

As mentioned before, the word *holy* means *unique, one-of-a-kind, separate.* The preceding verse could be read as:

> …*the unique God will show Himself unique in uprightness, honesty, and honor.*                    Isaiah 5:16 paraphrased

As we have progressed through the days of creation, we've learned how YAHWEH is truly one-of-a-kind. Now I want to enlarge the definition of *holy* by linking it to God's *righteous* character. These two words, *holy* and *righteous*, are almost interchangeable in meaning. They both speak of his moral perfection.

The absolute righteousness of the Creator cannot be over-emphasized. Keep this in mind as you continue to read. It's a piece that cannot be left out of the puzzle. Because the LORD is perfect, he could only make a perfect creation. Creation has changed, as we will see, but in the beginning it was just right! God said, *"It was good."* It was perfect.

## ANCIENT BUT ACCURATE

Although not a textbook on science, the Bible is accurate whenever it speaks about the physical universe. Whole books have been written on this subject, but here are a few items of interest.

Centuries ago, it was commonly believed that the earth was flat. This thinking never had its origins in the Bible. The Scripture uses a word that alludes to the spherical shape of the globe when it states:

*He sits enthroned above the circle of the earth . . .*

*Isaiah 40:22 NIV*

Some ancients speculated that the earth sat on a strong foundation or was supported by a god. The Bible says that the LORD . . .

*. . . hangs the earth on nothing.*          *Job 26:7 NKJV*

In the 2nd century, Ptolemy catalogued 1,022 stars—a number which was considered authoritative until Galileo's invention of the telescope in the 17th century. Though only about 5,000 stars are visible to the unaided eye, the Bible from its earliest pages relates the number of stars to . . .

*. . . the sand which is on the seashore . . .*  *Genesis 22:17 NASB*

Until a century ago, it was believed the ocean bottom was shaped like a great bowl, whereas the Bible speaks of the sea floor having both mountains and valleys.

*. . . down to the moorings of the mountains . . .*   *Jonah 2:6 NKJV*

*The valleys[4] of the sea . . .*          *2 Samuel 22:16 NIV*

In the mid-1800's Matthew Maury plotted the currents of the ocean and air. He was inspired by verses that spoke of . . .

*. . . the paths of the seas.*          *Psalm 8:8 NKJV*

*The wind blows to the south and goes around to the north; around and around goes the wind, and on its circuits the wind returns.*          *Ecclesiastes 1:6 ESV*

The monument raised in his honour shows him holding sea charts in one hand and a Bible in the other. It reads: *"Matthew Fontaine Maury, Pathfinder of the Seas, the genius who first snatched from the oceans and atmosphere the secret of their laws. His inspiration, Holy Writ, Psalm 8:8; Ecclesiastes 1:6."*

# 4 PERFECT AND CARING

## DAY SIX

The sixth day was the pinnacle of God's creative act. The LORD began the day by creating the land animals.

> Then God said, "Let the earth bring forth living creatures after their kind: cattle and creeping things and beasts of the earth after their kind"; and it was so.
>
> God made the beasts of the earth after their kind, and the cattle after their kind, and everything that creeps on the ground after its kind; and God saw that it was good.     Genesis 1:24-25 NASB

## KINDS

On days three, five, and six, it is respectively stated that plants, sea life, birds, and animals were to reproduce *"according to their kind."* What does it mean when it says, *"according to their kind?"* Simply put, it means that cats give birth to cats, horses to horses and elephants to elephants. We don't need to be concerned that, when we plant potatoes, palm trees might sprout.

Through breeding, creatures can develop into different varieties, but they will still be the same kind. The original dogs created by God were full of genetic information which could never be improved upon or added to. We derived different breeds by selectively reducing the amount of genetic information in each dog. Whether we ended up with a Wolf Hound or a Chihuahua, it was always a *reduction* in genetic information that gave rise to the new breed. And regardless of the breed, it was still a dog—it still belonged to the same *kind*. Because kinds are fixed, a farmer need not be concerned about the neighbour's milk cow interbreeding with his prize horse. Why? It's because the LORD embedded physical laws in the system to maintain order. We count on it. It makes life secure.

## HE CARES

The LORD didn't limit his creation of plant life to a few kinds. Instead, we see an overwhelming variety. The Bible says that YAHWEH …

> … richly provides us with everything to enjoy.     1 Timothy 6:17 ESV

A God who created an enjoyable world is a God who truly cares. To show care is to exhibit a form of love.

The LORD could have coloured all plants and animals blue, but instead he made everything with an endless variety of pigmentation and hues. Not only did he invent colour, but he also created eyes able to see the colour.

The Creator could have made all food to taste bitter! But no, YAHWEH created endless flavors, and he also provided us with taste buds able to enjoy the fine nuances of a whole host of cooking styles.

Along with many other things, he gave fragrance to flowers and created the nose with its ability to appreciate a multitude of scents. Everything could have smelled like rotten eggs, but that is not the way God designed it.

> ... The earth is full of the lovingkindness of the LORD.
>
> Psalm 33:5 NASB

Love is an attribute of the LORD YAHWEH—it's a part of the way he is—it's in his nature to love.

> ... the lovingkindness of the LORD is from everlasting to everlasting...
>
> Psalm 103:17 NASB

## A HOME

I have lived and travelled among cultures where it is expected that before a man can be married, he must first build a house for his intended bride. It's an interesting process to watch. The work is usually done with great thought and care. It's quite evident the young man has someone special in mind. Well, in the same way, the Bible tells us that...

> ... this is what the LORD says—he who created the heavens, he is God; he who fashioned and made the earth, he founded it; he did not create it to be empty, but formed it to be inhabited...
>
> Isaiah 45:18 NIV

From its unique atmosphere to its vast oceans of water, from its celestial clocks that *mark off time* to its diverse flora and fauna, from its laws that *make things safe* to its *great-tasting* food—all things great and small were made by a kind and caring God in preparation for man to inhabit the earth.

> The LORD is righteous in all his ways and loving toward all he has made.
>
> Psalm 145:17 NIV

In six days, the LORD YAHWEH made earth ready ... ready for someone with whom he could be a special friend.

# 5 THE IMAGE OF GOD

## DAY SIX (CONTINUED)

*Then God said, "Let us⁵ make man in our image, after our likeness. And let them have dominion over the fish of the sea and over the birds of the heavens and over the livestock and over all the earth and over every creeping thing that creeps on the earth." So God created man in his own image, in the image of God he created him; male and female he created them.*

*Genesis 1:26-27 ESV*

## THE IMAGE OF GOD

Man was created in the image of God. What did this mean? The ancient Egyptians believed Pharaoh was a god or at least half god. Did it mean man could be a god?

First of all, it is obvious that we are not exact duplicates of the LORD. None of us are all-knowing, all-powerful, or everywhere present at one time. Rather, man is like a mirror which reflects the image of the object but is not the object itself. In a sense, when you look at man, you see many things that resemble God.

Because the LORD is a person, God created us as *beings*—**persons** in our own right, with personalities and various traits, as those with whom the LORD could relate and be a friend.[6]

God also gave man part of his **eternal** nature—a spirit that would exist forever. YAHWEH wanted friendships that would last for time without end. The Scripture says,

*He has planted eternity in the human heart… Ecclesiastes 3:11 NLT*

Since the LORD is morally perfect, man was created innocent of all wrong-doing. That has all changed as we will see, but in the beginning man had a **sinless** nature.

Because God is the great Creator, he made man with the capacity to create. In a sense, the LORD gave man a dab of his intellect. Because man was given a **mind**, he could investigate and understand, abilities which God possesses—abilities which are an important part of being a person. Man could relate to God as an intelligent, thinking being.

Because God has feelings, he created man with **emotions**. Not only did the LORD want mankind to be able to experience kindness, he wanted man to have the ability to show heartfelt appreciation.

The ability to feel is a very important aspect of personhood. Without feelings, one's response to others would be like that of a robot—cold and calculated.

God also created man with a **will**. Man's ability to make decisions for himself is often taken for granted, but the capacity to choose and have preferences is what defines one as a person and not a robot. Man was given a will so he could freely respond to the LORD, not like a machine, but as a genuine friend.

All of these abilities are a reflection of *God's character*—sometimes referred to as *God's glory*. When the LORD created man in His image, He created man to reflect a little of what God is like.

> *For You have made him a little lower than the angels, And You have crowned him with glory and honor.*     Psalm 8:5 NKJV

Because humans are created in the image of God, we are set apart from any other living creature. Just as humans do not belong in the "God" category, neither do they fit in the "animal" category. We are distinct from each other. Mankind alone was made in the image of God, with the glory of God. It would be with men and women that the LORD would establish lasting relationships.

There are other aspects of God's image we could look at as well, but let's move on in the story.

| | Role | Category | Name(s) |
|---|---|---|---|
| Distinct from… | Creator | God | YAHWEH |
| Distinct from… | created | spirit being | Gabriel, Michael, The Shining One |
| Distinct from… | created | human beings | Kumar, James, Ali, Susan, etc. |
| | created | animals, birds, fish, insects, etc. | Arabian Horse, Bald Eagle, Bluefin Tuna, Monarch Butterfly, etc. |

**BREATH OF LIFE**

The Bible says,

> *…the LORD God formed man of the dust of the ground and breathed into his nostrils the breath of life, and man became a living being.*     Genesis 2:7 NKJV

The phrase *breath of life* is often associated with the spirit or non-material side of man. This is an additional reflection of God's image, for the LORD YAHWEH is a Spirit. As we stated before, spirits cannot be seen since they have no bodies. However, in man's case, in addition to creating him in God's image, the LORD chose to also provide a physical house of flesh and bones for man's spirit to dwell in—a house formed from the dust of the ground. Once formed, the body would have laid there, complete in every way but entirely lifeless. It was when God breathed the spirit into man that the body became alive. Only the LORD can impart life; no person or angel, no other god or goddess has that ability.

## A COMPANION

The first and only man God created was named *Adam*, which means *man*. God then created the woman.

> …the LORD God said, "It is not good for the man to be alone; I will make him a helper suitable for him." Genesis 2:18 NASB

> So the LORD God caused a deep sleep to fall upon the man, and while he slept took one of his ribs and closed up its place with flesh. And the rib that the LORD God had taken from the man he made into a woman and brought her to the man.

> And the man and his wife were both naked and were not ashamed. Genesis 2:21–22, 25 ESV

These few verses have generated heated arguments. Some have understood that when God made woman, he made her a second-class citizen. This is not consistent with what the Bible teaches. The LORD took woman out of man's side, to be a companion—not from man's heel, to be his slave. God wanted them to be each other's friend.

Adam gave his wife the name *Eve*, meaning *life-giver*.

## THE PERFECT GARDEN

> …the LORD God planted a garden in Eden in the east, and there he placed the man he had made. Genesis 2:8 NLT

In the Bible, Eden is spoken of as a perfect paradise—a place with luxuriant foliage, sparkling clear water teeming with fish, an incredible variety of animals—with beauty beyond description! It seems the weather was different too.

Though we have very little idea of what Eden was like, obviously God did not create a garden where Adam and Eve were struggling to survive. The garden had an abundance, and everything they could possibly need was adequately provided by the LORD. It was a perfect world in which to live. It was an expression of his love—his friendship.

> Know that the LORD, he is God! It is he who made us, and we are his; we are his people … *Psalm 100:3 ESV*

# 6 HIGH YET NEAR

When one ponders the immensity of the universe, the intricate detail of his creation, the structure of his laws—the LORD's greatness as a "living being" can leave one breathless.

### UNKNOWABLE

However, even at best, our understanding of YAHWEH is limited. Much is hidden.

> Great is the LORD, and greatly to be praised, And His greatness is unsearchable. *Psalm 145:3 NKJV*

> Do you not know? Have you not heard? The LORD is the everlasting God, the Creator of the ends of the earth. … and his understanding no one can fathom. *Isaiah 40:28 NIV*

### KNOWABLE

But what we do know about YAHWEH is amazing. And though God is very great, the LORD is not distant—uncommunicative.

> For thus says the LORD …"I have not spoken in secret, In a dark place of the earth … I, the LORD, speak righteousness, I declare things that are right." *Isaiah 45:18-19 NKJV*

He speaks—and, yes, he speaks to us lowly humans.

> For this is what the high and lofty One says—he who lives forever, whose name is holy: "I live in a high and holy place, but also with him who is contrite and lowly in spirit, to revive the spirit of the lowly and to revive the heart of the contrite."
> *Isaiah 57:15 NIV*

Yes, the unique God is seated in Heaven, but he also walks among us. He created us.

> The LORD is near to all who call upon Him, To all who call upon Him in truth. *Psalm 145:18 NASB*

## CREATOR-OWNER

Just as the angels belonged to God because he created them, so Adam and Eve belonged to God because the LORD was their Creator. (Remember the tribal illustration? He who makes the paddle also owns the paddle.) The Bible says,

> The LORD owns the earth and all it contains, the world and all who live in it …
> Psalm 24:1 NET

> Yours, O LORD, is the greatness and the power and the glory and the majesty and the splendor, for everything in heaven and earth is yours.
> 1 Chronicles 29:11 NIV

And just as the angels were given the position of being God's servants, so YAHWEH gave Adam and Eve and all their future children the responsibility of taking care of the earth.

> God blessed them; and God said to them, "Be fruitful and multiply, and fill the earth and subdue it; and rule over the fish of the sea and over the birds of the sky and over every living thing that moves on the earth."
> Genesis 1:28 NASB

> Then the LORD God took the man and put him into the garden of Eden to cultivate it and keep it.
> Genesis 2:15 NASB

## A FRIEND

The Scripture says God filled every need Adam and Eve had.

> Then God said, "I now give you every seed-bearing plant on the face of the entire earth and every tree that has fruit with seed in it. They will be yours for food. And to all the animals of the earth, and to every bird of the air, and to all the creatures that move on the ground—everything that has the breath of life in it—I give every green plant for food." It was so.
> Genesis 1: 29-30 NET

Probably, God visibly appeared to Adam and Eve as a man, as the Bible records instances of the LORD taking on human form so that people could see him. The Scripture speaks of YAHWEH coming in the evening to walk with Adam and Eve, as one would walk with a friend.

To stroll in the garden with the Creator must have been quite an experience! Perhaps God spent time explaining in detail how he made things, imparting profound knowledge of intricate flowers, calling down birds high in the treetops, and discussing the vast spectrum of animals. Perhaps he explained the laws that kept everything running so precisely. What an education and what an Educator! No one could have better instructed them on how to care for the garden.

Because Adam and Eve were innocent of any sort of evil or wrong, they had a perfection that allowed them to be in God's company. The Bible says only perfect people[7] can live in the presence of a perfect God.

At this time in history there was a bridge of friendship between God and man. The world was a perfect place in which to live. It was the way God created things to be.

## CREATION COMPLETED

*God saw all that he had made—and it was very good! There was evening, and there was morning, the sixth day.*
Genesis 1:31 NET

Creation was complete. People often start projects with great gusto and then lose interest over time. But God is different. The LORD always finishes what he sets out to do.

*…the plans of the LORD stand firm forever, the purposes of his heart through all generations.* Psalm 33:11 NIV

Some people have said that creation is on-going, that the gods continue to tinker with the world, but the Bible says that…

*…in six days the LORD made the heavens and the earth and the sea and all that is in them, and he rested on the seventh day…*
Exodus 20:11 NET

## DAY SEVEN

The LORD rested or ceased work on the seventh day, not because he was tired, but because his creation was complete. Perhaps he spent the day with Adam and Eve—we really don't know. What we do know is that the Bible says creation was the work of only one God, the God whose name is LORD YAHWEH.

## REVIEW

As we have read the *book of beginnings*, we have learned more about this unique God.

The LORD is **an eternal spirit**—the only Holy Spirit.

The LORD is a **person** or **being**, not a force.

The LORD is **all-knowing, all-powerful, and everywhere present at one time.**

The LORD is a God of **order**; he established laws that he faithfully maintains.

The LORD is a **perfect** God, morally pure and righteous.

The LORD is a **caring** God, one who shows love.

The LORD is exceedingly **great**, but he also **communicates with mankind.**

These characteristics of God form part of what is known as his *glory*. And it is the unique combination of YAHWEH's many attributes that makes for one very unique God. The Bible says,

*"No one is holy like the LORD, for there is none besides You..."*

1 Samuel 2:2 NKJV

---

### WHAT ABOUT DARWINIAN EVOLUTION?

The Bible does not mention evolution. This book is not written to address this topic, but here is a little food for thought.

It is not correct to simply designate Evolution as science and Creation as religion, as some do. Why not?

❖ There is no agreed-upon body of facts that explains origins. Since Charles Darwin first published the theory in 1859, classic Darwinism has been largely replaced by Neo-Darwinism and Punctuated Equilibrium—theories that differ greatly from each other.

Many scholars point out that these theories are inconsistent with known science. For example, they tell us...

• **Cosmic evolution violates known laws of physics.** For instance, our culture is taught that, with time, the universe moved from initial chaos to ever-increasing order. We now know the Second Law of Thermodynamics states the exact opposite—an isolated system[8] will become more disordered with time.

Continued on next page

Continued from previous page

- **Evolution is mathematically impossible.** Examples abound, but an interesting parallel was made by Sir Fred Hoyle, noted astrophysicist and mathematician who spent most of his working life at Cambridge. He compared the likelihood of even the simplest cell forming by natural processes to the probability of a tornado sweeping through a junk-yard and assembling a Boeing 747.[9] It would never happen.

- **Evolution is biologically untenable.** For example, Darwin wrote that the many varieties of dogs were an instance of evolution, not knowing that genetics would reveal the exact opposite—multiple "dogs" are the result of each breed having a reduction in genetic information—a *de*-evolution instead of evolution.[10]

❖ Ardent evolutionists have typically begun with the premise that there is no Creator. They believe that with sufficient time, evolution is possible. These are faith-based choices in thinking, identified more with religion than science.

On the other hand, to put Creation wholly in the religion category is not correct either. Why not?

❖ A significant community of scientists has concluded that this complex universe could only exist if there was a designer (such as God), or a team of designers. Solely using science, they point out that the world has an irreducible complexity at even the smallest level.[11] They demonstrate that such universal complexity and order could only exist if it were planned from the ground up—it could not evolve by random chance. Complexity demands a designer.

Since the mid-1960's, there has been an explosion of written material on the subject (see Appendix). Much of it is readable for those unschooled in advanced sciences.

Some wonder about the Creation account as it relates to dinosaurs. From a biblical viewpoint, there is no reason not to believe that God created them along with the rest of the animals. Evidence exists that dinosaurs lived at the same time as man. Later we will see what may have caused their demise.

Others wonder about the earth's age—to some it appears very old. It is true that scientists have developed various methods[12] to gauge the age of the universe, but while they employ reasoned calculations, the computed ages have left scientists scratching their heads. Depending on the method used, ages range from a few thousand years to billions of years. Darwin theorized 400 million years for biological evolution. Today, a common estimate starts at 4.6 billion years. Whose clock is right?

Is there a reasonable answer that fits the biblical account? Going strictly by the Bible, we know that God created a mature earth. On the day of his creation, Adam could have walked among towering trees, marvelled at immense animals, and gazed at stars in the night sky. Perhaps he thought, *"Wow! This place has been around for a long time."* However, God would have told him that it was, at most, six days old—he had created the whole universe in a fully functioning state. Scientists, in looking back, try to determine the past by what they observe—just like Adam would have. The Bible, however, records the origins of the earth from the perspective of an eyewitness—God himself.

So, did YAHWEH mean it when he said he created the universe? Who are we to believe? Whose word is to be trusted?

Centuries ago, a king pondered his place in the world:

> When I look up at the heavens, which your fingers made, and see the moon and the stars, which you set in place, Of what importance is the human race, that you should notice them?
>
> Of what importance is mankind, that you should pay attention to them, and make them a little less than the heavenly beings?
>
> You grant mankind honor and majesty; you appoint them to rule over your creation; you have placed everything under their authority, including all the sheep and cattle, as well as the wild animals, the birds in the sky, the fish in the sea and everything that moves through the currents of the seas. O LORD, our Lord, how magnificent is your reputation throughout the earth! *Psalm 8:3–9 NET*

# CHAPTER FOUR

# 1 TWO WAYS

As Moses recorded the first chapter of the Book of Genesis, it's not hard to imagine him deep in thought over these next words:

> God saw all that he had made—and **it was very good**!
> Genesis 1:31 NET

Creation had obviously ended with God's stamp of approval. From what Moses wrote, it was plain to see the LORD had created the world without pain and disease, without discord and death. Originally there was a unique relationship, a fellowship, a friendship between YAHWEH and mankind. Eden was a perfect place to live. Everything back then had been *very good*.

But that had all changed and Moses knew that change had affected everyone. He had experienced both the wealth of Pharaoh's court and the want of a fugitive. Neither privilege nor poverty left a person exempt from shame, fear, guilt, suffering, and death. Things were no longer *very good*. What happened? To answer that question, we must return to the topic of spirit beings.

## PROBATION

It seems that in the beginning, the LORD gave all his angels a probationary period—a time when they could willingly choose to follow their Creator-Owner or reject him as King. God did not want robotic obedience. His desire was for all angels to serve him freely because they wanted to—not because they had to.[1] It also seems clear from Scripture that once the probationary period was past, the angelic beings were locked into the choices they had made, whether good or bad.[2] We know that countless angels such as *Gabriel* and *Michael* joyfully chose to serve the LORD. However, there were other angels who made a different choice. Such was the case with *Lucifer*—the *Shining One*.

## PERFECT

We pick up the story where we left off, in the Garden of Eden. The Bible says of the *Shining One*:

> You were in Eden, the garden of God; Every precious stone was your covering… Ezekiel 28:13 NASB

The *Shining One*, you will remember, was the most powerful spirit that the LORD had created. He belonged to the angelic order called *cherubim* and was selected by God for special responsibilities.

> *"You were an anointed guardian cherub … you were on the holy*
> *mountain of God …"*                              *Ezekiel 28:14 ESV*

The *Shining One* was perfect, both in beauty and in wisdom.

> *"You were blameless in your ways from the day you were*
> *created …"*                                      *Ezekiel 28:15 ESV*

> *"You had the seal of perfection, full of wisdom and perfect*
> *in beauty."*                                     *Ezekiel 28:12 NASB*

### PRIDE

But then he made his choice. It was recorded with these words:

> *"O shining one, son of the dawn … you have said in your heart:*
> *'I will ascend into heaven, I will exalt my throne above the stars*
> *of God; I will also sit on the mount of the congregation On the*
> *farthest sides of the north; I will ascend above the heights of the*
> *clouds, I will be like the Most High.'"*   *Isaiah 14:12 YLT, 13-14 NKJV*

Not only did the *Shining One* want to take over Heaven, but he was determined to replace the *Most High* with himself. His rebellious heart was bursting with prideful ambition. God called the *Shining One's* attitude *sin*.

### WRONG

Some people equate sin with a crime, such as murder or thievery, but the Bible defines it in much broader terms. The Scripture says that *sin* is anything that is *wrong*—it is the opposite of *right*. In the Bible it is often translated as *unrighteousness*. The Bible says of the *Shining One* …

> *"You were blameless in your ways From the day you were created*
> *Until **unrighteousness** was found in you."*
>                                                   *Ezekiel 28:15 NASB*

Later on we will see how the Bible defines *right* and *wrong*. For now, all we need to know is that the *Shining One* made a *wrong* choice. It was not *right*. It was sin.

### ROTTEN

The Bible also says *sin* is like something good that has gone bad. It uses the word *corrupt*, literally meaning *rotted* or *ruined*. The Scripture says of the *Shining One*,

> *"… you sinned … you corrupted your wisdom for the sake of*
> *your splendor."*                                 *Ezekiel 28:16-17 ESV*

The *Shining One* had *gone bad*. He had become sinful.

## EXPELLED

Because God is perfect, he could not ignore the *Shining One*'s sin as if it did not matter. The LORD's response was immediate. He expelled the *Shining One* from his position in Heaven.

> "...you sinned. So I drove you in disgrace from the mount of God, and I expelled you, O guardian cherub...I threw you to the earth..."
> Ezekiel 28:16-17 NIV

He didn't go without a battle. *The Shining One* was still very powerful and, on top of that, many other angels followed him. The Bible gives some precise details of what happened. To help you understand the account, I have tied key parts of the verse together.

> Then another sign appeared in heaven: an enormous red dragon ... His tail swept a third of the stars out of the sky and flung them to the earth...
>
> And there was war in heaven. Michael and his angels fought against the dragon, and the dragon and his angels fought back. But he was not strong enough, and they lost their place in heaven.
>
> The great dragon was hurled down—that ancient serpent called the devil, or Satan, who leads the whole world astray. He was hurled to the earth, and his angels with him.[3]
> Revelation 12:3-4, 7-9 NIV

## DEVIL, SATAN, DEMONS

The text indicates that one-third of the angels followed the *Shining One* in his rebellion. These rebellious angels became known as *demons* or *evil spirits*. The *Shining One* would now be called the *Devil* or *Satan*. Just as the LORD's names describe his attributes, so the *Shining One*'s names reveal his character. Satan means *adversary* or *enemy*; Devil means *false accuser* or *slanderer*.

This powerful spirit would now be the root of all that is evil, all that is cruel, all that is wrong. He would be referred to as a *ruler* or *prince of demons*, ruling over the spirits that followed him. Some would still refer to him by his Latin name, *Lucifer*.

At this point we must ask ourselves, *"Does the Bible ever identify Satan as a god?"* The answer is, *"Yes, it does."* He is sometimes referred to as...

> The god of this age...
> 2 Corinthians 4:4 NKJV

Up to this point in the story everything about creation was perfect—without the taint of sin.

The Scripture also tells us of a future time when there will be...

> ...new heavens and a new earth, in which righteousness dwells.
> 2 Peter 3:13 NASB

But sandwiched between that perfect creation in the past and the perfect world to come is a block of time—an age—where Satan is a god. This does not mean *Lucifer* is anything close to Yahweh. The Devil is not all-knowing, all-powerful, or everywhere present. He is not flawless. Satan does not love; he hates. Nonetheless, the Bible refers to Satan as a *god*—spelled with a small "g."

### The Lake of Fire

When the Lord cast the Devil and his demons from Heaven, it was only the first phase in judging these rebellious spirits. The Bible says that God has a place of final punishment, an...

> ...eternal fire prepared for the devil and his angels.
> Matthew 25:41 ESV

This location is known as *Gehenna*, commonly called *Hell* or the *Lake of Fire*. The name *Gehenna* is derived from the Valley of Hinnom, a deep, narrow abyss directly south of Jerusalem. It was a cursed place, associated with the ancient practice of burning children alive in worship of a god. Over time, this valley became the city garbage dump where the bodies of criminals, carcasses of animals, and all sorts of rubbish were cast. Its narrow depths, filled with stench, flames and smoke, became an apt symbol for a different, yet equally real place—a place of punishment that God created specifically for Satan. Yahweh used the word *Gehenna* to speak of a future rubbish heap—the garbage bin of the universe—a place where the Devil and his demons will be confined for eternity.

Often cartoons are drawn depicting Satan and his demons standing waist-deep in flames, conniving and plotting mischief. However, the Bible tells us that Satan is not yet there. He was cast out of Heaven, but not into *Gehenna*. In the future, after many events take place involving him and his demons, Satan will be forever confined to this place of punishment.

Referring to this future time, the Bible says,

> The devil, who deceived them, was cast into the lake of fire... And they will be tormented day and night forever and ever.
>
> Revelation 20:10 NKJV

## Two Ways

When Satan rebelled against God, the probation period was over. The angelic beings had made their choices.

1. There was the way of those angels such as Gabriel and Michael, who continued to serve God and act as his messengers, and...

2. There was the way of the *Shining One*—the Devil and his demons—now enemies of the *Most High God*.

Just two ways.

Although *Yahweh* had expelled Satan and his demons from Heaven, they still retained their immense power and intellect. It would be all-out war. Satan would fight dirty. He would be against everything good, everything that God planned to do. His prey? God's pinnacle of creation—mankind.

# 2 The Test

When God created man, he didn't just place him on earth and walk away. The Bible says that the Lord visited Adam and Eve in the garden and, in the offhand way it is mentioned, one can assume this was a regular event. The Creator was a good friend to Adam and Eve and he took care of their every need.

Though God was their friend, the Bible says the Lord tested Adam and Eve. We will discuss why he did this in the pages to come, but first, let's look at what the test involved.

> ... In the middle of the garden were the tree of life and the tree of the knowledge of good and evil.
>
> Genesis 2:9 NIV

Nothing specific is mentioned regarding the first tree, however, the second tree came with a warning.

> And the Lord God commanded the man, saying, "Of every tree of the garden you may freely eat; but of the tree of the knowledge of good and evil you shall not eat, for in the day that you eat of it you shall surely die."
>
> Genesis 2:16-17 NKJV

Adam and Eve knew about good, but evil was another matter.

They had both been created as sinless beings and were innocent of all wrong. Their experience was limited to God's goodness. The Bible says that if they ate the fruit of this one tree, then not only would they know what was good but also what was evil.

Earlier on we saw that to defy one of God's physical laws, such as gravity, has repercussions. That principle—*a broken law has consequences*—applies to any of God's laws. In this case, God gave man one simple rule: *"Don't eat the fruit from that one tree."* The consequence of breaking that command was made just as plain—man would die. We will discuss death in detail later.

This test was not a hardship for Adam and Eve.

> …the Lord God made **all kinds of trees** grow from the soil, every tree that was pleasing to look at and good for food.
>
> Genesis 2:9 NET

There was obviously an abundance of fruit to eat. To ignore the one forbidden tree would be a simple command to obey.

### The Deceiver

But then Satan slinked into the garden. He did not arrive with a blast of trumpets, announcing who he was and what he was about. Satan is much too subtle for that. The Bible tells us that Satan is the great deceiver—the devil. He is incapable of telling uncorrupted truth.

> …the devil…was a murderer from the beginning, not holding to the truth, for there is no truth in him. When he lies, he speaks his native language, for he is a liar and the father of lies.
>
> John 8:44 NIV

The word *lie* in the original Greek text is *pseudos*—an intentional falsehood. We use the word ourselves. It implies *imitation*.

Several years ago I was reading an article about Satan in a popular news magazine. He was illustrated as having a red body with horns on his head, a pointed tail and carrying a pitchfork. The overall rendering was hideous. According to the Bible, that picture is deceptive to the extreme. The Bible says that…

> …Satan disguises himself as an angel of light.
>
> 2 Corinthians 11:14 NASB

Satan is still the *Shining One*. He comes in all his eye-catching splendor, mimicking Yahweh as closely as he can. A better picture of the Devil might have been a wise-looking elderly gentleman dressed in the finest religious robes. Satan and his demonic host love religion. They imitate the truth, but they cannot be trusted because, by their very nature, they are impostors—counterfeits—tellers of deliberate falsehoods. They always mix lies with truth. They are masters of deception.

I've heard stories of people who have had dreams or visions of a bright, shining spirit talking to them. The Bible says that this can be very dangerous as that *angel of light* could be the Devil or one of his demons. Later in the story we will learn how to tell the difference between a good and a bad angel.

## DECEPTION

So Satan arrived in the Garden of Eden with all the subtlety he could muster. No trumpets, no fanfare. He came in the embodiment of a snake, a reptile that is often identified with the Devil. The Bible records several incidents of evil spirits living inside both humans and animals, speaking through them or causing them to act abnormally. On this occasion Satan spoke through the reptile. He addressed Eve.

> Now the serpent … said to the woman, **"Did God really say**, `You must not eat from any tree in the garden'?"* Genesis 3:1 NIV*

The fact that a snake could speak did not seem to disturb Eve. No doubt every day she discovered a new and fascinating part of God's creation. Perhaps she thought this was just another one of those new creatures.

## DOUBT

The Bible says Satan approached Eve with a question about the LORD. He planted an idea in her mind that she had never considered—the idea that the creature can question the Creator. The question came in a slightly condescending tone, *"Did God really say …? I mean, come on—did God really say that?"*

With his *you've-got-to-be-kidding* approach, Satan implied that man was rather naive to accept the LORD's word at face value.

*"Perhaps Y*AHWEH *is holding back something good from you. I mean, how do you know? Maybe the* LORD *isn't as good a friend as he makes himself out to be."*

There was a hint that God wasn't being completely honest. Satan passed himself off as looking out for man's best interests—as a true friend. The Devil counterfeited the LORD's goodness. In addition, Satan grossly overstated God's prohibition—he mixed a lie with the truth. The LORD had *not* forbidden eating from every tree. He had only mentioned one tree.

> *The woman said to the serpent, "We may eat fruit from the trees in the garden, but God did say, `You must not eat fruit from the tree that is in the middle of the garden, and you must not touch it, or you will die.'"*
>
> *"**You will not surely die**," the serpent said to the woman.*
>
> *"For God knows that when you eat of it your eyes will be opened, and **you will be like God**, knowing good and evil."*
>
> Genesis 3:2-5 NIV

## DENIAL

First, Satan questioned God's Word—*"Did God really say…?"* Then he denied God's Word—*"You will not surely die."* Finally, he substituted his own lie—*"… you will be like God…"* The Bible says the Devil tempted Adam and Eve on the pretext that the fruit would be…

> *… desirable for gaining wisdom…*     Genesis 3:6 NIV

The Hebrew word translated *wisdom* includes the idea of gaining *insight* or *enlightenment*. Sometimes we use the words *self-actualization* or *self-realization*. Satan was enticing Adam and Eve with the idea of becoming *enlightened ones*.

## A CHOICE

Adam and Eve were now faced with a choice:

1. **They could believe the** LORD. He had clearly said that if they ate the forbidden fruit, they would die.

2. **They could believe the Devil.** Satan said if they ate the fruit, they would live. They would become like gods—enlightened ones.

Whose words should they believe? Who should they trust? Who was their true friend?

# 3 The Choice

We saw earlier that the Lord gave his angels a probationary period when they could choose to freely follow him. In the same way, God gave mankind a probationary option. The Lord would not force Adam and Eve to be his friends. They had a choice.

We may wonder why God gave them an alternative at all. Why didn't he create them to love the Lord unconditionally and skip the probationary period? The Bible doesn't answer that question in detail, but consider these factors:

❖ Suppose a young lady met a fellow who appeared to be the nicest person on earth. He showed real love for her—going out of his way to do special things for her, comforting her when she hurt, sharing in her humour, telling her he loved her. Then she found out he had no choice—that he was a robot, programmed to be loving. What a terrible disappointment! It would seem so artificial, so empty. And it would be.

The Lord did not want robots monotonously repeating, "I love God!" It would be meaningless. Man was given a simple choice, but this one choice made a huge difference, defining man as human—capable of showing genuine friendship.

❖ At some time or other, all of us have discovered to our dismay that someone we considered to be *a loyal companion* was really just *a fair-weather friend*—dependable only in good times. We all know that authentic friendships are those which have survived times of testing.

So, God tested his relationship with Adam and Eve; he gave them a genuine choice. And with the arrival of Satan in the garden, that choice had taken on a new dimension. God said one thing; Satan said another. Adam and Eve had to decide whether to trust Yahweh or Satan. Who was telling the truth? Whom should they believe? Who was their real friend?

> …when the woman saw that the fruit of the tree was good for food and pleasing to the eye, and also desirable for gaining wisdom [or enlightenment], she took some and ate it. She also gave some to her husband, who was with her, and he ate it.
>
> Genesis 3:6 NIV

Satan had succeeded! Adam and Eve had believed him! They had eaten the forbidden fruit thinking they would become gods! You can almost hear his howl of laughter echoing through the garden. Often the Devil comes across as a great friend—providing pleasure, fun, a good time—but it's only temporary and often very empty. In reality, Satan never gives. If he imparts anything, it's only gut-wrenching heartache. He's a malicious playmate, a cruel companion.

Over the years some have blamed the woman for this outright disobedience against God's command. However, throughout Eve's conversation with Satan, it seems that her husband was with her. Adam could have prevented his wife from eating the fruit, and certainly did not have to eat it himself. But they both ate.

### DISOBEDIENCE

This whole event can be compared to children playing on a busy street against their mother's instructions. The mother says, *"Stay off that street; you could be killed by a truck!"* But the youngsters think they know *better-than-mom* what is safe and fun, so they play on the street amid the traffic. They are showing that they don't entirely trust their mother's knowledge of safety. They are disregarding her loving authority. In the same way, Adam and Eve sinned when they felt they knew *better-than-God* what was good for them. Their choice made a statement. They didn't quite trust their Creator—they weren't sure YAHWEH was telling the truth. They considered Satan's word more reliable. In their mind, Satan made the better friend, and in making this choice, they sided with Satan against the LORD.

> They exchanged the truth of God for a lie … and served created
> things [such as Satan] rather than the Creator …[4]
>
> Romans 1:25 NIV

But such a choice had ramifications. We saw earlier that God is a God of order—he has established rules in the universe for mankind's safety. But wherever you have a law, you also have a consequence. God had given Adam and Eve one very simple rule to keep: *Don't eat from that one tree.* Now they had broken that one law. What would be the consequence?

# 4 WHERE ARE YOU?

It is important to understand that Adam and Eve's choice to sin was not the result of something they had been programmed to do. It wasn't their fate or some sort of karma. No. They had freely chosen to trust Satan all on their own! So they ate.

## FEAR, GUILT AND SHAME

Immediately, they sensed something was wrong. They had feelings they had never experienced before—very uncomfortable ones—feelings called *fear*, *guilt*, and *shame*. The Bible says,

> ... the eyes of both of them were opened, and they knew that they were naked ... *Genesis 3:7 NKJV*

Casting their eyes around for a solution,

> ... they sewed fig leaves together and made themselves coverings. *Genesis 3:7 NKJV*

Perhaps they thought that if they fixed up their outward appearance, God would never notice they had changed on the inside. They would just gloss things over and pretend everything was okay.

There was only one problem with the fig leaf solution—it didn't work. Having a good outward appearance did not remedy the inner reality. The feelings of fear, shame, and guilt still churned within. The Bible says that when ...

> ... they heard the sound of the LORD God walking in the garden in the cool of the day ... Adam and his wife hid themselves from the presence of the LORD God among the trees of the garden. *Genesis 3:8 NKJV*

You can imagine the pounding hearts, the sweaty palms, the dry mouths as they crouched out of sight in the garden, listening to YAHWEH approach. What would their Creator-Owner say?

What would an all-powerful God do with two disobedient humans?

> Then the LORD God called to Adam and said to him, "Where are you?" *Genesis 3:9 NKJV*

That question must have given Adam and Eve immense relief. Apparently Y*AHWEH* didn't know what had happened. He didn't even know where they were! Masking their faces with innocence, they poked their heads out. *"Ahh, are you looking for us?"* Adam spoke for them both.

> *"I heard the sound of You in the garden, and I was afraid because I was naked; so I hid myself."*　　　　Genesis 3:10 NASB

He spoke, but he erred. Like a boy playing hooky from school and then writing his own absentee note signed, "My mom," Adam overlooked the fact that he had never felt fear before, or that his nakedness had never bothered him. The L*ORD* said,

> *"Who told you that you were naked? Did you eat from the tree that I commanded you not to eat from?"*　　　　Genesis 3:11 NET

## QUESTIONS, QUESTIONS!

Why was Y*AHWEH* asking all these questions? Did an all-knowing God not know where Adam and Eve were hiding? And would he not know why they were feeling naked? Was the L*ORD* really so limited that he had to ask the culprits whether they had eaten of the forbidden fruit? The truth of the matter was that God knew exactly what had occurred—but he was asking questions to help Adam and Eve sort out in their minds precisely what had happened. They had betrayed their friend!

## BLAME GAME

The L*ORD*'s questions gave Adam and Eve an opportunity to seek reconciliation, but instead Adam blamed Eve—and God.

> The man said, "The woman whom YOU gave me—she gave me some fruit from the tree and I ate it."　　　　Genesis 3:12 NET

Adam was feeling victimized!

> So the L*ORD* God said to the woman, "What is this you have done?" And the woman replied, "The SERPENT tricked me, and I ate."　　　　Genesis 3:13 NET

So neither Adam nor Eve thought they were to blame!

The truth of the matter is that no one had forced them to disobey the L*ORD*. They had freely followed Satan, joining his side. Now Y*AHWEH* had given them an opportunity to admit their sin, and they had refused.

## A PROMISE

This initial sin had severe ramifications on the rest of mankind. As we will see, Adam and Eve were acting on behalf of the whole human race. But though they had failed their probation, God did not desert them.

> Because of the LORD's great love we are not consumed, for his compassions never fail.　　　　　*Lamentations 3:22 NIV*

God, in his great love, made a promise.

> ...the LORD God said to the serpent, "Because you have done this...I will put enmity between you and the woman, and between your offspring and hers; he will crush your head, and you will strike his heel."　　　　　*Genesis 3:14-15 NIV*

These sentences deserve a closer examination. Let's look again at what Moses wrote. The promise had two facets:

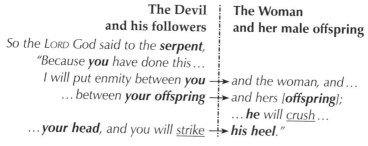

The LORD was saying that he would one day rescue mankind from Satan. The LORD promised that a *man* would come, born of the woman, who would crush the Devil's head—a fatal wound. True, Satan would one day hurt this *man*, but only with a strike at the heel—a temporary injury from which he would recover.

This was the first of many promises about this future offspring of Eve. This *man* would be known as THE ANOINTED ONE because of the special assignment given to him by God. The task the LORD had for this CHOSEN ONE was to *deliver* or *save* mankind from the consequences of sin. For this reason he would also be known as THE PROMISED DELIVERER.

| THE PROMISED DELIVERER would be ... |
|---|
| 1. The offspring of a woman |
| 2. A male |

This promise of a *DELIVERER* added another name to the list of terms that reveal this God's character. He would be known as *the one who saves* or *THE SAVIOUR*. Indeed, the Bible says only the LORD YAHWEH has the credentials to *save* mankind. No other god or goddess qualifies. The LORD tells us he is…

> *"A righteous God and a Savior; There is none except Me."*
> Isaiah 45:21 NASB

## A CURSE

As we said before, breaking one of God's laws has consequences. It always does. Just as defying the law of gravity brings broken bones, so violating God's word has ramifications. One sin brought more sin. The earth and everything in it suffered from a curse. The animals, the sea, the bird life, even the very ground was affected. No longer was creation perfect. As a result of the curse, the Bible says,

> *…the whole creation groans and labors…*  Romans 8:22 NKJV

Everything would run down, break down, or wear out. Life on this planet would be full of injustice, sweat, and misery. From every corner of the animal kingdom to all mankind, life would involve perpetual struggle. The world was no longer a very good place.

Fear, guilt, and shame would become hallmarks of a sin-cursed world. As I have travelled the world, I have noticed that eastern cultures are preoccupied with shame, western cultures are troubled by guilt, and tribal cultures are obsessed with fear. But in truth, people everywhere have the same problem because these feelings are the direct result of sin. We don't like shame, we hate guilt, and we abhor fear, but the thing we dread the most is the very thing the LORD YAHWEH warned mankind about. It's called *death*.

# 5 DEATH

In a very real sense, when Adam and Eve chose to defy God's warning, they tested the LORD to see if he would keep his word. Did God really mean what he said? Would man really die? Or was God just talking, uttering empty threats—bombast without teeth? The Scripture's reply is quite emphatic:

> *…it is easier for heaven and earth to pass away than for one stroke of a letter of the Law [that Moses wrote] to fail.*  Luke 16:17 NASB

We don't like talking about death. It's a taboo subject. In my travels I have visited some of the most remote people groups on the planet. I have never found a society that enjoyed death. I have stood at many open graves, some in cemeteries, some in jungles, but they all shared one common denominator—grief. It is burnt into the human psyche with the branding iron of reality that death means one thing—separation. The loved one has slipped out of our presence to never return. The sense of loss and separation we feel at that time brings us very close to the meaning of "death" as defined by Scripture. **In the Bible, death implies some sort of separation.**

The Bible speaks of death as a consequence of sin—a reward, payment, or penalty for wrongdoing. Just as a person is paid wages for working, so...

> ... *the wages of sin is death*...　　　　　*Romans 6:23 NASB*

The Scripture speaks about death in a number of different ways. We will look at three.

**1. Death to a Friendship** (A separation of man from God)
We saw that Adam and Eve...

> ... *heard the sound of the* LORD *God walking in the garden in the cool of the day, and the man and his wife hid themselves from the presence of the* LORD *God*...　　　*Genesis 3:8 ESV*

What was going on here? One doesn't hide from a friend. Well, that is true, but according to the Bible, trust is the basis for all relationships. When trust is broken, businesses break apart, associations dissolve, friends split up, and marriages end in divorce. If you distrust a person, it means you don't have faith in him, you don't believe him, and you don't take him at his word. When Adam and Eve put their faith in Satan's word, in essence, they said that YAHWEH had lied to them. Their friendship with God was shattered. So they hid.

But the consequences went even further. The children of Adam and Eve and their children's children—indeed all mankind to this day—have been born into this world...

> ... *alienated from God*...　　　　　*Colossians 1:21 NIV*

But there is another dynamic here that we must not miss. Let me illustrate.

I have spent a significant portion of my life living in tropical countries. For a time, my wife and I had a house set on low stilts. On one occasion a very large rat chose to crawl into the narrow space under our house and die. Unfortunately, the vermin expired right under our little bedroom. The carcass rotting in the hot, humid climate sent a stupefying odor into our bedroom, giving new meaning to the word *foul*. It smelled so rank that we found it impossible to sleep and were forced to retreat to another part of the dwelling.

The next morning my son, Andrew, volunteered to remedy the situation. He located a long stick, and reaching deep into the crawl space under the house, slowly worked the dead rat towards the opening. As it got close, Andrew pulled back in revulsion, grimaced and said, *"Dad! The beast is full of maggots."* Oh gag! Andrew took a plastic bag and sticking it over his hand, reached far under the house. Grabbing the miserable creature by its tail, he pulled the worm-infested cadaver out into the open. Holding the offending remains far from his body, he ran towards the jungle that bordered our property, and with a mighty swing, flung the rat far from his presence.

Now, if that rat had been able to read Andrew's thoughts as he was flung into the woods, he would have heard him say, *"Get out of here!"* And if the rat could have spoken and said, *"For how long?"* Andrew would have answered, *"Forever!"*

The dead rat illustrates two ways the Lord feels about sin.

❖ First, just as the rat drove my wife and me to sleep in another room, and just as Andrew flung that revolting carcass out of his presence, so …

ESTRANGED

> … your iniquities have separated you from your God; And your sins have hidden His face from you …　　　*Isaiah 59:2 NKJV*

Remember how we said that the Bible compares sin to something that has gone rotten? Well, sin is to the Lord what a rotten rat is to us. Just as sleeping in close proximity to that evil-smelling carcass was not normal for us, so it is not natural for a holy God to allow sin in his presence. His …

> … eyes are too pure to look on evil; [he] cannot tolerate wrong.
> 　　　*Habakkuk 1:13 NIV*

Since sin has tainted the life of every human, God has distanced himself from us. It is a consequence of sin.

❖ This brings us to the second point that the dead rat illustrates. Just how long does the LORD feel we should be separated from him? The answer is pretty clear. Forever! Sin has infinite and eternal ramifications. Just like we would not want to live with the rotten rat next week, or at any time, God will never allow sin to dwell in his presence.

So it was that sin destroyed that first friendship. A barrier, a chasm now existed between God and man. Man was...

> ...dead in...transgressions and sins. Ephesians 2:1 NET

**2. Death of the Body** (A separation of man's spirit from his body)
As a result of the sin-curse, man would now enter the world through the pain of childbirth and depart it by the agonies of death. God told Adam,

DEAD

> "By the sweat of your brow you will eat food until you return to the ground, for out of it you were taken; for you are dust, and to dust you will return." Genesis 3:19 NET

Physical death is not hard for us to grasp. But we need to understand something more as it relates to Adam and Eve.

When you cut a leafy branch off a tree, the leaves don't instantly wither and look dead. In the same way, when God told Adam *"for when you eat of it you will surely die,"* God did not mean that Adam would drop dead as soon as he ate the fruit. Rather, the LORD meant that Adam would be cut off from his source of life, and then, just like a branch, his body would eventually wear out and stop functioning. The body would...

> ...die and return to dust. Psalm 104:29 NET

You have probably heard the expression *"once you are dead, you are dead"* meaning that once your body dies your spirit ceases to exist as well, but this is not what the Bible teaches. It is true that...

> ...the body without the spirit is dead... James 2:26 NASB

...but the Scripture also clearly states that the human spirit, once born, exists forever, even apart from the body. Nowhere does the Bible teach extinction or *annihilation* of the soul.

Neither does the Scripture teach *assimilation*, the idea that, upon death, a person is absorbed into nature.

Rather, the Bible says that after death the human spirit continues to exist as a thinking, feeling being—yet without a physical body.

Though *annihilation* and *assimilation* are traditional or trendy concepts, they are not taught in Scripture. The same can be said of *reincarnation*, the idea that, after death, a departed spirit can return to the earth to live again in another form. Nowhere in the Bible's pages did Moses, or any of the 40 writers, record a "circle of life"—the birth, death, rebirth and redeath of a human spirit. Not only is reincarnation not taught in the Bible, the Scripture clearly teaches the opposite. Each person has only one life.

> *…people are appointed to die once, and then to face judgment…*
> Hebrews 9:27 NET

> *As the cloud disappears and vanishes away, So he who goes down to the grave does not come up. He shall never return to his house, nor shall his place know him any more.* Job 7:9-10 NKJV

At this point it would be logical to ask, *"If it is true that a person has only one life, and when the body dies the spirit continues to exist, then just where does the human spirit live after it departs this life? Where are our ancestors living at this moment in time? What does the Bible say?"* These are good questions that will be addressed in the coming chapters. For now, let us look at one more way that the Bible uses the word *"death."*

### 3. Death to a Future Joy—The Second Death

(A separation of man's spirit from God forever)

Some say, *"If a person asks you 'Where do you go when you die?' then answer with silence."* This sounds profound, but it avoids the issue. In contrast, the Bible addresses the matter head-on.

The Scripture tells us that God is preparing a wonderful home for man after he dies. It's called Heaven. Heaven is an incredible place, designed by YAHWEH for man's eternal joy. Just being free of sin, suffering and death will be wonderful.

ETERNAL
JUDGMENT

But just as there is eternal life, so there is eternal death. This death is also called *the second death*, probably because it occurs after physical death. This *second death* is reserved for those people who will not be living in the perfect world to come. Instead, the Bible says they will be sent to the Lake of Fire, an appalling place God created specifically for punishing Satan and his demons.

> *This is the second death—the lake of fire.* Revelation 20:14 NET

When mankind abandoned friendship with God, he joined the ranks of those who rebelled against their Creator; he joined hands with Satan, who is…

> *The god of this age…*    2 Corinthians 4:4 NKJV

> *…the ruler of this world…*    John 12:31 NKJV

The Bible says,

> *…whoever wishes to be a friend of the world makes himself an enemy of God.*    James 4:4 NASB

ENEMY

All the enemies of God—whether human or spirit—will one day be cast into the…

> *…eternal fire prepared for the devil and his angels.*
> Matthew 25:41 ESV

The Bible speaks of being ᵃ*thrown alive into the fiery lake of burning sulfur*, and of being ᵇ*tormented day and night forever and ever*. It will be a place of ᶜ*sorrow*, devoid of happiness. The Scriptures talk of ᵈ*worms* (literally *maggots*), of an intense ᵉ*darkness*, of people *weeping and gnashing their teeth* in anguish, of being parched with ᶠ*thirst*, and of remembering this life and wishing for no one to join them. Hell is a place of lonely suffering, not some buddy-buddy celebration of debauchery.

ᵃ Rev. 19:20 Though the physical body dies, the spirit continues to live.
ᵇ Rev. 20:10
ᶜ Psalm 116:3
ᵈ Mark 9:48
ᵉ Matthew 8:12; 22:13; 25:30
ᶠ Luke 16:24

> But cowards, unbelievers, the corrupt, murderers, the immoral, those who practice witchcraft, idol worshipers, and all liars—their fate is in the fiery lake of burning sulfur. This is the second death.
> Revelation 21:8 NLT

Later on we will see how it is decided where a person will live—whether in Heaven or Hell.

### A MARRED IMAGE

When Adam and Eve sinned, they marred the image of God in which they had been created—they dulled the glory of God in which they had been formed. One can still see aspects of that image—the glory is still there to a certain extent, but it is thoroughly blemished. That spoiling effect is like a fatal disease, extending to every aspect of man's being.

For example, some time ago a friend of mine was diagnosed with cancer. At first none of us could tell anything was wrong, but we all knew he had this problem—this condition. But then, slowly the cancer began to reveal itself with symptoms. His speech became slurred and his skin took on a yellowish colour. He no longer had the energy he once did. We all knew it was just a matter of time before the cancer would take his life. In the same sense, we can say that every human being has a lethal condition the Bible calls the *sin nature*, or *Adam's nature*. This cancerous sin condition will one day take away life.

Like an apple polished on the outside, but rotten at the core, people often hide their sin condition quite well. But now and then we see symptoms of rottenness—the sin nature reveals its presence every time a person does something wrong.

### All Mankind

In Sri Lanka there is a mountain called *Adam's Peak*. Some claim that the summit has on it a giant imprint of Adam's foot. We will see that the world Adam and Eve lived in was destroyed, so any footprints would have been obliterated, but the Bible does make one thing clear—since the days of Adam, all mankind has been "walking in his footsteps."

Because of his sin, all his offspring have inherited his sin nature. And because he died, all his offspring die.[5]

> *Therefore, just as sin came into the world through one man, and death through sin, and so death spread to all men because all sinned.* Romans 5:12 ESV

### An Honest God

If all this talk of sin and death seems morbid, it should be a reminder to us that God doesn't make unpleasant subjects pretty. As a good friend should, he tells us what we need to know. In contrast to the Lord's honesty, the Bible says,

> *…the god of this world [which is the Devil] has blinded the minds of the unbelieving…* 2 Corinthians 4:4 NASB

Satan speaks lies. He blinds the minds of people with half-truths, lulling them to sleep with deceptions just as subtle as those he used on Adam and Eve. Satan is no friend. Instead the Scripture says…

> *…the devil prowls around like a roaring lion, seeking someone to devour.* 1 Peter 5:8 ESV

This is all very discouraging, but read on; there is good news coming.

## WHAT HAVE GENETICISTS FOUND?

*"It makes us realize that all human beings, despite differences in external appearances, are really members of a single entity that's had a very recent origin in one place. There is a kind of biological brotherhood that's much more profound than we ever realized."* So said the late Stephen Jay Gould, the Harvard paleontologist and essayist in a NEWSWEEK *1988* cover article entitled, "The Search for Adam and Eve."[6]

According to the article, scientists *"...trained in molecular biology...looked at an international assortment of genes and picked up a trail of DNA that led them to a single woman from whom we all descended."..."There weren't even telltale distinctions between races."*

The Bible says,

> *...Adam called his wife's name Eve, because she was the mother of all living.*　　　　Genesis 3:20 NKJV

Then in 1995, TIME[7] had a brief article saying there was scientific evidence that *"...there was an ancestral 'Adam,' whose genetic material on the chromosome is common to every man now on earth."*

The Bible says,

> *From one man he created all the nations throughout the whole earth...*　　　　Acts 17:26 NLT

These studies of human DNA conclude that we all have one man and one woman in our ancestry. Some scientists agree; others disagree. Even those who agree are quick to point out that this may not be the biblical Adam and Eve. Whatever the case, it's interesting to note that the findings are consistent with the Bible. This and other discoveries of modern molecular biology confirm what the Scripture has indicated for thousands of years: that we are all very closely related.

## A Review —The Bridge of Friendship

In the beginning *Yahweh* and man were close friends, living in harmony in a perfect world. Only perfect people can live with a perfect God.

The relational bridge was broken when Adam and Eve believed Satan's word instead of the *Lord's*, and disobeyed God's clear instructions. The whole world changed. It became a place of fear, guilt, shame, sorrow, and death.

After Adam and Eve sinned, they tried to cover their sin by improving their outward appearance. But the fig leaves didn't work. The gulf remained. Sin and death now reigned in Adam's bloodline, seemingly passed on through the generations by the father. Like begets like—apples reproduce apples, cats reproduce cats, sinful man reproduces sinful man.

As we continue our story, we will see that it is in the nature of man to deny his true sinfulness, to devise ways to reach God, to seek a way back to a perfect world.

## A Review —To what is sin compared?

1. **Unrighteousness:** Thoughts and actions opposite of what is right; that which is wrong.

2. **Rottenness, Corruption:** When goodness has been lost in the spoiling effect of sin; when humility is replaced with arrogance and self-centeredness.

3. **Disobedience, Rebellion:** To disregard instructions because you think you know *better-than-God*.

4. **Disease:** A lethal illness or *condition* of the spirit, a cancerous sin nature that results in eternal death. Sinful acts are *symptoms* of that inner *condition*.

It has become popular to believe that children are born into the world as perfect infants, free of all sin. But what do the Scriptures teach? Are we really born with a sinless nature?

Not according to *King David*, one of the 40 prophets who wrote significant portions of Scripture:

> For I was born a sinner—yes, from the moment my mother conceived me.  *Psalm 51:5 NLT*

Not according to *Job*, whose book is found in the Bible:

> Who can bring a clean thing out of an unclean? No one!
> *Job 14:4 NKJV*

Not according to our own life experiences:

> What is causing the quarrels and fights among you? Don't they come from the evil desires at war within you?  *James 4:1 NLT*

Adam by nature had become a sinner—Adam would die.

We have to ask ourselves some tough questions. Did our parents have to teach us to lie and disobey, to be selfish and quarrelsome? No. Our human nature does not need to be taught how to sin. We do such things naturally.

Sin is like a contagious disease. The Scripture says that Adam's sin nature (along with all its symptoms and consequences) has spread to us all. Because Adam sinned, all of his children have inherited his sin nature.

All of Adam's descendants would have the sin nature—all would die.

# CHAPTER FIVE

# 1 A PARADOX

In the first chapters we learned a little about the character of YAHWEH. As we progress we will learn more, but first, we need to stop, strengthen the foundation and fit together some more pieces of the biblical puzzle.

It is helpful to understand that just as YAHWEH established physical laws to govern the universe, so he established spiritual laws to govern his relationship with man. And just as a basic knowledge of physics and chemistry helps us make sense of the world around us, so a knowledge of these spiritual laws helps us make sense of life and death. These spiritual rules are not difficult to understand. To begin with, we will look at man's situation.

## MAN'S SITUATION

Because of Adam and Eve's choice, mankind now faced a dilemma, a problem with two facets, like opposite sides of the same coin.

❖ We have something we don't want—**a sin-penalty**, and…

❖ We need something we don't have—**perfection**.

Let me explain in greater depth.

1. **We have a sin-penalty.** We all know that in sports, when a player breaks a rule, he is penalized. But what is a sin-penalty and just how is it paid? To answer these questions, the Bible makes comparisons with ancient **judicial** and **financial** traditions. Both use the concept of a *Certificate of Debt*.

> **Judicial Comparison:** In this case, misconduct is viewed as a *debt* to society that must be *paid* with an appropriate punishment.
>
>
> DEBTOR
>
> The seeds of this thinking can be found in ancient Rome, where a lawbreaker could not be brought to trial until formally charged with a written *Certificate of Debt* detailing the offense. If the accused was found guilty, the judge recorded the sentence on the Certificate (*e.g. "Prison—five years!"*). The Certificate, detailing *both the offense and the required payment*, was nailed to the door of the prison cell. There it remained until the sentence was *paid*, at which time it was taken down and presented to the authorities. They would write *"cancelled"* or *"paid in full"* across the indictment and the prisoner was set free.

In the same way, the Bible teaches that every human is faced with a written charge—*a Certificate of Debt*—upon which are written the individual's sins, whether big or small. Man is pictured as standing in a courtroom, found guilty of an offense against a holy God. The judge reads the verdict. According to the…

> …*law of sin and death*…  Romans 8:2 ESV

…the penalty to be paid is death.

> *The person who sins will die*…  Ezekiel 18:20 NASB

God had warned Adam and Eve about this law when he told them they would die if they disobeyed his word.

DEBTOR

**Financial Comparison:** Centuries ago in the Middle East, when one incurred a debt, an official IOU was drafted. That IOU was also called a *Certificate of Debt*. It stated the terms of the loan and what it would take to pay it in full.

In the same way, the Bible teaches that on the moral ledger, our sin incurs a debt—there is a price to be paid. Man is pictured standing before a loan officer holding a *Certificate of Debt* that has come due. The *Certificate* states that…

> …*the wages [or payment] of sin is death*…  Romans 6:23 NKJV

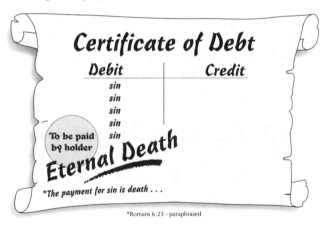

SEPARATED

Whether viewed as a *sin-penalty* or a *sin-debt*, the consequence for sin is the same—death in all its three-part meaning.

DEAD

The question then remains: *Is man able to pay that debt?* The answer is a qualified *yes*. But since the *Second Death* exists for eternity, it is hard to call it paid since the *Certificate of Debt* nailed to Hell's door has "*Eternal Death*" written on it. Sinful man is locked up forever—a person never stops paying.

ETERNAL
JUDGMENT

This is very bad news. Mankind is in an awful dilemma.

But this is only one side of the problem. There is the other side of the coin we must consider. You see, even if our sin-debt was *"erased"* or *"paid in full,"* we still could not live with God in Heaven because we need something we don't have.

**2. We need perfection.** Since only perfect people can live with a perfect God in a perfect Heaven, we need what Adam and Eve lost in the garden—we need to be remade in the unblemished image of God. The Scripture says,

> *…without holiness no one will see the Lord.*   Hebrews 12:14 NIV

This goodness, or righteousness, must be equal to the LORD's righteousness. Since no one even comes close to that sort of perfection, we have a problem.

### SUMMARY

As a result of Adam's sin, mankind was faced with a **two-sides-of-the-same-coin** question: *How can we get rid of our sin-penalty? And how can we gain a righteousness that is equal to God's righteousness, so that we can be accepted in his presence?*

Now that we have identified man's dilemma, let us turn our attention to YAHWEH and see how this affects him.

### THE LORD'S SITUATION

To appreciate the LORD's situation, we need to understand two attributes that are part of his character.

**1. YAHWEH is perfectly just:** We like justice. It bothers us when a bully takes advantage of a weaker individual. Even as children we knew it wasn't fair when people "got away" with being mean. But even if our sense of justice becomes distorted, that does not affect the way YAHWEH views things.

> *For the righteous LORD loves justice…*   Psalm 11:7 NLT

Since Y*AHWEH* is without sin, he is honest and fair in the way he deals with his created beings.

> He is the Rock; his deeds are perfect. Everything he does is just and fair. He is a faithful God who does no wrong; how just and upright he is! Deuteronomy 32:4 NLT

The L*ORD* is an ideal judge because he treats everyone the same.

> For the L*ORD* your God is the God of gods and the Lord of lords, the great, the mighty, and the awesome God who does not show partiality nor take a bribe. Deuteronomy 10:17 NASB

Whether dealing with prince or pauper, the L*ORD* enforces his rules equally and fairly. Here on earth a person may hide a crime, lie about it, bribe the judge, or simply not get caught. But with God, no perpetrator will get away with sin.

> For God will bring every act to judgment, everything which is hidden, whether it is good or evil. Ecclesiastes 12:14 NASB

Honesty and fairness are fundamental to God's perfect nature.

> Righteousness and justice are the foundation of Your throne… Psalm 89:14 NASB

SEPARATED

DEAD

ETERNAL
JUDGMENT

When Adam and Eve sinned, God could not say, "*Oh, forget it,*" or, "*We'll pretend it never happened,*" or, "*It was just one little sin.*" No. That would have gone against God's perfect character. The L*ORD* had to do something about man's sin—it had to be dealt with. It's indicative of just how seriously God views sin by the penalty assigned to it—death in its three-part meaning. Again, this is not good news. Thankfully, the other aspect of God's character must be kept in the picture.

**2. Y*AHWEH* is perfectly loving:** God is not only just, but by his very nature, he loves. We saw that the L*ORD* demonstrated his love when he made the world. It was shown in the care he gave to what he created and how he…

> …richly provides us with all things for our enjoyment. 1 Timothy 6:17 NET

It was Adam and Eve who broke the friendship with God, but God had not changed. Y*AHWEH* still loved them. What he did not love was their sin.

> Give thanks to the God of gods, For His lovingkindness is everlasting. Give thanks to the Lord of lords, For His lovingkindness is everlasting. Psalm 136:2-3 NASB

## THE PARADOX

God's just and loving nature creates a paradox when you consider it in light of mankind's dilemma— **sin equals death**. To be completely *just*, God must enforce his rules without exception. It means we all must pay our sin-debt—we all must die. But because God is *loving*, he has no desire to punish us. He wants us to live with him for eternity, as friends.

Both qualities of his character are equal—God is not more loving than he is just. Since YAHWEH always acts in a way that is consistent with his perfect nature, he will always express both attributes equally. The question is this: *"How can the LORD maintain justice and still be loving?"*

## SIN NEVER IGNORED

The Bible is clear that God punishes all sin either here on earth or after physical death. There is no escape. This is so certain, the Scripture says it's…

> *Like water spilled on the ground, which cannot be recovered, so we must die.*                    2 Samuel 14:14a NIV

But the verse does not stop there. Because God is also loving,

> *…he devises ways so that a banished person may not remain estranged from him.*                    2 Samuel 14:14b NIV

Although God allows our physical bodies to die, he has provided a way for our spirits to escape the *Lake of Fire*. He makes it possible for us to live in his presence again—as friends.

> *For the LORD…will have compassion according to the abundance of his steadfast love…*                    Lamentations 3:31-32 ESV

So how does the LORD judge sin and rescue us at the same time? How does God punish sin without punishing us? We will find the answers to those questions as we continue the story.

## PRIDE

One last thing before we move on. The Bible says that pride is what caused Satan to rebel. We often look at pride as being a good thing, but the Scripture says pride is what keeps us from coming to God for help. We are often too proud to humble ourselves and say that we need the LORD. The Scripture warns us that…

> *God opposes the proud but gives grace to the humble.*
> 1 Peter 5:5 ESV

Instead of being controlled by our pride and worrying about what others think of us, the LORD says ...

> "Let not the wise man boast in his wisdom, let not the mighty man boast in his might, let not the rich man boast in his riches, but let him who boasts boast in this, that he understands and knows me, that I am the LORD who practices steadfast love, justice, and righteousness in the earth. For in these things I delight, declares the LORD." Jeremiah 9:23-24 ESV

---

I come from a country where ice hockey is the big game. When a player breaks a rule, he is penalized. The offender must sit in a special box on the sidelines for a set period of time. Officially it is called the "penalty box," but sometimes referred to as the "sin-bin."

In the same way, we humans have broken God's rules. We will have to sit in the penalty box of Hell, not for a set period of time, but forever. When you stop and think about it, it's an awful future. However, good news is coming!

ETERNAL
JUDGMENT

---

# 2 TWO OFFERINGS

Now let's return to the events recorded in the book of Genesis.

Moses wrote that after eating the fruit, the first thing Adam and Eve did was to clothe themselves in fig leaves. In spite of these coverings, Adam told the LORD that he felt naked—exposed. There is a reason for this. The Bible tells us that ...

> ... God does not view things the way men do. People look on the **outward appearance**, but the LORD looks at the **heart**.
> 1 Samuel 16:7 NET

Adam and Eve had fixed up their **outward appearance** with fig leaves, but the Lord was looking at their **hearts** and saw them as they really were—disobedient and deceitful—sinful.

## A COVERING

God didn't argue with Adam and Eve over whether they needed a covering or not, but he did refuse to accept their fig leaf clothes. Instead ...

> The LORD God made garments of skin for Adam and his wife, and clothed them.
> Genesis 3:21 NASB

Why did God do this? The Scripture doesn't give us details at this point, but using the totality of God's Word we can see that this is the first hint of a concept called *atonement*.

The word *atonement* encompasses many concepts, but at its most basic level it has the idea of a *covering*—in a sense, having the *right clothes* for the heart. In the Scriptures, a sinful man is pictured as clothed in *filthy rags*, in contrast to a righteous man who is covered in *spotless garments*. These are not literal clothes, but mere pictures to help us understand spiritual truth. In the Bible there are only two coverings for the heart.

| Filthy rags | Spotless garments |
| --- | --- |
| Pictures mankind clothed in his own sin | Pictures mankind clothed in God's righteousness |
| No atonement-covering | Having atonement |
| All that man has | Provided by God |

God rejected Adam and Eve's fig leaves because they were the efforts of sinful people trying to make themselves good enough for God. Those efforts fit in the *filthy rag* category. Only when YAHWEH provided **his** *covering* were they accepted back into His presence.

| The fig leaf covering | The animal skin covering |
| --- | --- |
| The work of sinful man to gain acceptance with God | The work of God himself to provide a way of acceptance |
| Rejected by God | Accepted by God |

**MERCY**

> And the LORD God said, "Now that the man has become like one of us, knowing good and evil, he must not be allowed to stretch out his hand and take also from the tree of life and eat, and live forever." So the LORD God expelled him from ... Eden ...
>
> Genesis 3:22–23 NET

This was an act of mercy. God did not want men to live forever entrapped as sinners. Think what the world would be like if all the evil people down through the ages were still alive today. By putting Adam and Eve outside the garden, God allowed the consequence of sin to take its eventual toll, namely physical death. God was thinking beyond the grave. He was thinking of his plan to deliver man from the *Second Death*.

Moses wrote,

> Adam lay with his wife Eve, and she became pregnant and gave
> birth to Cain. She said, "With the help of the LORD I have brought
> forth a man." Later she gave birth to his brother Abel.
>
> Genesis 4:1-2 NIV

### CAIN AND ABEL

Both Cain and Abel were born outside of the garden. Because
they were conceived as a result of Adam's union with Eve, they
had Adam's sin problem—they were alienated from God. And
just like Adam and Eve, Cain and Abel would have to decide who
they were going to trust—the LORD or someone else?

> Abel took care of the flocks, while Cain cultivated the ground. At
> the designated time Cain brought some of the fruit of the ground
> for an offering to the LORD. But Abel brought some of the firstborn
> of his flock—even the fattest... Genesis 4:2-4 NET

### TWO OFFERINGS

These two offerings are very significant. One consisted of an
animal, the other—vegetables. Cain and Abel brought these
offerings, not because God was hungry, but because of specific
instructions YAHWEH had given them. At this point in the text
those directions are only alluded to, but later on they are given
in detail. For now it is enough to know that...

> ...the LORD was pleased with Abel and his offering, but with
> Cain and his offering he was not pleased. Genesis 4:4-5 NET

Why was this?

### ABEL

The Bible says Abel trusted the LORD—you'd
expect that in a friendship.

> By faith Abel offered to God a more
> acceptable sacrifice than Cain, through
> which he was commended as righteous,
> God commending him by accepting his
> gifts... Hebrews 11:4 ESV

Abel's offering had something in common
with the skin clothing that God had made for
Adam and Eve. It had to do with that concept
called *atonement*, the means whereby a holy God provides sinful man
with *spotless garments* so that mankind can be accepted by God.

God was pleased that Abel had faith in him. Because Abel trusted YAHWEH, the LORD, accepted Abel as one would accept a friend.

## CAIN

As for Cain, his offering had more in common with the fig leaves—his efforts fit in the *filthy rag* category. And like his parents, he wasn't sure whether he could trust God or not. But Cain *did* know someone in whom he had complete confidence— it was in himself!

Cain put faith in Cain. In essence, Cain elevated himself to the same level as God, as if he knew as much as YAHWEH. The Bible says the LORD disapproved of Cain's attitude. As a result,

> … Cain became very angry, and his expression was downcast.
> Genesis 4:5 NET

Cain was upset: *Didn't God realize what a big thing he had done? He had brought an offering that involved a lot of hard work! Abel could sit in the shade and watch his animals grow as they grazed, but gardening took backbreaking labour in the sun! How could God reject his sacrifice as if it was nothing? It was embarrassing. He had been shamed.*

Well, we don't know what Cain thought, but we do know that YAHWEH never asked him to work hard in order to be accepted. The LORD just wanted Cain to trust him as one would trust a friend. But Cain missed the point.

> Then the LORD said to Cain, "Why are you angry? Why is your face downcast? If you do what is right, will you not be accepted? But if you do not do what is right, sin is crouching at your door; it desires to have you, but you must master it." Genesis 4:6–7 NIV

God gently tried to show Cain that he was headed for trouble. He pointed out to Cain that he too would be accepted if he came the same way Abel had come. Cain now had a choice:

1. He could humble himself, simply trust the LORD and bring the same sacrifice as Abel, or…
2. He could continue to put faith in himself—in his own line of reasoning.

Cain made a choice. He ignored YAHWEH.

### Gentle Questions

*Cain said to his brother Abel, "Let's go out to the field." While they were in the field, Cain attacked his brother Abel and killed him.*

*Then the Lord said to Cain, "Where is your brother Abel?"*

Genesis 4:8-9 NET

Just as God quizzed Adam and Eve, so the Lord gave Cain a chance to admit his sin. But Cain lied. He said,

*"I do not know. Am I my brother's keeper?"*  Genesis 4:9 NKJV

And just like Adam and Eve, Cain avoided taking responsibility for his own actions. God said,

*"What have you done? The voice of your brother's blood cries out to Me from the ground."*  Genesis 4:10 NKJV

God put his finger on Cain—*"You murdered your brother!"* There is no record of Cain expressing remorse for his actions. The Lord could have destroyed him, but in his mercy, God moved him to another region. The human race had gotten off to a scandalous start.

### Seth

*And Adam had marital relations with his wife again, and she gave birth to a son. She named him Seth, saying, "God has given me another child in place of Abel because Cain killed him." And a son was also born to Seth, whom he named Enosh. At that time people began to worship the Lord.*  Genesis 4:25-26 NET

Although Seth was born with a sin nature, he trusted God just like Abel. It was through Seth and his descendants that God would send the Saviour. God was keeping his promise.

### Death

Well, it's time to leave Adam. The Bible says he had a large family and lived to be extremely old.

*After the birth of Seth, Adam lived another 800 years and he had other sons and daughters.*  Genesis 5:4 NLT

DEAD

Scientists increasingly believe that the length of one's life is genetically determined. Originally, that genetic limit could have been set for a longer life span. We will see later what may have caused the change. Whatever the reason, God's Word finally came true for Adam. Moses summed it up with these words:

*The entire lifetime of Adam was 930 years, and then he died.*

Genesis 5:5 NET

## SUMMARY

In this story we see two approaches to God:

| The way of Cain | The way of Abel |
|---|---|
| Offered vegetables from his garden | Offered an animal from his flock |
| Relied on his own ideas | Believed God knew what was best |
| Rejected by God | Accepted by God |

We saw that Cain fell into the same sin as Adam and Eve, trusting in someone other than the LORD. Neither Cain nor his parents were able to bridge the gap in the broken friendship.

Indeed, Cain's reliance on himself and his own ideas led to anger, lies, and murder. The Bible says,

> Do not be like Cain, who belonged to the evil one…his own actions were evil and his brother's were righteous. 1 John 3:12 NIV

## WHAT HAPPENED TO ABEL WHEN HE DIED?

Although the Bible does not explicitly mention where Abel's spirit went when he was murdered, we know from other Scriptures that those who trusted God went to a place called *Paradise*, a place God prepared for believing men and women. Some Bible scholars would differentiate between Paradise and Heaven during this time in history, but many believe that they have now merged into one location.

The Bible does not tell us a lot about Heaven, possibly because it is difficult for our fog-bound mortal brains to comprehend it. One of the 40 biblical writers who was given a peek at the place, was left wanting for concrete words, resorting to word pictures to get his point across. The Bible says Heaven is a real place with real people living there. It will be like Eden, only incomparably better.

Man's sin nature—his filthy rags—will be gone.

> Nothing impure will ever enter it, nor will anyone who does what is shameful or deceitful, but only those whose names are written in the … book of life.      Revelation 21:27 NIV

Man will be *clothed* in a righteousness that is completely acceptable to God. In thinking of seeing the LORD YAHWEH, one biblical writer wrote,

> … in righteousness I will see your face … I will be satisfied with seeing your likeness.      Psalm 17:15 NIV

Man's unique relationship with God will be restored.

> "… He will live among them, and they will be his people, and God himself will be with them."      Revelation 21:3 NET

Everything about life will be perfect.

> "[God] will wipe away every tear from their eyes, and death will not exist any more—or mourning, or crying, or pain, for the former things have ceased to exist." And the one seated on the throne said: "Look! I am making all things new!"
> Revelation 21:4-5 NET

There will be no funerals or fractured relationships, no graves or broken-hearted good-byes, no hospitals or homelessness, no crippled bodies or ailing health, no crutches, or canes.

Instead, Heaven will be a place of endless joy and pleasure.

*...you will fill me with joy in your presence, with eternal pleasures at your right hand.*　　　*Psalm 16:11 NIV*

Our bodies will not be limited by time or space. It seems we will be able to move about instantly. Evidently, we will also be able to recognize people we have known or heard about here on earth. We will be thinking, feeling, rational beings equipped with a special body created for a life in Paradise.

At least part of Heaven will be occupied by a large city. It has been calculated that if only 25% of the city was used, 20 billion people could be accommodated with plenty of room to spare. This city is called the *New Jerusalem.*

*And he...showed me the holy city, Jerusalem...having the glory of God. Her brilliance was like a very costly stone, as a stone of crystal-clear jasper. It had a great and high wall, with twelve gates, and at the gates twelve angels...*
*Revelation 21:10-12 NASB*

*In the daytime (for there will be no night there) its gates will never be closed...*　　　*Revelation 21:25 NASB*

*And the street of the city was pure gold, like transparent glass.*
*Revelation 21:21 NASB*

*Then [the angel] showed me a river of the water of life, clear as crystal, coming from the throne of God...*
*Revelation 22:1 NASB*

This will be a city like none we have ever known—no pollution, no rust, no decay, no thieves, no crime, no fear—perfect in every detail. All residents of Heaven will live there for eternity.

ETERNAL LIFE

*They will need no light of lamp or sun, for the Lord God will be their light, and they will reign forever and ever.*
*Revelation 22:5 ESV*

Perhaps we can end this section with the following verse which, though not limited to heavenly realms, certainly carries the idea of what YAHWEH has in store.

*No eye has seen, no ear has heard and no mind has imagined what God has prepared for those who love him.*
*1 Corinthians 2:9 NLT*

# 3 THE BOOK OF LIFE

Heaven is an incredible place, but not everyone will live there after death. The Bible says that there will be a judgment—a courtroom setting—to reveal who will and who will not enter Heaven. In a broad sense, such a concept is not unique to the Bible.

## THE ANCIENT EGYPTIANS

For example, the ancient Egyptians believed that upon death, the deceased was led into a courtroom and confronted with 42 gods to whom the dead must give account. It was very important that these gods be addressed properly. To remember the exact protocol, a wealthy Egyptian would commission a scribe to write a manuscript which included:

1. The Egyptian's personal name inserted in the text

2. Pictures illustrating what he could expect in the next life

3. Magical prayers to manipulate the gods in the afterlife

When the Egyptian died, his family would insert this book of instructions into his coffin. Known as the "*Book of the Dead*," this papyrus could be as long or as short as required.[1]

A page from the Book of the Dead, written for Hunifer, an Egyptian official.

To an ancient Egyptian, having your name in the *Book of the Dead* was very significant—only a fool would have died unprepared for the afterlife. Other ancient religions have similar stories.

But what does the Bible say?

## A GREAT WHITE THRONE

The Scripture does talk about a final judgment occurring at the end of this sin-cursed age, just before the perfect universe is restored.

Many of the 40 writers who recorded Scripture, wrote of this coming final judgment. One stated:

> Then I saw a great white throne and Him who sat upon it...
> *Revelation 20:11 NASB*

Instead of 42 judges as portrayed in the Egyptian *Book of the Dead*, the Bible says there will be only one throne and one judge—the LORD YAHWEH himself. As to incantations, there is no mention of them as YAHWEH is perfectly just—he cannot be manipulated.

> And I saw the dead, the great and the small, standing before the throne, and books were opened; and another book was opened, which is the **book of life**; and the dead were judged from the things which were written in the books, according to their deeds.
> *Revelation 20:12 NASB*

Everyone from kings to paupers will be present at this final judgment. Each must give an account of his past life. The only exception will be those who have had their names written in the *Book of Life*. According to the Bible, having your name in the *Book of Life* is what counts, not in the *Book of the Dead*.

> And if anyone's name was not found written in the **book of life**, he was thrown into the lake of fire."
> *Revelation 20:15 NASB*

## TWO HOMES

The Bible says that after death there are only two locations in which the human spirit can reside.

1. Those *clothed in righteousness* will live with YAHWEH in Heaven.

   > Nothing impure will ever enter it, nor will anyone who does what is shameful or deceitful, but only those whose names are written in the **Lamb's book of life.**
   > *Revelation 21:27 NIV*

ETERNAL LIFE

2. People still clothed in the *filthy rags of sin* will join Satan in Hell. As we saw before, *Gehenna* is that horrifying "garbage pit" where everything bad will be sealed up for all eternity.

ETERNAL JUDGMENT

At the final judgment, those who do not have their names recorded in the *Book of Life* will hear words similar to these, announcing their *Second Death*:

> *"Depart from me, you cursed, into the eternal fire prepared for the devil and his angels."*  Matthew 25:41 ESV
>
> *This is the second death—the lake of fire.*  Revelation 20:14 NASB

Obviously, no rational person would ever want to live there, but for those who do not want to live in Heaven with the LORD, the *Lake of Fire* is the only alternative. There is no neutral ground. So the two big questions are these, "How can a person get his name written in the *Book of Life*? How do we get *clothed in righteousness*?"

As we continue our overview of the Bible, we will learn the answer. Good news is coming, but don't jump ahead. It is important you build your understanding carefully. As you do, you will learn why this *Book of Life* is called the **Lamb's** *Book of Life*.

# 4 The Big Boat

Adam lived to be 930 years old, so for nearly a millennium, people could have learned about God and His ways directly from the original man and woman. The Scripture says that God...

> *... did not leave himself without witness.*  Acts 14:17 ESV

Though hundreds of years passed, the LORD did not forget His commitment to send the PROMISED DELIVERER—the one who would save mankind from the penalty of sin and the power of Satan. Though the population of the world was increasing by leaps and bounds, the number who trusted God did not increase at the same rate. Moses recorded that all but a handful turned their backs on the LORD.

ADAM ┌ *Cain*
EVE ─┤ ABEL
     └ SETH
        │
      Enosh
        │
      Kenan
        │
      Mahalaleel
        │
      Jared
        │
      **Enoch**
        │
      Methuselah
        │
      Lamech ┌ *Japheth*
        │
      NOAH ─┤ *Ham*
             └ SHEM

## VIOLENCE

Mankind had not only rejected the LORD but had chosen to follow Satan with an unholy fervor. Moses summed up the spirit of that day with these words:

*The LORD saw how great man's wickedness on the earth had become, and that every inclination [or intention] of the thoughts of his heart was only evil all the time.*

*Now the earth was corrupt in God's sight and was full of violence. God saw how corrupt the earth had become, for all the people on earth had corrupted their ways.*          Genesis 6:5,11-12 NIV

The world had become corrupt or rotten—a deadly place in which to live. In addition, the Bible declares that the society of that day was focused on living for self.[2] What God said wasn't important anymore. Man had scorned God's plan and had developed a philosophy of life that excluded any desire to seek after Him. Man had no interest in reflecting YAHWEH's glory. Man wasn't even attempting to bridge the gap.

One of the 40 writers penned these words to describe man's deadly spiral into sin:

*For although they knew God, they did not glorify him as God or give him thanks, but they became futile in their thoughts and their senseless hearts were darkened. Although they claimed to be wise, they became fools and exchanged the glory of the immortal God for an image resembling mortal human beings or birds or four-footed animals or reptiles.*

*Therefore God gave them over in the desires of their hearts to impurity, to dishonor their bodies among themselves. They exchanged the truth of God for a lie and worshiped and served the creation rather than the Creator, who is blessed forever! Amen.*

*For this reason God gave them over to dishonorable passions. For their women exchanged the natural sexual relations for unnatural ones, and likewise the men also abandoned natural relations with women and were inflamed in their passions for one another. Men committed shameless acts with men and received in themselves the due penalty for their error.*

*And just as they did not see fit to acknowledge God, God gave them over to a depraved mind, to do what should not be done.*

*They are filled with every kind of unrighteousness, wickedness, covetousness, malice. They are rife with envy, murder, strife, deceit, hostility. They are gossips, slanderers, haters of God, insolent, arrogant, boastful, contrivers of all sorts of evil, disobedient to parents, senseless, covenant-breakers, heartless, ruthless. Although they fully know God's righteous decree that those who practice such things deserve to die, they not only do them but also approve of those who practice them.[3]*

*Romans 1:21–32 NET*

At this juncture in history, man had chosen the easy path, following the example of Satan rather than seeking a way to reflect the image of God. But as we have seen before, sin has its consequences. It always does. Just as defying the law of gravity results in bruises and broken bones, so ignoring God's word has ramifications. Consistent with his nature, God could not condone sin.

*So the Lord said, "I will destroy man whom I have created from the face of the earth …"*  *Genesis 6:7 NKJV*

Man may have had a philosophy of life that excluded God, but the Creator still held man accountable for his behavior.

### Noah

However, one man was different. The Scripture says that…

*… Noah found favor in the eyes of the Lord … Noah was a righteous man, blameless in his generation. Noah walked with God.*

*Genesis 6:8–9 ESV*

Although Noah was a sinner, he had faith that God was reliable. As a result, his name was written in the *Book of Life*.

*So God said to Noah, "I have decided to destroy all living creatures, for they have filled the earth with violence."*  *Genesis 6:13 NLT*

*"I am going to bring floodwaters on the earth to destroy all life under the heavens, every creature that has the breath of life in it. Everything on earth will perish."*  *Genesis 6:17 NIV*

## THE WAY OF ESCAPE

God was going to judge sin. But whenever YAHWEH brings judgment, he also provides a way of escape. God told Noah,

> "Make for yourself an ark of cypress wood. Make rooms in the ark, and cover it with pitch inside and out."  Genesis 6:14 NET

The word *ark* is another word for *box* or *container*. In this case, God instructed Noah to make a large container—a ship in which to live while the world was destroyed in a flood. The LORD said,

> "You will enter the ark—you, your sons, your wife, and your sons' wives with you.
>
> You must bring into the ark two of every kind of living creature from all flesh, male and female, to keep them alive with you."
> Genesis 6:18-19 NET

Noah now had a choice:

1. He could be like Adam and Eve, **doubt God's word** as being true and trust Satan or some other god to give him more reliable information. He could imitate Cain, build the boat his own way—perhaps two or three boats might be better, or…

2. Noah could simply **believe the LORD** as one would believe a friend and follow his instructions to build the ark.

The Bible says Noah chose to trust YAHWEH and his Word. He made the right choice.

> So Noah did everything exactly as God had commanded him
> Genesis 6:22 NLT

## THE ARK

The ark that Noah constructed was a large ship, similar to modern ocean-going freighters. It was made out of wood and covered with a coat of tree pitch, a common means in past centuries of sealing a ship.[4] It had several decks, a built-in ventilation system, and a door—only one door. It remained the largest vessel ever built until its size and ratio were almost duplicated in 1844 by the ship *Great Britain*. The dimensions of the ark are still considered ideal for a large stable boat. It was not built for speed, only to preserve life.

During the years of construction, Noah not only oversaw the building of the ship, but he also warned all who would listen that judgment was coming.[5] Other than his family, not one person responded to his message.

*The Lord then said to Noah, "Go into the ark, you and your whole family, because I have found you righteous in this generation."*

Genesis 7:1 NIV

*And Noah did all that the Lord had commanded him.*

Genesis 7:5 ESV

*On that very day Noah and his sons, Shem, Ham and Japheth, together with his wife and the wives of his three sons, entered the ark.*

*They had with them every wild animal according to its kind, all livestock according to their kinds, every creature that moves along the ground according to its kind and every bird according to its kind, everything with wings. Pairs of all creatures that have the breath of life in them came to Noah and entered the ark. The animals going in were male and female of every living thing, as God had commanded Noah…*

Genesis 7:13–16 NIV

In addition to the pairs of each animal, God said,

*"You shall take with you seven each of every clean animal…"*

Genesis 7:2 NKJV

"Clean" animals were commonly used in making sacrifices.

## ONE DOOR

The ark took seven days to load. Even allowing for now-extinct creatures, the ship had adequate room to house them all with the animals occupying only an estimated 60% of the vessel.[6] The remaining space probably carried feed. Taking the young of large beasts may have been another space-saver. To conserve food, some may have hibernated. Of course, the Lord was able to sustain them in any way he chose. After the loading was completed,

*Then the Lord closed the door behind them.* Genesis 7:16 NLT

When judgment came and the waters began to rise, no amount of banging on the ark could move Noah to open the hatch. Nor did Noah and his family need fear that the door might be torn open in the pounding deluge. They were perfectly safe because the Lord had shut the door—the one and only door. He had shut in those who believed and shut out the rebellious.

The Scripture says Yahweh is very patient. He had given man many years to turn from sin and partake of his love. Now the time was up. Judgment came just as God had promised. Man sometimes threatens and never delivers, but the Lord always keeps his Word.

Chapter Five ❖ 105

**MIGHT MAKES RIGHT!?**

During the years the ark was being built, Noah and his family were lonely voices in a world where everyone else believed he was a fool.

This is something to note. The majority is not always right. Some folks believe that if a religion has a lot of adherents, then it must be true. But stop and think for a moment. Remember how in the time of Moses the Egyptian religion was considered a prestigious religion? Back then almost everyone thought it was right. But nowadays no one follows that ancient religion. Just because a lot of people believe something, doesn't make it true. As a matter of fact, the Bible warns us that...

> ...wide is the gate and broad is the road that leads to destruction, and many enter through it. But small is the gate and narrow the road that leads to life, and only a few find it.                    Matthew 7:13-14 NIV

# 5 CATASTROPHE

According to the Bible, the LORD intervenes in the law and order of his universe only under special circumstances. These are called *miracles*. When miraculous events are recorded, they need to be looked at seriously as the Bible says miracles are one way God gets our attention.

> In the six hundredth year of Noah's life, on the seventeenth day of the second month—on that day all the springs of the great deep burst forth, and the floodgates of the heavens were opened. And rain fell on the earth forty days and forty nights. Genesis 7:11-12 NIV

The Hebrew word that Moses used to describe this event means a *catastrophic deluge*. In the Bible that Hebrew word is solely used in reference to the Flood. No other inundation has ever come close to equaling it. So how did it happen? Where did all the water come from and where did it go?

## THE SPRINGS AND FLOODGATES

First of all, the Bible says the earth ruptured, releasing massive amounts of underground water. It says,

> ...all the fountains of the great deep burst open... Genesis 7:11 NET

It has been theorized that water under extreme pressure was jetted high into the sky. Then it, along with other water in the atmosphere, came down as...

> ... the floodgates of the heavens were opened.   Genesis 7:11 NET

Such a rupturing of the planet's crust had to have included enormous volcanic activity. Oceanographers estimate that there are as many as one million volcanoes on the Pacific Ocean floor alone—not all active, but residue from the past.

It is possible that at this time the whole process known as *continental drift* occurred. Using super-computers, one of the world's leading researchers in plate tectonics has modeled in 3-D the whole process of continental drift occurring in a few months.[7] As fissures tore open the crust of the earth, it is possible that huge slabs of the surface were thrust deep into the earth's interior, recycling the ocean basins and continental land.

Though many of the things that happened in the cataclysm can be explained by natural science, we must remember that an all-powerful God could create the Flood circumstances and the attending catastrophic results without any limitation.

The rain lasted for 40 days, but it seems from the text that water continued to flow out of the underground fountains for 150 days.

> *For forty days the flood kept coming on the earth, and as the waters increased they lifted the ark high above the earth. The waters rose and increased greatly on the earth, and the ark floated on the surface of the water.* Genesis 7:17–18 NIV

As Moses wrote of these events, he was no doubt quite familiar with the flood stories taught by the Egyptians, Babylonians, and other ancients. But now he was hearing the details of the Flood from one who claimed to be an eyewitness—the LORD himself. Moses recorded that the water...

> *...rose greatly on the earth, and all the high mountains under the entire heavens were covered.* Genesis 7:19 NIV

It is believed that prior to the flood, the mountains were not as high as they are now. Today, if you were able to take the surface of the globe and smooth it out, the water would cover the earth to a depth of approximately three kilometres (2 miles). Moses wrote:

> *Everything on dry land that had the breath of life in its nostrils died... Only Noah was left, and those with him in the ark.* Genesis 7:22-23 NIV

## THE WATERS RECEDE

> *But God remembered Noah... and the waters receded.* Genesis 8:1 NET

> *The waters were standing above the mountains. At Your rebuke they fled... The mountains rose; the valleys sank down To the place which You established for them. You set a boundary that they may not pass over, So that they will not return to cover the earth.* Psalm 104:6–9 NASB

This is interesting. Apparently, the multi-layered mountains we see today were formed under water, and then while the earthen material was still soft, they were thrust up, folding and splitting as they rose. As the water flowed off the rising mountains, it cut through the soft material, rapidly forming large valleys and canyons. Once the mountains reached their present position, they solidified into rock. This explains the many geological formations we see today and why we often find fossils, even of sea life, at high altitudes.

## A DIFFERENT PLANET

Noah and his family were in the boat for 371 days before God opened the door. By this time, the waters had receded and the ark had lodged in a mountainous region.

> *Then God said to Noah, "Come out of the ark, you and your*
> *wife and your sons and their wives. Bring out every kind of living*
> *creature that is with you—the birds, the animals, and all the*
> *creatures that move along the ground—so they can multiply on*
> *the earth and be fruitful and increase in number upon it."*
>
> *So Noah came out, together with his sons and his wife and his*
> *sons' wives.* Genesis 8:15–18 NIV

When they left the ark, the ground was not only dry but producing again. It was a very different planet from before the Flood. It was the earth on which we now live.

Before the flood people lived hundreds of years, but after the deluge, lives were shortened considerably so that a man of 90 was regarded as very old.

### An Offering

> *Then Noah built an altar to the LORD and, taking some of all the*
> *clean animals and clean birds, he sacrificed burnt offerings on it.*
> Genesis 8:20 NIV

Noah made an offering of *clean* animals to God, just like Abel had. Once again, these offerings were not for the purpose of feeding God. YAHWEH does not get hungry—he does not need food. Rather, these animal sacrifices were connected with the concept of *atonement*. We said earlier that, at the most basic level, the word *atonement* carries the idea of a *covering*—it is the same Hebrew word used to describe Noah coating the ark with pitch. In that sense the Bible speaks of sin being symbolically *covered* so that a holy God could look upon man favourably.

> *Blessed is he whose transgression is forgiven, whose sin is covered.*
> Psalm 32:1 KJV

As we progress in the story, we will see that the word *atonement* summarizes the whole means whereby a holy God provides sinful man with *right clothes* for the heart—a covering of righteousness equal to his righteousness.

## AN ALTAR

The Bible says Noah offered the animals on an altar. Altars were made of uncut stones, placed in a pile to form a platform. They were constructed under the LORD's direction and used as designated places to meet with YAHWEH. In making his offering, Noah confessed himself as a sinner in need of an *atonement-covering*. The LORD was pleased that Noah trusted him.

> Then God blessed Noah and his sons and said to them, "Be fruitful and multiply and fill the earth."　　　*Genesis 9:1 NET*

Noah and his descendants now had a choice:

1. They could **obey** God, "fill the earth" as the LORD had instructed, or...

2. They could be like Adam and Eve—and **doubt** that YAHWEH really meant what he said—trusting in their own enlightened judgment.

In the next section, we will see the choice they made.

## A PROMISE

God said,

> "...Never again will all life be cut off by the waters of a flood; never again will there be a flood to destroy the earth."

> "This is the sign of the covenant [or promise] I am making between me and you...I have set my rainbow in the clouds, and it will be the sign of the covenant between me and the earth."
> *Genesis 9:11–13 NIV*

The LORD promised to never destroy the earth with a flood again. Whenever it rained, the rainbow would be a reminder of that promise. Although thousands of years have passed since the Flood, YAHWEH has kept his word.

> The sons of Noah who came out of the ark were Shem, Ham and Japheth. These were the three sons of Noah, and from them came the people who were scattered over the earth.
> *Genesis 9:18-19 NIV*

Man now had a fresh start. Moses summed up this section of Genesis by writing:

> Altogether, Noah lived 950 years, and then he died.
> *Genesis 9:29 NIV*

## What about Dinosaurs, Fossils, Coal, and Oil?

We do not find the word *dinosaur* in the Bible—the word is recent, invented in 1841 by an English anatomist. However, the early books of the Bible do record references to animals that have no present parallels. Two of the larger animals mentioned have an intriguing resemblance to the fossil record.[8]

From what the Scripture says, one can assume that the dinosaurs were created by God and lived with man from the beginning. Dinosaurs appear to have been reptiles, most of which continue to grow throughout their lifetime. If they had the long life spans humans had before the Flood, it could account for the huge size some attained.

The Bible indicates that two of every *kind* of land animal were ordered into the Ark. It makes sense that only the young were taken, not only to conserve space, but also to maximize breeding time in the post-flood years. Since the average size of a dinosaur was that of a small pony, and even the largest dinosaurs at birth were no bigger than a football, calculations show that there was ample room for them on the Ark.

As to what caused their demise, we can only conjecture. In the last few decades, many creatures have become extinct but even then, it's hard to nail down the exact cause. Going back thousands of years makes it even more difficult. Since the climate changed radically after the Flood, it has been theorized that it would have been difficult for such animals to survive.

The conditions created by the deluge answer many questions we see in the natural world. For example, the massive amount of sediment created by the Flood, the extreme weight of the water, the tremendous amount of erosion—all could account for the deposits of coal, oil, and fossils we now find. Many of the fossils show overwhelming evidence that they were swiftly and catastrophically buried, frequently in vast fossil graveyards that we find today. The very existence of any well-preserved fossil, such as a fish, means it was buried rapidly with the encasing sediment hardening quickly before scavengers and decay destroyed its features.

See Appendix for more resources.

# 6 CONFUSION

The tenth chapter of the book of Genesis is often called *"The Table of Nations."* It tells us where the major ethnic groups came from, beginning with Noah's three sons. The chapter ends with this verse:

> These are the clans of Noah's sons, according to their lines of descent, within their nations. From these the nations spread out over the earth after the flood.             Genesis 10:32 NIV

All nations of the earth came from this one family. Originally, everyone knew about YAHWEH, his creative acts and the origin of sin and death. But that has changed. What happened?

The answer is found in a series of events that occurred several centuries after the Flood. By then the earth's population had increased dramatically and was concentrated in Mesopotamia, the cradle of civilization, now modern-day Iraq.

> Now the whole world had one language and a common speech. As men moved eastward, they found a plain in Shinar and settled there.
>
> They said to each other, "Come, let's make bricks and bake them thoroughly." They used brick instead of stone, and tar for mortar. Then they said, "Come, let us build ourselves a city, with a tower that reaches to the heavens, so that we may make a name for ourselves and not be scattered over the face of the whole earth."
>
> Genesis 11:1–4 NIV

## MAN'S AGENDA

Now there are some obvious problems here. After the Flood, God had told man to…

> …increase in number and fill the earth.             Genesis 9:1 NIV

But these people had determined that everyone should stay in one place and build a big city. This was in direct disobedience to the LORD's instruction. Obviously, they didn't care what God thought! Once again, man felt he knew *better-than-God* what was best. Man was perpetuating the wrong choice made in Eden.

As you can see, man has a problem with obedience. Have you ever wondered why you don't need to teach little children to disobey Mom and Dad? It comes very naturally because defiance is natural to the human heart. Basically, as humans we don't want to be told what to do. We prefer doing our own thing. Mankind is extremely self-centered. This was the core problem with the people staying in one place to build a city.

The Bible says the people also wanted to build a tower to...

"...make for ourselves a name..."                    *Genesis 11:4 NASB*

Man was seeking his own glory rather than looking for a way to reflect God's glory. The LORD was left out of the picture. Mankind likes it better that way.

### RELIGION

The exact spelling of this city's name is uncertain since many ancient languages did not use vowels, but some scholars translate the ancient text as *Babili*.[9] It's a name with strong religious overtones. It means *the Gate of God*.

There is solid evidence that the tower had religious significance too. Most likely it was an early ziggurat,[10] meaning *temple-tower*. This imitation mountain was connected to a temple complex and culminated with a small shrine on its peak. The temple was the focal point of the city and involved priests, sacrifices, idols and festivals. It was all highly structured. In the Bible, *Babili* is recorded as having the first organized religion.

The Bible defines religion as **man's efforts to reach out to a deity with the hopes of gaining favour or removing misfortune.**

Think about it. A ziggurat was huge! To undertake erecting such a structure, the builders definitely had to be devoted to satisfying their god. You can imagine the people slaving away in the heat as they collected mud, baked the bricks, and cemented them together with tar.

Even once the ziggurat was built, if they intended to visit the temple on its peak, they had to trudge up a massive flight of stairs. The people of *Babili* had devised a way of reaching their god—but it sure took a lot of hard work.

The Bible says that *self-effort* is the nature of all man-made religions— the more "steps" there are, the better the religion. These religions demand time, money, devotion, sometimes even physical pain to please a deity. Of course, it is hoped that this devotion will earn a person good luck or help evade evil. It is felt that after death, things will go better in the next life if one has been devout in a religion.

Now we need to ask ourselves a question: *What did the LORD think about this?* Suppose the people of *Babili* had dedicated their tower-temple solely to the LORD YAHWEH. Would all the blisters gained in construction, the sore feet from tromping up and down the vast staircase, the fatigue of listening to the demands of the priests, the cost of perpetual sacrifices, the weariness of prayers—would all this devotion have opened the *Gate to God?* Would YAHWEH say, *"Okay, we can be friends again"?* The Bible says, *"No."*

Why not? Because the issue at stake wasn't about following a religion. Rather, it was about trusting a person—the LORD himself. It was not how hard one worked to win God's favour, but whether a person simply trusted the LORD as one would trust a friend. It wasn't about manipulating God to get your way, but having a personal friendship with the Creator of the universe. Trust was the issue.

Religion makes one feel spiritual, but it is like swimming against the current in a river—it takes a lot of work, you may feel great when you are done, but you really haven't gone anywhere. A person's heart is still clothed in the filthy rags of sin.

## GOD'S VIEW

So the LORD wasn't impressed with all the religious fervor. He had told mankind to fill the earth and man was staying in one place.

> … the LORD came down[11] to see the city and the tower that the men were building. The LORD said, "If as one people speaking the same language they have begun to do this, then nothing they plan to do will be impossible for them." *Genesis 11:5-6 NIV*

The Creator knew what history has proven to be true—with a common language, man's progress in technology is much faster. It seems to be a pattern. The more advanced and comfortable things are, the less man feels he needs God as a friend. Though Yahweh had given man the freedom of choice, he did not want man living independently of him.

### Scattered

The Lord took action to confront man's defiance. God said,

> "Come, let us go down and confuse their language so they will not understand each other."
>
> So the Lord scattered them from there over all the earth, and they stopped building the city. Genesis 11:7-8 NIV

When God dispersed them, he gave them new languages. He definitely did a thorough job! Many of the languages the Lord created are so complex they take years for linguists to grasp, and even then, they do not completely understand them.

### Confusion

Though the people had named their city *Babili* [9], the *Gate of God*, after the Lord scattered them abroad, he renamed the city *Babel* and gave it a new definition. It means *to mingle, mix, confuse, confound*. Moses wrote,

> Therefore its name was called Babel,[12] because there the Lord confused the language of all the earth. And from there the Lord dispersed them over the face of all the earth. Genesis 11:9 ESV

The Lord wanted every one to know that this city and its religious doctrines were not proclaiming God's truth; it was not a gate to Yahweh—its message and rituals could not mend the broken friendship with the Lord.

From this point on, *Babel*, or what became known as *Babylon*, was used in the Scripture as an example of man's religious efforts.

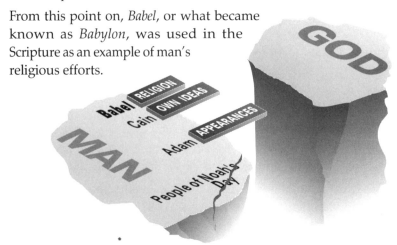

## SUMMARY

The Bible says it is a hopeless pursuit for a man or woman to devise a religion that purports to be a *gate to God*. Mankind is in a spiritual wilderness—he is lost—he cannot find a way back to God on his own. Apart from the LORD showing the way, man has no idea where to find that gate. But the LORD knows the way; he knows the gate, and it is he who…

> …*devises ways so that a banished person may not remain estranged from him.*
> 2 Samuel 14:14 NIV

If folks would only trust the LORD, he would show them the way back to a right relationship with him.

The people who remained in Babylon did not stop building ziggurats. Historians tell us other towers were constructed to honour gods and goddesses who had names like *Ishtar, Marduk,* and *Dagan*. These deities, along with others, showed up throughout history in other lands with other names. *Ishtar* was paralleled by the Egyptian *Isis,* the Greek *Athena* or *Aphrodite,* and the Roman *Venus*. *Marduk* had associations with the sun-god, and in the pages to come we will meet *Dagan* in another setting. We will learn the origin and identity of these deities once we build additional foundations for our understanding.

Looking back at the last two stories we can make an interesting comparison. There are two ways of thinking with two very different results.

| The way of Babel | The way of Noah |
| --- | --- |
| Trusted in religious effort | Trusted in YAHWEH |
| Many towers, gates to Heaven | God provided one boat, one door |
| People judged, dispersed | Noah and family saved |
| God called the place *confusion* | God called Noah *righteous* |

Perhaps Moses was thinking of this when he wrote,

> *"Who among the gods is like you, O LORD? Who is like you—majestic in holiness, awesome in glory, working wonders?*
> Exodus 15:11 NIV

YAHWEH is unique, truly one-of-a-kind, holy.

# CHAPTER SIX

# 1 FAITH

After the confusion of languages at Babel, Moses recorded the passing of several more generations. All through these years the LORD did not forget his promise to send a DELIVERER. Though the majority of people lived with little thought of God, each generation had those who believed his promises. Abram and Sarai were one such couple.

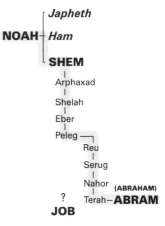

We pick up the story in Ur, a city just south of Babel. It was around this time[1] that the citizens of Ur also built a famous temple-tower, a ziggurat dedicated to the moon god. It was probably the worship of such gods that led the LORD to tell Abram:

> *"Leave your native country ... and go to the land that I will show you."* Genesis 12:1 NLT

Telling Abram and Sarai to move preserved them from a false religious system. (After all, the moon is a big rock, not a god.) Abram and Sarai now had a choice:

1. They could be disobedient like the people of Babel and stay put in Ur—in effect, trusting their judgment as being *better-than-God's*, or ...

2. They could believe that YAHWEH knew best, pack their bags and do as the LORD directed.

You can imagine the advice given to them by family and friends. *"Abram, you are financially secure! Life is great here! Don't be a fool!"* But ...

> *... Abram went, as the LORD had told him ... Abram was seventy-five years old ...*[2] Genesis 12:4 ESV

This was a big step for Abram. He couldn't consult an atlas, research the country on the Web, or discuss plans with a travel agent. He didn't even know where he was going! God had not told him. But Abram had faith in the LORD to lead him one step at a time.

**WHAT IS FAITH?**

People have odd notions about faith, often confusing the biblical puzzle. But the Scripture uses the life of Abram to define exactly what YAHWEH means by "faith." Here are some guidelines.

The words or concepts of *belief, faith, trust,* and *confidence* are often used interchangeably:

| | |
|---|---|
| Abram **believed** the LORD. | He **believed** what YAHWEH said. |
| Abram put **faith** in the LORD. | He had **faith** in YAHWEH's word. |
| Abram **trusted** the LORD. | He knew YAHWEH to be **trustworthy**. |
| Abram had **confidence** in the LORD. | His **confidence** was in God alone. |

The old saying, *"Never trust a stranger,"* is particularly applicable to the subject of faith. To trust someone you don't know is risky. Adam and Eve trusted a stranger (Satan) and it had terrible ramifications.

Before you trust a person you need to find out two things:

1. **Identity:** What is his name? Where is he from? Who does he claim to be—prince or pauper, poet or plumber, politician or priest?

2. **History:** What is his reputation? Does he keep his word? Is he reliable? For this you will need to investigate his past.

It is important to know these two things before you place your faith in a person. In light of that, the Bible says Scripture was written so mankind might become acquainted with YAHWEH.

We saw that Moses was to tell everyone that YAHWEH is the Supreme Being, the Creator-Owner of the Universe. That is his **Identity**.

As to his **History**, Scripture was written so mankind could learn that YAHWEH is reliable—he tells the truth. When he makes promises, he keeps them. We are still in the early stages of learning God's history, but with time we will see that YAHWEH's...

> *...promises have been thoroughly tested...*     Psalm 119:140 NLT

The Bible encourages us to check out God's history for ourselves. A special promise is given for those seeking him. It says if we believe *HE* exists, and if we seek to know *HIS* history, then he will reward us with additional information about *HIMSELF*.

> *But without faith it is impossible to please Him, for he who comes to God must believe that He is, and that He is a rewarder of those who diligently seek Him.*     Hebrews 11:6 NKJV

## BLIND FAITH

There is such a thing as blind faith—people trust strangers every day. We all agree it is risky, and yet it is done.

1. **Identity:** Abram would have known many people in the city of Ur who trusted the moon god.

2. **History:** Yet the moon god had no history, no reliable reputation. He never made promises, let alone kept them. He couldn't—the moon is just a big rock which orbits the earth, unable to think, speak, or make promises.

Yet people still trusted in the moon as a god. This sort of faith is a *"leap in the dark"* equivalent to *"trusting a stranger."* It is often based on opinion rather than reliable information.

In the Bible Abram and Sarai are used as examples of faith. Their whole lives were marked by faith, but it wasn't a leap in the dark. They knew YAHWEH had a reliable history, and...

> *...regarded the one who had given the promise to be trustworthy.*
> Hebrews 11:11 NET

## BIBLICAL FAITH

Some people talk about faith as if it were a gift that God gives you, like a present. But when you study the lives of Abram and Sarai, you see that their faith towards God functioned like any other day-to-day expression of trust. They believed YAHWEH was telling the truth and acted upon that belief.[3]

> By faith Abraham, when called to go to a place he would later receive as his inheritance, obeyed and went, even though he did not know where he was going.    Hebrews 11:8 NIV

Their unknown destination was the land of Canaan, today the home of the Arabs and the Israelis.

> By faith he made his home in the promised land like a stranger in a foreign country; he lived in tents...
> Hebrews 11:9 NIV

Abram and Sarai led semi-nomadic lives. The locals called them *hebrews*, a name which carried the connotation of *a wanderer, the one from beyond.* From this time on, their descendants were referred to as *Hebrews.*

# 2 PROMISES

When God told Abram to leave Ur, he also gave him four specific promises. Now this is interesting for two reasons:

First of all, in Abram's country it was unheard of for a deity to make promises. Babylonian gods never made commitments. Since the gods were always fighting among themselves, people never knew which deity would be in power for the long run—to fulfill a promise.

Secondly, if YAHWEH made promises and consistently kept those promises, it would put him in a category that no other god or goddess was known to occupy. He would be unique. It would also build a reliable history for future people considering whether or not to trust him.

The LORD promised Abram...

1. *I will make you into a great nation...*[4]
2. *I will make your name great...*[5]
3. *I will bless those who bless you, and whoever curses you I will curse...*[6]
4. *...all peoples on earth will be blessed through you.*

*Genesis 12:2-3 NIV*

God's first promise was good news to Abram because...

*Sarai was barren; she had no child.*     *Genesis 11:30 NASB*

In order to become a great nation, he would have to father children. However, since Sarai was sixty-five years of age and he had no offspring, Abram was perplexed as to how this would happen. Once again he would need to trust the LORD to keep his word.

The last promise hinged on the first and was a direct reference to THE DELIVERER. God was telling Abram that one of his descendants would be THE ANOINTED ONE, and that He would be a blessing to everyone. The Bible says Abram believed God and rejoiced at "the thought of seeing" the day of THE DELIVERER's arrival.[7]

| THE PROMISED DELIVERER would be... |
| --- |
| 1. The offspring of a woman |
| 2. A male |
| 3. A descendant of Abram |

## A PROMISED SON

*After this, the word of the LORD came to Abram in a vision: "Do not be afraid, Abram. I am your shield, your very great reward."*

*But Abram said, "O Sovereign LORD, what can you give me since I remain childless…?"*

*[God] took him outside and said, "Look up at the heavens and count the stars—if indeed you can count them." Then he said to him, "So shall your offspring be."*

*Abram believed the LORD, and he credited it to him as righteousness.*

Genesis 15:1-2,5-6 NIV

This last sentence is loaded with meaning. We will look at three words: *righteousness*, *credited*, and *believed*.

### RIGHTEOUSNESS

As we saw earlier, the word *righteousness* is used in reference to God's perfect character; he is totally without blemish or sin.

To live in the presence of the LORD, one needs what Adam and Eve lost in the garden—one needs righteousness. Humanly speaking, it is impossible. Yet the Bible says Abram ended up with this sort of righteousness, not because he had it within himself, but because God *credited* it to him.

### CREDITED

The word *credited* means *to count, to consider*. The original rendering of this verse uses an accounting term for the word credited. It is a word that deals with a reality. For example, if you are flat broke, but a friend tells you he has credited your bank account with $10,000, it is a certainty you have $10,000. The word refers to facts, not suppositions. It is something you can rely upon.

The Scripture says the LORD *credited* righteousness to Abram. It wasn't that Abram all of sudden began to live a perfect life here on earth, but rather God looked upon Abram as if he was clothed in righteousness, already standing in Heaven. It was a done deal. The transaction was completed. He could count on it.

The question is, *"Just how did Abram obtain this righteousness that allowed him to stand before the LORD?"* The Bible's answer is that,

*Abram **believed** the LORD, and he credited it to him as righteousness.*

Genesis 15:6 NIV

### BELIEVED

Abram did what Adam and Eve should have done back in the Garden of Eden. He simply believed the LORD.

*But hold it! How could a simple "belief in the LORD" clothe a person in righteous garments? Surely a person had to live a good life, do the right thing and think the right thoughts. Believing was just too simple. There had to be a catch.* We will answer these questions as we continue, but for now it is enough to know that Abram had such faith in YAHWEH keeping his word, that he…

> …*was looking for the city which has foundations, whose architect and builder is God.* Hebrews 11:10 NASB

Although Abram's body would eventually die, he believed that God would make a way for him to live in Heaven as a friend.

> *"Abraham believed God, and it was credited to him as righteousness," and he was called God's friend.* James 2:23 NIV

# 3 SON OF UNBELIEF

As the years passed and Abram and Sarai still didn't have the son promised by YAHWEH, they began to wonder … they struggled.

> *Now Sarai, Abram's wife, had not given birth to any children, but she had an Egyptian servant named Hagar. So Sarai said to Abram, "Since the LORD has prevented me from having children, have sexual relations with my servant. Perhaps I can have a family by her."* Genesis 16:1-2 NET

This was the culturally accepted way of dealing with childlessness. Sarai offered her servant girl to Abram.

> *[Abram] slept with Hagar, and she conceived.* Genesis 16:4 NIV

> *So Hagar gave birth to Abram's son, whom Abram named Ishmael. (Now Abram was 86 years old when Hagar gave birth to Ishmael.)* Genesis 16:15-16 NET

### ISHMAEL

Abram finally had a descendant! But there was a problem. They had done things their way, not God's way.

> *Now when Abram was ninety-nine years old, the LORD appeared to Abram and said to him, "…No longer shall your name be called Abram, But your name shall be Abraham; For I have made you the father of a multitude of nations."* Genesis 17:1,5 NASB

Abram, now called Abraham, had no problem with what God was saying. After all, he had a descendant—Ishmael!

> And God said to Abraham, "As for Sarai your wife, you shall not call her name Sarai, but Sarah shall be her name. I will bless her, and moreover, I will give you a son by her. I will bless her, and she shall become nations; kings of peoples shall come from her."
>
> Genesis 17:15-16 ESV

Why was Yahweh mentioning Sarah at all? Did the Lord not know about Hagar? Surely it was possible for The Promised Deliverer to come through Ishmael.

> Abraham fell facedown; he laughed and said to himself, "Will a son be born to a man a hundred years old? Will Sarah bear a child at the age of ninety?"
>
> And Abraham said to God, "If only Ishmael might live under your blessing!"
>
> Genesis 17:17-18 NIV

Abraham pointed out to the Lord that Ishmael could be the promised son.

> Then God said, "Yes, but your wife Sarah will bear you a son, and you will call him Isaac. I will establish my covenant with him as an everlasting covenant for his descendants after him. And as for Ishmael, I have heard you: I will surely bless him … and I will make him into a great nation. But my covenant I will establish with Isaac, whom Sarah will bear to you by this time next year."
>
> Genesis 17:19-21 NIV

So there it was. God would bless Ishmael, but he was not the promised son. God would only honour that which was done His way. Sarah was to have a child in one year's time and his name would be Isaac.

Though Abraham and Sarah believed that God would keep his promise, their faith went through ups and downs. At times they struggled with doubt. But God says he will even honour faith the size of a mustard seed.[8] Mustard seeds are very small. What makes the difference is **not the amount of faith** you have, but **in whom** you are placing your faith.

A lot of faith in the moon god would not have helped Abraham, but even wavering faith in Yahweh made the difference. It is the **object** of one's faith that is important—not faith itself. Abraham and Sarah were trusting the Lord Yahweh.

# 4 Grace

After Abraham arrived in Canaan, he moved…

> …to the mountain east of Bethel, and he pitched his tent with
> Bethel on the west…                    Genesis 12:8 NKJV

Bethel became associated with YAHWEH and his blessings, a place
to seek the LORD. Even though I'll only mention Bethel a couple
more times, remember this place. It was here Abraham…

> …built an altar to the LORD and called on the name of the LORD.
>                                         Genesis 12:8 NKJV

As we saw before, altars had been in use since the time of Abel.
They were designated as special places to meet God. As a man
approached the LORD, he would offer an animal, often a sheep or
goat. The offering would be killed and its remains burned. These
altars and offerings were very significant as they were connected
to the concept of atonement. It was the means whereby God
restored a sinner to a right relationship with Himself. Later, we
will explain this concept in detail.

## LOT

Abraham had a nephew named *Lot* who had accompanied him
from Ur. Not long after they settled in Canaan, it became obvious
that there was not enough pastureland for both of their flocks.

> So Abram said to Lot, "Please let there be no strife between you
> and me … for we are brethren. Is not the whole land before you?
> Please separate from me. If you take the left, then I will go to
> the right; or, if you go to the right, then I will go to the left."
>                                         Genesis 13:8-9 NKJV

Lot had a choice. He could choose the lush, fertile valley or the
stark, rugged mountains. On the other hand, he could split both
the fruitful and barren land with Abraham, each taking half.

> And Lot lifted his eyes and saw all the plain of Jordan, that it
> was well watered everywhere … Then Lot chose for himself all
> the plain of Jordan …                  Genesis 13:10-11 NKJV

Lot took the whole valley—all of it!

> And they separated from each other. Abram dwelt in the land of
> Canaan, and Lot dwelt in the cities of the plain and pitched his tent
> even as far as Sodom. But the men of Sodom were exceedingly
> wicked and sinful against the LORD.    Genesis 13:11-13 NKJV

## SODOM

Lot settled in Sodom, a city with a questionable reputation.

> *"Now this was the sin of ... Sodom: She and her daughters were arrogant, overfed and unconcerned; they did not help the poor and needy. They were haughty and did detestable things before me."*
> Ezekiel 16:49-50 NIV

The people of Sodom had given themselves over to self-indulgence. They were self-centered, reveling in ease and luxury while ignoring the hunger and poverty around them. They were a proud people whom God said were exceedingly sinful. **God told Abraham that the sin of Sodom and her sister cities was so great and blatant that he was going to destroy them.**

Abraham was concerned for Lot and wanted to know what would happen to the godly—those in the city who had their names written in the *Book of Life*.

> *Abraham approached [the LORD] and said, "Will you sweep away the godly along with the wicked? What if there are fifty godly people in the city? Will you really wipe it out and not spare the place for the sake of the fifty godly people who are in it? Far be it from you to do such a thing—to kill the godly with the wicked, treating the godly and the wicked alike! Far be it from you! Will not the judge of the whole earth do what is right?"*
> Genesis 18:23-25 NET

Abraham probably figured he was pushing YAHWEH to the limit by asking him to spare the city for fifty God-honouring people, but then on the other hand, Lot was a good man and had been in Sodom quite a while. Surely he had influenced at least fifty.

> *So the LORD replied, "If I find in the city of Sodom fifty godly people, I will spare the whole place ..."*
> Genesis 18:26 NET

You can almost hear Abraham's sigh of relief. But then he got to thinking. Some of the things he had heard about Lot did not speak too well of his life. Maybe he wouldn't have influenced that many people. Abraham began bargaining. He said,

> *"Since I have undertaken to speak to the LORD (although I am but dust and ashes), what if there are five less than the fifty godly people? Will you destroy the whole city because five are lacking?" He replied, "I will not destroy it if I find forty-five there."*
>
> *Abraham spoke to him again, "What if forty are found there?" He replied, "I will not do it for the sake of the forty."*

> Then Abraham said, "May the Lord not be angry so that I may
> speak! What if thirty are found there?" He replied, "I will not
> do it if I find thirty there."
>
> Abraham said, "Since I have undertaken to speak to the Lord,
> what if only twenty are found there?" He replied, "I will not
> destroy it for the sake of the twenty."
>
> Finally Abraham said, "May the Lord not be angry so that I
> may speak just once more. What if ten are found there?" He
> replied, "I will not destroy it for the sake of the ten."
>
> Genesis 18:27-32 NET

Abraham must have breathed a sigh of relief. He knew Sodom. If God destroyed the people of Noah's day, Sodom had no chance. Yet God said he would spare the city if ten godly people were found. Abraham must have been astonished.

Earlier we saw that Yahweh revealed a type of love when he created the world. It was a love characterized by **care and concern**. We can see it in the diversity, the beauty, the fragrances, and the tasty food.

But when God said he would spare Sodom for the sake of a handful, God demonstrated love in a different light, to a different depth. It was an **undeserved love**. The Bible refers to *undeserved love* using the words *grace* and *mercy*.

Abraham had learned another aspect of God's character. As Moses recorded this event, he learned it too—and so do we.

# 5 Judgment

Although the Lord Yahweh is gracious, he does not allow his love to be trampled upon forever. Sinful living is contagious and God did not want Sodom's life-style spreading beyond the valley. So God sent angels to destroy these cities.

Angels are invisible spirits, so to be seen they had to take on the form of men.

> The two angels came to Sodom in the evening while Lot was
> sitting in the city's gateway. When Lot saw them, he got up to
> meet them and bowed down with his face toward the ground.
>
> Genesis 19:1 NET

Somehow Lot recognized the angels for who they really were. He knew they had been sent by God.

*He said, "Here, my lords, please turn aside to your servant's house. Stay the night and wash your feet. Then you can be on your way early in the morning." "No," they replied, "we'll spend the night in the town square."*
Genesis 19:2 NET

Lot knew the sinfulness of Sodom. He feared for them sleeping out in the open.

*But he urged them persistently, so they turned aside with him and entered his house. He prepared a feast for them, including bread baked without yeast, and they ate. Before they could lie down to sleep, all the men—both young and old, from every part of the city of Sodom—surrounded the house. They shouted to Lot, "Where are the men who came to you tonight? Bring them out to us so we can have sex with them!"*

*Lot went outside to them, shutting the door behind him. He said, "No, my brothers! Don't act so wickedly! Look, I have two daughters who have never had sexual relations with a man. Let me bring them out to you, and you can do to them whatever you please. Only don't do anything to these men, for they have come under the protection of my roof."*

*"Out of our way!" they cried, and "This man came to live here as a foreigner, and now he dares to judge us! We'll do more harm to you than to them!" They kept pressing in on Lot until they were close enough to break down the door.*

*So the men inside reached out and pulled Lot back into the house as they shut the door. Then they struck the men who were at the door of the house, from the youngest to the oldest, with blindness. The men outside wore themselves out trying to find the door. Then the two visitors said to Lot, "Who else do you have here? Do you have any sons-in-law, sons, daughters, or other relatives in the city? Get them out of this place because we are about to destroy it. The outcry against this place is so great before the LORD that he has sent us to destroy it."*
Genesis 19: 3-13 NET

*At dawn the angels hurried Lot along, saying, "Get going! Take your wife and your two daughters who are here, or else you will be destroyed when the city is judged!"*

*When Lot hesitated, the men grabbed his hand and the hands of his wife and two daughters because the LORD had compassion on them. They led them away and placed them outside the city. When they had brought them outside, they said, "Run for your lives! Don't look behind you or stop anywhere in the valley! Escape to the mountains or you will be destroyed!"* Genesis 19: 15-17 NET

Although Lot trusted YAHWEH as a friend, Lot was a terrible embarrassment to the LORD. Nevertheless, God showed him grace—undeserved love—in spite of his ungodly character.

*The sun had just risen over the land as Lot reached Zoar. Then the LORD rained down sulfur and fire on Sodom and Gomorrah. It was sent down from the sky by the LORD. So he overthrew those cities and all that region, including all the inhabitants of the cities and the vegetation that grew from the ground.* Genesis 19:23-25 NET

*Abraham got up early in the morning and ... looked out toward Sodom and Gomorrah and all the land of that region. As he did so, he saw the smoke rising up from the land like smoke from a furnace.* Genesis 19:27-28 NET

God had said he would destroy these sinful cities and he kept his word. He always does. People may react to this story, but we must remember, it is YAHWEH who sets the rules for how mankind should live. He did this for our well-being. We jeopardize ourselves when we ignore or try to change God's laws. The Bible says,

*Woe to those who call evil good, and good evil ... Woe to those who are wise in their own eyes, And prudent in their own sight!* Isaiah 5:20-21 NKJV

While YAHWEH is gracious, he must be taken seriously. The Scripture says that the events at Sodom remind us that the LORD does judge all sin—here on earth or in the Lake of Fire.

*... Sodom and Gomorrah and the surrounding towns gave themselves up to sexual immorality and perversion. They **serve as an example** of those who suffer the punishment of eternal fire.* Jude 7 NIV

| Sodom | Bethel |
|---|---|
| A place to indulge in sin | A place to meet with God |
| Associated with men of sin | Associated with men of faith |
| An example of judgment | An example of blessing |

# 6 Son of the Promise

*Now the Lord was gracious to Sarah as he had said, and the Lord did for Sarah what he had promised. Sarah became pregnant and bore a son to Abraham in his old age, at the very time God had promised him. Abraham gave the name Isaac to the son Sarah bore him.*
*Genesis 21:1–3 NIV*

God kept his promise to Abraham and Sarah in spite of their age.

We now jump forward in the story. Isaac has matured and is the only son at home. Ishmael has moved to Egypt.

*Some time later God tested Abraham. He said to him, "Abraham!"*

*"Here I am," he replied.*

*Then God said, "Take your son, your only son, Isaac, whom you love, and go to the region of Moriah."*
*Genesis 22:1-2 NIV*

Abraham was told to take Isaac to the region of Moriah. Today the city of Jerusalem occupies this entire area, but back then it would have been sparsely inhabited. Abraham was told to…

*"Sacrifice him there as a burnt offering on one of the mountains I will tell you about."*
*Genesis 22:2 NIV*

*Hold it! Could this be right!? Was God really telling Abraham to kill Isaac and then burn his body on an altar?* Yes, the instructions were clear. Abraham now had to make a choice:

1. He could **ignore** God, renounce him as hard-hearted and cruel, or…
2. He could **believe** that Yahweh knew something he did not know and obey the Lord as instructed.

**Abraham Reasoned**

God's request must have bewildered Abraham. In all probability he had witnessed the human sacrifices practiced by other nations of his day and knew it was a common form of appeasing gods. Yet God's command to sacrifice Isaac went against everything Abraham knew about Yahweh. Not only that, but God had promised Isaac as a descendant who would bear many children. There was no earthly way to harmonize the Lord's previous promise with His present command. The Bible does not leave us guessing as to what went on in Abraham's mind. It tells us that…

*…Abraham reasoned that God could raise the dead…*
*Hebrews 11:19 NIV*

Abraham was convinced that if he sacrificed Isaac, the LORD would bring him back to life.

### FAITH

So Abraham went, putting his faith in God's goodness. He even started his journey *early* the next day.

> Early in the morning Abraham got up and saddled his donkey. He took two of his young servants with him, along with his son Isaac. When he had cut the wood for the burnt offering, he started out for the place God had spoken to him about.
>
> On the third day Abraham caught sight of the place in the distance. So he said to his servants, "You two stay here with the donkey while the boy and I go up there." *Genesis 22:3-5 NET*

Abraham was so sure that both of them would **return home alive,** he even told his servants,

> "We will worship and then return to you."  *Genesis 22:5 NET*

### A QUESTION

> Abraham took the wood for the burnt offering and put it on his son Isaac. Then he took the fire and the knife in his hand, and the two of them walked on together. Isaac said to his father Abraham, "My father?"
>
> "What is it, my son?" he replied.
>
> "Here is the fire and the wood," Isaac said, "but where is the lamb for the burnt offering?"  *Genesis 22:6-7 NET*

No doubt, Isaac had witnessed many altar sacrifices and it didn't take a university degree for him to realize that one of the essentials was missing. Where was the offering?

> Abraham said, "God will provide for himself the lamb for a burnt offering, my son." So they went both of them together.
>
> When they came to the place of which God had told him, Abraham built the altar there and laid the wood in order and bound Isaac his son and laid him on the altar, on top of the wood.
>
> *Genesis 22:8-9 ESV*

Isaac was no infant. The Hebrew word translated *boy* was used of young males all the way up to military age. He was certainly old enough to put up a fight—remember, he had carried the wood up the mountain. Yet in spite of the fact that Abraham was an old man, there is no record of a struggle. It is obvious that Isaac willingly submitted to his father, an act which showed implicit confidence in his dad whom he knew to be a follower of YAHWEH.

Once bound on the altar, Isaac was helpless. He was under direct orders from God to be slain. There was no way he could save himself. The Bible says Abraham then...

> *...stretched out his hand and took the knife to slay his son.*
>
> Genesis 22:10 NKJV

You can see the old man's hand shake. His jaw sags. His heart is about to break. The strain of the moment is incredible. Slowly the trembling arm is raised and in the somber light of the day, the cold metal of the knife glints. Deliberately, the mind commits itself to the plunge, and then... and then...

> *...the LORD called to him from heaven and said, "Abraham, Abraham!"*
>
> *So he said, "Here I am."*

*And He said, "Do not lay your hand on the lad, or do anything to him; for now I know that you fear God, since you have not withheld your son, your only son, from Me."* Genesis 22:11-12 NKJV

There must have been tears of relief. The sentence of death was gone—at least for Isaac it was gone. But there still was a death.

*Then Abraham looked up and saw a ram caught by its horns in a thicket. So he took the ram and sacrificed it as a burnt offering in place of his son.* Genesis 22:13 NLT

What was going on here? Why sacrifice an animal after releasing Isaac? What was this all about? We will answer that question in the next section, but let's conclude the story first.

### THE LORD WILL PROVIDE

This event so imprinted itself on Abraham's mind that he named the mountain as a reminder of what God is like.

*So Abraham called that place **The LORD Will Provide**. And to this day it is said, "On the mountain of the LORD it will be provided."* Genesis 22:14 NIV

Notice that Abraham called the place, *"The LORD **Will** Provide."* Why didn't he name it *"The LORD **Has** Provided?"* Had not the LORD already provided an offering? Why should Abraham talk about a future provision? The difference is intentional, but we will have to wait until a later chapter to learn its implication.

*... the LORD called to Abraham from heaven a second time and said, "I swear by myself, declares the LORD, that because you have done this and have not withheld your son, your only son, I will surely bless you ... and through your offspring all nations on earth will be blessed, because you have obeyed me."* Genesis 22:15-18 NIV

The story ends with God reaffirming his promise that THE ANOINTED ONE would be one of the descendants of Abraham and Isaac. It was said THE DELIVERER would be a blessing to all people.

| THE PROMISED DELIVERER would be ... |
|---|
| 1. The offspring of a woman |
| 2. A male |
| 3. A descendant of Abraham |
| 4. A descendant of Isaac |

# 7 WHAT IT WOULD TAKE

As you read the Bible you see altars and offerings mentioned frequently. We need to understand their significance or our biblical puzzle will be missing crucial pieces. Remember that *two-sides-of-the-same-coin* question?

1. How can we get rid of our sin-penalty with its horrific consequences, and ...

2. How can we gain a righteousness that is *equal* to God's righteousness so we can be accepted in his presence?

Understanding the purpose for offerings and altars in Scripture gives us needed background to answer those two questions.

## THE SIN-PENALTY

As we said before, the LORD YAHWEH had to do something about man's sin—he could not ignore it as if it had never happened. All sin had to be punished. That is only fair and just.

But God loved mankind and did not want us to spend an eternity in the Lake of Fire. So the question was asked, *"How could God punish sin without punishing us?"* Here's part of the answer. It involved a rather vivid visual aid.

## ATONEMENT

God told people to take an animal, kill it and let its blood run out on an altar.

> For the life of a creature is in the blood, and I have given it to you to make atonement for yourselves on the altar; it is the blood that makes atonement for one's life. *Leviticus 17:11 NIV*

We saw that the word *atonement* encompasses the idea of man's sin being symbolically *covered* before God's eyes. Ultimately, the word describes *what it would take* for the LORD to be satisfied that the sin-debt had been justly paid. The atonement for sin required blood to be spilled upon an altar, for the Scripture says...

> ... without shedding of blood there is no forgiveness. *Hebrews 9:22 NASB*

Let's unpack that verse. Here it is again with explanatory inserts.

> ... without [death through] the shedding of blood there is no forgiveness [of the sin-debt]. *Hebrews 9:22 NIV*

The Lord said that **man's sin-debt could only be forgiven if there was death**. Normally, man would die for his own sin. But now, based on certain future events, the Lord was saying that **he would accept an innocent animal's death in man's place**—as a substitute. It would be a life for a life, the innocent dying in place of the guilty. The sacrifice pictured *the law of sin and death* being obeyed and justice being fulfilled. Sin was not ignored—it was punished.

### A SUBSTITUTE

Just as Isaac had fallen under God's direct order to die, so all mankind is under the sentence of death.[9] Isaac could not save himself from God's judgment. Bound, he was helpless. But Abraham trusted the Lord, believing that somehow his loving God would make the difference. And the Lord did intervene. He provided a way of escape through a substitute. The Scripture says Abraham…

> …took the ram and sacrificed it as a burnt offering in place of
> his son.                                                        *Genesis 22:13 NLT*

He sacrificed the ram *"in place of"* Isaac. There was a death all right, but it was the ram's death instead of Isaac's. Isaac went free because a ram died. Yahweh had provided a substitute.

These sin offerings extended from Isaac all the way back to the very beginning of history. Just as the ram died in Isaac's place, so Abel had offered an animal sacrifice to die in his place. And just as the Lord provided a ram as an acceptable sacrifice in Isaac's place, so God had viewed Abel's sacrifice as acceptable. Since the time of Eden, man had brought substitutionary offerings for sin. When man came to God in God's way, believing his word, man found acceptance and friendship with YAHWEH.

These offerings illustrated *what it would take* to have the sin-debt paid in full. In essence, they were visual aids. For this reason God had rejected Cain's offering, as vegetables do not shed blood.

> ... *without shedding of blood there is no forgiveness.*
>
> Hebrews 9:22 NASB

Cain had brought an offering that was not in harmony with God's visual aid. The vegetables did not picture *what it would take* to have sin punished and forgiven.

## TWO SIDES OF THE COIN

With all this in mind let's return to our *two-sides-of-the-same-coin* questions. We now have some answers we can insert.

**Question:** "How could mankind escape the penalty for sin?"

**Answer:** "The penalty for sin could be paid by a substitute."

**Question:** "How can we gain back the perfect nature Adam and Eve lost in the Garden? How do we obtain *right clothes*—a righteousness that is equal to God's righteousness—so we can be accepted in his presence?"

**Answer:** "When ...

> *Abraham believed God ... it was credited to him as righteousness, and he was called God's friend."*
>
> James 2:23 NIV

*Now hold it! How could that be? How could this man with all his faults be considered righteous? He was far from perfect. And as to the matter of a substitute, does this mean we need to find an animal?*

The answers to these questions will be found in the pages to come. But for now, don't worry about finding an animal. To use the words of Abraham,

> *"God himself will provide the lamb ... "*
>
> Genesis 22:8 NIV

# CHAPTER SEVEN

# 1 ISRAEL AND JUDAH

God had promised both Abraham and Isaac that THE DELIVERER would be one of their descendants. Both these men lived long lives and then died.

**JACOB**

Isaac had two sons, Esau and Jacob. Esau was like Cain, trusting his own ideas, doing his own thing. On the other hand, Jacob trusted God and the LORD considered him a friend. Jacob knew he needed a substitute to die for his sin and often came to God offering blood sacrifices on an altar.

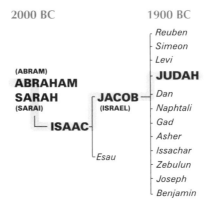

2000 BC      1900 BC

Reuben
Simeon
Levi
**JUDAH**
Dan
Naphtali
Gad
Asher
Issachar
Zebulun
Joseph
Benjamin

(ABRAM) **ABRAHAM** **SARAH** (SARAI) — **ISAAC** — **JACOB** (ISRAEL) — *Esau*

> So Jacob came to Luz (that is, Bethel), which is in the land of Canaan, he and all the people who were with him. He built an altar there, and called the place El-bethel, because there God had revealed Himself to him ...  *Genesis 35:6-7 NASB*

Jacob believed the LORD, taking him at his word. Through the altar sacrifices, he demonstrated his agreement with YAHWEH that ...

> ... without [death through] the shedding of blood there is no forgiveness [of the sin-debt].  *Hebrews 9:22 NIV*

Although Jacob often failed in life, God was the ultimate focus of his trust. Later his name was changed to *Israel*, meaning *God prevails*. Today the nation of Israel which descends directly from Jacob, is named after this man.

Among the promises God made to Jacob, he renewed the commitment he had made to Abraham and Isaac. YAHWEH told Jacob,

> "I am the LORD, the God of your father Abraham and the God of Isaac ... in you and in your descendants shall all the families of the earth be blessed."  *Genesis 28:13-14 NASB*

God was saying that one of Jacob's descendants would be a blessing to every nation—a reference to THE DELIVERER.

Jacob (or Israel) had twelve sons from whom descended twelve tribes.[1] Before Jacob died, he told his son Judah that it would be through his tribe that THE CHOSEN ONE would come.

| The Promised Deliverer would be ... |
|---|
| 1. The offspring of a woman |
| 2. A male |
| 3. A descendant of Abraham |
| 4. A descendant of Isaac |
| 5. A descendant of Jacob (Israel) |
| 6. From the tribe of Judah |

In the final years of Jacob's life, famine hit the country. He, along with his extended family, moved into Egypt. At the time they numbered only seventy.[2] Egypt received and treated them well— they were no threat to

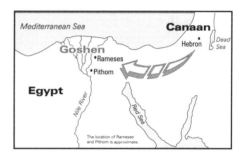

such a great nation. Jacob settled his family in the Nile delta, planted crops, and prepared to wait out the famine.

Three hundred and fifty years later they were still living in Egypt, but by then it is estimated that there were 2 ½ million Israelites. The descendants of Abraham, Isaac, and Jacob had indeed become a great nation, but there was a problem—they were in the wrong country. They had been promised the land of Canaan, not Egypt. However, the LORD had told Jacob long before the seventy had fled the famine in Canaan,

> *"I am with you and will keep you wherever you go, and I will bring you back to this land. For I will not leave you until I have done what I have promised you."* Genesis 28:15 ESV

God was about to fulfill that pledge. It would be recorded in the next book Moses was to write—the book of Exodus.

Exodus is the second book in the Bible, out of 66 that comprise all of Scripture.

### SLAVERY

It is at this point in history that we return to where our story began. Remember how in chapter one we read about Pharaoh enslaving the Israelites to control their rapidly growing population? We saw that the King of Egypt decided to ...

> *... oppress them with hard labor ...* Exodus 1:11 NET

Remember how it was into this setting that Moses was born of Israelite parents? He was condemned to die at birth, then through God's intervention rescued, raised, and educated as a member of Pharaoh's household. We saw that, as an adult, Moses murdered an Egyptian and fled as a fugitive into the desert, and then after forty years as a shepherd, met with YAHWEH at the burning bush. It was here, at this "burning bush meeting" the LORD said,

> "I have surely seen the oppression of My people who are in Egypt, and have heard their cry because of their taskmasters, for I know their sorrows. So I have come down to deliver them out of the hand of the Egyptians, and to bring them up from that land to a good and large land, to a land flowing with milk and honey…"  Exodus 3:7-8 NKJV

Moses was told to go back to Egypt and seek the release of the Hebrew slaves. To help him in his task, the LORD arranged for Aaron, Moses' brother, to function as a spokesman. They began by asking the Israelite's permission to approach Pharaoh. Moses…

> …gathered together all the elders of the children of Israel. And Aaron spoke all the words which the LORD had spoken to Moses. … So the people believed…  Exodus 4:29-31 NKJV

The Scripture says the Hebrew slaves agreed to trust YAHWEH, as one would agree to trust a friend.

# 2 PHARAOH AND MOSES

In the time of Moses the Egyptians were one of the strongest nations on earth whereas the Israelites were common slaves. Pharaoh was a world leader; Moses, a fugitive from justice. A whole list of problems must have entered Moses' mind as he considered the prospect of meeting Pharaoh face-to-face. When the time finally came, Moses recorded that he simply told Pharaoh,

> "Thus says the LORD, the God of Israel, `Let My people go…'"  Exodus 5:1 NASB

Pharaoh's reply was not encouraging.

> "Who is the LORD that I should obey His voice to let Israel go?"  Exodus 5:2 NASB

Pharaoh knew about *Ra, Isis,* and many other Egyptian gods, but he had never heard of the LORD YAHWEH. He probably figured that whoever this YAHWEH god was, he couldn't be very significant.

He would not waste his time with the god of the slaves. Besides Pharaoh already had a religion, one that was esteemed by the rest of the world.

But the real issue was financial. To release the Israelite slaves would be devastating to the economy. That would not do! So, trusting in his own wisdom, Pharaoh made the wrong choice. He told Moses,

> *"I don't know the LORD, and I will not let Israel go."*
>
> *Exodus 5:2 NLT*

> *Then the LORD said to Moses, "Now you will see what I will do to Pharaoh … I will bring you out from under the yoke of the Egyptians. I will free you from being slaves to them … with mighty acts of judgment."* *Exodus 6:1,6 NIV*

The LORD told Moses that He would bring judgment on Egypt in the form of plagues. Only under these conditions would Pharaoh relinquish his hold and let the Israelites depart Egypt. At the same time, YAHWEH said he would teach the Israelites so that they would…

> *"… know that **I am the LORD** your God, who brought you out from under the burdens of the Egyptians."* *Exodus 6:7 NASB*

But the lesson would not be just for them.

> *"The **Egyptians** will know that **I am the LORD** when I stretch out my hand against Egypt and bring the Israelites out of it."*
>
> *Exodus 7:5 NIV*

God was going to teach both the Israelites and the Egyptians the same thing, that he was YAHWEH—a God who had more power than all the Egyptian gods and goddesses combined, a God who was able to deliver his *Chosen People* from the strongest nation on earth.

But it would not be just these two people groups who would learn these lessons. The Scripture says all the nations of the world would watch and receive an education.

### THE CHOSEN PEOPLE

The LORD told the Israelites,

> *"I will take you to be my people, and I will be your God… I will bring you into the land that I swore [or pledged] to give to Abraham, to Isaac, and to Jacob. I will give it to you for a possession. I am the LORD."* *Exodus 6:7-8 ESV*

By choosing one nation, the LORD made it easier for all nations to know what the Creator was like and how he related to man.

*YAHWEH made promises. But did he keep them?*

*YAHWEH said he would force Pharaoh to release his slaves. Did he really have that power?*

*YAHWEH said he would sustain the whole nation of Israel—2 ½ million strong—on a trip from Egypt to Canaan. Was it possible?*

These and a multitude of other questions would be answered. All that the world would need to do is look at Israel and they would see a full-colour, surround-sound, living lesson of how the LORD dealt with mankind! From this point on, the Israelites would be known as the *Chosen People*. God had kept his promise to Abraham, Isaac, and Jacob.

> …you, Israel, are My servant, Jacob whom I have chosen, The descendants of Abraham My friend.　　　*Isaiah 41:8 NKJV*

## THE GLOBAL CLASSROOM

This analogy, though not found in the Bible, is instructive.

Many ages ago word went out to the nations of the world that they were to assemble representatives in a global classroom. The meeting was being called by the *Unique God*, YAHWEH.

On the important day, the students gathered. Near the front sat Mr. Egypt, old and erect, greatly respected for his architectural achievements. Further back was the representative for Babylon, well known for his knowledge in astronomy. Persia, India, China, all the Asian nations, European nations, African nations—all corners of the globe—had sent their best and brightest, dressed in their finest.

When the LORD YAHWEH entered the auditorium, a hush settled over the crowded room. With little ado, he stated that he would choose one of the nations to help him in his presentation. It was an important position and must not be taken lightly. A slight rustle echoed in the hall as each representative sat a little straighter. There was an almost palpable unspoken wish coming from every student, *"I hope it is me!"*

*continued next page*

continued from previous page

As those gathered waited in eager anticipation, the *Unique God* left the platform and walked up and down the rows. Then, near the back, he bent over a small chair and taking a little student by the hand, led him down to the front. There was a collective gasp; a wave of whispering swept the room. *"He's so young. Who is he? What has he achieved?"* It seemed no one knew the name of the little nation that had been chosen.

But then word spread through the classroom. According to Mr. Egypt, the little nation was made up of slaves—nobodies, really. It was not spoken, but the question could be felt. *"Why had not* YAHWEH *chosen an important nation to help with the teaching—a nation respected for its age? Why had he chosen slaves?"*

But the *Unique God* was unmoved by the classroom buzz. He pulled out a stool and hoisting the little representative onto the chair, YAHWEH placed chalk in his hand. Then turning to the assembled students, he motioned for silence. *"There is a lot of confusion in the world about what is right and what is wrong. People have questions about life and death, about what I am like or whether I exist at all."* Indicating the little fellow on the stool, YAHWEH continued, *"I am going to have my chosen student write on the chalk board things you all need to know. I want you to watch, listen, and above all, learn. This is very important."*

With that God turned to little Israel, for that was the chosen nation, and said, *"Write what I tell you, and only what I tell you."*

**THE CHOSEN NATION**

The Bible says that YAHWEH chose one nation through whom he would speak to the world so ...

> ... that all the peoples of the earth may know that the LORD is God; there is no other.          1 Kings 8:60 ESV

It wasn't because Israel was more worthy. God loves all nations equally.

> *"The LORD did not set His love on you nor choose you because you were more in number than any other people, for you were the least of all peoples; but because the LORD loves you, and because He would keep the oath which He swore to your fathers ... "*          Deuteronomy 7:7-8 NKJV

# 3 Plagues and Prophecy

When Moses and Aaron demanded the release of God's *Chosen People*, Pharaoh simply turned them a deaf ear. So the Lord told Moses,

> "Go to Pharaoh in the morning, as he is going out to the water. Stand on the bank of the Nile to meet him ... And you shall say to him, 'The Lord, the God of the Hebrews, sent me to you, saying, "Let my people go ... But so far, you have not obeyed." Thus says the Lord, "By this you shall know that I am the Lord ... I will strike the water that is in the Nile, and it shall turn into blood. The fish in the Nile shall die, and the Nile will stink, and the Egyptians will grow weary of drinking water from the Nile."'"
>
> *Exodus 7:15-18 ESV*

The Lord struck right at the heart of the Egyptian religion by making one of their gods, the Nile, turn to blood. The Lord made their god stink—he made the river abhorrent to them! In so doing, the Lord drew a line in the sand—he made a statement. Yahweh was not like the deities of Egypt! He was different, a lot different! Everyone needed to understand that the Lord was far more powerful than the god of the Nile.

Pharaoh could have stopped right then and there and said, *"Whoa! I better find out more about this Yahweh God. He sure has power. Where is this Moses guy? I need to talk to him right now."* But no, Pharaoh continued to trust in his own line of reasoning.

> ... Pharaoh's heart became hard; he would not listen to Moses ... and did not take even this to heart.   *Exodus 7:22-23 NIV*

> Then the Lord said to Moses, "Go to Pharaoh and tell him, 'Thus says the Lord: " ... if you refuse to release them, then I am going to plague all your territory with frogs. The Nile will swarm with frogs, and they will come up and go into your house, in your bedroom, and on your bed, and into the houses of your servants and your people, and into your ovens and your kneading troughs."'"   *Exodus 8:1-3 NET*

## Prophets

We need to stop here and consider something that has immense implications. Think what would happen if two men showed up in a major capital of the world and said that all the water in a local river was going to turn to blood. If it made the newspaper at all, it would probably be a small column near the back, and these guys would be labeled "quacks." But if this event actually happened, then overnight it would be front page news! Everyone would be watching to determine if they were sensible men or just simpletons that had hit it lucky.

Imagine then, if those same men said that next week the country would be overrun with frogs. Everyone would be talking and watching very carefully. And if the plague of frogs actually occurred, well, it would be incredible! From then on, whatever they said would be taken very seriously, whether it was prophetic or not.

That is what happened with Moses and Aaron, not only twice, but with dozens of prophecies, specifically stated, then accurately fulfilled. To make it even more foolproof, God had Moses foretell events, some that would be fulfilled immediately after his death, and others throughout the centuries even to this very day. In the pages to come, we will read about some of those events. Mathematicians agree that the probability of this occurring by chance is so infinitesimally small, it is impossible.[3]

What makes this so significant is that this is the way God authenticated all 40 writers of the Bible. When God told them the message to write, he included prophetic elements that, when fulfilled, validated the whole message. This is why they were called *prophets*. In referring to these 40 men, one Hebrew writer wrote,

> *In the past God spoke to our forefathers through the prophets…*
>
> Hebrews 1:1 NIV

Fulfilled prophecy was the potent test to determine whether a writer was genuine or not. If the prophecies they recorded actually came to pass, then everything else they wrote was considered true. For example, because the prophecies of Moses were fulfilled with pinpoint accuracy, then everything else he wrote—how the universe was created, how sin entered the world, the judgment to come—all these events were considered to be reliable facts as well.

To prevent con-artists from concocting their own prophecies and then passing them off as Scripture, the LORD commanded that…

> *…when a prophet speaks in the name of the LORD, if the thing does not happen or come to pass, that is the thing which the LORD has not spoken.*
>
> Deuteronomy 18:22 NKJV

They had to be 100% correct every time—without error.

*"But the prophet who presumes to speak a word in My name, which I have not commanded him to speak, or who speaks in the name of other gods, that prophet shall die."*

*Deuteronomy 18:20 NKJV*

In other words, a prophet had to be 100% accurate or he was not considered to be speaking on behalf of the LORD. His message was to be viewed as derived from his own imagination or possibly from other gods or goddesses. In such cases, the penalty was severe—the prophet was put to death. This absolute standard obviously discouraged false prophets.

Because each of the 40 prophets made specific predictions that were remarkably fulfilled, the information they recorded regarding the key to a joyful life, the solution to the sin-debt, what to expect after death—all these things were also considered reliable information, coming directly from YAHWEH.

This is another reason why the Bible is so incredibly unique. It should also cause us to consider seriously what we are reading.

### ACCURATE

Moses was 100% accurate in his prophecies. When he said the LORD would bring a plague of frogs,

*…frogs came up and covered the land of Egypt.* Exodus 8:6 NET

Moses and Aaron would have made headline news in the *Egyptian Times*. As a result, the people not only believed their prophecies, but they also believed what Moses told them about life and the way it should be lived. Later on, Moses wrote,

*When Israel saw the great power which the LORD had used against the Egyptians, the people feared the LORD, and they believed in the LORD and in His servant Moses.* Exodus 14:31 NASB

### THE LORD VERSUS GODS

These plagues began a cycle. The LORD would warn Pharaoh to let the Israelites go; Pharaoh would say, *"No,"* and God would bring a plague, each one targeting another of the Egyptian gods. Not every god is clearly identifiable, but I will list the most likely deity.

First, the water was turned to **blood**, humiliating *Hapi*, the god of the Nile River.

Then the LORD sent a scourge of **frogs**—in every nook and cranny. In food, in beds—everywhere. This plague defeated *Heqet*, the frog-headed goddess of life, birth, and rebirth. It was like the LORD was saying, *"If you insist on worshipping a frog, then here are a lot of them!"* Everyone must have been a little weary of *Heqet* by the time this plague passed.

The frogs were followed by swarms of aggressive **gnats**.[4] Then **flies** supplanted the gnats. These insects would have defiled the Egyptians—a dreadful blow, as they were required to be ceremonially clean to worship their deities.

Then an epidemic struck the **cattle**—they all died. The Egyptians worshipped several cattle deities—*Apis*, the sacred bull and *Hathor*, the cow-goddess, to name two. But when YAHWEH destroyed the cattle, these animal gods and goddesses were shown to be powerless in preventing the unique God's judgment. The LORD YAHWEH was greater than them all.

After the devastating plague on the cattle, the people were tormented with festering **boils**, a direct hit at the many deities said to preserve good health. The LORD showed the people that their personal lives, their very cleanliness, depended on him.

## So You May Know

The Bible takes many pages to report the plagues, but for the sake of brevity, it is enough to know that each followed a similar scenario. For example, Moses confronted Pharaoh,

> *"Thus says the LORD, the God of the Hebrews, 'Let My people go, that they may serve Me. For this time I will send all My plagues on you and your servants and your people, so that you may know that there is no one like Me in all the earth.*
>
> *Still you exalt yourself against My people by not letting them go. Behold, about this time tomorrow, I will send a very heavy hail, such as has not been seen in Egypt from the day it was founded until now.'"* Exodus 9:13-14,17-18 NASB

This plague struck at *Shu*, the god of the sky; *Set*, the god of wind and storms; and maybe even *Baal*, the god of thunder.

As each plague unfolded, it became increasingly clear that YAHWEH not only ruled the earth, but was master of the universe.

## Yahweh Keeps His Word

By this time, some of the Egyptians were beginning to take notice. When they heard of the impending **hail**,

*Some of Pharaoh's officials were afraid because of what the LORD
had said. They quickly brought their servants and livestock in
from the fields.*                                      Exodus 9:20 NLT

They had learned that Yahweh keeps his word.

*And the LORD rained hail on the land of Egypt. So there was hail,
and fire mingled with the hail, so very heavy that there was none
like it in all the land of Egypt since it became a nation.*
                                                      Exodus 9:23-24 NKJV

Even Pharaoh was forced to face the facts.

*Then Pharaoh sent and called Moses and Aaron and said to
them, "This time I have sinned; the LORD is in the right, and I
and my people are in the wrong. Plead with the LORD, for there
has been enough of God's thunder and hail. I will let you go,
and you shall stay no longer."*                       Exodus 9:27-28 ESV

But Pharaoh did not keep his word. Although he was often
considered an *avatar*—a god in human form—he was not like
the LORD. He lied.

*But when Pharaoh saw that the rain and the hail and the thunder
had ceased, he sinned yet again and hardened his heart, he and
his servants. So the heart of Pharaoh was hardened, and he
did not let the people of Israel go, just as the LORD had spoken
through Moses.*                                       Exodus 9:34-35 ESV

## MORE PLAGUES

So the LORD sent another plague. What the hail had left behind
was devoured by a horde of **locusts**. This hit *Osiris* particularly
hard. He was the god of agriculture and fertility—one of Egypt's
most cherished deities. Yet Pharaoh's response was the same. He
would not release the *Chosen Nation*.

Finally, the LORD struck at *Ra*, the sun god, supposedly the god
of gods. The LORD sent a curse of **darkness** so thick it could be
felt. Moses wrote that…

*No one could see another person, and no one could rise from
his place for three days. But the Israelites had light in the places
where they lived.*                                    Exodus 10:23 NET

*Ra* was shamed—utterly powerless in the face of Yahweh. In just
nine plagues, the LORD Yahweh demolished the people's confidence
in the Egyptian deities. As all the nations of the world watched, the
Egyptian gods and goddesses fell from their exalted position.

Later, one of the 40 prophets recorded the reaction of another nation who watched the events from afar. He wrote,

> ... the terror of you has fallen on us, and ... all the inhabitants of the land are fainthearted because of you ... our hearts melted; neither did there remain any more courage in anyone because of you, for the LORD your God, He is God in heaven above and on earth beneath. Joshua 2:9,11 NKJV

However, Pharaoh still wasn't moved. So God sent one more plague, the tenth—the most devastating one yet to come.

# 4 The Bread and the Lamb

And the LORD said to Moses, "I will bring one more plague on Pharaoh and on Egypt. Afterward he will let you go from here. When he lets you go, he will surely drive you out of here altogether.

"Thus says the LORD: 'About midnight I will go out into the midst of Egypt; and all the firstborn in the land of Egypt shall die, from the firstborn of Pharaoh who sits on his throne, even to the firstborn of the female servant who is behind the handmill ...'"
Exodus 11:1,4-5 NKJV

The last plague was indeed the worst, falling on Egyptians and Israelites alike if they did not follow God's instructions. To prevent this disaster, God told Moses to tell the people to:

**Take a lamb ...**

> "... on the tenth day of this month each family must choose a lamb or a young goat for a sacrifice." Exodus 12:3 NLT

**It must be a male, without blemish.** It couldn't be deformed or defective in any way. God was asking for a perfect lamb.

> "The animal you select must be a one-year-old male, either a sheep or a goat, with no defects." Exodus 12:5 NLT

**Kill the lamb at the appointed time.**

> "Take special care of this chosen animal until the evening of the fourteenth day of this first month. Then the whole assembly of the community of Israel must slaughter their lamb or young goat at twilight." Exodus 12:6 NLT

**Apply the blood to the door posts and the lintel.**

> "They will take some of the blood and put it on the two side posts and top of the doorframe of the houses where they will eat it." Exodus 12:7 NET

**Do not break any of the lamb's bones.**

> *"Each Passover lamb must be eaten in one house. Do not carry any of its meat outside, and do not break any of its bones."*
>
> Exodus 12:46 NLT

**Bake and eat bread prepared without yeast.**

> *"That same night they must roast the meat over a fire and eat it along with … bread made without yeast."*     Exodus 12:8 NLT

**Stay inside the house until morning.**

> *"None of you shall go out of the door of his house until the morning."*     Exodus 12:22 ESV

**I will pass over.**

> *"On that same night I will pass through Egypt and strike down every firstborn—both men and animals—and **I will bring judgment on all the gods of Egypt**. I am the LORD.*
>
> *The blood will be a sign for you on the houses where you are; and when I see the blood, **I will pass over you**. No destructive plague will touch you when I strike Egypt."*     Exodus 12:12-13 NIV

When God came in judgment to kill the firstborn, the LORD said he would pass over every house where the blood was applied.

## A Choice

The Israelites now had a choice:

1. They could trust the Lord and obey his instructions, or...
2. They could trust their own notions and put their faith in the weak gods of the Egyptians.

In whom would they trust?

The Bible tells us the slaves made the right choice. They may have been scared—the firstborn son may have sat on his daddy's lap nervously biting his upper lip; others may have wondered and worried—but all was well. Deliverance was not based on their feelings, but on concrete facts. That is the nature of biblical faith. It is based on facts found in the Bible—not on ever-changing emotions. The Israelites did not need to worry. They had done...

> ...just as the Lord had commanded through Moses and Aaron.
>
> Exodus 12:28 NLT

## Death

> It happened at midnight—the Lord attacked all the firstborn in the land of Egypt, from the firstborn of Pharaoh who sat on his throne to the firstborn of the captive who was in the prison...
>
> Pharaoh got up in the night, along with all his servants and all Egypt, and there was a great cry in Egypt, for there was no house in which there was not someone dead.
>
> Pharaoh summoned Moses and Aaron in the night and said, "Get up, get out from among my people, both you and the Israelites! Go, serve the Lord as you have requested! Also, take your flocks and your herds, just as you have requested, and leave. But bless me also."

> So all the Israelites did exactly as the Lord commanded Moses and Aaron. And on this very day the Lord brought the Israelites out of the land of Egypt...
>
> Exodus 12:29–32, 50-51 NET

God had been gracious with Pharaoh. He had given him many opportunities to let the Israelites go, but Pharaoh had refused. God said he would judge the Egyptians and he did just that. YAHWEH is not like us. We may threaten to discipline our children and not follow through, but the LORD always keeps his word.

On the other hand, the Israelites experienced the LORD's kindness because they believed him. When he came in judgment, wherever he saw the blood applied, he passed over. *The firstborn lived—but only because a lamb died.* It had been this way from the very beginning. **God had accepted Abel's sacrifice as a death payment** *in Abel's place.* **When Abraham offered Isaac as a sacrifice, the ram died** *in Isaac's place.* **Now with the Passover, the lamb died** *in the place of* **the firstborn.**

These substitutionary sacrifices were visible statements of each person's trust in YAHWEH as their Saviour. Because they believed the LORD was truthful, they obeyed him. God said,

> "This is a day to remember. Each year, from generation to generation, you must celebrate it as a special festival to the LORD."
>
> Exodus 12:14 NLT

> "In the future, when your son asks you 'What is this?' you are to tell him, 'With a mighty hand the LORD brought us out from Egypt, from the land of slavery.'" Exodus 13:14 NET

Each year as the Israelites celebrated the Passover, they would be reminded that the LORD was a powerful God who faithfully kept his word. He could be trusted. He had a proven, reliable history. He was the sort of God you would want as your friend.

But it was not only the Israelites who would be reminded of these facts. All the nations that witnessed these events would be reminded as well. The *Chosen Nation* had begun to fulfill its purpose in the *Global Classroom*.

| The gods of Egypt | The LORD YAHWEH |
| --- | --- |
| Believed by Pharaoh | Believed by Moses |
| Had nothing to offer | Provided a substitute Lamb |
| Egyptians judged | Israelites delivered |

# CHAPTER EIGHT

# 1 THE RED SEA

The Israelites were a dishevel-ed crowd as they started off on their long journey. The Egyptians sped their departure by loading them down with valuables. With no time to pack in an orderly fashion, they left in a mighty rush, driving their livestock before them. Multiply those factors with their approximate number—2 ½ million—and you have confusion! Moses was the leader, but how do you yell, *"This way!"* to such a multitude? God solved the dilemma.

> *And the LORD went before them by day in a pillar of cloud to lead them along the way, and by night in a pillar of fire to give them light, that they might travel by day and by night.*
>
> Exodus 13:21 ESV

With this guiding beacon, everyone was able to organize themselves immediately. All they had to do was look ahead and follow the special cloud, trusting the LORD to lead them. This was crowd-control on a grand scale!

## SECOND THOUGHTS

But hardly had the Israelites started on their journey than Pharaoh had second thoughts. He said,

> *"What in the world have we done? For we have released the people of Israel from serving us!"* Exodus 14:5 NET

Pharaoh was losing his slaves—all his free labor!

> *Then he prepared his chariots and took his army with him … The Egyptians chased after them, and all the horses and chariots of Pharaoh and his horsemen and his army overtook them camping by the sea …* Exodus 14:6,9 NET

The Israelites were fenced in by the sea on one side and the Egyptian army on the other side. They were trapped.

> … the Israelites looked up, and there were the Egyptians marching after them, and they were terrified.
>
> Moses said to the people, "Do not fear! Stand firm and see the salvation of the LORD that he will provide for you today…"
>
> Exodus 14:10,13 NET

### SALVATION

Moses reminded the people that YAHWEH is an ever-present Saviour. The Scripture says,

> … and the pillar of cloud moved from before them and stood behind them. It came between the Egyptian camp and the Israelite camp; it was a dark cloud and it lit up the night so that one camp did not come near the other the whole night.
>
> Moses stretched out his hand toward the sea, and the LORD drove the sea apart by a strong east wind all that night, and he made the sea into dry land, and the water was divided. So the Israelites went through the middle of the sea on dry ground, the water forming a wall for them on their right and on their left.
>
> Exodus 14:19-22 NET

While the LORD held the Egyptians off, the Hebrews crossed the sea on dry ground. Once they were safely across,

> The Egyptians chased them and followed them into the middle of the sea… In the morning… the LORD… threw the Egyptian army into a panic. He jammed the wheels of their chariots so that they had difficulty driving…
>
> The LORD said to Moses, "Extend your hand toward the sea, so that the waters may flow back on the Egyptians, on their chariots, and on their horsemen!"
>
> The water returned and covered the chariots and the horsemen and all the army of Pharaoh that was coming after the Israelites into the sea—not so much as one of them survived!
>
> When Israel saw the great power that the LORD had exercised over the Egyptians, they feared the LORD, and they believed in the LORD and in his servant Moses.       Exodus 14:23-26,28,31 NET

YAHWEH demonstrated to a watching world that he was a God who could be counted on in time of trouble—in the same way one could rely upon a good friend.

# 2 Bread and Water

When the Israelites left Egypt,

> …God did not lead them along the main road that runs through Philistine territory, even though that was the shortest route to the Promised Land. God said, "If the people are faced with a battle, they might change their minds and return to Egypt." So God led them…through the wilderness… *Exodus 13:17-18 NLT*

This desolate wasteland was devoid of enemies, but there was also very little food.

> Then the whole congregation of the children of Israel complained against Moses and Aaron in the wilderness…"Oh, that we had died by the hand of the LORD in the land of Egypt, when we sat by the pots of meat and when we ate bread to the full! For you have brought us out into this wilderness to kill this whole assembly with hunger." *Exodus 16:2-3 NKJV*

The people complained and even wanted to return to slavery. Their attitude toward God was saddening, for the LORD had shown vigilant care for them and he wasn't about to abandon them. They should have asked the LORD for food, but no, they grumbled!

## Bread and Quail

> And the LORD said to Moses, "I have heard the grumbling of the people of Israel. Say to them, 'At twilight you shall eat meat, and in the morning you shall be filled with bread. Then you shall know that I am the LORD your God.'"
>
> In the evening quail came up and covered the camp, and in the morning dew lay around the camp. And when the dew had gone up, there was on the face of the wilderness a fine, flake-like thing, fine as frost on the ground. When the people of Israel saw it, they said to one another, "What is it?" For they did not know what it was. And Moses said to them, "It is the bread that the LORD has given you to eat." *Exodus 16:11–15 ESV*

God provided them with meat and bread and they didn't even have to work for it. As they gathered the daily bread, they would be reminded: *a faithful and reliable God is providing for us.*

The bread also had a purpose greater than food. God said,

> "I will test them in this to see whether or not they will follow my instructions." *Exodus 16:4 NLT*

It was another one of those "trust me" tests. God told the people to gather only as much bread as they could eat in one day. It was an easy test, equivalent to what God had given to Adam and Eve in the Garden of Eden.

> But they did not listen to Moses; some kept part of it until morning, and it was full of worms and began to stink… *Exodus 16:20 NET*

It was a simple lesson with only minor repercussions, but through it the people learned that YAHWEH meant what he said and was to be trusted. Disobedience was fraught with hazards.

> This is what the LORD says… the Holy One of Israel: "I am the LORD your God, who teaches you what is best for you, who directs you in the way you should go." *Isaiah 48:17 NIV*

## WATER

> Then all the congregation of the sons of Israel journeyed… according to the command of the LORD, and camped at Rephidim, and there was no water for the people to drink. Therefore the people quarreled with Moses and said, "Give us water that we may drink… Why, now, have you brought us up from Egypt, to kill us and our children and our livestock with thirst?"
>
> So Moses cried out to the LORD, saying, "What shall I do to this people? A little more and they will stone me."
> *Exodus 17:1-4 NASB*

So much for learning from past experiences. The people were back in the grumble and gripe mode, only this time it had to do with water.

> And the LORD said to Moses, "… take in your hand the staff… I will stand before you there on the rock at Horeb, and you shall strike the rock, and water shall come out of it, and the people will drink."
>
> And Moses did so, in the sight of the elders of Israel.
> *Exodus 17:5-6 ESV*

On occasion you see an artist's rendition of this miracle. Moses is portrayed as standing by a rock holding his staff, with a little stream of water spurting onto the ground. The truth of the matter is that there must have been quite a gush. There was a vast throng of thirsty people to water, plus all their livestock. This was not a trickle, but a mighty torrent! The Bible says,

> He opened the rock, and water gushed out; it flowed through the desert like a river. *Psalm 105:41 ESV*

## GRACE

Again, the LORD provided for the people's needs even though they were rude and demanding. God could have cracked the whip—told them to sit up and behave themselves, but the LORD showed them grace—undeserved love. He was giving them an opportunity to get to know him better.

We may judge the Israelites harshly for acting like misbehaving children, but a big part of Israel's problem was that they did not know *how* they should act. It was not clear to them what was right or wrong. Like little children, they needed these facts explained. And God was about to do just that.

# 3 THE TEN RULES

Why is it that some actions are considered right and others wrong? What constitutes sin? This is an ancient debate. To clear up the confusion, the LORD embarked upon the next major revelation of his character. Using the *Global Classroom* analogy, the *Chosen Nation* was about to write on the chalkboard the Unique God's definition of words like *righteous, sinless,* and *pure.* Man was about to learn what it meant to reflect the image of God.

### A VISUAL AID

> In the third month after the Israelites went out from the land of Egypt … they came to the Desert of Sinai … Israel camped there in front of the mountain. *Exodus 19:1-2 NET*

The LORD told Moses to …

> "Mark off a boundary all around the mountain. Warn the people, 'Be careful! Do not go up on the mountain or even touch its boundaries.'" *Exodus 19:12 NLT*

The boundaries pictured the separation between God and man because of sin. Anyone crossing the line faced death.

> On the morning of the third day there were thunders and lightnings and a thick cloud on the mountain and a very loud trumpet blast, so that all the people in the camp trembled. *Exodus 19:16 ESV*

Just as movie makers use music and backdrops to enhance the theme of their productions, so YAHWEH carefully set the stage to establish the fact that he is a great God, and his purity is not to be taken lightly.

*Now Mount Sinai was all in smoke because the Lord descended upon it in fire;*

*Now the Lord said to Moses, "Come up to Me on the mountain and remain there, and I will give you the stone tablets, with the law and commandment which I have written for their instruction."*
*Exodus 19:18; 24:12 NASB*

Moses ascended the mountain and stayed there for 40 days. While there God gave Moses two stone tablets upon which were engraved ten rules. Four of the rules targeted man's relationship with God; the other six—how people should relate with one another.

Each one of the rules described the way to create and maintain trust. As we saw before, *trust* is the basis for every friendship—whether in a family, business, or government. Without trust, relationships fall apart, resulting in anger and anxiety, hurt and hardship, bitterness and battles. Ultimately, these ten commands described what the Lord considered to be right and wrong. Here's the list Yahweh gave to Moses:

## Rule # 1

*"I am the Lord your God … You shall have no other gods before Me."*
*Exodus 20:2-3 NASB*

Obviously, Yahweh would forbid the worship of Satan, who is …

*The god of this age…*
*2 Corinthians 4:4 NKJV*

The Devil is a liar, the destroyer of relationships—families, friends, even entire nations. To revere him would be extremely foolish. You can't trust him. But this command went beyond Satan. It was like the Lord was telling the Israelites, *"It is right for you to honour me as your God, for I am Yahweh, but don't trust those Egyptian gods or any other gods. To do homage to other deities is wrong. It's what I call sin."* But why was the Lord Yahweh so opposed to the worship of other gods? Surely one could revere the Lord along with other gods at the same time.

The answer to that question is related to the identity of the gods and goddesses—who they are and where they came from. We will address that issue in a moment, but for now all we need to know is that Yahweh made it clear that …

*… the Lord is the true God; He is the living God and the everlasting King…*
*Jeremiah 10:10 NASB*

To reflect the image of God, one must honour Y*AHWEH* alone—the one who made promises to Abraham, Isaac, and Jacob. To trust in any other deity was wrong. It was sin.

> Some people believe that all the gods and goddesses are the multiple manifestation of just one Supreme Being. As we shall see, the Scripture rules out that possibility.
>
> Others worship the spirits of trees, streams, or departed ancestors. The Bible emphatically declares that the L*ORD* alone is to be worshipped. Only he is to be honoured in this way.

## RULE # 2

*"You shall not make for yourself an idol in the form of anything in heaven above or on the earth beneath or in the waters below. You shall not bow down to them or worship them..."*

Exodus 20:4-5 NIV

This command has two aspects.

❖ God prohibited mankind from bowing down to images, icons, or pictures which represented himself.

*"I am the L*ORD*; that is my name! I will not give my glory to anyone else, nor share my praise with carved idols."*

Isaiah 42:8 NLT

Some religions claim to follow the Bible but include the adoration of idols, pictures, and icons in their worship. They say that the image only represents the L*ORD*. But God was opposed to people worshipping a depiction of himself, as man's natural inclination seems to be to revere the image instead of the L*ORD*.

*They worshiped their idols, which became a snare to them.*

Psalm 106:36 NET

Also, the L*ORD* was a spirit. Any picture or image of him was a fabrication of the mind.

❖ The L*ORD* also forbade people from worshipping pictures, icons, or idols of other gods.

*You must not make gods of silver alongside me, nor make gods of gold for yourselves.*

Exodus 20:23 NET

The reason the L*ORD* forbade the worship of spirits, idols, and other deities was because of their identity. When the *Shining One* rebelled against Yahweh, one-third of the angelic host joined him in his revolt. We saw that these rebellious spirits were cast out of Heaven—the *Shining One* becoming the *Devil* and the defiant angels, *demons*. The Lord prohibited the worship of other gods and goddesses because they were really demons.

> *"…these sacrifices are offered to demons, not to God. And I don't want you to participate with demons. 1 Corinthians 10:20-21 NLT*

We saw earlier that…

> *…Satan disguises himself as an angel of light.*
> 2 Corinthians 11:14 NASB

In the same way, demons masquerade as gods and goddesses—as idols. I've been shown idols that had holes in the back of them so the spirit could enter and leave at will. In a way, the idols functioned as a mask for the demons. But masks have only one purpose—to cover up and deceive. Both Satan and the demons are deceivers. They cannot be trusted. It is for our own good that the Lord doesn't want people to…

> *…follow deceiving spirits and things taught by demons.*
> 1 Timothy 4:1 NIV

Instead, people should trust the Lord, the…

> *…God, who cannot lie…*           Titus 1:2 NASB

The problem with idols is that they are part of the demonic deception. The Scripture tells us to stop and think! When a man makes an idol,

> *Half of the wood he burns in the fire; over it he prepares his meal, he roasts his meat and eats his fill. He also warms himself and says, "Ah! I am warm; I see the fire." From the rest he makes a god, his idol; he bows down to it and worships. He prays to it and says, "Save me; you are my god."*
>
> *No one stops to think, no one has the knowledge or understanding to say, "Half of it I used for fuel; I even baked bread over its coals, I roasted meat and I ate. Shall I make a detestable thing [an idol] from what is left? Shall I bow down to a block of wood?"…"Is not this thing in my right hand a lie?"*
> Isaiah 44:16-17, 19-20 NIV

The Bible says an idol is a lie concocted by demons.

> *…idols are silver and gold, The work of men's hands.*
> *They have mouths, but they do not speak;*

*Eyes they have, but they do not see;*
*They have ears, but they do not hear;*
*Noses they have, but they do not smell;*
*They have hands, but they do not handle;*
*Feet they have, but they do not walk;*
*Nor do they mutter through their throat.*
*Those who make them are like them;*
*So is everyone who trusts in them.*　　　*Psalm 115:4-8 NKJV*

The LORD wants people to trust him, not demonic gods and goddesses hiding behind lifeless idols.

Well, we could go on and on, for the Bible has much to say on this subject. It is clear that to show respect and honour to an idol is wrong—it is demon worship—it is sin. It mars the image of God which man was designed to reflect.

---

Idols can be very diverse. They need not be images of deities or spirits. One can also worship birds, animals, stones, the earth, money, music, family, status, education, business, house, or car—an endless number of "things."

---

### RULE # 3

*"You shall not misuse the name of the LORD your God, for the LORD will not hold anyone guiltless who misuses his name."*
　　　　　　　　　　　　　　　　　　*Exodus 20:7 NIV*

Mankind was to respect the LORD in his holiness. We saw earlier that the word *holy* means *unique, one-of-a-kind, separate.* It's the opposite of the word *profane* which means *common.* God didn't want people to use his name as profanity—he didn't want to be treated as a common swear word. To do so is disrespectful. It is sin.

Rule #3 was clear. To reflect YAHWEH's righteous image, one must esteem the *Most High.*

---

If you have ever said, *"I will do such and such, God willing!"* without intending to keep your word, then you have shown disrespect for God's name and broken this law. If you have ever said, *"By God, I did not do such and such!"* when you knew you were guilty, then you have misused His name.

---

### RULE # 4

*"Remember the Sabbath day, to keep it holy. Six days you shall labor, and do all your work, but the seventh day is a Sabbath to the Lord your God. On it you shall not do any work…"*

*Exodus 20:8-10 ESV*

God was telling the Israelites that they were to keep the seventh day, Saturday, as a rest day. This special day would remind everyone in the *Global Classroom* that God had chosen them as his unique, one-of-a-kind messengers. The Bible says,

*"Say to the Israelites, 'You must observe my Sabbaths. This will be a sign between me and you for the generations to come, so you may know that I am the Lord, who makes you holy.'"*

*Exodus 31:13 NIV*

God wanted the Israelites to honour the Sabbaths as a special mark of distinction.

### RULE # 5

*"Honor your father and your mother…"*     *Exodus 20:12 ESV*

Not only was the Lord to be respected, but children were to esteem their parents. For a family to function in the right way, it was to be free of talking back, ignoring, arguing, pouting, the silent treatment, criticism—all actions and attitudes marked by disrespect. The family was to be a place of peace, not hostility. Children were to trust their parents, and parents were to be trustworthy. God wanted a family environment where children thrived, where things were safe and secure.

### RULE # 6

*"You shall not murder."*     *Exodus 20:13 ESV*

God had created man in his image, and so it was wrong for one man to take the life of another. It wasn't as some believe, that if you kill a person, he would simply be reborn somewhere else. Each individual had only one life and each life was to be treated with great care. It was wrong to murder another human.

But the Lord had more than the act of murder in mind—he was targeting the intent behind the act. The Bible tells us that…

*God…judges the thoughts and attitudes of the heart.*

*…Nothing in all creation is hidden from God's sight. Everything is uncovered and laid bare before the eyes of him to whom we must give account.*     *Hebrews 4:12-13 NIV*

Because Y*AHWEH* looks on the heart, he interprets murder on a much broader plane than we do.

> *"You have heard that it was said … `Do not murder, and anyone who murders will be subject to judgment.'*
>
> *But I tell you that anyone who is angry with his brother will be subject to judgment … anyone who says, `You fool!' will be in danger of the fire of hell."* Matthew 5:21–22 NIV

From God's viewpoint, if someone lost his temper or was angry without just cause, he had assumed the role of a murderer. His temper and anger would have "killed" any relationship that existed with the victim. Trust would be gone, and in its place—fear, shame, and guilt.

## RULE #7

*"You shall not commit adultery."* Exodus 20:14 ESV

God was saying that the only acceptable time to have sex is after a person is married, and the only rightful person to share that intimacy with is your marriage partner. To cheat on your partner is to break faith with a close friend who has trusted you. Broken faith leads to broken families, ruining the trusting environment in which children thrive. This is why adultery is wrong.

But then the L*ORD* goes one step further. Because he looks at the heart, he knows when someone has sinful thoughts.

> *"… anyone who even looks at a woman with lust has already committed adultery with her in his heart."* Matthew 5:28 NLT

To desire to have sex with someone to whom you are not married, is disrespectful to that person—a person whom God created in his image. To lust in the heart means you have broken this law—you have sinned. In order to live as one reflecting God's image, one must have a pure mind as well as pure actions.

## RULE #8

*"You shall not steal."* Exodus 20:15 NET

God did not want a society occupied with thieves—fear of robbery breeds distrust. The L*ORD* is the one who gives each person the right to own property and he wants that right respected. Of course, theft includes cheating—whether on an exam or on taxes. To steal, even something that is very small, is to sin. God isn't a thief, so he doesn't want people living as thieves.

### Rule #9

*"You shall not give false testimony against your neighbor."*

Exodus 20:16 NET

Man should always be honest for God will have no part in deceitfulness. Earlier we saw that Satan and his demons are liars—by their very nature, dishonest. But God is the direct opposite. Truthfulness is his very essence. When the LORD tells us something, we can count on it to be true, because …

*… it is impossible for God to lie …*        Hebrews 6:18 ESV

Only when people tell the truth can you trust them. Anything less than absolute honesty creates suspicion and misgivings. False accusations, slander, libel, gossip—all of these are sinful according to God's law. Since the LORD is not a liar, he did not want those he had created in his image telling lies either.

### Rule #10

*"You shall not covet your neighbor's house; you shall not covet your neighbor's wife or … anything that belongs to your neighbor."*

Exodus 20:17 NASB

Man must not envy another's possessions, abilities, looks, or whatever they may have. Envy leads to other sin—it breaks down trust.

Satan had said, *"I will be like the Most High,"* coveting God's position. To covet, to be greedy or jealous, is to sin and it is unacceptable to the LORD. It's the path that Satan followed. Envy is not a trait of God and neither should it be part of our lives.

### Now I Know

So the giving of the Ten Commands was concluded. Just as God placed physical laws in the universe to create a safe and secure world, these ten relational laws were given to create a safe and secure environment for every friendship. Each rule was given in the light of who God is and what he is like. Man now knew what was needed to reflect God's image—his sinless character.

Unfortunately, man had a tendency to change the law to accommodate sin, so God wrote the Ten Commandments on stone. Over the process of time, man might convince himself that a little cheating was okay, but the Law would still say it was wrong.

Now man knew what the LORD YAHWEH considered to be right or wrong, good or bad, righteous or sinful.

# 4 WOE TO ME!

A study of the world's religions reveals that each has its own list of what is right and what is wrong. Some of the lists are relatively short; others occupy volumes and are extremely detailed.

Lists are funny things—especially a list of *do's* and *don'ts*. We find ourselves going down each item, mentally checking off how we are doing at keeping each rule. But the purpose for the Ten Commands is different than any other moral code. Using the full body of Scripture, we can see how the LORD directed his prophets to address questions like these:

> *Just how strictly were the Ten Commands to be obeyed?*
>
> *Were there any exceptions?*
>
> *Suppose a person had worshipped an idol or a spirit, would God hold that against him forever?*
>
> *As a perfect lawgiver, what did the LORD expect?*

## WHAT IT TAKES

When Adam and Eve sinned, they marred the *sinless image* in which they had been created. Since the Ten Commandments reveal God's *perfect character*, simply obeying them should make man acceptable to God once again. That seems easy enough! But to have God's *sinless image*:

1. A person must observe all ten of the commandments—every one of them!

   *I testify again to every man … that he is obligated to obey the whole law.* Galatians 5:3 NET

   You can't pick four and ignore the rest. The LORD is specific. To have God's *sinless image* you have to obey all of them.

2. A person must also observe all ten of the commands consistently, for he …

   *… who obeys the whole law but fails in one point has become guilty of all of it.*
   James 2:10 NET

   If you disobey one command—just ONCE—you are *less* than "perfect" in God's eyes. The image has been marred. Man's righteousness must *equal* God's righteousness or the relationship cannot be restored.

3. Not only must one keep the whole Law, but a person is accountable for sin, even if he is not aware of it. Moses wrote,

   *If a person sins and does what is forbidden in any of the LORD's commands, even though he does not know it, he is guilty and will be held responsible.* Leviticus 5:17 NIV

Breaking the Law is like cutting a string with ten knots. You only have to cut one knot for the whole string to be broken. In the same way, you only have to break one law to no longer be perfect.

On one occasion I was teaching a couple and upon reaching this point in the lesson, the man banged his fist on the table and swore. (His girlfriend pointed out to him that he had just broken one of God's laws by misusing the LORD's name!) He said, "*God is not fair! If this is the only way I can be accepted by God, he's made it impossible. There is no way I can keep that list of rules perfectly!*" The young man was right. To have God's image mankind had to be perfect, just as God is perfect.

So, what is the solution for our predicament? How can we be accepted by God? How can we gain a perfection that is equal to God's perfection so we can live in his holy presence?

## SELF-RIGHTEOUSNESS

To begin with, we need to understand that the giving of the Ten Commandments dealt a blow to a problem that has gripped mankind since the beginning of creation. It's called *self-righteousness*. Self-righteousness is a result of doing a mental check of *do's* and *don'ts*, and concluding that one is getting along just fine. In a sense, we re-create God in our image with all our sin. A "god" that is "like us" allows us to feel good about the way we are living.

As self-righteous people, we may not strut and swagger, but nonetheless we feel we are "pretty good." Even those who have "gone wrong" will often think they *would* be "good" if given a chance. This notion is so strong in human thinking, it's almost universally assumed that if you live a good life now then things will be better after death.

Moses would have known this was true of the ancient Egyptians. They believed that after a person died, the soul was led into a courtroom where he faced 42 judges. The departed soul would review his past life, confidently calling out to each god and stating the sins he had not committed. One Egyptologist called it *"Proclaiming One Righteous in the Kingdom of the Dead."*[1] In the course of his defense, the deceased would declare, *"I am pure, pure, pure, pure!"*[2] To the ancient Egyptian way of thinking, this was the correct thing to do.

In contrast to this mindset, one of the 40 biblical prophets who had the rare opportunity to view God's throne room, wrote,

> ... I saw the Lord sitting on a throne, lofty and exalted, with the train of His robe filling the temple. Seraphim stood above Him, each having six wings: with two he covered his face, and with two he covered his feet, and with two he flew. And one called out to another and said, "Holy, Holy, Holy, is the LORD of hosts, The whole earth is full of His glory."  Isaiah 6:1-3 NASB

It was the LORD YAHWEH who was declared *holy, holy, holy,* not a man. Indeed when the prophet saw the LORD, he said,

> "Woe is me! For I am lost; for I am a man of unclean lips, and I dwell in the midst of a people of unclean lips; for my eyes have seen the King, the LORD of hosts!"  Isaiah 6:5 ESV

Instead of confidently declaring himself righteous, the prophet declared himself a sinner. Though he faithfully obeyed the Ten Commandments, upon seeing Y*AHWEH* in all his holiness, he knew that...

> ...no one will be **declared righteous** in his sight by observing the law...
> Romans 3:20 NIV

Mankind had marred the image in which he was created, and unless he could recover perfect righteousness, he would never be able to live in God's presence. In God's eyes...

> ...a man is not **declared righteous** by works of law...
> Galatians 2:16 YLT

## THE GULF

As the *Global Classroom* watched the events at Mount Sinai, every nation learned that the L*ORD*'s throne room was different than what the Egyptians believed. Instead of man standing arrogantly in a judgment hall with many gods, declaring that he was *"pure, pure, pure, pure,"* man was pictured on his knees before a single throne and one God with very different words on his lips:

> *"O Sovereign L*ORD*; I will proclaim **your** righteousness, **yours** alone."*
> Psalm 71:16 NIV

Yes, Y*AHWEH*'s righteousness was far beyond man's reach—unattainable. The chasm caused by sin was wider than man expected. Because no one could obey the Ten Rules perfectly, the Law could not bridge the gap. Man was stuck.

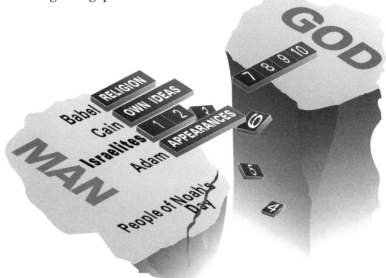

# 5 MISSING THE MARK

So then, why did God give us the Ten Commandments if he knew that none of us could keep them perfectly?

To answer that question I am going to use an illustration from medieval history.[3] Whenever an archer practiced his skill, he would place a scorekeeper to one side of his target. When the arrow was shot, if it *missed the mark*, the scorekeeper would call out *"sin!"*

Even if he scored very close to the bull's-eye, it made no difference. A miss was still a miss—it was *"sin!"* In the Bible one of the words translated "sin" means *to miss the mark*.

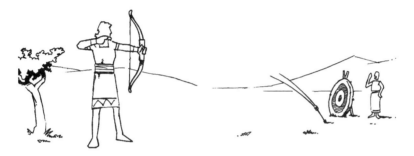

In that sense, the perfect character of God is the bull's-eye, and is referred to as *God's glory*.

Since only a perfect life could hit the bull's-eye of God's perfection, man finds himself *falling short* or *missing the mark*. We "sin!" The Bible uses that particular Greek word when it says,

> …for all have **sinned** [missed the mark] and fall short of the glory of God.　　　　　　　　　　　　　　　Romans 3:23 NASB

We may try hard to live a good life, but all of our goodness falls short of attaining the uncorrupted image that Adam and Eve possessed in the Garden. We can't even come close to living a perfect life.

## PURPOSE OF THE LAW

Since we are often blinded by self-righteousness, God gave us the law to make us aware of our sin.

Many years ago, my wife and I were on vacation with my parents. As I drove our car around a bend in the road, a policeman flagged me down and informed me that I was speeding. Now, to be honest, I did not feel I had been driving too fast. (I guess you would call that self-righteousness!) The policeman's response to my protest was to show me what his radar gun had recorded, and then he pointed down the road to a traffic sign that I had passed. It gave the posted limit! I was stuck with nothing to say. I had gone from being vacation-minded to a guilty law-breaker in less than a minute!

The Scripture tells us that the Ten Commandments are like a policeman pointing to the traffic sign. Just as the officer made me aware that I had broken the law, so the Scripture tells us that...

> ... through the law we become conscious of sin.    Romans 3:20 NIV

The Ten Commandments show us that we are lawbreakers.

> Everyone who sins breaks the law; in fact, sin is lawlessness.
> 1 John 3:4 NIV

## A Mirror

In many ways, the Ten Commandments are to us as a mirror is to a dirty face. If you are alone, you can't tell whether or not your face is clean. Someone could point at you and say, *"Your face is filthy,"* but you could deny it outright and say, *"My face isn't dirty—I don't see anything!"* and you might truly believe it. (Self-righteousness again!) But if given a mirror, you could see that your face was indeed grimy and you would no longer be able to deny the fact.

It's the same way with sin. We didn't really know what sin was until the LORD gave us the Law. Just as the mirror exposed the dirt, so the ten rules made us aware of our sin, and we see that our hearts are clothed in filthy rags. One of the 40 prophets wrote,

> ... it was the law that showed me my sin. I would never have known that coveting is wrong if the law had not said, "Do not covet."
> Romans 7:7 NLT

The Law is like a thermometer—it shows us that we are sick with sin, but it does not contribute to making us well.

## God's Viewpoint

Remember how we compared our view of a maggot-infested rat to God's viewpoint on sin? Well, trying to please the LORD by keeping the Ten Commandments—or for that matter any other list of *do's* and *don'ts*—is comparable to spraying perfume on a rotten rat—it doesn't make it any more appealing. The rat is still rotten. In the same way, obeying a list of rules doesn't make us any more acceptable to God. We are still sinners.

The reason God gave the Ten Laws was…

> … so that through the commandment sin would become utterly sinful.
> Romans 7:13 NASB

God wanted us to see all sin, big or small, the way he sees it—utterly sinful, totally destructive, grossly offensive, thoroughly repulsive, appalling, malignant, filthy. He wanted us to comprehend that his purity far exceeds any righteousness we might achieve on our own. He wanted us to understand that even at the best of times, our goodness is not equal to his holiness. It doesn't even come close.

Until this time a man could have boasted that God loved him more than another, because he thought himself to be a better person. But with the giving of the Ten Commandments, God was bringing everyone to the point of realizing that…

> … I was born a sinner—yes, from the moment my mother conceived me.
> Psalm 51:5 NLT

## IN TROUBLE

In the beginning Yahweh had been man's best friend. But when Adam and Eve disobeyed the Lord God, he laid aside his mantle of friendship and donned a magistrate's cloak. Now, instead of Yahweh being a friend, he was a judge, summoning man to the courtroom bench. The court fell silent.

No lawyer rose to defend man's cause. None could. No advocate, no matter how clever, could lead the court to believe that the condemned was anything but what he was. There would be no hung jury. No bribes. The perfect Judge had spoken. The verdict was in. Man was *guilty* of breaking God's Law.

GUILTY

> Now we know that whatever the law says, it says… [so] that every mouth may be stopped, and all the world may become guilty before God.
> Romans 3:19 NKJV

## Two Types Only

Most people will agree that they are not perfect. Some even say they are *sinners*. However, few will admit that they are *helpless sinners*. There is a big difference.

### A Sinner

A *sinner* will admit he is not perfect, but he believes there is something he can do to make himself good enough for the afterlife. He may think that going to a temple, praying to an idol, offering food and money, meditating, giving to charity, or being nice to neighbours will build more good merit than bad. He may think that observing the Ten Commandments, keeping the Golden Rule, going to church, saying the rosary, being baptized—will result in his **good outweighing his bad**.

The weigh scale notion is an ancient concept. The Egyptians believed that when a person died, the heart of the deceased was taken by the gods and placed on one side of a weigh scale. On the other side was placed the *Feather of Truth*.

If the deceased was found to be righteous, then he could enter the "fields of peace." If he was an unworthy person, his heart was eaten by a strange beast. It needs to be understood that this was not an actual weighing of the heart done by the Egyptians, but a ceremony they believed was performed by the gods in the afterlife.

Variations of this weigh scale idea abound. Perhaps the most common notion is that, *"When I die, if I have enough good karma, if I've done more good things than bad things, if my good outweighs my bad, then whatever happens after death, I'll be just fine."*

But there is a major flaw with the weigh scale concept—it doesn't stand up to analysis. No earthly court of law would forgive a thief because the crook said, *"Judge, you are right, I should not have stolen this one item, but just think of all the things I did not steal! My good far outweighs my bad!"*

When you think about it, the weigh scale idea is ridiculous. If such an idea offends our sense of fairness, then we can't expect a God of perfect justice to use it either. No, the Bible is quite emphatic. There is no weigh scale in YAHWEH's courtroom.

**GOOD**            **BAD**

**CONCEPT NOT FOUND IN THE BIBLE**

**A HELPLESS SINNER**

In contrast to a *sinner*, a *helpless sinner* knows there is nothing he can do to make himself acceptable to the LORD YAHWEH—he cannot get rid of his filthy rags. The dead rat of sin has contaminated his heart.

No matter how hard we try, no matter how much good karma we build, no matter the strength of our good deeds, we cannot meet God's level of righteousness. In fact, even our good acts are far from perfect in his sight.

> For all of us have become like one who is unclean, And all our righteous deeds are like a filthy garment ... And our iniquities, like the wind, take us away. *Isaiah 64:6 NASB*

Even our righteous deeds are like filthy rags stained by the rotten rat of sin. Our lives have "dirtied" the image of God in which we were created. We have a cancerous sin-nature that repels the pure, perfect LORD. We are stuck—unable to escape the stain of sin and all its consequences!

Once again this is *not* good news. But keep reading. Good news is coming.

# 6 The Golden Calf

With the giving of the Ten Rules, the Israelites knew exactly what the Creator-Owner regarded as right and wrong. And for those who had never heard of the Ten Commandments, God wrote their general outline on the tablet of man's heart.

The Scripture says Moses remained on Mount Sinai for 40 days.

> *When the people saw that Moses delayed in coming down from the mountain, they gathered around Aaron and said to him, "Get up, make us gods that will go before us. As for this fellow Moses, the man who brought us up from the land of Egypt, we do not know what has become of him!"* Exodus 32:1 NET

The Israelites were asking Aaron to make gods—idols!

> *And Aaron said to them, "Break off the golden earrings which are in the ears of your wives, your sons, and your daughters, and bring them to me."*
>
> *So all the people broke off the golden earrings which were in their ears, and brought them to Aaron. And he received the gold from their hand, and he fashioned it with an engraving tool, and made a molded calf.* Exodus 32:2-4 NKJV

The Bible doesn't specifically identify the god Aaron crafted, but we do know the Egyptians worshipped several different calf-gods, at least one of which was connected with fortune-telling. Today, these sacred bulls have been found in Egypt, embalmed and entombed with the same attention given to royalty. Whichever god was in question, when Aaron presented the golden calf to the Israelites, the people exclaimed,

> *"This is your god, O Israel, that brought you out of the land of Egypt!"* Exodus 32:4 NKJV

The Israelites were giving Egyptian gods credit for delivering them from slavery in Egypt! That didn't make sense! For the LORD YAHWEH, it certainly was a slap in the face!

*When Aaron saw this, he built an altar before it. And Aaron made proclamation and said, "Tomorrow shall be a feast to the LORD."*

*Exodus 32:5 ESV*

Aaron was mixing the worship of demon-gods with the worship of the LORD God! This is called *syncretism*, the combining of two belief systems.

## SYNCRETISM

One time to illustrate this point, I asked a volunteer to break the seal on a fresh bottle of water, pour a glass and drink it. As he lifted the pure water to his lips, I stopped him. I took the glass and reaching under the table, pulled out a bottle of cleaning solvent. After putting a couple of drops in the water, I offered it back to my volunteer. He refused to drink it.

In the same way the contaminated water repulsed my volunteer, so mixing the worship of idols and YAHWEH repulsed the LORD God. The LORD had told Moses,

*"You must not make gods … alongside me …"* Exodus 20:23 NET

Another prophet recorded God's thoughts when he wrote about what is sacrificed to idols:

*"… these sacrifices are offered to demons, not to God. And I don't want you to participate with demons. You cannot drink from the cup of the Lord and from the cup of demons, too. You cannot eat at the Lord's Table and at the table of demons, too.*

*1 Corinthians 10:20-21 NLT*

Some people create their own belief system, drawing from other religions and mixing together a salad bowl of ideas. But the Bible is clear that this is not acceptable with the LORD—you cannot worship the golden calf and the Creator at the same time. Aaron had led his people deep into error.

In the meantime, back on the mountain,

*… the LORD spoke to Moses, "Go down at once, for your people, whom you brought up from the land of Egypt, have corrupted themselves. They have quickly turned aside from the way which I commanded them. They have made for themselves a molten calf, and have worshiped it and have sacrificed to it and said, 'This is your god, O Israel, who brought you up from the land of Egypt!'"*

*Then Moses turned and went down from the mountain with the two tablets of the testimony in his hand…* Exodus 32:7-8,15 NASB

These were the stones on which God had written the Ten Laws.

> *...as soon as Moses came near the camp...he saw the calf and the dancing; and Moses' anger burned, and he threw the tablets from his hands and shattered them at the foot of the mountain.*
>
> Exodus 32:19 NASB

Moses was angered at the sin, and smashed the two tablets on the ground as a graphic picture of the people having broken God's Law. Then Moses...

> *...took the calf which they had made, burned it in the fire, and ground it to powder; and he scattered it on the water and made the children of Israel drink it. And Moses said to Aaron, "What did this people do to you that you have brought so great a sin upon them?"*
>
> *Then Moses returned to the LORD and said, "Oh, these people have committed a great sin, and have made for themselves a god of gold!"* Exodus 32:20-21,31 NKJV

Moses recognized that although the LORD had taken Israel out of Egypt, the Israelites needed to have "Egyptian thinking" taken out of their minds. They needed to learn that Egypt did not have the answers to life, death, and life after death.

> *...the LORD sent a great plague upon the people because they had worshiped the calf Aaron had made.* Exodus 32:35 NLT

It was like the LORD was saying, *"If you place your trust in Egyptian gods, you will suffer the same fate as the Egyptians."* It was also a reminder that sin's effects are very costly, the ultimate consequence being death in all its three-part meaning.

### NEW TABLETS

> *And the LORD said to Moses, "Cut two tablets of stone like the first ones, and I will write on these tablets the words that were on the first tablets which you broke."* Exodus 34:1 NKJV

Once again the Israelites were given the Ten Laws. Though the Commandments were unable to restore the broken relationship with God, it did not mean they were without value. When man does what is "right," the result can only be beneficial.

> Do what is right and good in the LORD's sight, so all will go well with you ...
> Deuteronomy 6:18 NLT

In the same way that physical laws make the universe an orderly and secure place in which to live, so spiritual laws bring order and security to a nation. Many countries have rejected the biblical code of conduct in a quest to live in a morally-neutral society. But to take no stand is, in effect, to take a stand. The rejection of biblical absolutes has resulted in a callousness towards wrong, with each generation becoming more comfortable with sin. The Bible teaches that this will eventually lead to chaos.

God wanted people to obey the rules, not so they would be smug in their own goodness, but because the rules were a reflection of God's character. Just as the LORD does not lie, cheat or envy, so he didn't want those he had created in his image to lie, cheat or envy.

It is time to move on to the next story. It is a very significant one. YAHWEH was about to show those in the *Global Classroom* the *only* way to acceptance by him.

---

### REVIEW — TWO COVERINGS

In the Bible the heart of sinful man is pictured clothed in *filthy rags*. In contrast, the heart of a righteous man is covered in *spotless garments*. These are not literal clothes, but mere pictures to help us understand spiritual truth. In the Bible there are only two coverings. Never are these two "clothes" mixed together.

| Filthy rags | Spotless garments |
|---|---|
| Pictures mankind clothed in his own sin | Pictures mankind clothed in God's righteousness |
| No atonement-covering | Having atonement |
| All that man has | Provided by God |

# CHAPTER NINE

# 1 THE TENT

At Mount Sinai the LORD revealed the impossibility of following rules to restore the broken friendship with YAHWEH. Now the people were ready to learn God's way to acceptance.

> Then the LORD spoke to Moses, saying, "…let them make Me a sanctuary, that I may dwell among them." *Exodus 25:1,8 NKJV*

### A VISUAL AID

The Israelites were to build a sanctuary,* called the *Tabernacle* or the *tent of meeting*. God was not asking them to do this because he needed a house.

| |
|---|
| *Not to be confused with a church. They are unrelated. |

> The God who made the world and everything in it, who is Lord of heaven and earth, does not live in temples made by human hands… *Acts 17:24 NET*

Rather, the LORD was creating an elaborate visual aid to help explain what it would take to remove the sin-penalty.

> "You must build this Tabernacle and its furnishings exactly according to the pattern I will show you." *Exodus 25:9 NLT*

The Tabernacle could be disassembled and moved. The tent-like portion had solid walls with rug-like coverings for the roof. It was divided into two parts: one-third forming a room called the *Holy of Holies* or the *Most Holy Place*, and the other two-thirds forming the *Holy Place*. A heavy curtain, sometimes referred to as the *veil*, was used to…

> …separate the Holy Place from the Most Holy Place. *Exodus 26:33 NLT*

The Tabernacle was completed with an external courtyard which, in turn, was surrounded by a fence two metres (seven feet) in height. Access to the entire compound was gained through a single gate.

There were seven pieces of furniture inside the tent and outside in the courtyard.[1]

# The Courtyard

**❶ THE BRONZE ALTAR:**

Just inside the courtyard gate was the first piece of furniture. It was quite large, made of wood overlaid with bronze, having four horns on the corners, and long poles on each side so that it could be carried. This altar replaced the previous stone or earthen altars that had been in use since Abel. By this time in history, the altar had become firmly associated with death—as a place where atonement was made for sin.

**❷ THE BASIN:**

This large bronze bowl was situated halfway between the Bronze Altar and the *Holy Place*. Filled with water, it was used for ceremonial washing, and signified that man must be pure when he approached the LORD God.

**❸ THE LAMPSTAND:**

The dimensions of the lampstand were not defined by God, although we are told its weight.[2] It was crafted of pure gold, with a main shaft branching into seven arms.

**❹ THE ALTAR OF INCENSE:**

This altar was placed squarely before the curtain that divided the *Holy of Holies* from the *Holy Place*. Incense was offered on it as the Israelites gathered outside to pray. The scent wafting toward the sky was symbolic of prayers going up to God.

**The Holy Place**

The Curtain (Veil)

**The Holy of Holies**

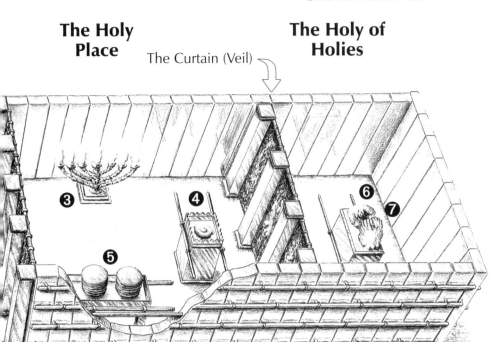

**❺ THE TABLE WITH THE BREAD:**

On this table were placed twelve loaves of bread, each representing a tribe of Israel.

**❻ THE ARK OF THE COVENANT:**

This small wooden box overlaid with pure gold was designed in part to function as a chest. Inside the Ark were the two tablets of stone upon which were written the Ten Commandments.

**❼ THE ATONEMENT COVER:**

The Ark of the Covenant had an intricate gold lid or cover complete with two angels having outstretched wings. The Ark with its Atonement Cover were the only pieces of furniture placed in the *Holy of Holies*.

## The Priests

God told Moses,

*"Now take Aaron your brother, and his sons with him, from among the children of Israel, that he may minister to Me as priest..."*

Exodus 28:1 NKJV

Moses was to appoint Aaron and his sons as priests in the Tabernacle with Aaron as the High Priest. God set these men apart from the others, not because they were special in themselves, but because the LORD wanted the people to respect His holiness. God didn't want an unorganized rabble taking care of the Tabernacle. The priests were trained to carry out God's instructions and functioned as custodians, taking care of the Tabernacle as the nomadic Israelites moved from one place to another.

## The Tabernacle Completed

The entire structure was finished nine months after the Israelites arrived at Mount Sinai.

*Then Moses looked over all the work, and indeed they had done it; as the LORD had commanded...*  Exodus 39:43 NKJV

With the Tabernacle completed, the cloud that led the Israelites moved into position above the *Holy of Holies* right over the *Ark of the Covenant*. **It signified** YAHWEH's **presence dwelling in the midst of his people.**

*Then the cloud covered the tent of meeting... Moses was not able to enter the tent of meeting because the cloud settled on it, and the glory of the LORD filled the tabernacle.*
Exodus 40:34-35 NET

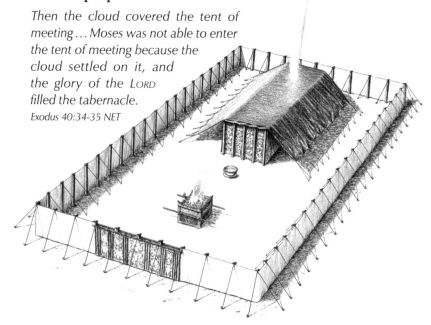

## THE SACRIFICE

With the Tabernacle and its furniture in place, it was time to implement this large visual aid. God said to Moses,

> *"Speak to the Israelites and say to them: 'When any of you brings an offering to the LORD, bring as your offering an animal from either the herd or the flock ... '"*      Leviticus 1:2 NIV

God was telling man to bring a sacrifice to the Tabernacle and offer it on the Bronze Altar.

The sacrifice had to be *"... of the herd ... "*      Leviticus 1:3 KJV

It could be a sheep, goat, or bullock, but it could not be any other animal such as a pig, horse, or camel.

They were to *"... offer a male ... "*      Leviticus 1:3 KJV

It was to be *"... without defect ... "*      Leviticus 1:3 NASB

There could be no disease or lameness. The individual bringing it was to ...

> *"... put his hand on the head of the ... offering, and it [would] be accepted on his behalf to make atonement for him ... "*
>      Leviticus 1:4 NKJV

In placing his hand on the head of the offering, the man identified himself with the sacrifice. The hand on the head symbolized the individual's sin and guilt being transferred from the man to the animal. Because the animal now carried the man's sin, it had to die.

Death is the penalty for sin. The one offering the sacrifice slit its throat, a final acknowledgment that it was his sin that caused the death of the animal. It was a case of the innocent dying in place of the guilty—as a substitute. The Bible says that God accepted the sacrifice on his behalf.

This must have sounded very familiar to the Israelites. Had not their forefathers come to the LORD offering substitutionary sacrifices on an altar? Indeed they had. Once again, the LORD was reminding everyone in the *Global Classroom* that only he could provide the way to acceptance. He is a …

> … *righteous God and a Savior* …
>
> Isaiah 45:21 NASB

## THE DAY OF ATONEMENT

In fulfilling their duties, the priests had complete freedom within the Tabernacle compound, with one exception. They were forbidden to enter the *Holy of Holies*.

The *Holy of Holies* was where God's presence symbolically lived with man. As long as the cloud covered the Tabernacle, sinful man was not to enter the room. Even Aaron, as High Priest, was not to enter the *Holy of Holies* except on the *Day of Atonement*.[3]

> *But only the high priest entered the inner room, and that only once a year, and never without blood, which he offered for himself and for the sins the people had committed in ignorance.*
>
> Hebrews 9:7 NIV

To ignore these instructions was to disrespect YAHWEH's majesty. It would be treating the LORD as someone common rather than unique or holy. Such contempt was fatal.

> *The LORD said to Moses: "Tell your brother Aaron not to come whenever he chooses into the Most Holy Place behind the curtain in front of the atonement cover on the ark, or else he will die, because I appear in the cloud over the atonement cover."*
>
> Leviticus 16:2 NIV

## SUMMARY

The Tabernacle, the furniture, the priests, the sacrifices—all were part of God's elaborate visual aid. At this point they may not make a whole lot of sense, but as we progress you will see that they are key pieces to the biblical puzzle. For now, we will move on in the story.

# 2 BLESSING OR CURSING

Moses lived long enough to lead the people right up to the border of the Promised Land. Before his death, he gathered the Hebrews together one last time to remind them to...

> Ask now about the former days, long before your time, from the day God created man on the earth; ask from one end of the heavens to the other. Has anything so great as this ever happened, or has anything like it ever been heard of? Has any other people heard the voice of God speaking out of fire, as you have, and lived?
>
> Has any god ever tried to take for himself one nation out of another nation, by testings, by miraculous signs and wonders, by war, by a mighty hand and an outstretched arm, or by great and awesome deeds, like all the things the LORD your God did for you in Egypt before your very eyes?
>
> You were shown these things so that you might know that **the LORD [YAHWEH] is God; besides him there is no other.**
>
> Deuteronomy 4:32-35 NIV

The Israelites had experienced an unprecedented number of miracles. As we saw before, when the LORD uses miracles, everyone in the *Global Classroom* had best listen. Moses continued,

> "Now it shall be, if you diligently obey the LORD your God, being careful to do all His commandments which I command you today... All these blessings will come upon you and overtake you if you obey the LORD your God." Deuteronomy 28:1-2 NASB

If the people were obedient, the LORD would make their lives and their land safe and secure, full of joy and rejoicing. But YAHWEH didn't ignore the fact that Israel could freely choose to reject his blessing and indulge in the temporary pleasures of sin.

Sin is destructive—it always hurts somebody. To prevent people from being hurt, God established painful consequences for wrong-doers. Often those consequences would drive a person back to obedience and faith in God—but not always. As Moses continued his speech, he reminded Israel of the pain they would face if they, as the *selected nation*, collectively chose to reject God.

> "But it shall come to pass, if you do not obey the voice of the LORD your God, to observe carefully all His commandments and His statutes [laws] which I command you today, that all these curses will come upon you and overtake you..." Deuteronomy 28:15 NKJV

Disobedience would bring sickness, drought, famine, and death … and if they persisted in rebellion, Moses told them,

*"The Lord will cause you to be defeated before your enemies."*
Deuteronomy 28:25 NKJV

If they still did not learn,

*"Then the Lord will scatter you among all peoples, from one end of the earth to the other … there the Lord will give you a trembling heart, failing eyes, and anguish of soul."*
Deuteronomy 28:64-65 NKJV

The Israelites were now faced with a choice:

1.  They could trust the Lord as one who tells the truth—as one who has faithfully kept his promises, or …
2.  They could trust their own wisdom, and ignore the Lord as if he was exaggerating the consequences.

We will soon see who they would trust.

### MOSES

Well, it is time to say goodbye to Moses. Without doubt, his life left a mark on the *Global Classroom*. The words he recorded laid the foundations for understanding all Scripture. Probably the greatest thing that could be said about him is that …

*… the Lord spoke to Moses face to face, as a man speaks to his friend.*
Exodus 33:11 NKJV

### JOSHUA

After Moses died, he was replaced by an able general named *Joshua*. Joshua led the people into the land that God had promised them. The land was divided according to tribes, each tribe representing, for the most part, one of Jacob's (or Israel's) twelve sons.

After Joshua died, there was a period of time when the Israelites trusted God, and the Lord blessed them abundantly even as he said he would. But then they began to drift and ended up worshipping idols and trusting other gods.

*… the children of Israel did evil in the sight of the Lord. They forgot the Lord their God, and served the Baals and Asherahs.*
Judges 3:7 NKJV

*Baals* and *Asherahs* were Canaanite deities. In the past Yahweh had repeatedly overlooked the Israelites' sin.[4] He had shown them grace—undeserved love. But the Israelites were no longer beginners in their relationship with their Creator-Owner. They had learned many things about the LORD. They now knew the Ten Commandments, and that knowledge made them accountable.

> From everyone who has been given much, much will be required, and from the one who has been entrusted with much, even more will be asked. *Luke 12:48 NET*

So God could not condone the people's sin and say, *"Oh forget it. We'll pretend it never happened."* No, sin has its consequences. It always does. Just as defying God's physical law of gravity results in fractured bones, so violating God's spiritual law has ramifications.

> Therefore the anger of the LORD was hot against Israel, and He sold them into the hand of Cushan-Rishathaim king of Mesopotamia; and the children of Israel served Cushan-Rishathaim eight years.
> *Judges 3:8 NKJV*

This king's name means "twice-wicked Cushan."

Cush and Canaan had a common ancestry. Ironic, isn't it? The Israelites were worshipping Canaanite deities, but were enslaved by a king who had a Canaanite connection. In other words, worshipping demon-gods led to slavery by those controlled by demons.

### REPENT

God allowed this slavery to occur as a means of bringing about a change of attitude—*a change of mind*. In the Bible this change is described by the word *repent*.

The word *repent* is often misunderstood. Some people feel if you aren't *weeping and feeling sorry* then you haven't repented. But tying the word to such feelings confuses the issue. A correct understanding of repentance simply defines the word as a *change of mind*. You turn from one thing to something else. The Israelites *changed their minds* when they ...

> ... turned to God from idols to serve the living and true God ...
> *1 Thessalonians 1:9 NKJV*

They went from unbelief to belief. They trusted God again. That *change of mind* may have been accompanied by weeping, but even if not, it was the right choice to make—choosing to repent.

> When the children of Israel cried out to the LORD, the LORD raised up a deliverer for the children of Israel, who delivered them: Othniel the son of Kenaz ... The Spirit of the LORD came upon him, and he judged Israel. *Judges 3:9-10 NKJV*

## Judges

God raised up a man named Othniel to lead the people to victory. He was called a *Judge.*

> He went out to war, and the Lord delivered Cushan-Rishathaim king of Mesopotamia into his hand … So the land had rest for forty years.          Judges 3:10-11 NKJV

So began a cycle that was to last approximately 300 years. The Israelites would worship other gods, God would bring in a foreign nation to conquer them, they would repent and call on Yahweh to deliver them from their oppressors. God would raise up a *Judge* to lead them and they would throw out the alien conquerors. This cycle occurred over and over again. In all, there were fifteen Judges.

## 3 The God Dagon

The fact that Israel followed other gods did not mean they forsook the Lord entirely. They still wanted Yahweh to bless them—to protect them from their enemies, to bring bounty to their farms. But they also wanted to partake in loose living—free sex and self-indulgence—something that was promoted by the demonic gods. But there was a snag with that sort of living—Yahweh made them feel guilty. It was almost easier to not have him around at all. The Bible says that when people want to sin, they …

> … suppress the truth in unrighteousness          Romans 1:18 NASB

Of course, it's easier to sin if those around you are also sinning.

> … they not only continue to do these very things [sin] but also approve of those who practice them.          Romans 1:32 NIV

So the Israelites mixed a veneration of demon-gods with the worship of Yahweh, worshipping whichever deity met the carnal desires of the heart. It was a mess. One prophet told the Lord how he …

> … warned them to return to your law, but they became arrogant and disobeyed your commands. They sinned … Stubbornly they turned their backs on you, became stiff-necked and refused to listen.
> Nehemiah 9:29 NIV

As a result, the Lord allowed the Hebrews to be overrun by foreign nations to show them it was a vain thing to trust in demon-gods.

One country that repeatedly enslaved Israel was from the region known today as Gaza. It was the nation of Philistia.

## THE PHILISTINES

> The Philistines deployed their forces to meet Israel, and as the battle spread, Israel was defeated by the Philistines…
>
> When the soldiers returned to camp, the elders of Israel asked, "Why did the LORD bring defeat upon us today before the Philistines?"
>
> I Samuel 4:2-3 NIV

If the Israelites had only read God's Word they would have known the answer to their own question. They were worshipping gods and idols! But instead of repenting, they said,

> "…Let us bring the ark of the LORD's covenant…so that it may go with us and save us from the hand of our enemies."
>
> I Samuel 4:3 NIV

The *Ark of the Covenant* was that special gold box kept in the *Holy of Holies*. It was being suggested that the Israelite army take the Ark out of its holy location and carry it into battle. There was a procedure for moving this sacred box, but it was not to be carried around like a charm to ward off evil. Nonetheless…

> …they brought back the ark of the covenant of the LORD Almighty, who is enthroned between the cherubim.
>
> When the ark of the LORD's covenant came into the [Hebrew military] camp, all Israel raised such a great shout that the ground shook. Hearing the uproar, the Philistines asked, "What's all this shouting in the Hebrew camp?"
>
> When they learned that the ark of the LORD had come into the camp, the Philistines were afraid. "A god has come into the camp," they said. "We're in trouble! Nothing like this has happened before. Woe to us! Who will deliver us from the hand of these mighty gods? They are the gods who struck the Egyptians with all kinds of plagues in the desert."
>
> I Samuel 4:4-8 NIV

The Philistines were quite mixed up as to who the LORD was and what the *Ark of the Covenant* was all about, but they did recognize that it was somehow connected to the God who had brought the Israelites out of Egypt. They said,

> Be strong and conduct yourselves like men, you Philistines, that you do not become servants of the Hebrews, as they have been to you. Conduct yourselves like men, and fight!"

*So the Philistines fought, and Israel was defeated… Also the ark of God was captured…*                                    *I Samuel 4:9-11 NKJV*

From the Israelites' perspective, the situation could not have been worse. They had been defeated in battle and their precious Ark had been captured! But this had not taken God by surprise. He had allowed the Ark's capture so he could teach everyone in the *Global Classroom* another lesson.

> *After the Philistines had captured the ark of God… they carried the ark into Dagon's temple and set it beside Dagon.*
> *I Samuel 5:1-2 NIV*

### DAGON

We met *Dagon* before at the Tower of Babel. *Dagon's* true identity was demonic—he was a false front for evil spirits, a clever deception. He was often depicted as being half human and half fish.[5] The blurring of two bodies into one is very common with demon-gods. It is an effort by Satan to smudge the distinction between the Creator and his creation. Satan wants people to be confused about the nature of the true God. To create such confusion is wrong—it is sin.

The Bible says the Philistines took the captured *Ark of the Covenant* to Ashdod, a city in Philistia, and placed it before an idol of Dagon.

> *And when the people of Ashdod arose early in the morning, there was Dagon, fallen on its face to the earth before the ark of the LORD.*                    *I Samuel 5:3 NKJV*

What a shock to the Philistines. *Dagon* was flat on his face before the Ark!

We need to understand that the Ark was not an idol—it was only a physical object or location where the LORD symbolically made his presence known. The Ark was definitely not God, nor an idol of God. Yet here was *Dagon*, who claimed to be a real god, flat on his face before a mere symbol. You can imagine the confusion and turmoil it caused. *It had to have been a coincidence!* No doubt efforts were made to make sure it would not happen again.

> *They took Dagon and put him back in his place. But the following morning when they rose, there was Dagon, fallen on his face*

*on the ground before the ark of the LORD! His head and hands had been broken off and were lying on the threshold; only his body remained.* I Samuel 5:3-4 NIV

It wasn't an accident! *Dagon* had fallen again, only this time his head and hands had broken off!

This should have caused people to think: Does a real god have to be picked up off the ground—twice—and then sent out to a local shop for repairs? Does a real god fall apart? Should a real god have to be glued back together? Of course not! *Dagon* belonged on a rubbish heap, not in a temple. Even though Israel had been defeated in battle, the LORD was using his *Chosen Nation* to teach those in the *Global Classroom* that...

*I am the First and I am the Last; besides Me there is no God.*
Isaiah 44:6 NKJV

But the Philistines did not recognize the real God for who he was. Instead they began to worship the threshold on which the false god, *Dagon*, had smashed his face! Surely, this is an example of human foolishness.

*Therefore neither the priests of Dagon nor any who come into Dagon's house tread on the threshold of Dagon in Ashdod to this day.* I Samuel 5:5 NKJV

If we were to continue the story, we would see that the Philistines returned the Ark to Israel. In time, the Israelites turned back to the LORD and he began to bless them again. But...

*...when they were at rest again, they went back to doing evil before you. Then you abandoned them to their enemies, and they gained dominion over them. When they again cried out to you, in your compassion you heard from heaven and rescued them time and again.* Nehemiah 9:28 NET

The Israelites had left Egypt, but they struggled for centuries to leave behind their trust in many gods.

Idols can be things other than images, pictures, or icons. Whatever possesses our mind basically becomes the object of our worship—our idol. The following can be idolatry:

❖ Obsession with the opposite sex.

❖ Grasping after money and material possessions.

❖ Fixation with our bodies, our clothes, our diet, or anything that belongs to us. Mind-altering chemicals or beverages could also fit into this category.

❖ Obsession with status, education, power, and control.

❖ Self-serving causes in which we invest immense amounts of time.

> *...sexual immorality, impurity, passion, evil desire, and covetousness, which is idolatry.*     Colossians 3:5 ESV

When we refuse to put faith in the LORD and instead trust in our abilities, intellect, and strength, we in essence worship ourselves as if we were a god.

> *But they will be held guilty, they whose strength is their god.*     Habakkuk 1:11 NASB

# 4 THE PROPHETS

Of all the nations of the world, Israel was unique, for God himself was their Leader and King. But as time passed they rejected God and demanded a human king. YAHWEH granted their request, but their propensity to wander off and trust other gods remained.

> *...they mingled with the nations and adopted their customs. They worshiped their idols, which became a snare to them. They sacrificed their sons and their daughters to demons. They shed innocent blood, the blood of their sons and daughters, whom they sacrificed to the idols...*
>
> *Therefore the LORD... handed them over to the nations, and their foes ruled over them. ... Many times he delivered them, but they were bent on rebellion and they wasted away in their sin.*     Psalm 106:35-38,40-41,43 NIV

So the cycle of earlier years continued only instead of a Judge, they now had a King.

## DAVID AND SOLOMON

Undoubtedly, the greatest and best known of Israel's monarchs was King David. Unlike many of the other kings who ruled over the *Chosen Nation*, King David truly trusted God. David called YAHWEH "my Saviour."

David is noted for the songs or *Psalms* he wrote, praising God for His great love and mercy. He also wrote prophecy about the coming DELIVERER, and God made a pledge that this ANOINTED ONE would be one of David's descendants.[6]

| THE PROMISED DELIVERER would be... |
|---|
| 1. The offspring of a woman |
| 2. A male |
| 3. A descendant of Abraham |
| 4. A descendant of Isaac |
| 5. A descendant of Jacob (Israel) |
| 6. From the tribe (a descendant) of Judah |
| 7. A descendant of King David |

King David had great ambition to replace the portable Tabernacle with a permanent structure of similar design. It would be called the *Temple*. He wanted to build it in Jerusalem, which had become the capital of the country during his reign. But it was his son, Solomon, who actually saw the Temple built.

King Solomon is known for at least two things: his great wisdom and the Temple he built. This magnificent structure was constructed in Jerusalem on Mount Moriah, possibly on the same site where Abraham was prepared to offer Isaac. Once again, this building was not a place for YAHWEH to live. King Solomon said,

> "... the heaven of heavens cannot contain You. How much less this temple which I have built!"  1 Kings 8:27 NKJV

The Temple replaced the Tabernacle as God's visual aid.

After Solomon's death, the nation split in two: the northern ten tribes retained the name *Israel*, while the southern two tribes became the nation of *Judah*. This division seemed to be the Israelites' first step towards a semi-permanent distance from God. The northern tribes led the way. The people went through the motions of following the LORD, but their hearts were far from God.

*"The multitude of your sacrifices—what are they to me?" says the Lord. "I have more than enough of burnt offerings, of rams and the fat of fattened animals; I have no pleasure in the blood of bulls and lambs and goats. Stop bringing meaningless offerings!"*

Isaiah 1:11,13 NIV

Yahweh hates mindless ritual. He does not want robots for friends.

*"I consider your incense detestable! You observe new moon festivals, Sabbaths, and convocations, but I cannot tolerate sin-stained celebrations! I hate your new moon festivals and assemblies; they are a burden that I am tired of carrying… when you offer your many prayers, I do not listen, because your hands are covered with blood."*

Isaiah 1:13-15 NET

The Israelites had lost sight of Yahweh as a person. The Lord wanted people to enjoy him—to be his friends forever. He wasn't interested in mechanical obedience, in hollow friendships.

## False Prophets

To complicate matters further, false prophets—inspired by Satan—churned the spiritual scene. Even though Yahweh provided clear instructions to enable his people to discern the difference between truth and error, the false prophets were much more popular, for they were telling the people the very things they wished to hear.

*Thus says the Lord of hosts: "Do not listen to the words of the prophets who prophesy to you, filling you with vain hopes. They speak visions of their own minds, not from the mouth of the Lord."*

Jeremiah 23:16 ESV

But the Israelites didn't listen—and they continued to drift.

## True Prophets

As a wake-up call, God sent prophets who thundered against Israel, warning the nation that the Lord would judge them for their mindless ritualism. But the people continued to wander away from God, losing their moral compass in the process. They became callous, insensitive, and morally corrupt.

LOST

*This is what the Lord says: "… They sell the righteous for silver, and the needy for a pair of sandals. They trample on the heads of the poor as upon the dust of the ground and deny justice to the oppressed. Father and son use the same girl and so profane my holy name. They lie down beside every altar on garments taken in pledge. In the house of their god they drink wine taken as fines."*

Amos 2:6-8 NIV

## TRUSTWORTHY

Along with their warnings against sin, the true prophets also gave specific information about the coming PROMISED DELIVERER. In the following pages, wherever you see a scroll icon, it refers to a prophecy being fulfilled, a prophecy that was given hundreds of years before the fact.

> *"I am God, and there is no other; I am God, and there is none like me. I make known the end from the beginning, from ancient times, what is still to come."* Isaiah 46:9-10 NIV

Each fulfilled prophecy reminded the people that YAHWEH was reliable—he could be counted on—he was trustworthy. As we saw before, only YAHWEH had the capability to make and keep such promises.

But the Israelites were too busy to investigate and understand the immense ramifications of fulfilled prophecy. It is something that is all too common to this very day. Somehow, collectively, mankind misses the point. Our neglect is to our own peril.

---

### HOW THE PROPHETS WROTE

The Bible states that the LORD guided the 40 writers in such a way that what was recorded was precisely what he wanted written. At the same time, YAHWEH allowed the human writer to record *Scripture* in the prophet's own unique style, but to do so without error. These men were not free to add their own private thoughts to the Bible. Scripture was not something they dreamed up on their own.

> *...recognize this: No prophecy of scripture ever comes about by the prophet's own imagination, for no prophecy was ever borne of human impulse; rather, men carried along by the Holy Spirit spoke from God.* 2 Peter 1:20-21 NET

The phrase *carried along* is used elsewhere in the Bible in reference to the transporting of a paralyzed man.[7] Just as a disabled man could not walk by his own power, so the prophets did not write the Scripture at their own inclination. Nor did the LORD put his stamp of approval on some literary effort of man. The Bible is clear—it was the LORD's message from beginning to end.

## How do we know the Bible is right?

Using the five books written by Moses as an example, one can draw out of their content two sub-categories: **Must know Information** and **Prophetic Information**.

The **Must Know Information** answers questions about the origin of the universe and mankind, the origin of evil, sin and death, how to escape sorrow, the source of joy, and things pertaining to eternal life. It also gives practical guidance for everyday living. But the big question remains, *"How can we know the Bible is correct in what it has to say about these things?"*

The answer to that question resides in the unique architecture of Scripture. The **Must Know Information** written by Moses was considered reliable only if his **Prophetic Information** was 100% accurate. If he was correct in the **Prophetic Information** then it was highly probable that he was accurate in the **Must Know Information**. If his prophecy was not precisely fulfilled then the entire message was to be rejected. (Reread pages 143 to 145.)

Not only were Moses' prophecies fulfilled in his lifetime, but they continue to be fulfilled right down to this present day. Though I have used Moses as the example, this would apply to the other prophets as well.

### A Living Example

Moses wrote many prophecies, but some of the most fascinating have to do with the history and the future of the Israelites. The details he foretold were not vague or abstract.

There is a story that in the 17th century, King Louis XIV of France asked Blaise Pascal, the great mathematician and philosopher, to give him proof of the supernatural. Pascal answered: *"Why, the Jews, your Majesty, the Jews."* [8]

It is clear from Pascal's writings that he studied the ancient prophecies, and no doubt he combined that study with his knowledge of mathematics—he was the father of probability theory. He would have known that the odds of the Jews fulfilling the prophecies was infinitesimally small, to the point of being impossible—and yet their fulfillment is historical fact! (See sample of prophecies on opposite page.)

| Must Know Information | Prophetic Information | | |
|---|---|---|---|
| | Example | Prophecy written by Moses (1400 BC) | Fulfillment |
| **Origin of Universe** | | | |
| **Origin of Mankind** | Moses said that soon after his death the Israelites would rebel against YAHWEH. | "...after my death you are sure to become utterly corrupt and to turn from the way I have commanded you." *Deuteronomy 31:29 NIV* | 1400 BC to 70 AD: History reveals that Israel did rebel, a process that deepened as the years passed. |
| **Origin of Evil, Sin** | | | |
| **Origin of Death** | Moses said that eventually Jerusalem would be destroyed and the Israelites scattered to the four corners of the globe. | "You will be uprooted from the land... Then the LORD will scatter you among all nations, from one end of the earth to the other." *Deuteronomy 28:63-64 NIV* | In 70 AD, the Romans destroyed Jerusalem, fulfilling a detailed prophecy given by Moses.[9] The people were scattered to the nations. |
| **How to escape Sorrow** | | | |
| **The source of Joy** | Moses said that the Israelites would suffer constant persecution among the nations to which they were scattered. Today we call this anti-Semitism. | "Among those nations you will find no repose, no resting place for the sole of your foot. ...You will live in constant suspense, filled with dread both night and day, never sure of your life." *Deuteronomy 28:65-66 NIV* | 70 AD to 1948 AD: They became known as the "wandering Jew." Regarding persecution, no other race has suffered as much as the scattered Israelites.[10] |
| **Eternal Life** | | | |
| **Practical advice on Life** | Historically, nations in exile are assimilated—they cease to exist. Moses wrote that the Israelites would retain their identity. | "...when they are in the land of their enemies, I will not reject them or abhor them so as to destroy them completely..." *Leviticus 26:44 NIV* | The fact that, against all odds, the Jews have maintained their identity over 2000 years of dispersal, is still considered miraculous.[11] |
| | Moses wrote that near the end of this evil age, God would return the Israelites to their country. | "...then the LORD your God will ...gather you again from all the nations where he scattered you. ...and bring you back. He will bring you to the land that belonged to your fathers, and you will take possession of it." *Deuteronomy 30:3-5 NIV* | 1948 AD to Present: For the last 100 years, Jews have been flooding back to their ancient home. It would seem we are in some stage of seeing this ancient prophecy fulfilled.[12] |

# 5 The god Baal

Many of the LORD's prophets risked their lives in face-to-face confrontations with false prophets. Elijah was one such Hebrew. He warned the Israelites, telling them to *repent*—to have *a change of mind*—to turn from their unbelief back to faith in God. Ahab, a king of Israel, resisted Elijah and scoffed at his message.

> When Ahab saw Elijah, Ahab said to him, "Is this you, you troubler of Israel?"
>
> He said, "I have not troubled Israel, but you and your father's house have, because you have forsaken the commandments of the LORD and you have followed the Baals. *1 Kings 18:17-18 NASB*

*Baal* was a major god in the Middle East, considered to be a son of *Dagon*. The religion surrounding his worship was pornographic and sadistic. Elijah confronted this false god. He told King Ahab,

> "Now then send and gather to me all Israel at Mount Carmel, together with 450 prophets of Baal and 400 prophets of the Asherah, who eat at Jezebel's table." *1 Kings 18:19 NASB*

*Asherah*, a goddess with roots in Babel, was considered to be the consort of *Baal*. The idolatry and worship surrounding her were also sensual and debased.

## Bigger is Better

It's worth noting that Elijah was only one man surrounded by 850 false prophets. It's a common misconception today that if a lot of people believe something, then it must be right. But the Bible cautions us. It says,

> Enter through the narrow gate; for the gate is wide and the way is broad that leads to destruction, and there are many who enter through it. For the gate is small and the way is narrow that leads to life, and there are few who find it. Beware of the false prophets, who come to you in sheep's clothing, but inwardly are ravenous wolves. You will know them by their fruits. *Matthew 7:13-16 NASB*

False prophets can be known by their fruits—their teachings—whether or not they agree with God's word. In this case, YAHWEH provided clear instructions to the Israelites, enabling them to discern the difference between truth and error. However the prophets of *Baal* and *Asherah* were more popular because they told the people the very things they wished to hear.

## MOUNT CARMEL

Elijah challenged Ahab to a showdown on Mount Carmel. Since there is evidence that this mountain was a site for the worship of *Baal*, Elijah gave the false prophets home ground advantage.

> So Ahab sent for all the children of Israel, and gathered the prophets together on Mount Carmel. And Elijah came to all the people, and said, "How long will you falter between two opinions? If the LORD is God, follow Him; but if Baal, follow him."
>
> *1 Kings 18:20-21 NKJV*

Following both *Baal* and the LORD at the same time was not an option. It never has been and never will be. God does not allow room for mixing truth and error. He detests syncretism.

> Then Elijah said to the people, "...Let two bulls be given to us, and let them choose one bull for themselves and cut it in pieces and lay it on the wood, but put no fire to it. And I will prepare the other bull and lay it on the wood and put no fire to it. And you call upon the name of your god, and I will call upon the name of the LORD, and the God who answers by fire, he is God."
>
> *1 Kings 18:22-24 ESV*

Elijah told the prophets of *Baal* to "go first."

> So they... called on the name of Baal from morning even till noon, saying, "O Baal, hear us!" But there was no voice; no one answered. Then they leaped about the altar which they had made.
>
> And so it was, at noon, that Elijah mocked them and said, "Cry aloud, for he is a god; either he is meditating, or he is busy, or he is on a journey, or perhaps he is sleeping and must be awakened." So they cried aloud, and cut themselves, as was their custom, with knives and lances, until the blood gushed out on them.
>
> *1 Kings 18:26-28 NKJV*

The worship of demon-gods often involves the piercing or slashing of the body. It is a hallmark of their false religions.

> They raved all afternoon until the time of the evening sacrifice, but still there was no sound, no reply, no response.
>
> *1 Kings 18:29 NLT*

Elijah wanted the watching crowd, including those in the *Global Classroom*, to come to the point of saying,

> "Of what value is an idol, since a man has carved it? Or an image that teaches lies? For he who makes it trusts in his own creation; he makes idols that cannot speak." *Habakkuk 2:18 NIV*

### No Lord, No Fire

*Then Elijah said to all the people, "Come near to me."… Elijah took twelve stones according to the number of the tribes of the sons of Jacob… So with the stones he built an altar in the name of the Lord, and he made a trench around the altar, large enough to hold two measures of seed.*        1 Kings 18:30-32 NASB

The trench would have held about 15 litres [4 gallons].

*He piled wood on the altar, cut the bull into pieces, and laid the pieces on the wood.*        1 Kings 18:33 NLT

Elijah said,

*"Fill four water jars and pour the water on the offering and the wood." When they had done so, he said, "Do it again." So they did it again. Then he said, "Do it a third time." So they did it a third time. The water flowed down all sides of the altar and filled the trench.*        1 Kings 18:34-35 NET

They doused the altar and wood with twelve large jars of water. The message was clear—if there was no real God, then there would be no real fire.

*And it came to pass, at the time of the offering of the evening sacrifice, that Elijah the prophet came near and said, "Lord God of Abraham, Isaac, and Israel, let it be known this day that You are God in Israel and I am Your servant, and that I have done all these things at Your word. Hear me, O Lord, hear me, that this people may know that You are the Lord God, and that You have turned their hearts back to You again."*

*Then the fire of the Lord fell and consumed the burnt sacrifice, and the wood and the stones and the dust, and it licked up the water that was in the trench. Now when all the people saw it, they fell on their faces; and they said, **"The Lord, He is God! The Lord, He is God!"***        1 Kings 18:36-39 NKJV

Yahweh is God! It was him they must trust.

# 6 THE EXILE

The Israelites' Mount Carmel experience didn't prevent them from resuming their worship of idols. Before Moses had died, he had prophesied that the day would come when it would be said that the Israelites provoked the LORD...

> ...with other gods, they enraged him with abhorrent idols. They sacrificed to demons, not God, to gods they had not known; to new ones who had recently come along, gods your ancestors had not known about.    Deuteronomy 32:16-17 NET

Even then, one of YAHWEH's prophets wrote:

> Yet the LORD longs to be gracious to you; he rises to show you compassion. For the LORD is a God of justice...    Isaiah 30:18 NIV

But when the Israelites persisted in bowing down to demon-gods, the LORD did what he had promised—he sent judgment. The Assyrians invaded the ten northern tribes in 722 BC and took them into captivity. The Bible does not record an organized return of these people to the land of Israel.

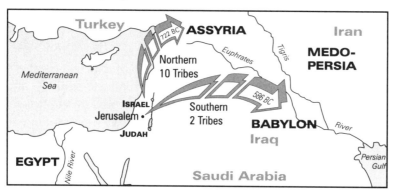

The two southern tribes continued as a distinct political entity until 586 BC when the Babylonians* ravaged the city of Jerusalem, demolished the great Temple of Solomon, and took them into exile.

*People from the area where the Tower of Babel was built.

## JEWS

While in exile the people began to be called *Jews*, a reference to the fact that most of them were from the tribe of Judah. With the temple destroyed, the Jews introduced the synagogue* as a place for social interaction, for teaching, and studying the Scriptures.

*Greek for the word *assemblies*.

While in captivity, one of the 40 prophets wrote,

> "Lord, you are righteous, but this day we are covered with shame—the men of Judah and people of Jerusalem and all Israel, both near and far, in all the countries where you have scattered us because of our unfaithfulness to you. O Lord … we have sinned against you.
>
> The Lord our God is merciful and forgiving, even though we have rebelled against him; we have not obeyed the Lord our God or kept the laws he gave us through his servants the prophets. All Israel has transgressed your law and turned away, refusing to obey you.
>
> Therefore the curses and sworn judgments written in the Law of Moses, the servant of God, have been poured out on us, because we have sinned against you. **You have fulfilled the words** spoken against us and against our rulers by bringing upon us great disaster…
>
> **Just as it is written** in the Law of Moses, all this disaster has come upon us, yet we have not sought the favor of the Lord our God by turning from our sins and giving attention to your truth. The Lord did not hesitate to bring the disaster upon us, for the Lord our God is righteous in everything he does; yet we have not obeyed him."                    Daniel 9:7-14 NIV

The exile continued for 70 years, but in 536 BC the two southern tribes began to trickle back to their homeland to settle in and around Jerusalem, in the area formerly occupied by the tribe of Judah. The temple was rebuilt, though not in the grandeur of Solomon's day, and the sacrificial system was reinstituted.

### THE GREEKS

Around 400 BC, the biblical record pauses and remains silent for a period of some four centuries. History didn't stand still though. Alexander the Great, the brilliant general of the Greeks, swept through the Middle East, engulfing the Jews in the process. His emissaries introduced *Greek* as the universal trade language and the Hellenistic culture became a status symbol for centuries to follow.

Some Jews freely embraced the Greek culture, combining it with their beliefs about God. These people were called *Sadducees*. Though small in number, they were people of wealth and influence. They tended to control the high priest, a position that had come to be bought and sold. They also denied parts of the Bible as being true. **The Sadducees took *away* from God's Word.**

For about 200 years, the Jews knuckled under to a succession of Greek occupying forces, and then in 166 BC they revolted. Judas Maccabeus led the people into a period of autonomy.

During this time, a party of Jewish religious zealots, called *Pharisees*, came to the forefront. The Pharisees fought the influence of the Greek culture and clung to the Law given to Moses. In their zeal, they created a protective ring of other laws around Moses' law so that none of the real law would be broken. These additional laws became an authority of their own, assuming equal weight with the Law of Moses. **The Pharisees *added* to God's Word.**

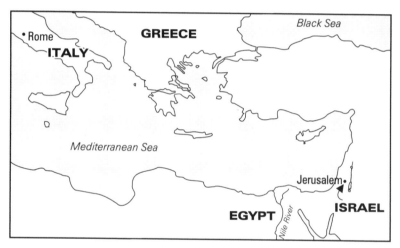

## THE ROMANS

The Jews' liberty under the Maccabean leadership lasted barely 100 years. The iron heel of Rome crushed the Jews' freedom in 67 BC when General Pompey entered Jerusalem.

Rome was quite accommodating of the Jewish religion as long as the Jews paid their taxes and did not encourage rebellion. The civilized world of the day had entered into an *uneasy peace*.

Starting in 27 BC and continuing barely 200 years, this peace, or what was called the *Pax Romana*, settled the turbulent political scene that had ruled the world since Babel. With peace came increased trade and travel, courtesy of well-built Roman roads and bridges. Socially, the world now had a common trade language, *Koine Greek*. Never before had the conditions been so ripe for a messenger and a message to be spread to the four corners of the globe.

## A Prepared World

For the Israelites, their preparation had included slavery in Babylon. The exile had been a jarring experience, a sort of flashback to what it had been like in Egypt. But through it, the Hebrews had learned a hard lesson—they had finally ceased to worship other gods. The following verse became the confession of faith for all Jews. It is called the *Shema*.

> *"Hear, O Israel: The Lord our God, the Lord is one!"*
> Deuteronomy 6:4 NKJV

The Shema literally reads *"Yahweh our God is Yahweh alone."* He is totally unique—he is holy. The Scriptures are replete with similar statements about the Lord:

> *"There is no one holy like the Lord, Indeed, there is no one besides You, Nor is there any rock like our God."*
> 1 Samuel 2:2 NASB

> *"Thus says the Lord, the King of Israel, And his Redeemer, the Lord of hosts: 'I am the First and I am the Last; Besides Me there is no God.'"*
> Isaiah 44:6 NKJV

> *"I am the Lord, and there is no other; Besides Me there is no God."*
> Isaiah 45:5 NASB

> *"Before me no god was formed, nor shall there be any after me."*
> Isaiah 43:10 ESV

The Israelites were now ready for the next major revelation of the Lord's character. The question was this: *Would they believe him? Would the watching world believe him?*

## A Faithful God

The preceding centuries had also proven to the Israelites—indeed to the entire *Global Classroom*—that the Lord Yahweh was a promise-keeping God. King David had written,

> *Your promises have been thoroughly tested…* Psalm 119:140 NLT

When a person has a long and reliable history of keeping his word, that is the sort of person who can be trusted. You can believe what he says. Yahweh, at work in history, had proven to the waiting Hebrews—and to the world at large—that they no longer had an excuse not to trust him.

## Herod the Great

Though the world was now at peace, life was not easy for the common Jew on the street. Since the Roman Empire was far too large to be administered effectively from Rome, local leaders were selected to rule the different regions. In Judea, now a province of Rome, a man named Herod was appointed as a puppet king. He would come to be known as *Herod the Great*. Cruel beyond belief, Herod was a follower of the Jewish religion in name only. Under Rome's authority, he and his descendants ruled the resentful Jewish world for the next one hundred years. The people yearned for rescue—for one who could give them relief.

### THE PROMISED ONE

More than 2,000 years had passed since God first promised Abraham that one of his descendants would be THE PROMISED DELIVERER. Throughout the centuries, God had those people—sometimes only a few—who believed His Word and trusted him. They waited in eager anticipation for THE ANOINTED ONE to come. In these early years of the Pax Romana, those who clung tenaciously to God's promises were still waiting to see them fulfilled. The time had come, but they were unaware of it.

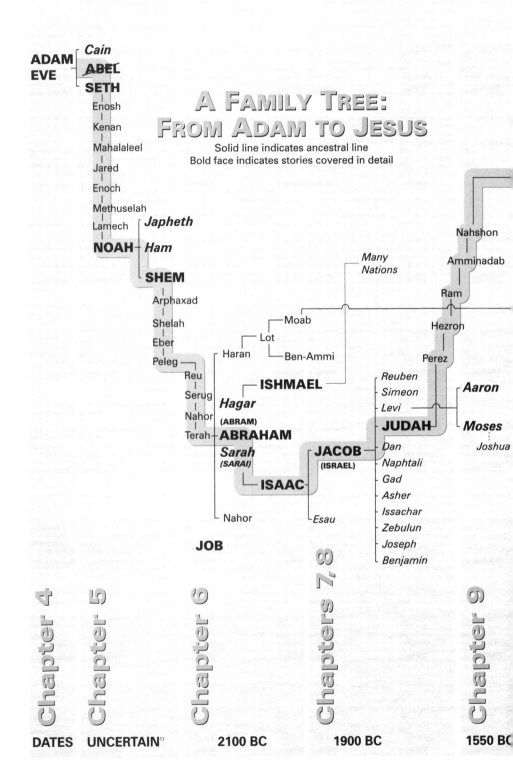

# A FAMILY TREE:
# FROM ADAM TO JESUS

Solid line indicates ancestral line
Bold face indicates stories covered in detail

ADAM
EVE

Cain
ABEL
SETH
Enosh
Kenan
Mahalaleel
Jared
Enoch
Methuselah
Lamech

Japheth
NOAH — Ham
SHEM
Arphaxad
Shelah
Eber
Peleg
Reu
Serug
Nahor
Terah — ABRAHAM
Sarah
(SARAI)
Nahor

Haran
Lot
ISHMAEL
Hagar
(ABRAM)

Moab
Ben-Ammi

JACOB
(ISRAEL)
ISAAC
Esau

Many
Nations

Reuben
Simeon
Levi
JUDAH
Dan
Naphtali
Gad
Asher
Issachar
Zebulun
Joseph
Benjamin

Nahshon
Amminadab
Ram
Hezron
Perez

Aaron
Moses
Joshua

JOB

Chapter 4

Chapter 5

Chapter 6

Chapters 7, 8

Chapter 9

DATES    UNCERTAIN[13]         2100 BC          1900 BC          1550 BC

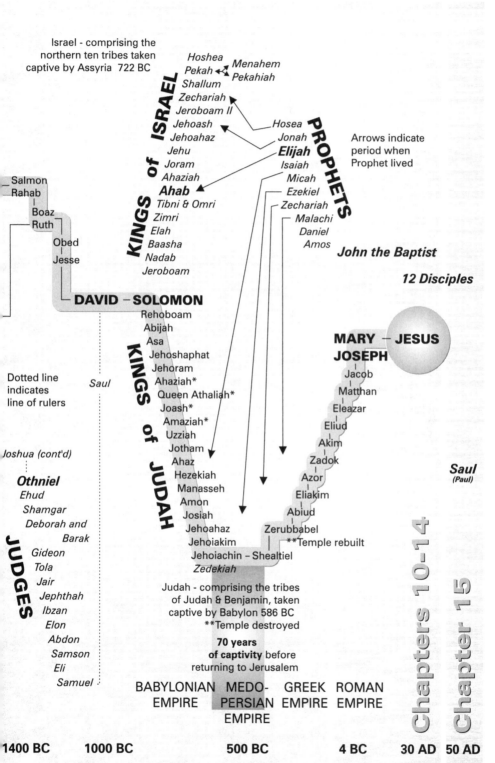

Israel - comprising the northern ten tribes taken captive by Assyria 722 BC

**ISRAEL**

Hoshea
Pekah ↔ Menahem
Pekahiah
Shallum
Zechariah
Jeroboam II
Jehoash
Jehoahaz
Jehu
Joram
Ahaziah
**Ahab**
Tibni & Omri
Zimri
Elah
Baasha
Nadab
Jeroboam

**KINGS of ISRAEL**

**PROPHETS**

Hosea
Jonah
*Elijah*
Isaiah
Micah
Ezekiel
Zechariah
Malachi
Daniel
Amos

Arrows indicate period when Prophet lived

**John the Baptist**

**12 Disciples**

Salmon
Rahab
Boaz
Ruth
Obed
Jesse

**DAVID – SOLOMON**

Rehoboam
Abijah
Asa
Jehoshaphat
Jehoram
Ahaziah*
Queen Athaliah*
Joash*
Amaziah*
Uzziah
Jotham
Ahaz
Hezekiah
Manasseh
Amon
Josiah
Jehoahaz
Jehoiakim
Jehoiachin – Shealtiel
Zedekiah

**KINGS of JUDAH**

Dotted line indicates line of rulers

Saul

Joshua (cont'd)

**Othniel**
Ehud
Shamgar
Deborah and Barak
Gideon
Tola
Jair
Jephthah
Ibzan
Elon
Abdon
Samson
Eli
Samuel

**JUDGES**

**MARY – JESUS**
**JOSEPH**
Jacob
Matthan
Eleazar
Eliud
Akim
Zadok
Azor
Eliakim
Abiud
Zerubbabel
**Temple rebuilt

**Saul**
(Paul)

Judah - comprising the tribes of Judah & Benjamin, taken captive by Babylon 586 BC
**Temple destroyed

**70 years of captivity** before returning to Jerusalem

BABYLONIAN EMPIRE | MEDO-PERSIAN EMPIRE | GREEK EMPIRE | ROMAN EMPIRE

**Chapters 10–14**

**Chapter 15**

1400 BC　　1000 BC　　　　500 BC　　　　4 BC　　30 AD　50 AD

*Rulers that do not appear in Matthew's account of Jesus' ancestral line.

# Chapter Ten

# 1 FOR PERSPECTIVE

Every now and then you hear of individuals who announce dogmatically that they are the special DELIVERER promised in the Bible. How are we to know that they're not right? Well, the Scripture gives us a means to test the truth of these claims. Let me explain it this way.

## CLEAR IDENTITY

You may have read spy stories that go something like this: A secret agent is supposed to meet with an unknown contact. The spy is told to go to a certain city, catch a bus to an outlying suburb, and upon arriving, take a seat in the public square at 3:00 p.m. according to the town hall clock. He would be met by a man wearing a long, dark gray coat carrying a newspaper. This man would ask the agent for the time of day. The agent was to point at the town clock and ask the man if he knew "Dr. Kim." Of course, all this is done to remove any confusion in identifying the right contact.

Well, as incredible as it may sound, the LORD had the prophets write similar details about THE PROMISED DELIVERER. His means of transport, the town he was to arrive in, his "code" name…all sorts of information was given to make sure no one would miss his identity.

Dr. Peter Stoner, Professor Emeritus of Science at Westmont College, calculated [1] the probability factor if only eight pieces of identification were used.[2] He chose eight prophecies in the Bible all having been fulfilled by THE ANOINTED ONE. Twelve different classes representing 600 university students discussed each prophecy and examined circumstances that might indicate men had conspired to fulfill any one of those prophecies. For example, picking your place of birth is outside of one's control, so such a prophecy was considered legitimate. The student's collective estimates were conservative enough that even the most skeptical scholars gave unanimous consent to the conclusions.

Taking his students' data, Professor Stoner drew an even more conservative conclusion, encouraging skeptics to examine his deductions to see if they were fair. The conclusion? According to the law of probability, if one event fulfilled just eight prophecies, then that probability was 1 in 100,000,000,000,000,000.[3] Dr. Stoner illustrated the probability with the following supposition:

Take 100,000,000,000,000,000 silver dollars and lay them…

*"… on the face of Texas [a region bigger than France or Thailand]. They will cover all of the state two feet [or a half metre] deep. Now mark one of these silver dollars and stir the whole mass thoroughly, all over the state. Blindfold a man and tell him that he can travel as far as he wishes, but he must pick up one silver dollar and say that this is the right one."*

If one person fulfilled all eight prophecies, it would be the same likelihood as the blindfolded man finding the right coin. It is virtually impossible! As we progress with the story, we will see that The Promised One fulfilled more than eight prophecies, so needless to say, there was no mistaking his identity.

### Doctor Luke

Over the last nine chapters, we have followed Moses as he recorded God's word, fleshing out the message with excerpts from other prophets. For the rest of this book we will join another prophet and let him lead us to the conclusion. This man's name is *Luke*, and out of the 40 prophets who recorded Scripture, he was the only one who was not a Jew. By profession, Luke was a medical doctor but he was also a meticulous historian.

### Equal Value

For centuries man had struggled along, burdened by sin, with only one hope on the horizon—a Promised Deliverer. It was true that God in his mercy had allowed an innocent animal to die in man's place—as a substitute, but that only provided a temporary covering for sin. In the full scope of eternity, it was…

*… impossible for the blood of bulls and goats to take away sins.*
Hebrews 10:4 NASB

Man had been created in God's image, so for man's sin-debt to be paid, it would take someone equal to man—it would take a human being. An animal would not do.

For example, if you had borrowed a Mercedes Benz and then totalled it in a car accident, it would not be acceptable to give the owner a toy car in its place. No, you would need to replace the car with its full-blown equal or something even better.

In the same way, for man's sin-debt to be paid, it would take someone who had God's image—a human—an animal did not qualify.

### Two Men, Same Pit

Perhaps one man might be willing to pay the sin-debt for another man, but even then, that wasn't a solution. One sinner could not save another sinner.

It would be like two men who had fallen into an old mine shaft. Struggling in the darkness and mud at the bottom of the pit, the one said to the other, *"Get me out of this appalling place; I am sinking in this foul slime."* The other man replied, *"Are you crazy? I'm drowning too! I can't help you."* In the same way, it is impossible for one sinner to pull another sinner out of the abyss of sin. It would take someone who was sinless to save mankind.

But in searching the face of the globe, no perfect man could be found. Whether prophet or priest, every man from the beginning of time had been born as a son of Adam—born clothed in Adam's filthy rags of sin. No man could function as a Deliverer, because every man had his own sin-penalty to contend with.

### Summary

So man needed a saviour from outside the pit, one who had no sin. That saviour needed to be a human—not an animal. But who could this Deliverer be? Where would Yahweh find a person without sin? To answer these questions, Doctor Luke began by writing:

> Now many have undertaken to compile an account of the things that have been fulfilled among us, like the accounts passed on to us by those who were eyewitnesses … from the beginning. So it seemed good to me as well, because I have followed all things carefully from the beginning, to write an orderly account for you … **so that you may know for certain the things you were taught.** Luke 1:1-4 NET

# 2 The Angel

Before The Promised Deliverer arrived on the scene, the Lord prepared the Jewish people by sending a special messenger to announce the impending event. Doctor Luke wrote:

> During the reign of Herod king of Judea, there lived a priest named Zechariah … and he had a wife named Elizabeth, who was a descendant of Aaron. They were both righteous in the sight of

*God, following all the commandments and ordinances of the Lord blamelessly. But they did not have a child, because Elizabeth was barren, and they were both very old.*

*Now while Zechariah was serving as priest before God when his division was on duty, he was chosen … to enter the holy place of the Lord and burn incense.*

*Now the whole crowd of people were praying outside at the hour of the incense offering. An angel of the Lord, standing on the right side of the altar of incense, appeared to him. And Zechariah, visibly shaken when he saw the angel, was seized with fear.* Luke 1:5–12 NET

We need to stop for a moment and ask ourselves a question. How was Zechariah to know if this angel came from the LORD? Perhaps the angel was from the Devil!? Indeed, how can anyone know if a vision of bright, shining spirits is genuine or not? After all, the Scripture says Satan also comes as an "angel of light." [4]

To differentiate the good from the bad, YAHWEH had his angels give specific prophecies that would be immediately fulfilled. If there were no prophecies, then the message was not trusted. If prophecies were given and they were precisely fulfilled, then the rest of the message was factual. In Zechariah's case, the angel foretold several events:

*… the angel said to him, "Do not be afraid, Zechariah, for your prayer has been heard, and your **wife Elizabeth will bear you a son**; you will name him John. Joy and gladness will come to you, and many will rejoice at his birth, for he will be great in the sight of the Lord.[5] … He will turn many of the people of Israel to the Lord their God. And he will go as forerunner before the Lord … to turn the hearts of the fathers back to their children and the disobedient to the wisdom of the just, to make ready for the Lord a people prepared for him."*

*Zechariah said to the angel, "How can I be sure of this? For I am an old man, and my wife is old as well." The angel answered him, "I am Gabriel, who stands in the presence of God, and I was*

*sent to speak to you and to bring you this good news. And now, because you did not believe my words, which will be fulfilled in their time, **you will be silent, unable to speak, until the day these things take place.** "* Luke 1:13–20 NET

The angel gave Zechariah four specific prophecies along with his message:

1. Elizabeth was going to have a child, and …
2. The child would be a male.

That news must have bewildered the old man. His wife was "up in years." But it was the announcement that the LORD was coming to earth that must have really stunned Zechariah. Being informed that YAHWEH was THE PROMISED DELIVERER—well, it was simply unbelievable! To help Zechariah overcome his unbelief:

3. Gabriel said he would be unable to talk, and …
4. He would remain that way until the baby was born.

It is true that Zechariah struggled with disbelief, but even then, he would have known that 400 years before his time, the prophet Malachi had written about such an event.

> *"See, **I** will send my messenger, who will prepare the way before **me**. Then suddenly the Lord you are seeking will come to his temple; the messenger of the covenant, whom you desire, will come," **says the LORD Almighty**.* Malachi 3:1 NIV

There it was in plain words. Zechariah must have wondered why he had not seen it before. It was obvious! The LORD Almighty had said, "*I will send a messenger to prepare the way before **me**!*" YAHWEH himself would be coming as THE ANOINTED ONE. Moreover, the angel had said that the messenger who would prepare his way would be the priest's own son—John.

## WAS IT TRUE?

*But was Gabriel telling the truth?* Only if the four prophecies were fulfilled should Zechariah believe the news about YAHWEH.

> *Now the people were waiting for Zechariah, and they began to wonder why he was delayed in the holy place. When he came out, **he was not able to speak to them.** They realized that he had seen a vision in the holy place, because he was making signs to them and **remained unable to speak**.*
> Luke 1:21-22 NET

Prophecy number three had been fulfilled!

> *After some time his wife **Elizabeth became pregnant**, and for five months she kept herself in seclusion. She said, "This is what the Lord has done for me at the time when he has been gracious to me, to take away my disgrace among people.*
>
> Luke 1:24-25 NET

Prophecy number one was fulfilled! It looked like the whole message may be true, including the part about the LORD coming to earth!

But a question must have nagged away at the back of Zechariah's mind. Just how would the Creator come to earth? Would he come in a golden chariot driving seven white steeds, surrounded with legions of angels all dressed in brilliant light? Would he unseat the Roman rulers—dump Herod off his throne? The angel had not said.

### MARY

The scene now shifts. The angel, Gabriel, made another visit, this time to a young lady by the name of Mary.

> *In the sixth month of Elizabeth's pregnancy, the angel Gabriel was sent by God to a town of Galilee called Nazareth, to a virgin engaged to a man whose name was Joseph, a descendant of David, and the virgin's name was Mary.* Luke 1:26-27 NET

The Bible says that both Joseph and Mary were direct descendants of King David who had lived 1000 years earlier. Luke wrote that...

> *The angel came to her and said, "Greetings, favored one, the Lord is with you!"*
>
> *But she was greatly troubled by his words and began to wonder about the meaning of this greeting. So the angel said to her, "Do not be afraid, Mary, for you have found favor with God! Listen: **You will become pregnant** and give birth to a son, and you will name him Jesus."* Luke 1:28-31 NET

Now it was Mary's turn to be speechless. When she finally found her tongue, she asked a very logical question.

> *Mary said to the angel, "How can this be, since I am a virgin?"*
>
> *The angel answered and said to her, "The Holy Spirit will come upon you, and the power of the Most High will overshadow you; and for that reason the holy Child shall be called the Son of God."* Luke 1:34-35 NASB

YAHWEH was entering the world as a baby! Why? Why not come in all his dazzling glory? Well, as we saw before, the saviour must be a human. So YAHWEH came as a man. He would still be God, but he would also be a flesh-and-bones man—the one and only God-man. According to the angel, this God-man would be born of a virgin. This was not without significance.

Way back in the Garden of Eden, the LORD had told Eve that THE PROMISED DELIVERER would be *her* offspring. It did not say *their* offspring, referring to both man and woman. Now the promise was about to be fulfilled, and the child would be born of a virgin—it would be her offspring only. Ever since creation, all children born in the world were *Sons of Adam*, belonging to Adam's bloodline, and because they were Sons of Adam they had Adam's nature—the sin nature.[6]

But this child, miraculously conceived by the power of the LORD would be called the *Son of God*—he would have the nature of the God *Most High*. No wonder the angel referred to the baby as the *Holy One*. This child would be sinless, just as the LORD YAHWEH is sinless. Jesus would be a perfect human from conception.

So YAHWEH would not be coming with all of Heaven's pomp and grandeur. Rather, he would arrive on the planet as all humans have and ever will—as a baby!

Gabriel gave Mary three prophecies. The first one stated that she would become pregnant while still a virgin. The second and third prophecies involved the wife of Zechariah.

> "And look, your relative **Elizabeth has also become pregnant with a son** in her old age—although she was called barren, she is now in her sixth month! For nothing will be impossible with God." Luke 1:36-37 NET

Mary knew Elizabeth was too old to have a child. Surely, if it was possible for an old woman to conceive, then it was just as believable for a virgin to give birth. Mary chose to trust God.

> So Mary said, "Yes, I am a servant of the Lord; let this happen to me according to your word." Then the angel departed from her. Luke 1:38 NET

## ZECHARIAH AND ELIZABETH

> Now the time came for Elizabeth to have her baby, and she gave birth to a son. Luke 1:57 NET

**JOHN**

**Elizabeth gave birth to a son**, not a daughter—the second prophecy fulfilled! It was quite an occasion for in those days a stigma was attached to those who could not bear children. Following the naming ceremony, **Zechariah's voice returned**—the fourth prophecy fulfilled! Bursting into a speech of praise, he recalled the LORD's promises to send a Saviour.

> *"Praise the Lord, the God of Israel, because he has visited … his people …*                                    *Luke 1:68 NLT*

Speaking of the child still in Mary's womb, Zechariah continued. The LORD …

> *…has sent us a mighty Savior from the royal line of his servant David, just as he promised through his holy prophets long ago. He has been merciful to our ancestors by remembering his sacred covenant—the covenant he swore with an oath to our ancestor Abraham."*                        *Luke 1:69-70,72-73 NLT*

You can see the elderly Zechariah holding the child high, fixing his eyes on baby John's face as he said,

> *"And you, child, will be called the prophet of the Most High. For you will go before the Lord to prepare his ways."*
>                                                     *Luke 1:76 NET*

John would be the messenger who would announce the arrival of the LORD YAHWEH to the whole world—the whole *Global Classroom.*

# 3 MANY NAMES

The angel, Gabriel, had announced that …

> *"… the child to be born will be holy; he will be called the Son of God."*                                       *Luke 1:35 NET*

As we have seen before, God has many names, each describing something of his character. This list lengthens as God descends to earth as a man. We will look at three of these names:

**1. The Son of God:** Some have understood the term *Son of God* to mean that God had sexual relations with Mary. The Bible *does not* teach such a concept anywhere. The Scripture clearly tells us that Mary was a virgin until *after* Jesus was born.[7] Jesus was conceived, not through physical union, but by a miracle. God empowered Mary's body to do that which is not natural—to give birth to a baby while still a virgin.

Others have concluded that since Mary was the mother of Jesus, therefore, Mary was God's mother—implying that Mary was a god. Some call Mary the *Queen of Heaven* which is a mistake, as the *Queen of Heaven* is a pagan goddess mentioned five times in Scripture and always with a warning. The prophet Jeremiah recorded the LORD saying,

> *"The children gather wood, the fathers kindle fire, and the women knead dough, to make cakes for the **queen of heaven**. And they pour out drink offerings to other gods, to provoke me to anger.* Jeremiah 7:18 ESV

Obviously Mary could not have been the Queen of Heaven!

Though Mary trusted God and honoured his Word, she was not equal with God in any way. Yes, she was the human vehicle God used to enter the world but only that and nothing more. Mary herself was a sinner and recognized her need for a Saviour.

> *And Mary said, "My soul magnifies the Lord, and my spirit rejoices in God **my Savior** ..."* Luke 1:46-47 ESV

So, if the term *Son of God* does not have physical implications, what does it mean?

Many languages use the term *son* in ways that do not confine it to a physical descendant. For example, if a person is referred to as a *son of the road*, it is understood that the individual is a *traveller*. (Roads do not give birth to children!) The Bible uses this same form of expression to make a point about a person's character. Here are three examples from Scripture:

> ❖ *Joseph ... who was also called Barnabas ... (which translated means Son of Encouragement).* Acts 4:36 NASB

We understand by this that Joseph's life was distinguished by the encouragement he gave to others, not that his father's name was *Encouragement*.

> ❖ *... the sons of disobedience.* Ephesians 5:6 NASB

Obviously this does not mean that a fellow called *Disobedience* had several sons. Instead it is referring to those who by nature are disobedient.

> ❖ *... you son of the devil, you enemy of all righteousness ...* Acts 13:10 NASB

Satan did not take a wife and have a son! Instead the passage is referring to a *wicked person*.

In the same way, when the Bible talks about Jesus as the *Son of God*, we need to understand that it refers to his perfect nature—the nature of God, in contrast to a human who has a corrupt nature—as expected of a *Son of Adam*. The Bible says,

> The Son is the radiance of God's glory and the exact representation of his being...                                        Hebrews 1:3 NIV

Jesus, the *Son*, is the exact representation of God's being. Yahweh's character—his glory—was revealed in Jesus. Much more could be written on this, but let's proceed to the next name.

**2. The Son of Man**: This name does not imply that Jesus had a human father. Joseph was Mary's husband but not Jesus' father.

a.   **The name *Son of Man* emphasizes his humanity:** Although Jesus did not have a human father, he was completely man and lived as a human lived—yet was without sin. Jesus' references to himself as the *Son of Man* were statements of humility.

b.   **It's a name that declares his true identity:** For centuries, scholars of the Scripture recognized this name as referring to THE ANOINTED ONE. Five hundred years before the birth of Jesus, the prophet Daniel had written about THE PROMISED ONE when he said:

> "I saw in the night visions, and, behold, one like the **Son of man** came... And there was given him dominion, and glory, and a kingdom, that all people, nations, and languages, should serve him."                                        Daniel 7:13-14 KJV

### NAMES COMBINED

When the two names, *Son of God* and *Son of Man*, are tied together, they find their complete expression in the fact that...

> He [God] was made visible in human flesh... 1 Timothy 3:16 AMP

Yahweh did not cease to be God when he became man. Nor did he become sinful when he took on the form of a man. Although he accepted certain self-imposed limitations, he was still all-powerful, still all-knowing, and still perfect in righteousness.

Neither was he a demi-god—part God and part human. Rather he was 100% God and 100% human—simultaneously. How he could restrict himself to a human body and still be complete in all his attributes is difficult for us to understand, but this is what the Scripture teaches. As we go on in the story, it will make sense as to why God chose to do things this way.

**3. The Word:** We saw earlier that Scripture is often referred to as *God's Word*. But now we are going to take the definition a step further. *The Word* is one of God's names. The Scripture says,

> *In the beginning was the Word … and the Word was God.*
> John 1:1 NKJV

It then goes on to tell us that God came to earth, became a man and lived with mankind.

> *And the Word became flesh and dwelt among us …*
> John 1:14 NKJV

The word *dwelling* is an interesting word in the Greek. It means *tabernacle*. A literal translation of the same verse reads like this:

> *And the Word became flesh, and did **tabernacle** among us …*
> John 1:14 YLT

Just as the Israelites pitched the Tabernacle in the middle of their camp as a sign of God's presence dwelling in their midst, so God left Heaven and *tabernacled* with man—he dwelt in our midst.

Using the common definition, this would distinguish Jesus from an avatar. Avatars are said to be gods that take the *form* of a being, whereas Jesus truly became human *flesh* and *tabernacled* among us. Additionally, avatars are said to appear, disappear, and appear again in different forms, sometimes as humans but often as animals or part animals. In contrast, Jesus was born only once and only as a human.

## MANY NAMES

Seven hundred years before the birth of Jesus, Isaiah, one of the 40 writers prophesied,

> *For to us a **child** is born, to us a son is given … and his name shall be called Wonderful Counselor, Mighty God, Everlasting Father, Prince of Peace.*
> Isaiah 9:6 ESV

Notice the *child* is called *Mighty God, Everlasting Father*—two names that can mean nothing other than the LORD YAHWEH Himself.

Jesus not only had the image of God, he was God—God in human flesh. He was sinless with no sin-debt to pay. He was the one from outside of the slime pit, clothed in spotless clothes, the one who could rescue mankind from the penalty of sin. He was eminently qualified to be a saviour. The Bible says,

> *… Jesus came into the world to save sinners …*   1 Timothy 1:15 NASB

# 4 THE SAVIOUR

*This is how Jesus … was born. His mother, Mary, was engaged to be married to Joseph. But before the marriage took place, while she was still a virgin, she became pregnant through the power of the Holy Spirit. Joseph, her fiancé, was a good man and did not want to disgrace her publicly, so he decided to break the engagement quietly.*            Matthew 1:18-19 NLT

You can imagine for a moment the anguish Joseph felt. *Mary was pregnant and the child wasn't his. To reveal the truth publicly would label Mary for what she must be—an adulteress!—unless Mary's explanation about an angel appearing to her was right. No, that was absurd. The poor girl must be losing her mind. Joseph loved her, but he could not marry a girl who had cheated on him and was obviously trying to cover it up with an insane story.* What Joseph thought we don't really know, but he painfully decided to break off the engagement.

> *But when he had considered this, behold, an angel of the Lord appeared to him in a dream, saying, "Joseph, son of David, do not be afraid to take Mary as your wife; for the Child who has been conceived in her is of the Holy Spirit.*
>
> *"She will bear a Son; and you shall call His name Jesus, for He will save His people from their sins."*
>
> *Now all this took place to fulfill what was spoken by the Lord through the prophet:*
>
> *"Behold, the virgin shall be with child, and shall bear a Son, and they shall call His name Immanuel," which translated means, "God with us."*            Matthew 1:20–23 NASB

Joseph could not have heard it any more plainly. Mary was still a virgin and she was going to have a son! The child's name would be *Jesus* which means YAHWEH *is our Deliverer* or YAHWEH *is our Saviour.* He would *deliver* or *save* people from the sin-penalty. Jesus would also be called *Immanuel*, meaning *God with us.*

 The prophet, Isaiah, had used this name when he had written about this event 700 years before.

> *Therefore the Lord Himself will give you a sign: Behold, a virgin will be with child and bear a son, and she will call His name Immanuel.*            Isaiah 7:14 NASB

The virgin birth would make a bold statement to the *Global Classroom* that this baby was different—he was *God with us.*

*And Joseph awoke from his sleep and did as the angel of the Lord commanded him, and took Mary as his wife, but kept her a virgin until she gave birth to a Son; and he called His name Jesus.*

Matthew 1:24-25 NASB

## THE CENSUS

*In those days Caesar Augustus\* issued a decree that a census should be taken of the entire Roman world.*

Luke 2:1 NIV

\*Caesar Augustus was ruler of the Roman empire.

Caesar needed money, and if the Romans got an accurate census, more people would have to pay taxes. Joseph was required to take his wife 120 kilometres (or 70 miles) from Nazareth to Bethlehem which 1000 years before had been King David's home.

*And everyone was on his way to register for the census, each to his own city.*

*Joseph also went up from Galilee, from the city of Nazareth, to Judea, to the city of David which is called Bethlehem, because he was of the house and family of David, in order to register along with Mary, who was engaged to him, and was with child. While they were there, the days were completed for her to give birth. And she gave birth to her firstborn son; and she wrapped Him in cloths, and laid Him in a manger, because there was no room for them in the inn.*

Luke 2:3-7 NASB

So Jesus was born in Bethlehem, far from Joseph and Mary's home. The town was so crowded that it seems the only place where they could find lodging was in a stable. Jesus' first bed was a manger, a trough for feeding cattle. But in spite of the conditions, Joseph must have sensed that everything was right. Very much right.

*And he called his name Jesus.*         Matthew 1:25 ESV

THE PROMISED ONE had finally arrived. The Bible says the LORD,

> *"Who, being in very nature God … made himself nothing, taking the very nature of a servant, being made in human likeness."*
>       Philippians 2:6-7 NIV

---

### TWO KINDS OF GREATNESS

Some folks say, *"Impossible! Almighty God would never stoop so low as to be born as a helpless baby … in a dirty stable. He would never become a man! God is great, he would never do that!"*

Perhaps we need to redefine the word *great*. Consider this:

❖ There is the greatness of a king who lives in his imperial palace, surrounded by wealth and luxury and slaves to keep himself comfortable. Rarely does he get his hands dirty. He knows little of the hardships and concerns faced by his subjects day after wearying day.

❖ Then there is the greatness of the skilled doctor who forsakes a lucrative medical practice in his homeland to set up a clinic in a foreign country. Surrounded by disease and poverty, he serves the people, helping them, healing them, and finally laying down his life for them.

Which kind of greatness do you think is most worthy of a merciful and gracious God?

> *For you know the grace of our Lord Jesus Christ, that though He was rich, yet for your sakes He became poor, that you through His poverty might become rich.*
>       2 Corinthians 8:9 NKJV

---

Some have wondered why it took so long for the LORD to come to earth. The Bible does not say. Perhaps it was because it took centuries to convince just one nation to worship YAHWEH alone. Or maybe it had to do with the fact that you should *"never trust a stranger."* If that was the issue, the LORD had taken thousands of years to build a long and reliable history so man would have no excuse not to trust him. Whatever the reason, the Bible says THE PROMISED DELIVERER had finally arrived.

## THE SHEPHERDS

> *In the same region there were some shepherds staying out in the fields and keeping watch over their flock by night. And an angel of the Lord suddenly stood before them, and the glory of the Lord shone around them; and they were terribly frightened.*

> *But the angel said to them, "Do not be afraid; for behold, I bring you good news of great joy which will be for all the people; for today **in the city of David** there has been born for you a Savior, who is Christ the Lord. This will be a sign for you: you will find **a baby wrapped in cloths and lying in a manger**."*
>
> Luke 2:8-12 NASB

The shepherds were given no less than four specific signs to verify the message.

> *And suddenly there appeared with the angel a multitude of the heavenly host praising God and saying,"Glory to God in the highest, And on earth peace among men with whom He is pleased."*　　Luke 2:13-14 NASB

The shepherds had been minding their own business, tending their sheep. Often sheep from their flocks were used in the temple sacrifices in Jerusalem only a few miles north of Bethlehem. Life was predictable. But now the angels had come, and the shepherds' whole world was shaken, not only by the event of the Saviour's birth but also by his identity! They must have excitedly queried each other, *"Did you hear what I heard? The Christ is the LORD!"*

## CHRIST / MESSIAH

The Greek word *Christ* is the same as the Hebrew word *Messiah*—a word meaning *the anointed one*. For centuries the title "Messiah" had been applied to THE PROMISED DELIVERER. Now the angels were saying that the Messiah/Christ—was YAHWEH himself.

> When the angels had gone away from them into heaven, the shepherds began saying to one another, "Let us go straight to Bethlehem then, and see this thing that has happened which the Lord has made known to us." So they came in a hurry and found their way to Mary and Joseph, and the baby as He lay in the manger. When they had seen this, they made known the statement which had been told them about this Child. Luke 2:15-17 NASB

## WISE MEN

> Now after Jesus was born in Bethlehem of Judea in the days of Herod the king, magi from the east arrived in Jerusalem, saying, "Where is He who has been born King of the Jews? For we saw His star in the east and have come to worship Him."
>
> Matthew 2:1-2 NASB

The Magi were experts in the study of the stars, probably coming from Persia (Iran). At great personal expense, they had travelled over treacherous mountains and deserts to see the newborn child. The king enthroned in Judea at this time was Herod the Great who, no doubt, had been alerted to this rather prestigious company. Their visit could not have been perceived as a threat as they were not leading armies. All they had was a question: "*Where is the newborn King?*"

> When Herod the king heard this, he was troubled, and all Jerusalem with him. Matthew 2:3 NASB

That single question really rocked Herod. He held his authority as king in a tightly clenched fist and would crush anyone who dared try to wrench it from him. No doubt the whole city was a little shaken as well. Herod was known to be cruel to his citizens especially when he was upset. Who knew what he might do? Herod called his religious advisors.

*When he had called together all the people's chief priests and teachers of the law, he asked them where the Christ was to be born.*
Matthew 2:4 NIV

You can see an agitated scribe blowing dust off a small scroll. His fellow sages bend over the papyrus and with rheumy eyes, scan the text. They are a little rattled. They want Herod to understand that they are *not* the ones who had said these things. A prophet by the name of Micah had written it over 700 years earlier. A shaky finger points to a well-worn part of the document. Herod refuses to look. A scribe clears his raspy throat and reads:

*"But you, Bethlehem Ephrathah, Though you are little among the thousands of Judah, Yet out of you shall come forth to Me The One to be Ruler in Israel, Whose goings forth are from of old, From everlasting."*
Micah 5:2 NKJV

The prophecy was very specific. It said the baby must be born in Bethlehem Ephrathah. Since there were two towns called Bethlehem, one near Nazareth and another south of Jerusalem in the region of Ephrathah, the distinction was important.

Herod wanted to see if the Prophet Micah had recorded more. He had! The prophecy clearly stated that the One to be born had lived *from everlasting*. Herod must have been ashen. It couldn't be. Only God was eternal. The Creator would never come to earth as an infant, especially to be born in the backwoods of Bethlehem. He would arrive with trumpets and chariots—in Jerusalem. Aha! Perhaps the scribes were intentionally trying to alarm him, to manipulate him. It wouldn't hurt to humour them. He would show them what sort of worship new kings could expect. He shooed out his priests...

*Then Herod called the Magi secretly and found out from them the exact time the star had appeared. He sent them to Bethlehem and said, "Go and make a careful search for the child. As soon as you find him, report to me, so that I too may go and worship him."*

*After they had heard the king, they went on their way, and the star they had seen in the east went ahead of them until it stopped over the place where the child was. When they saw the star, they were overjoyed. On coming to the house, they saw the child with his mother Mary, and they bowed down and worshiped him. Then they opened their treasures and presented him with gifts of gold and of incense and of myrrh.[8]*
Matthew 2:7-11 NIV

**WORSHIP**

These men of wealth and status worshipped Jesus. The Law was very specific—only the God *Most High* was to be worshipped. Joseph and Mary knew the Ten Commandments well and yet they did not intervene. They must have known deep down inside that the Magi were worshipping the LORD.

> *And having been warned by God in a dream not to return to Herod, the magi left for their own country by another way.*
>
> *Now when they had gone, behold, an angel of the Lord appeared to Joseph in a dream and said, "Get up! Take the Child and His mother and flee to Egypt, and remain there until I tell you; for Herod is going to search for the Child to destroy Him."*
>
> *So Joseph got up and took the Child and His mother while it was still night, and left for Egypt.*
>
> *He remained there until the death of Herod.* Matthew 2:12-15 NASB

Consistent with what history records of him, Herod did make an all-out effort to kill Jesus, but the child remained safe in Egypt. Eventually Herod died, and so Joseph, Mary, and Jesus moved back to Nazareth where Joseph worked as a carpenter. Doctor Luke wrote,

> *And the child grew and became strong, filled with wisdom, and the favor of God was upon him.* Luke 2:40 ESV

| According to the prophets,<br>THE PROMISED DELIVERER would be … | Fulfilled by … |
|---|---|
| 1. The offspring of a woman | Jesus |
| 2. A male | Jesus |
| 3. A descendant of Abraham | Jesus |
| 4. A descendant of Isaac | Jesus |
| 5. A descendant of Jacob (Israel) | Jesus |
| 6. From the tribe of Judah | Jesus |
| 7. A descendant of King David | Jesus |
| 8. Preceded by a messenger (John) | Jesus |
| 9. Born in Bethlehem Ephrathah | Jesus |
| 10. Known as a Nazarene | Jesus |

# 5 Baptism

Jesus grew up and lived as any commoner of that era—working with his hands, living in a humble home, and travelling little. The only exception was that he never married.

> *Jesus was about thirty years old when he began his public ministry.*
>
> Luke 3:23 NLT

Thirty was considered the minimum age at which a man could command an audience and be heard. As those three decades came to a close, news of the Messiah's arrival began spreading far and wide. It was happening just as the prophets had foretold.

> *In those days John the Baptist came preaching in the wilderness of Judea, and saying, "Repent, for the kingdom of heaven is at hand!" For this is he who was spoken of by the prophet Isaiah, saying:*
>
> *"The voice of one crying in the wilderness: 'Prepare the way of the Lord; Make **His** paths straight.'"*      Matthew 3:1-3 NKJV

John, the son of Zechariah, was being referred to as *the Baptist* because he was baptizing people. The ritual of baptism was not uncommon to the Middle Eastern people of that day. It was full of meaning. Today, however, throughout the world much confusion surrounds this word.

For example, I had the opportunity to visit a country where the local people had been exposed to fragments of biblical thought. They had adopted baptism, believing their sins were washed away by the water. They were so convinced of its literal nature that they would not go into the river after a baptism for fear they would take on the sin left in the water.

The Bible is clear that baptism does not make us acceptable to God. It is only an outward picture of what has transpired inwardly. Today, many "theologians" inadvertently give baptism much more meaning than the Bible warrants.

Part of the confusion is a result of not having a word in the English language that precisely translates the Greek word *baptizo*. The translators resolved the problem by creating the word *baptism*. That's okay, but it doesn't help the average person understand its original meaning.

## IDENTIFICATION

Baptism implies *identification*. A common meaning of the word *baptizo* originated in the early Greek textile industry. In the process of dying fabric, a piece of cloth was plunged into a vat of dye whereby it took on the colour of the pigment. The cloth was totally identified with the dye.

## PHARISEES AND SADDUCEES

John taught that the Jews had strayed from the Scripture, embracing man's ideas. He said they needed to change their mind about their wandering ways and return to God; in short, *repent*. The Jews who were baptized showed that they identified (or agreed personally) with his message of repentance.

> Then people from Jerusalem, as well as all Judea and all the region around the Jordan, were going out to him, and he was baptizing them in the Jordan River as they confessed their sins.
>
> But when he saw many Pharisees and Sadducees coming to his baptism, he said to them, "You offspring of vipers! Who warned you to flee from the coming wrath [God's judgement of sin]? Therefore produce fruit that proves your repentance…"
>
> Matthew 3:5–8 NET

John the Baptist saw that some in his audience were Pharisees and Sadducees. Remember, they were the ones who *added to* or *took away from* the Bible. These two sects despised each other, but they had one thing in common—they were proud. John called them a *bunch of snakes* because they enforced unbearably strict rules on others but did not practice what they preached. He told them to *repent*, to have *a change of mind*.

## JESUS' BAPTISM

> Then Jesus came from Galilee to John to be baptized by him in the Jordan River. But John tried to prevent him, saying, "I need to be baptized by you, and yet you come to me?"
>
> Matthew 3:13-14 NET

John recognized who Jesus was—he was the Messiah. Jesus did not need to repent of anything because he was perfect. John knew that *he* was the one who needed to be baptized, not Jesus.

> So Jesus replied to him, "Let it happen now, for it is right for us to fulfill all righteousness." Then John yielded to him.
>
> Matthew 3:15 NET

Jesus insisted on being baptized because he wanted to be identified with John's message of righteous living. He wanted to affirm John's message as being true.

> As soon as Jesus was baptized, he went up out of the water. At that moment heaven was opened, and he saw the Spirit of God descending like a dove and lighting on him. And a voice from heaven said, "This is my Son, whom I love; with him I am well pleased."
> Matthew 3:16-17 NIV

In a moment we will look at this verse in more depth, but first, let us finish the story.

> On the next day John saw Jesus coming toward him and said, "Look, the Lamb of God who takes away the sin of the world! This is the one about whom I said, 'After me comes a man who is greater than I am, because **he existed before me.**'"
> John 1:29-30 NET

John identified Jesus as THE PROMISED SAVIOUR, the one who would take away the sin of the world. He called him the *Lamb of God*, a name often used of Jesus. We will see later why Jesus was identified with this harmless animal. Even though John had been born before Jesus, John also stated that Jesus had lived before him—eternally. He concluded,

> "And I have seen and testified that this is the Son of God."
> John 1:34 NKJV

# 6 A COMPLEX ONENESS

For 1000 years the LORD had worked with Israel to bring them to a point of not trusting other gods. It took invasions and exile to get idolatry out of their system. Finally Israel worshipped only one God—the LORD YAHWEH.

But now the LORD wanted his *Chosen People* and all the other nations in the *Global Classroom* to understand something more about himself, something they had not been ready for until they learned that…

> … The LORD our God, the LORD is **one.**       Deuteronomy 6:4 ESV

Remember how in the early chapters, we mentioned the unknowable part of God—the things Scripture says we cannot fathom? Well, this latest revelation touched deeply on an aspect of God's character that is truly beyond our understanding.

When the preceding Scripture says the Lᴏʀᴅ is *one*, the word used in the original Hebrew is *echad*.[9] It means a *complex* "one" versus an *absolute or mathematical* "one."

For example, the Bible uses *echad* when it speaks of men who…

> …cut down a branch with **one** cluster of grapes…
>
> Numbers 13:23 NKJV

There is only *one* cluster, but there are *many* grapes. We use this grammatical construct in the English language when we talk about a university or hospital complex. We know there is only *one* university, but it has *many* buildings; there is just *one* hospital, but it is comprised of *many* wards. That makes sense when we're talking about buildings and grapes, but the idea of a *complex oneness* is harder to understand when referring to persons. Can two persons be one? The Scripture says *yes*, and uses marriage as an example.

> …a man leaves his father and mother and is joined to his wife, and the two are united into **one**.    Genesis 2:24 NLT

This is not specifically referring to a sexual act. The Hebrew word translated "one" is *echad*. It speaks of *two* persons being united into *one* family. It is not an *absolute or mathematical* "one," but a *complex* "one." The Scripture says that a married couple…

> …are no longer two, but **one**…    Mark 10:8 NKJV

The Bible calls this oneness…

> …a profound mystery…    Ephesians 5:32 NIV

On a much greater and deeper scale, the Scriptures affirm that God is *echad*—he is one, but comprised of three persons.[10] Each one of these three persons has many names but they can be readily identified as the *Father, Son,* and *Holy Spirit.* In theological terms, this is referred to as a *trinity* or *tri-unity*—"tri" meaning *three*, and "unity" meaning *one*—a *three in one.*

Over the centuries the prophets had touched on the plurality of God's oneness. When God created man, Moses had written,

> God said, "Let **Us** make man in **Our** image, according to **Our** likeness…"    Genesis 1:26 NKJV

When Adam sinned,

> …the Lᴏʀᴅ God said, "…the man has become like one of **us**, knowing good and evil…"    Genesis 3:22 NET

When the people of Babel were dispersed, the LORD said,

> "Come, let **us** go down and confuse their language so they will not understand each other." So the LORD scattered them …
>
> Genesis 11:7-8 NIV

Even the Hebrew word the prophets used for God—*Elohim*—communicated a complex oneness. In Hebrew grammar, *Elohim* uses the plural form which allows for complexity, but the word itself is singular, meaning *one*.

With the coming of the LORD to earth as the God-man, the LORD revealed in greater detail his *complex oneness*. Doctor Luke wrote that when the angel talked to Mary, he said,

> "The **Holy Spirit** will come upon you, and the power of the **Most High** will overshadow you; and for that reason the holy Child shall be called the **Son of God**." Luke 1:35 NASB

Here are three persons, yet one God. From this point on in Scripture, it is common to find verses referring to the Trinity.

> As soon as **Jesus** was baptized, he went up out of the water. At that moment heaven was opened, and he saw the **Spirit of God** descending like a dove and lighting on him. And a **voice from heaven** said, "This is my Son, whom I love; with him I am well pleased." Matthew 3:16-17 NIV

We have three persons here: *Jesus*, the *Spirit of God*, and a *voice from heaven*. Together they form a tri-unity—one God whose personal name is the LORD YAHWEH.

Over the years various attempts have been made to explain the tri-oneness of God:

1. **The egg:** Each egg has a shell, a white, and a yolk; three distinct parts, but only one egg.

2. **Dimensions:** A box has height, width, and length. They are not the same, cannot be separated, nor are they "parts." The concept of space is meaningless without all three.

3. **Multiplication:** $1 \times 1 \times 1 = 1$

For some, these illustrations may be helpful but they fall far short in explaining the Trinity. We need to be careful that we don't try to drag God down to our level. The LORD says part of the reason we don't understand him is because …

> You thought that I was just like you … Psalm 50:21 NASB

We need to recognize that our ability to reason cannot fit an infinite God into our finite minds. Rightly understood, God, as revealed in the Bible, is a God who leaves us astonished. There are things about the LORD that are beyond our scope of reason; incredible complexities that are difficult for us to fathom.

For example, the whole concept of an eternal God is not easy to digest. In the same way, trying to conceptualize a God who is *everywhere at the same time* is baffling. Getting a solid handle on just these two truths is impossible for our finite minds to comprehend. It's no different with the Trinity.

> The secret things belong unto the LORD our God: but those things which are revealed belong unto us...　　Deuteronomy 29:29 KJV

### THE TRIUNE ONE

Although it is correct to refer to any person of the Trinity as *God*, a distinction can be made as follows:

The Most High = The Father
Jesus Christ　= The Son
The Spirit　　= The Holy Spirit

The Trinity is sometimes referred to as *the Godhead*. The Scripture says of Jesus:

> For in Him dwells all the fullness of the Godhead bodily...
> 　　　　　　　　　　　　　　　　　Colossians 2:9 NKJV

### FULLY GOD

Jesus was not "part of God"—he was fully God.

In this book we focus on Jesus, but the same emphasis could have been directed toward the Father and the Holy Spirit. They are personalities in their own right—they are not abstract forces. Some have understood the Holy Spirit to be a divine fluid, but this is an error. What we've learned about YAHWEH up to this point applies to each person in the Godhead. The accompanying diagram has been used for centuries to explain the Trinity.[11]

### ANSWERS

The Trinity does answer many questions we have about God. For example, the Bible speaks of YAHWEH on his throne in Heaven, and yet, at the same time, dwelling in the Tabernacle. To complicate it even further, God is *everywhere present at one time.* How can this be? Mathematically, it does not make sense.

But YAHWEH's oneness is not a *mathematical oneness*—biblically, we can't think in terms of an *absolute "one."* Rather, as a *complex one,* the Father rules from Heaven, the Son dwelt (literally *tabernacled*) among the human race, and the Spirit by his presence is *everywhere at the same time.* God can be both great and lofty (unknowable) and near and lowly (knowable) at the same time. The *three in one* God makes it possible.

Although the concept of a triune God explains much of what we find in scripture, we still need to be reminded that the Godhead is a mystery. For centuries scholars have struggled to find the right words to adequately express this truth. There really are none. When we think of YAHWEH's greatness, this should not surprise us.

**What the Bible does not teach:**

❖ **Tri-theism:** This was believed by the ancient Egyptians. They grouped their gods in triads—three gods in a cluster. Usually they were a family: *Osiris* the father, *Isis* the mother, and *Horus* the son. Today a serious misunderstanding of the Trinity places God as father, Mary as mother, and Jesus as son. The idea of the Tri-murti (three chief gods) would also be considered Tri-theism.

The commonness of tri-theism in ancient religions could be a reflection that, after Noah's flood, everyone knew the truth about the three-in-one God. Later when the first religions began to develop at Babel, the Trinity was misrepresented as tri-theism.

❖ **Modalism:** Three roles are played by one person, such as a man being known as a son, husband, and father. This would also apply to job descriptions, such as one person being a doctor, lawyer, and computer programmer. The Trinity is not one person, three roles; but one God, three persons, who each play a unique role.

❖ The Bible does not teach **three individual Gods existing as one**, but rather three Persons who are inseparable, co-eternal, co-equal, and eternally united in one Divine Being.

# CHAPTER ELEVEN

# 1 TEMPTED

The four men who recorded the life of Christ all stated that Jesus lived a very humble life. Jesus himself said,

> "The foxes have holes and the birds of the air have nests, but the Son of Man has nowhere to lay His head."    Luke 9:58 NASB

Jesus made no attempt to use his Godness to soften life or to shelter himself from difficulty. He experienced hardships and temptations like any other human.

> Then Jesus was led up by the Spirit into the wilderness to be tempted by the devil.* And after fasting forty days and forty nights, he was hungry.
>
> Matthew 4:1-2 ESV

*Devil means false accuser, slanderer

Although he was God, Jesus was also a real man with real physical needs. His body was crying out for food.

> And the tempter came and said to him, "If you are the Son of God, command these stones to become loaves of bread."
>
> Matthew 4:3 ESV

## SUSTENANCE

The same tempter who had seduced Adam and Eve into eating the forbidden fruit was now suggesting that Jesus do something that everyone would understand, namely, take care of his physical well-being. It also seemed like a prime opportunity for Jesus to prove who He really was. If he was YAHWEH then he had created the world simply by speaking it into existence. To turn stones into bread would be a simple matter. But there was a catch. To do so, he would be following Satan's orders.

> But [Jesus] answered, "It is written, 'Man shall not live by bread alone, but by every word that comes from the mouth of God.'"
>
> Matthew 4:4 ESV

Jesus responded to Satan by quoting the Bible, God's written word. He said it was more important to follow the LORD than to take care of physical needs. This is a significant statement, as many people are so concerned about this physical life that they ignore their spiritual well-being. Jesus said,

> "For what will it profit a man if he gains the whole world, and loses his own soul?"    Mark 8:36 NKJV

### Safety

*Then the devil took him to the holy city [or Jerusalem] and had him stand on the highest point of the temple. "If you are the Son of God," he said, "throw yourself down. For it is written: `He will command his angels concerning you, and they will lift you up in their hands, so that you will not strike your foot against a stone.'"*
Matthew 4:5-6 NIV

This time the challenge was blatant. *"Prove it! Prove that you are God! If you fall, the angels will save you!"*

Satan was quoting a passage found in the Psalms of King David. The Devil loves religion, and quoting the Bible is a favourite trick of his. The problem was that Satan was not quoting Scripture accurately. He was selecting only the portion that suited his purposes. He had previously done this with Adam and Eve in the Garden of Eden and now he was trying it on Jesus.

Once again Jesus answered Satan's temptation by quoting the Bible, only he quoted it correctly. He did not need to prove to Satan that he was God—Satan was acutely aware of that fact!

*Jesus said to him, "Again it is written, 'You shall not put the Lord your God to the test.'"*
Matthew 4:7 ESV

### Status

*Again, the devil took him to a very high mountain and showed him all the kingdoms of the world and their glory. And he said to him, "All these I will give you, if you will fall down and worship me."*
Matthew 4:8-9 ESV

*Wasn't this what Jesus wanted—for people to follow him?* Yes it was, but what wasn't mentioned was the fact that if Jesus worshipped Satan then Jesus would also be serving the Devil. Worship and service always go together. You can't divide the two. But Satan's ploy did not work. Again, Jesus quoted Scripture:

*Jesus said to him, "Away from me, Satan! For it is written: 'Worship the Lord your God, and serve him only.'"*
Matthew 4:10 NIV

Doctor Luke wrote that...

*When the devil had finished all this tempting, he left him until an opportune time.*
Luke 4:13 NIV

Satan was still determined to destroy Jesus. Though the Devil had failed in this attack, in his overall scheme to defeat Y*AHWEH*, it must have seemed to him that he had experienced a measure of success—John the Baptist had been thrown into jail.[1]

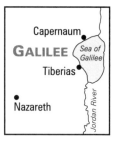

> Now when Jesus heard that John had been imprisoned, he went into Galilee … he moved from Nazareth to make his home in Capernaum by the sea …  Matthew 4:12-13 NET

---

### SINLESS

The Scripture says that Jesus was …

> … tempted in every way, just as we are—yet was without sin.
> Hebrews 4:15 NIV

True and false prophets have come and gone but none have claimed to be sinless. The Bible records the lives of many people who confessed their sinfulness or were revealed as sinners. But Jesus never did. Even those who were closest to him and were most likely to know of any character flaws, wrote that Jesus …

> … committed no sin, Nor was deceit found in His mouth.
> 1 Peter 2:22 NKJV

When speaking Jesus neither exaggerated nor understated. As he lived life, his righteousness was evident for all to see. Just as we saw that Y*AHWEH* was perfect, so Jesus was sinless.

---

# 2 POWER

People are not inclined to trust a person who claims to be God. Such a declaration is generally received with skepticism, derision, and questions about one's mental stability. Even having a prophet like John the Baptist announce your arrival would not make it easier. The Israelites of Jesus' day were not gullible—they firmly believed that Y*AHWEH* was a spirit and they must worship him alone. They would not be prone to worshipping a "man."

When Jesus first pointed out to a crowd how he had fulfilled a Messianic prophecy,

> *All the people in the synagogue were furious … They got up, drove him out of the town, and took him to the brow of the hill on which the town was built, in order to throw him down the cliff. But he walked right through the crowd and went on his way.*  Luke 4:28-30 NIV

It's not an overstatement to say that Jesus was facing a very skeptical audience.

From the very beginning Jesus didn't push his *Godness* on people. Rather, he allowed people to slowly come to that conclusion by observing his sinless life, his incredible miracles, and the way he fulfilled prophecy. In the pages to come we can only touch on a few of the amazing things Jesus did, but the Bible records enough to fill four books. According to one prophet:

> *Jesus did many other things as well. If every one of them were written down, I suppose that even the whole world would not have room for the books that would be written.*  John 21:25 NIV

**Authority**

After John was put in prison Jesus went into Galilee, proclaiming the good news of God.

> *Then they went to Capernaum. When the Sabbath came, Jesus went into the synagogue and began to teach. The people there were amazed by his teaching, because he taught them like one who had authority, not like the experts in the law.*
> Mark 1:21-22 NET

Those who heard Jesus knew there was something very unusual about him. He spoke with authority—as one in the know, as one in charge. But what's so great about that!? We've all tangled with sales people who are so convincing, they could sell a bald man a comb! What made Jesus so different?

> *In the synagogue there was a man possessed by a demon, an evil spirit. He cried out at the top of his voice, "Ha! What do you want with us, Jesus of Nazareth? Have you come to destroy us? I know who you are—the Holy One of God!"*  Luke 4:33-34 NIV

One of Satan's angels was living inside this man—with the man's consent. The evil spirit knew who Jesus was, calling him *"the Holy One of God!"*

> *Jesus cut him short. "Be quiet!"*  Luke 4:35 NLT

Since demons always twist the truth, Jesus did not want them perceived as a reliable source for his true identity. Jesus shut the demon up and told the evil spirit to…

> "Come out of the man!"                                    *Luke 4:35 NLT*

Jesus did not request the demon to leave of his own free will; he ordered him out! No doubt all those present watched closely. Who was stronger—Jesus or the demon? Who had the real power? Doctor Luke wrote:

> …the demon threw the man to the floor as the crowd watched; then it came out of him without hurting him further.
>                                                           *Luke 4:35 NLT*

What made Jesus' words so different was that his life and actions backed up what he said.

> All the people were amazed and said to each other, "What is this teaching? With authority and power he gives orders to evil spirits and they come out!"                      *Luke 4:36 NIV*

Casting a demon out of a man was no problem for Jesus. At the beginning of time he had cast one-third of the angels out of Heaven because they had sinned. But even this "small" miracle made the headlines.

> And the news about him spread throughout the surrounding area.
>                                                           *Luke 4:37 NIV*

For those who were watching—and the crowds were immense—his miracles revealed that Jesus was not just a man. He had to be something more.

---

The struggle between good and evil is not a balanced one. Jesus, the Creator God, is far more powerful than Satan, a created being.

---

### POWER

One type of miracle Jesus performed on a regular basis was the healing of the sick. As I have travelled the world, it has been common to find those who claim to be faith healers, shamans, medicine men or medicine women. Whether through incantations or prayer, placing hands on the sick or tying on charms, shouting *"Be healed!"* or mumbling secret power words, they appear to have some success.

I have noticed, however, of those who claimed to have been healed, none of them were disfigured before the healing. They weren't crippled or missing limbs. Usually they had an internal problem making it difficult to verify that true healing had occurred.

So the question we must ask ourselves is this, *"Was Jesus any different than a faith healer?"* It's something we need to think about as we look at his life. Perhaps it is significant that a doctor recorded the following story. Luke wrote:

> And it happened when he was in a certain city, that … a man
> who was full of leprosy saw Jesus.          Luke 5:12 NKJV

There was no mistaking that this man was very ill. He was ridden with leprosy—a horribly mutilating disease that in ancient times had no cure. It was a death sentence—a slow one. Doctor Luke wrote that when the leper saw Jesus, he …

> … fell on his face and implored him, saying, "Lord, if you are
> willing, You can make me clean."          Luke 5:12 NKJV

It was commendable of the leper to say this of Jesus, but people have been saying this of healers for centuries. To say that Jesus could heal him was one thing, but was it true? Did Jesus have the power to remove such a disease—to bring healing?

> Then Jesus, moved with compassion, stretched out His hand
> and touched him, and said to him, "I am willing…"
> Mark 1:41 NKJV

That touch and those words must have electrified the on-lookers.

## THE TOUCH

According to the culture of that day, a leper was required to shout *"unclean"* whenever anyone approached. If a leper was downwind, then you could come within 2 metres (6 feet) of him, but if the leper was upwind, then not even 60 metres (130 feet) was considered safe enough. Lepers were not to be touched. They lived in a vacuum, empty of any expression of love. Yet, the Bible says Jesus was filled with compassion and he deliberately reached out and touched the leper. The Greek word translated *touched* has the idea of *adhering to, clinging to*. Perhaps Jesus put his arm around the leper and pulled him close. We don't know for sure, but you can imagine what that little gesture of affection meant to this love-starved man. Of course, *caring love* is part of the LORD's perfect nature. It's just the way he is.

But just because Jesus said he was willing to heal the leper, and just because he was compassionate did not mean the sick man would be healed.

I remember visiting a huge leper colony. I agonized over the sight of disfigured people, but even if the whole colony believed I could heal them, it would have been misplaced trust. I was willing, I was compassionate, but I was powerless. So, the big question was, *"Did Jesus also have the **power**?"*

## THE WORDS

You can see the crowd pressing around, jostling to stay the required distance from the leper, yet straining to see. Would there be incantations, charms, or secret words? The answer was, "No." Instead, Jesus simply spoke. He said to the leper,

> *"Be clean!" The leprosy left him at once, and he was clean.*
> Mark 1:41-42 NET

This was no partial healing of some internal disease. What had happened was obvious to all. The leper had been instantly and completely healed. Of course, as far as the LORD was concerned, this was nothing extraordinary—he had created man in the first place, so healing a body was nothing dramatic to him. But it certainly had an impact on those watching. They had witnessed something very remarkable.

There is one more point of interest here. According to Jewish law, when Jesus touched the leper, *Jesus* would have been considered *unclean*, but instead the opposite happened. Jesus touched the leper, and the *leper* became *clean*. Doctor Luke wrote that…

> *…the news about Him was spreading even farther, and large crowds were gathering to hear Him and to be healed of their sicknesses.*
> Luke 5:15 NASB

The prophets went on record as having witnessed Jesus heal all sorts of nasty ailments of people who were obviously ill or severely crippled. No man was ever sent away because his disease was incurable. Jesus even raised the dead!

But his miracles were not entertainment for the local populace. Jesus' teachings and compassion revealed his character, and the miracles verified that both he and his message were from Heaven. Yes, he was a man, but he was also God.

# 3 BORN AGAIN

*Now [there was] a certain man, a Pharisee named Nicodemus,*
*who was a member of the Jewish ruling council.* John 3:1 NET

Nicodemus was a man of status. He was a member of the Sanhedrin, the Jewish ruling council that advised the Romans on local law.

*[He] came to Jesus at night and said to him, "Rabbi,\* we know that you are a teacher who has come from God. For no one could perform the miraculous signs that you do unless God is with him."* John 3:2 NET

\*Rabbi is the name for a Jewish religious teacher. To call a person *Rabbi* implied respect.

Nicodemus was skeptical but he also knew there was something different about Jesus. He figured God had to enter into the equation somehow, but he still had a lot of questions.

But Jesus was concerned about something different—Nicodemus' soul. He knew Nicodemus thought he was *good-enough-for-God*—that he was trusting in his own goodness because he kept the Law of Moses meticulously. He also knew that Nicodemus prided himself in being part of the *Chosen People*.

*Jesus declared, "I tell you the truth, no one can see the kingdom of God unless he is born again."* John 3:3 NIV

## BORN AGAIN?

This was not as some think—Jesus was not speaking of reincarnation. Rather, Jesus knew that Nicodemus was trusting in his Jewish ancestry to make himself acceptable to God. Jesus wanted to show him that his faith was placed in the wrong object—the wrong birth. So Jesus told him, *"You must be born again."* This really unsettled Nicodemus.

*"How can a man be born when he is old?" Nicodemus asked. "Surely he cannot enter a second time into his mother's womb to be born!"*

*Jesus answered, "I tell you the truth, no one can enter the kingdom of God unless he is born of water and the Spirit. Flesh gives birth to flesh, but the Spirit gives birth to spirit. You should not be surprised at my saying, `You must be born again.'"*
John 3:4-7 NIV

When Nicodemus was born as an infant—born of water or born of the flesh—he had entered the world in a spiritually dead condition.

Nicodemus needed a second birth if he was to go to Heaven. He needed new life—a spiritual beginning. Jesus continued by explaining just how that second birth occurred.

> *"For God so loved the world that he gave his one and only Son, that whoever believes in him shall not perish but have eternal life."*
> John 3:16 NIV

When Nicodemus transferred *trust in himself* to *faith in Jesus*, then he would be born again with a spiritual birth—he would have eternal life.

## EVERLASTING LIFE

ETERNAL LIFE

But there was more. Jesus was promising eternal life not just to Nicodemus, but to *whoever believes* in him! The angel had instructed Mary and Joseph to name their son *Jesus* because that name meant YAHWEH is our DELIVERER. And now Jesus was saying he would deliver mankind from the penalty of sin—eternal punishment in the Lake of Fire.

> *"For God did not send his Son into the world to condemn the world, but that the world should be saved through him."*
> John 3:17 NET

Jesus had not come to earth to judge it. Rather, he had come to save the world from all the tragedy that Satan, sin, and death had brought. All people needed to do was reverse the choice Adam and Eve had made in the Garden of Eden. Instead of trusting Satan and self, they needed to trust the LORD JESUS CHRIST.

> *"The one who believes in him is not condemned. The one who does not believe has been condemned already, because he has not believed in the name of the one and only Son of God."*
> John 3:18 NET

## NO MIDDLE GROUND

Jesus said that those who put their faith in him would not be judged as sinners. But those who did not trust in him were already under judgment. There was no middle ground. One could not say, *"I'll think about it,"* and comfortably remain in a gray zone. One either chose to believe, or remained an unbeliever. To make no choice was, in effect, to make a choice.

ETERNAL JUDGMENT

Also, there was no need to wait until death to find out one's eternal destiny. Jesus was emphatic. People were under judgment, bound for the Lake of Fire, until they put their trust in Jesus to deliver them. Then they would have eternal life. This was the promise Jesus was making, and as we have seen along the way, the Lord has a long history of keeping promises.

> *"I tell you the … truth, the one who hears my message and believes the one who sent me has eternal life and will not be condemned, but has crossed over from death to life."*
>
> John 5:24 NET

Jesus was not ignoring the judgment of sin. He knew that not everyone would trust in him. Many would choose not to do so for their own reasons. But he was offering a choice. He was offering eternal life.

# 4 The Light

Jesus continued his conversation with Nicodemus.

> *"This is the judgement, that the Light has come into the world, and men loved darkness rather than the Light, for their deeds were evil."*
> John 3:19 NASB

Nicodemus knew that the ancient prophets had written that in the new world to come,

> *… the Lord will be your everlasting light …*    Isaiah 60:20 NKJV

It was clear that Yahweh was that "everlasting light." And yet here Jesus was saying that,

> *"Light has come into the world …"*    John 3:19 NASB

You can see Nicodemus trying to process this information. *What did Jesus mean by this? Had God entered the world in some special way?* Nicodemus needed time to think.

Later, Jesus was to put it in plain words. He said,

> *"I am the light of the world."*    John 8:12 NKJV

Jesus was the *light* who had come into the world. Just as Yahweh created light so we could see our way along a physical path, now he had come to earth to light the way to the spiritual path that leads to Heaven. Mankind had a choice—we could continue to stumble around in the darkness, trusting our own ideas and religions, or we could trust what Jesus said and have the darkness removed from our understanding. Jesus promised,

> *"Whoever follows me will not walk in darkness, but will have the light of life."*
> John 8:12 ESV

## I Am

One can sympathize with the Jewish people as they tried to grasp the identity of Jesus. After all, here he was, looking very much like any other man, but … well … he just wasn't a mere man. And his claims?! Why, they were outrageous. For example, he said he had lived forever!

On one occasion Jesus supported this claim by harkening back to the time of Abraham, mentioning that he had existed back then. The Pharisees were appalled.

> *"You are not yet fifty years old, and have you seen Abraham!"*
>
> *Jesus said to them, "Truly … I say to you, before Abraham was, I am!"*                                John 8:57-58 ESV

Those listening to Jesus knew that he was claiming to be the LORD YAHWEH himself—the eternal self-existent *I AM!* They now had three choices:

1.   They could believe Jesus was telling the truth and worship him as the LORD YAHWEH, or …

2.   They could reject him and his message; in essence, call him a liar, a fake, an evil man—in which case, according to their law, they should stone him to death for claiming to be God, or …

3.   They could label him as mad, insane, a lunatic whose mind was gone—a sad case where pity would be in order.

These were the choices the Pharisees had to grapple with. Today there are those who would want to add a fourth choice:

4.   They want to believe that Jesus was a great moral teacher, an ascended master, a guru of the highest order, but nothing more—certainly not the Supreme Being.

But this fourth option is not an option at all. C. S. Lewis (1898-1963), author of the *Chronicles of Narnia* and distinguished professor at Cambridge University, clearly articulated this when he wrote:

*I am trying here to prevent anyone saying the really foolish thing that people often say about Him: "I'm ready to accept Jesus as a great moral teacher, but I don't accept His claim to be God." That is the one thing we must not say. A man who was merely a man and said the sort of things Jesus said would not be a great moral teacher. [Jesus said he was YAHWEH, the only way to Heaven.] He would either be a lunatic—on*

*a level with the man who says he is a poached egg—or else he would
be the Devil of Hell. You must make your choice: Either this man was,
and is, the Son of God, or else a madman or something worse.*

Then Lewis added:

*You can shut Him up for a fool, you can spit at Him and kill Him as
a demon; or you can fall at His feet and call Him Lord and God. But
let us not come up with any patronizing nonsense about His being
a great human teacher. He has not left that open to us. He did not
intend to.*

Lewis had once been an agnostic—one who claims it is impossible
to know whether there is a God or not—but through his study of
Scripture he became convinced that Jesus was God himself.

The Pharisees made their choice about Jesus' claim to be YAHWEH.
The Bible says,

> *… they picked up stones to throw at him, but Jesus hid himself
> and went out …*                                                    John 8:59 ESV

# 5 REJECTED

> *A few days later, when Jesus again entered Capernaum, the
> people heard that he had come home. So many gathered that
> there was no room left, not even outside the door, and he
> preached the word to them. Some men came, bringing to him
> a paralytic, carried by four of them.*                           Mark 2:1–3 NIV

This was a familiar scenario wherever Jesus went. As soon as he
put in an appearance, the sick and lame began to arrive. In this
case, four men brought a paralyzed friend.

> *Since they could not get him to Jesus because of the crowd,
> they made an opening in the roof above Jesus and, after digging
> through it, lowered the mat the paralyzed man was lying on.*
> Mark 2:4 NIV

The houses of the time were typically flat-roofed. Stairs led to
the top, making it a cool place to relax in the evening. When
the four men could not get close to Jesus, they simply went up
on the roof, tore it open and lowered the paralyzed man down
in front of Jesus. I say "simply," but that only applies to getting
up on the housetop. Tearing up a roof of sun-baked clay must
have been an ordeal. You can imagine the dust and chunks
of packed earth that rained down on those inside. Of course,

Jesus' lesson was interrupted. Everyone stared at the ceiling wondering what was going on. As the faces of the determined men came into view, probably Jesus' audience took to yelling and carrying on: *"For crying out loud! Where's your respect?! We're covered in dust! You're wrecking the house!"* But Jesus saw something different.

> When Jesus saw their faith he said, "Friend, your sins are forgiven."
>
> Luke 5:20 NET

Jesus was first concerned about the inward person, the heart. It was no problem for him to forgive sin. He is God. But some of his audience had trouble accepting that fact. Though they did not express anything out loud, their thoughts were hostile.

> Then the experts in the law and the Pharisees began to think to themselves, "Who is this man who is uttering blasphemies? Who can forgive sins but God alone?"    Luke 5:21 NET

They were right—only God can forgive sin!

> But Jesus, aware of their reasonings, answered and said to them, "Why are you reasoning in your hearts?"    Luke 5:22 NASB

Since the LORD is all-knowing, Jesus knew what they were thinking and he told them so. You can imagine the Pharisees' mortification. They probably reeled back in their minds trying to remember their thoughts during the previous ten minutes. One thing was certain—Jesus could read their minds! But Jesus wasn't trying to impress them. He had a question:

> "Which is easier, to say to the paralytic,
>
> 1. `Your sins are forgiven,' or to say,
>
> 2. `Stand up, take your stretcher and walk'?"    Mark 2:9 NET

## TO FORGIVE SIN

A lawyer could not have framed a more difficult question. You can see the Pharisees trying to grasp the inevitable conclusions. Jesus answered their query without them asking.

> "But that you may know that the Son of Man has authority on earth to forgive sins"—he said to the man who was paralyzed—"I say to you, rise, pick up your bed and go home." And immediately he rose up before them and picked up what he had been lying on and went home, glorifying God. And amazement seized them all, and they glorified God and were filled with awe, saying, "We have seen extraordinary things today."    Luke 5:24-26 ESV

## Working on the Sabbath

Jesus' constant rebukes must have been galling to the Pharisees. They were losing face. Hoping to catch Jesus in some act of blatant sin, they began to keep a close eye on him.

> Another time he went into the synagogue, and a man with a shriveled hand was there. Some of them were looking for a reason to accuse Jesus, so they watched him closely to see if he would heal him on the Sabbath. *Mark 3:1-2 NIV*

According to the Law, no one was to work on the Sabbath. To do such work was to break God's Law and that would be sin. In the Pharisees' minds, *work* included such things as performing the service of a doctor. The Law did not say it was wrong to tend the sick on this day, but the Pharisees had encircled the Ten Commandments with their own list of rules, and those precepts had taken on the authority of Scripture. So they watched to see if Jesus would heal the man, if he would work on the Sabbath. Knowing the Pharisees' scheme to entrap him, Christ could have avoided a confrontation, but he did not back off.

> Jesus said to the man with the shriveled hand, "Stand up in front of everyone." *Mark 3:3 NIV*

You can see Jesus slowly turn and gaze at those who had plotted to accuse him. The moment is frozen.

> Then Jesus asked them, "Which is lawful on the sabbath: to do good or to do evil, to save life or to kill?" *Mark 3:4 NIV*

There he went again, asking awkward questions! The Pharisees seethed with resentment.

> But they remained silent.

> He looked around at them in anger and, deeply distressed at their stubborn hearts, said to the man, "Stretch out your hand." He stretched it out, and his hand was completely restored. *Mark 3:4-5 NIV*

## Caught in the Act

Jesus had done it. He had worked on the Sabbath! The Pharisees had caught him in the act.

> Then the Pharisees went out and began to plot with the Herodians how they might kill Jesus. *Mark 3:6 NIV*

Normally such an alliance would have been unthinkable. The Herodians were a political party that supported the rule of Herod and the Romans. On the other hand, the Pharisees despised the Romans—but they hated Jesus even more. If they were going to kill him, they would need Rome's help.

The religious leaders had rejected Jesus. As far as they were concerned, he could not be THE PROMISED DELIVERER.

# 6 THE TWELVE

*Jesus withdrew … and a great crowd followed … When the great crowd heard all he was doing, they came to him.*
*Mark 3:7-8 ESV*

Vast throngs followed Jesus around the countryside—some for the teaching, others to see miracles. Out of these many, Jesus chose twelve with whom to spend extra time. At first, people called them *disciples*, or simply *the Twelve*, but eventually they were referred to as *apostles*, meaning *sent ones*—a name given to them by Jesus.

*Jesus went up on a mountainside and called to him those he wanted, and they came to him. He appointed twelve—designating them apostles …*

*Simon (to whom he gave the name Peter); James son of Zebedee, and his brother John (to them he gave the name Boanerges, which means Sons of Thunder); Andrew, Philip, Bartholomew, Matthew, Thomas, James son of Alphaeus, Thaddaeus, Simon the Zealot and Judas Iscariot, who betrayed him.*
*Mark 3:13-14,16-19 NIV*

The disciples were a mixed lot, comprised of a Rome-employed tax collector on one end of the spectrum and, on the other end, a zealot pledged to overthrow the Romans. The remainder included an assortment of fishermen.

Doctor Luke wrote that the disciples shared many experiences with the Messiah.

*Now on one of those days Jesus and His disciples got into a boat, and He said to them, "Let us go over to the other side of the lake." So they launched out. But as they were sailing along He fell asleep; and a fierce gale of wind descended on the lake, and they began to be swamped and to be in danger.*
*Luke 8:22-23 NASB*

We need to remember that many of the disciples were veteran fishermen. They had often weathered storms on the Sea of Galilee, but this storm was unusually violent. You can imagine the dark sky, the raging wind, the furious waves, the driving rain. With foaming water flooding the boat, the terrified...

> ...disciples went and woke him up, shouting, "Master, Master, we're going to drown!"
> Luke 8:24 NLT

You can see the frightened disciples babbling almost incoherently as they shook Jesus awake. He sat up, pulled himself to his feet, and then with a firm, authoritative voice,

> ...rebuked the wind and the surging waves, and they stopped, and it became calm.
> Luke 8:24 NASB

In the startling silence you can hear the rigging squeak, the lap of calm water gently sloshing against the hull of the still-rocking boat. Though the wind and waves were calm, the disciples' hearts were still thumping. As the boat peacefully drifted, Jesus...

> ...asked them, "Where is your faith?"
> Luke 8:25 NLT

In other words, *"Don't you trust me?"* You can see the disciples, drenched in perspiration, swallowing hard, looking at Jesus, then squinting out at the lake, and then back again at the tranquil Messiah. Who broke the silence first, Doctor Luke did not record, but...

> They were fearful and amazed, saying to one another, "Who then is this, that He commands even the winds and the water, and they obey Him?"
> Luke 8:25 NASB

In God's way of thinking it wasn't much of a miracle, not when you consider he had created the wind and the waves in the first place. But Jesus calmed more than wind and waves—he also calmed pounding hearts. Jesus said,

> "Do not let your hearts be troubled. Trust in God; trust also in me."
> John 14:1 NIV

All they needed to do was trust him.

The English language has an interesting expression. We say if something *"walks like a duck and quacks like a duck, then it must be a duck."* This expression is far too frivolous to apply to Jesus, but it does illustrate the process of thinking that drove the disciples to certain conclusions. *Jesus displayed the power of God, he spoke with the authority of God, he was sinless like God—therefore he must be God.* In theological terms, Jesus Christ was:

❖ True Humanity—Not just a body indwelt by God.

❖ Undiminished Deity—Not a minor scaled-down God.

❖ United in one person—100% God and 100% human at the same time—but sinless.

❖ Without Confusion—Not part animal, part God, or any other combination. The Creator-creation distinction remained.

## 7 THE BREAD

The Bible says the LORD restricted the God-side of his nature when he became man. Nonetheless, you see it shining through his humanity over and over again as he went about his daily life.

*After this Jesus went away to the other side of the Sea of Galilee, which is the Sea of Tiberias. And a large crowd was following him, because they saw the signs that he was doing on the sick. Jesus went up on the mountain, and there he sat down with his disciples. Now the Passover, the feast of the Jews, was at hand.*

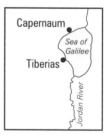

*Lifting up his eyes, then, and seeing that a large crowd was coming toward him, Jesus said to Philip, "Where are we to buy bread, so that these people may eat?"* John 6:1-5 ESV

Jesus was asking questions again. He wanted Philip to analyze the situation. It was another one of those *will-you-trust-me* tests.

*Philip answered him, "Two hundred denarii [eight months wages] would not buy enough bread for each of them to get a little."*

*One of his disciples, Andrew, Simon Peter's brother, said to him, "There is a boy here who has five barley loaves and two fish, but what are they for so many?"* John 6:7-9 ESV

You can't help but wonder if Andrew was like a small boy hinting to his father, hoping that Jesus could do something.

*Jesus said, "Have the people sit down." (Now there was a lot of grass in that place.) So the men sat down, about five thousand in number. Then Jesus took the loaves, and when he had given thanks, he distributed the bread to those who were seated. He then did the same with the fish, as much as they wanted.*

*John 6:10-11 NET*

The biblical account is stated so matter-of-factly that you almost miss what happened. Jesus had just fed a massive crowd with a boy's lunch. This is not a lesson in exponential multiplication. Jesus divided the bread and fish among his twelve disciples, and they apportioned it to five thousand men—the women and children would have been in addition to this number. Although this miracle was nothing big for the LORD—he had created the wheat and the fish in the first place—it had staggering implications.

*Now when the people saw the miraculous sign that Jesus performed, they began to say to one another, "This is certainly the Prophet who is to come into the world." John 6:14 NET*

### MAKE JESUS A KING

The people were so impressed by what they had seen that they decided they would forcibly install Jesus as their king. But Jesus was not interested in starting an earthly kingdom though there would be a time for that in the future. For now he was seeking to rule people's hearts.

*Then Jesus, because he knew they were going to come and seize him by force to make him king, withdrew again up the mountainside alone.*

*When they found him on the other side of the lake, they said to him, "Rabbi, when did you get here?"*

*Jesus replied, "I tell you the solemn truth, you are looking for me not because you saw miraculous signs, but because you ate all the loaves of bread you wanted. John 6:15,25-26 NET*

## WRONG MOTIVES

Well, there you have it. Jesus could see that the people only wanted him to be king so that they could get free food. Jesus said,

> "Do not work for food that disappears, but for food that remains to eternal life—the food which the Son of Man will give to you. For God the Father has put his seal of approval on him."
>
> John 6:27 NET

The food they ate could only sustain life for a short time. Sooner or later, they would all die. Therefore, Jesus said their goal in life should be to pursue that which would give them eternal life.

> So then they said to him, "What must we do to accomplish the deeds God requires?"
>
> John 6:28 NET

The people wanted to know what sort of work they would have to do to earn everlasting life.

> Jesus replied, "This is the deed God requires—to believe in the one whom he sent."
>
> John 6:29 NET

Jesus said that they only needed to *believe*; they only needed to trust in him to be their Saviour. That was all. It was simply reversing the choice made in the Garden of Eden. Instead of trusting themselves or Satan, the people needed to trust the LORD.

> So they said to him, "Then what miraculous sign will you perform, so that we may see it and believe you?"
>
> John 6:30 NET

What was that? They were asking Jesus for a sign to prove that he was God, as if feeding the five thousand with a boy's lunch was not enough! What they were really asking for was another free meal, another loaf of bread.

> Then Jesus said to them, "Most assuredly, I say to you … My Father gives you the true bread from heaven. For the bread of God is He who comes down from heaven and gives life to the world."
>
> Then they said to Him, "Lord, give us this bread always."
>
> And Jesus said to them, "I am the bread of life. He who comes to Me shall never hunger, and he who believes in Me shall never thirst.
>
> John 6:32-35 NKJV

Just as the Maker of all things had created food and water to fill our hungry bellies, so now, as the *Bread of Life,* he had come down from Heaven to fill the hunger that gnaws at the soul—the hunger to somehow be made right with our Creator.

# CHAPTER TWELVE

# 1 THE PLAN

As you study the life of Jesus, you see him slowly revealing to the disciples his plan and purpose in coming to earth. But there came a day when it was said …

> From that time Jesus began to show his disciples that He must go to Jerusalem, and suffer many things from the elders and chief priests and scribes, and be killed, and be raised up [to life] on the third day.                                   Matthew 16:21 NASB

Jesus did something that is humanly impossible. He foretold how and where he would die. He also described events leading up to his death. But why was Jesus saying this? We will understand more as we continue.

## THE TRANSFIGURATION

One week after Jesus spoke of his death, he took Peter, James and John up a mountain to give them a glimpse of his true being.

> And he was transfigured before them, and his face shone like the sun, and his clothes became white as light. Matthew 17:2 ESV

Jesus' outward form was transformed into the same dazzling light that had filled the *Most Holy Place* of the Tabernacle. The radiance of his majesty had been there all along, but people could not see it.

> …two men were talking with [Jesus], Moses and Elijah, who appeared in glory and spoke of his departure, which he was about to accomplish at Jerusalem.            Luke 9:30-31 ESV

Moses and Elijah discussed with Jesus his coming departure from earth. Peter was astounded by it all. It seems he blurted out whatever idea came to his mind.

> And Peter said to Jesus, "Lord, it is good that we are here. If you wish, I will make three tents here, one for you and one for Moses and one for Elijah." He was still speaking when, behold, a bright cloud overshadowed them, and a voice from the cloud said, "This is my beloved Son, with whom I am well pleased; listen to him."                                  Matthew 17:4-5 ESV

God the Father had spoken from Heaven.

> When the disciples heard this, they fell on their faces and were terrified. But Jesus came and touched them, saying, "Rise, and have no fear." And when they lifted up their eyes, they saw no one but Jesus … as they were coming down the mountain,

> *Jesus commanded them, "Tell no one the vision, until the Son of Man is raised from the dead."*     *Matthew 17:6-9 ESV*

At that time the disciples didn't know what to make of it all, but years later Peter would write:

> *We did not follow cleverly invented stories when we told you about the power and coming of our Lord Jesus Christ, but we were eyewitnesses of his majesty. For he received honor and glory from God the Father when the voice came to him from the Majestic Glory, saying, "This is my Son, whom I love; with him I am well pleased." We ourselves heard this voice that came from heaven when we were with him on the sacred mountain!*
>     *2 Peter 1:16-18 NIV*

# 2 ONE GATE

As Jesus continued his teaching, he often used common day-to-day experiences to illustrate spiritual truths. On one occasion Jesus reminded his listeners of the sort of pen in which sheep were kept. The enclosure was constructed using stones upon which thorny vines were encouraged to grow. The purpose of these brambles was to dissuade wild animals or thieves from crawling over the wall. The pen had only one entrance.

During the day the shepherd would lead his flock out to the pasture for grazing. At night the flock returned to the pen and the shepherd would sleep in the entrance. No one could enter the fold without disturbing the guardian. The shepherd's body literally became the door to the pen.

> *Therefore Jesus said again, "I tell you the truth, I am the gate for the sheep."*     *John 10:7 NIV*

Many centuries before Christ the people of Babel had named their city the *Gate to God*. But on closer examination we saw that the *Gate* they created was simply an elaborate religion based on satanically-inspired ideas.

In contrast to the people of Babel, Jesus said he was the true *Gate to God* and spoke of those who trust him as being sheep, safely secured in the sheep pen of Heaven.

> *"Yes, I am the gate. Those who come in through me will be saved…"*
> John 10:9 NLT

Jesus said that he alone was the gate—there were no other doors. It was only through him that one could be saved from the terrible consequences of sin. It was only through him that one could have eternal life.

> *"The thief comes only to steal and kill and destroy. I came that they may have life and have it abundantly."* John 10:10 ESV

Thieves do not care about the welfare of sheep. The Bible calls them *false teachers.* Some use the Bible to feed a power trip or thicken their wallets. Others claim enlightenment or special revelations and gather followers that purport to know the way to safety. Some deny the spiritual realm as ridiculous and worship science instead. Whatever the case, these "thieves" fabricate a way to live…

> *…a way that seems right to a man, but in the end it leads to death.* Proverbs 14:12 NIV

On the other hand, Jesus said he came to give a full life to those who would trust in Him, a life abundant with joy. Jesus said,

> *"I am the **way**, and the **truth**, and the **life**. No one comes to the Father except through me."*
> John 14:6 ESV

Jesus said:   He is the only *way* to God.
His Word is the only *truth*.
Eternal *life* can only be found in Him.

The Lord emphasized that no one could come to him any other way. Some people believe that all religions are like the many rivers that lead to the sea—it doesn't matter which one you follow, they all arrive at the same place. This idea is very popular, but to be honest and fair to what the Bible teaches, I must point out that Scripture tells us otherwise. It says that just as the shepherd was the only gate to the sheepfold, so Jesus is the *only* way to God. Although Doctor Luke was not a Jew, he wrote that...

> *...there is salvation in no one else, for there is no other name under heaven given among men by which we must be saved.*
> Acts 4:12 ESV

Only Jesus could save a person from the penalty of sin.

# 3 Hell

We do not like being reminded that there is a *penalty for sin*, but the Bible does not pull punches on this subject. On one occasion Jesus related this sad chain of events.

> *"There was a rich man who was clothed in purple and fine linen and who feasted sumptuously every day. And at his gate was laid a poor man named Lazarus, covered with sores, who desired to be fed with what fell from the rich man's table ... even the dogs came and licked his sores. The poor man died and was carried by the angels to Abraham's side.*
> Luke 16:19-22 ESV

ETERNAL
LIFE

For the intent of this study, *Abraham's side* is equivalent to Heaven and is sometimes referred to as *paradise*. Lazarus went to paradise, not because he was poor, but because he trusted the Lord.

> *The rich man also died and was buried. In hell, where he was in torment, he looked up and saw Abraham far away, with Lazarus by his side. So he called to him, 'Father Abraham, have pity on me and send Lazarus to dip the tip of his finger in water and cool my tongue, because I am in agony in this fire.'*
> Luke 16:22-24 NIV

The rich man had gone to Hell, not because he was wealthy, but because he ignored God and lived only for himself while on earth. He begged Abraham for help.

ETERNAL
JUDGMENT

> *"But Abraham said, 'Child, remember that you in your lifetime received your good things, and Lazarus in like manner bad things; but now he is comforted here, and you are in anguish. And besides all this, between us and you a great chasm has been fixed, in order that those who would pass from here to you may not be able, and none may cross from there to us.'"*     Luke 16:25-26 ESV

## IT IS FINAL

The Bible makes it clear that one can only repent—have a change of mind—while here on earth. After a person dies there is no second chance, no opportunity to escape Hell for Heaven. Those who die and do not have their names written in the *Lamb's Book of Life* remain separated from the LORD forever in the Lake of Fire. Nowhere does the Scripture suggest that one can escape from this place of suffering. Even though the rich man cried out for a measure of relief from his torment, there was none. Mercy can only be received during this lifetime. The rich man continued:

> *"'Then I beg you, father, to send him to my father's house—for I have five brothers—so that he may warn them, lest they also come into this place of torment.'"*     Luke 16:27-28 ESV

Even though this man was in terrible agony, he could remember his life on earth. He knew that his five brothers were not right with God and wanted them to be warned. But in spite of his desire to communicate an urgent warning to his still living brothers, he could not connect with them. The Bible is clear that our departed ancestors can neither help nor harm us, nor can they communicate with us—they cannot hear or speak to us. However, demons can pose as departed ancestors and lead us astray.

It is also worth noting that the rich man did not want to be joined by his brothers upon their death. The idea of partying with one's friends in Hell is foreign to the Bible. Those in Hell would not wish it on their worst enemies.

> *"But Abraham said, 'They have Moses and the Prophets; let them hear them.'"*     Luke 16:29 ESV

Abraham told the rich man that his brothers should read the Scripture written by Moses and the prophets—and listen to what they wrote.

*"And he said, 'No, father Abraham, but if someone goes to them from the dead, they will repent.'*

*[Abraham] said to him, 'If they do not hear Moses and the Prophets, neither will they be convinced if someone should rise from the dead.'"*　　　　　　　　　　　　Luke 16:30-31 ESV

The Bible says that if people reject what is written within its pages, they will even reject a messenger returned from the dead.

---

Just as language lacks words to describe Heaven, so it is difficult to describe Hell. It is definitely not a happy place to be. The Bible clearly speaks of it as a real place of eternal punishment—where the occupants never cease to exist, never have a second chance. It is also evident that some are punished more severely than others, based on how they lived life on earth.

---

# 4 Come Out!

*Now a certain man named Lazarus was sick. He was from Bethany, the village where Mary and her sister Martha lived ... So the sisters sent a message to Jesus, "Lord ... the one you love is sick."*　　　　　　　　　　John 11:1,3 NET

This Lazarus was a different man than the one named in the last story. This Lazarus, along with Mary and Martha, were close friends of Jesus. They lived in a little village a couple of kilometres east of Jerusalem. At the time of this event Jesus was on the other side of the Jordan River, a full day's journey from Bethany.

*(Now Jesus loved Martha and her sister and Lazarus.) ... when he heard that Lazarus was sick, he remained in the place where he was for two more days.*　　　　　　　　　John 11:5-6 NET

From a purely human point of view, this made no sense. In our day of quick-response rescue teams, everyone knows that when someone is seriously ill, delays can be fatal. But Jesus stayed where he was for another two days! What was he thinking?

*Then ... he said to his disciples, "Let us go to Judea again."*

*The disciples replied, "Rabbi, the Jewish leaders were just now trying to stone you to death! Are you going there again?"*

*Then Jesus told them plainly, "Lazarus has died, and I am glad for your sake that I was not there, so that you may believe. But let us go to him."*

*When Jesus arrived, he found that Lazarus had been in the tomb four days already. (Now Bethany was less than two miles from Jerusalem, so many of the Jewish people of the region had come to Martha and Mary to console them over the loss of their brother.) So when Martha heard that Jesus was coming, she went out to meet him, but Mary was sitting in the house.*

*Martha said to Jesus, "Lord, if you had been here, my brother would not have died. But even now I know that whatever you ask from God, God will grant you."*   John 11:7-8,14-15,17-22 NET

We are not told what Martha thought Jesus might ask of God, but one thing is abundantly clear—she had faith in him.

*Jesus replied, "Your brother will come back to life again."*

*Martha said, "I know he will come back to life again in the resurrection at the last day."*   John 11:23-24 NET

Martha was not surprised at Jesus' statement. She knew from the Scripture that all people will come back to life, but *that* would occur at the end of this sinful age when everyone will be judged by the LORD. Until then, a person only dies once.

*Jesus said to her, "I am the resurrection and the life; he who believes in Me will live even if he dies, and everyone who lives and believes in Me will never die. Do you believe this?"*

John 11:25-26 NASB

Jesus was saying that Lazarus did not have to wait until the day of judgment to be raised back to life. The LORD was the one who gave life in the first place and therefore had the power to restore life to Lazarus at any moment. Jesus said, *"Do you believe this?"* Martha now had a choice:

1.  She could trust Jesus, believing that what he said was true, or ...
2.  She could consider it foolish talk, the prattle of a lunatic.

Martha made her choice.

*"Yes, Lord," she told him, "I believe that you are the Christ, the Son of God, who was to come into the world."*   John 11:27 NIV

Martha not only believed Jesus, she also affirmed that he was the Christ—*THE PROMISED MESSIAH.*

*And [Jesus] said, "Where have you laid [Lazarus]?"*
*They said to Him, "Lord, come and see."*
*Jesus wept.*                                     John 11:34-35 NKJV

The Bible does not tell us why Jesus cried, but the fact that he wept does show us that Jesus experienced human feelings.

*So the Jews said, "See how he loved him!"*

*But some of them said, "Could not he who opened the eyes of the blind man also have kept this man from dying?"*

*Then Jesus, deeply moved again, came to the tomb. It was a cave, and a stone lay against it.*          John 11:36-38 ESV

The traditional Jewish burial of the day often involved placing the body in a tomb which, over time, became the last resting place of successive generations. A natural cave was commonly used, though sometimes the sepulcher was hewn out of solid rock. These tombs were large; you could stand upright in the ❶ weeping chamber. Inside, ❷ shelves were carved on which to lay the ❸ bodies. A ❹ wheel-shaped rock, weighing several tons, was hewn to tightly seal the entrance. Resting in a ❺ trench, this door could be rolled back and forth. When closed, the door rested in a small hollow in front of the entrance, preventing the stone from rolling open.

*Jesus said, "Remove the stone."*

*Martha, the sister of the deceased, said to Him, "Lord, by this time there will be a stench, for he has been dead four days."*
                                                John 11:39 NASB

There was no doubt that Lazarus was dead, as his body was decaying. Understandably, Martha was reluctant.

*Jesus said to her, "Did I not tell you that if you believed you would see the glory of God?"*

> So they took away the stone. And Jesus lifted up his eyes and said, "Father, I thank you that you have heard me. I knew that you always hear me, but I said this on account of the people standing around, that they may believe that you sent me."
>
> When he had said these things, he cried out with a loud voice, "Lazarus, come out." *John 11:40-43 ESV*

The watching crowd must have held their breath. Was Jesus stronger than death itself? Did he really have power to raise a dead man back to life? A collective gasp swept the crowd!

> The man who had died came out, his hands and feet bound with linen strips, and his face wrapped with a cloth.
>
> Jesus said to them, "Unbind him, and let him go." *John 11:44 ESV*

It was a good thing that Jesus said, "*Lazarus, come out!*" Perhaps if he had only said, "*Come out!*" the whole cemetery would have emptied its dead! Lazarus was alive! His friends had to unwind the long strips of burial clothes before Lazarus was free to walk. There was no doubt that Jesus had performed a tremendous miracle.

> Many of the Jews therefore, who had come with Mary and had seen what he did, believed in him, but some of them went to the Pharisees and told them what Jesus had done.
>
> So the chief priests and the Pharisees gathered the Council* and said, "What are we to do? For this man performs many signs. If we let him go on like this, everyone will believe in him, and the Romans will come and take away both our place and our nation."
>
> *The Council in question was called the Sanhedrin, a group of 71 Jewish leaders.
>
> So from that day on they made plans to put him to death.
> *John 11:45-48,53 ESV*

Some believed, but others plotted. And just as Jesus had said, not even a man returned from the dead could convince those who had rejected the Scriptures. The chief priests and Pharisees had too much at stake—their power and their pride.

---

### Resurrection or Reincarnation

Lazarus genuinely died and then miraculously came back to life in the same body. Later on this body died again and did not return to this life.

Speaking biblically, a *resurrection* is different. A resurrection involves coming back to life in a new body that will never die. That body will spend eternity either in Heaven or in Hell.

*Reincarnation*, the belief that after death a departed soul returns to the earth to live again in the form of another human or animal, is not taught in the Bible. The Scripture clearly teaches the opposite. It says that each person has only one life.

> ...it is appointed for men to die **once** and after this comes judgment...
> *Hebrews 9:27 NASB*

---

# 5 Two Ways

As Jesus travelled the breadth of the land, he often taught parables to make a point. A parable is a story that contains a message.

> ...He spoke this parable to some who trusted in themselves that they were righteous, and despised others: "Two men went up to the temple to pray, one a Pharisee and the other a tax collector.
> *Luke 18:9-10 NKJV*

In the Jewish culture of that day, Pharisees were viewed as being very religious. In contrast, the tax collectors were considered to be crooks. Now here were two people from opposite ends of the moral spectrum, praying in the same place.

> "The Pharisee, standing by himself, prayed thus: 'God, I thank you that I am not like other men, extortioners, unjust, adulterers, or even like this tax collector. I fast* twice a week; I give tithes of all that I get.'

*His fasting, or doing without food, was to give time to prayer. He also gave a tenth of his income to a charitable cause.

> But the tax collector, standing far off, would not even lift up his eyes to heaven, but beat his breast, saying, 'God, be merciful to me, a sinner!'"
> *Luke 18:11-13 ESV*

Jesus used the parable to define the two paths which people walk. There was the *way of the Pharisee* and the *way of the tax collector*.

## THE PHARISEE

The *way of the Pharisee* was followed by those who relied on their own goodness to make themselves acceptable to the LORD. Jesus had strong words for such people.

> *"Isaiah was right when he prophesied about you hypocrites; as it is written: 'These people honor me with their lips, but their hearts are far from me. They worship me in vain; their teachings are but rules taught by men.' You have let go of the commands of God and are holding on to the traditions of men."*    Mark 7:6–8 NIV

The Pharisees believed that by observing religious traditions handed down through the centuries, they could be right with God. Their prayers and offerings, though often done with great fervor, were nothing but ritualism—repetitive, strict adherence to detail and form—empty and dry. But God did not want "robot-like" worship. We saw right from the beginning that God only wanted those who would genuinely worship and trust him. Jesus warned them,

> *"Thus you nullify the word of God by your tradition that you have handed down."*    Mark 7:13 NET

Their religious ceremonies undercut the truth of God's word, making worship a mechanical formula to be followed. Jesus said that these rituals do nothing to make a person acceptable to the LORD, because evil…

> *… come[s] from within, and [defiles] a person.*
> Mark 7:23 ESV

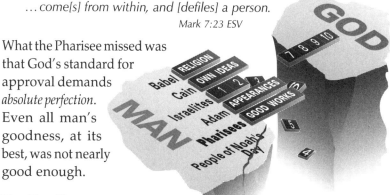

What the Pharisee missed was that God's standard for approval demands *absolute perfection.* Even all man's goodness, at its best, was not nearly good enough.

## THE TAX COLLECTOR

On the other hand, the tax collector was overwhelmed by his sin. He knew that he desperately needed the LORD's forgiveness. That he ought to be punished was not in question—he knew he was wrong. Nonetheless, he begged God to show him mercy— undeserved love. Jesus said of the tax collector,

*"I tell you, this man went down to his house justified,\* rather than the other. For everyone who exalts himself will be humbled, but the one who humbles himself will be exalted."* Luke 18:14 ESV

\*Justified means to be declared righteous.

It is interesting to note that the LORD connects a humble heart to being right with God. It is often pride which causes people to hold back from admitting they are helpless sinners in need of a Saviour. Pride can be an awful pitfall. Think about it! Would not it be a terrible thing to know the truth, but spend eternity in the Lake of Fire because one was too proud to admit that he was wrong and God was right?

Although more people travel the *way of the Pharisee* than the *way of the tax collector,* on occasion you find those who view themselves as exceedingly sinful—convinced that they deserve hell. The truth is, no matter where one is on the moral spectrum, everyone needs to be rescued. Most importantly, Jesus promised that…

*"…the one who comes to Me I will by no means cast out."*
John 6:37 NKJV

*He is also able to save to the **uttermost** those who come to God through Him…* Hebrews 7:25 NKJV

Yes, the LORD will accept even the greatest of sinners who put trust in him. Jesus himself was said to be…

*…a friend of tax collectors and sinners!* Matthew 11:19 NASB

Although Jesus did not love their sin, he did love the sinner. Doctor Luke wrote that…

*…the Son of Man has come to seek and to save that which was lost.* Luke 19:10 NKJV

| The Way of the Pharisee | The Way of the Tax Collector |
| --- | --- |
| Saw himself as righteous | Saw himself as a sinner |
| Trusted in his own goodness | Trusted in God's goodness |
| Offered empty prayers | Begged for mercy |
| Proud | Humble |
| God rejected him | God accepted him |

# 6 SLAVES

The Bible says that sin has a grip on us in a way we often do not recognize. The sorry truth is that all people, whether they are aware of it or not,

> … are slaves to sin, which leads to death … Romans 6:16 NIV

We often get frustrated trying to live a good life. The harder we try to do what is right, the more we seem to fail. Just as we get one part of life under control, we find ourselves falling short in another area. In every way, the sin nature works against our efforts to live right. Sin has wrapped its chains around the life of every human.

> "I tell you the truth, everyone who sins is a slave of sin.
> John 8:34 NLT

Not only are we slaves to sin, the Bible speaks of man as being a slave to Satan. The Devil manipulates man by temptation and pride to accomplish his ends. Indeed, Satan works very hard to convince man that he is inherently good, just like the Pharisee in the preceding story. The Scripture says that people need to …

SLAVE

> … come to their senses and escape from the trap of the devil, who has taken them captive to do his will. 2 Timothy 2:26 NIV

Just because man is a slave to sin and Satan, does not justify a devilish lifestyle. God still holds everyone responsible for the choices they make.

## DETESTABLE

Although one does not need to meddle in the occult to be considered a slave to Satan, the Bible does give a special warning against dabbling with demons. Satan's web of deceit is wide and involves many different forms.

> Let no one be found among you who … practices **divination** or **sorcery**, interprets **omens**, engages in **witchcraft**, or casts **spells**, or who is a **medium** or **spiritist** or who **consults the dead**. Anyone who does these things is detestable to the LORD …
> Deuteronomy 18:10-12 NIV

I will elaborate on each one of these forbidden activities:

❖ **Divination** involves foretelling future events or discovering hidden knowledge. Consulting horoscopes, palm-readers, face-readers, numerology, phrenology, wheels of fortune, the use of crystal balls, dice, shells or cards in fortune-telling, all forms of astrology including the use of the zodiac, every type of trial by ordeal—all are considered divination.

*... diviners envision lies And tell false dreams; They comfort in vain.*
*Zechariah 10:2 NKJV*

❖ **Sorcery** takes divination a step further. It involves the use of power gained from demons especially for the purpose of divining or witchcraft. The evil spirits may be viewed as assistants or they may be invited to possess the sorcerer and use the human body to do the will of the demon.

*Do not practice divination or sorcery.*　　*Leviticus 19:26 NIV*

❖ **Omens** are believed to indicate future events, such as an infant's future personality. Visions, dreams, hunches, presentiments, body twitches, sneezes, animal or plant behavior, the flight of birds or the howling of animals can all be taken as omens. Superstitions related to the right day for a wedding or when to travel would also fall in this category.

❖ **Witchcraft** or **shamanism** involves magic and is often employed to cure sicknesses or relieve stress. Incantations, trances, charms and hallucinogenic drugs are common. Yoga, Reiki, contemplative prayer, and mantras are means of connecting with evil spirits. God forbids both white and black magic.

*... he practiced witchcraft, used divination, practiced sorcery and dealt with mediums and spiritists. He did much evil in the sight of the LORD ...*　　*2 Chronicles 33:6 NASB*

❖ **Spells** are usually some form of spoken words thought to have magical power to bring protection or disaster. Sometimes a lock of hair or a fingernail clipping is employed.

❖ A **Medium** or **Spiritist** functions as a channel of communication between the earthly world and the realm of spirits. Since the Bible says that dead ancestors cannot be contacted by the living, the only spirit a medium can talk to is a demon. Any supposed contact with the dead is the result of a demon pretending to be the deceased.

*"Do not turn to mediums or spiritists; do not seek them out to be defiled by them. I am the LORD your God."* *Leviticus 19:31 NASB*

Often many of the above are combined in a deadly cocktail. To participate in any of these activities is to seek power provided by Satan, who loves and craves the attention. He uses these means to extend his slavery over the individual's life. It's a horrible pit that the LORD warns us to avoid.

## FALSE MESSIAHS

We need to remember that Satan and his legions of demons are masters at deception. They imitate the truth as closely as possible and in the process they deceive multitudes.

> And Jesus answered and said to them: "Take heed that no one deceives you. For many will come in My name, saying, 'I am the Christ,' and will deceive many."  Matthew 24:4-5 NKJV

History books, both ancient and recent, record the stories of those who have claimed to be the Messiah. Scripture says that this is to be expected and will increase as we approach the end of this evil age. Jesus said,

> "Then if anyone says to you, 'Look, here is the Christ!' or 'There!' do not believe it. For false christs and false prophets will rise and show great signs and wonders to deceive…"

> "Therefore if they say to you, 'Look, He is in the desert!' do not go out; or 'Look, He is in the inner rooms!' do not believe it."
> Matthew 24:23-24, 26 NKJV

Remember the story we referred to earlier, about the spy who was to meet another agent in the town square? We stated how certain pieces of identification were used to authenticate the genuine contact. Well, Satan and his demons will perform miracles imitating the true Messiah, but we need not be confused. The real Messiah can be identified by the accurate fulfillment of the ancient prophecies. Only the Jesus of the Bible has ever qualified. The Scripture warns us that…

> … the work of Satan [will be] displayed in all kinds of counterfeit miracles, signs and wonders, and in every sort of evil that deceives those who are perishing. They perish because they refused to love the truth and so be saved.
> 2 Thessalonians 2:9-10 NIV

Just because a person or spirit performs incredible miracles does not mean he is from God. It is healthy to be skeptical.

As we have seen before, the Bible does give guidelines to distinguish truth from error. We are told:

> ... do not believe every spirit, but test the spirits to see whether they are from God, because many false prophets have gone out into the world.　　　　　　　　　　　　　1 John 4:1 NASB

Jesus said,

> "Beware of the false prophets, who come to you in sheep's clothing, but inwardly are ravenous wolves. You will know them by their fruits."　　　　　　　　　　Matthew 7:15-16 NASB

Jesus said we could discern a false prophet by *what he teaches* and *the way he lives*—one or the other will be inconsistent with the Bible. The "fruit" of a prophet's mouth and life will reveal his true identity.

# 7 Betrayed

For three years Jesus taught all who would listen. It seems an incredibly brief span of time, considering everything that happened. Doctor Luke wrote that near the end, Jesus ...

> ... took the twelve aside and said to them, "Behold, we are going up to Jerusalem, and all things that are written by the prophets concerning the Son of Man will be accomplished. For He will be delivered to the Gentiles and will be mocked and insulted and spit upon. They will scourge Him and kill Him. And the third day He will rise again."　　　　　　　Luke 18:31-33 NKJV

No human being can foretell the exact events surrounding his own death. But Jesus was more than a man. He was God. He said he would be the one to fulfill all the events foretold by the ancient prophets.

> The disciples did not understand any of this.　　Luke 18:34 NIV

> After He had said these things, He was going on ahead ... to Jerusalem. When He approached Bethphage and Bethany, near the mount that is called Olivet, He sent two of the disciples, saying, "Go into the village ahead of you; there, as you enter, you will find a colt tied on which no one yet has ever sat; untie it and bring it here. If anyone asks you, 'Why are you untying it?' you shall say, 'The Lord has need of it.'"

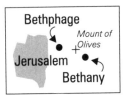

*So those who were sent went away and found it just as He had told them. As they were untying the colt, its owners said to them, "Why are you untying the colt?"*

*They said, "The Lord has need of it."*

*They brought it to Jesus, and they threw their coats on the colt and put Jesus on it.*

*As He was going, they were spreading their coats on the road.*

*As soon as He was approaching, near the descent of the Mount of Olives, the whole crowd of the disciples began to praise God joyfully with a loud voice for all the miracles which they had seen, shouting:"'Blessed is the King who comes in the name of the LORD!' Peace in heaven and glory in the highest!"*

*Luke 19:28-38 NASB*

The enthusiastic crowd was giving Jesus a spur-of-the-moment parade usually reserved to welcome a triumphant Roman conqueror. They were applauding and praising him in hopes that he would oust their Roman oppressors.

Unbeknown to them, they were fulfilling a 500-year-old prophecy. The Prophet Zechariah had written that the Lord Jesus would receive such a welcome.

*Rejoice greatly, O Daughter of Zion! Shout, Daughter of Jerusalem! See, your king comes to you, righteous and having salvation, gentle and riding on a donkey, on a colt, the foal of a donkey.*  *Zechariah 9:9 NIV*

But not everyone was happy with these events. Luke wrote:

*…some of the Pharisees in the crowd said to him, "Teacher, rebuke your disciples." He answered, "I tell you, if they keep silent, the very stones will cry out!"*

*Now when Jesus approached and saw the city, he wept over it, saying, "… the days will come upon you when your enemies will build an embankment against you and surround you and close in on you from every side.*

*They will demolish you—you and your children within your*
*walls—and they will not leave within you one stone on top of*
*another, because you did not recognize the time of your visitation*
*from God."*                                                   Luke 19:39-44 NET

Jesus was foretelling a series of specific events that would happen in 70 AD. As unlikely as it seemed at this point in time, in less than 40 years, Titus, a Roman general, would surround the city of Jerusalem, crush its fortifications, and destroy the Temple to a point where literally not one stone would be left on another.

### The Plot

*It was now two days before the Passover and the Feast of*
*Unleavened Bread. And the chief priests and the scribes were*
*seeking how to arrest him by stealth and kill him, for they said,*
*"Not during the feast, lest there be an uproar from the people."*
                                                              Mark 14:1-2 ESV

From the perspective of the shouting crowd, it was time for Jesus to announce that he was the true King of Israel. But for the religious leaders who were plotting his death, it was an awkward situation. If Jesus needed to be put off the stage, now was the time, but they were afraid of the public reaction. It was obvious that Jesus was very popular.

The city was crammed with people for the Passover, many of whom were expectantly watching Jesus in the hope that he would evict the Romans. But as the hours passed with no official proclamation of his kingship, his hero-status was fast fading.

### The Passover Meal

Jesus instructed two disciples to arrange a room for the feast.

*When it was evening He came with the twelve. As they were*
*reclining at the table and eating, Jesus said, "Truly I say to you*
*that one of you will betray Me—one who is eating with Me."*

*They began to be grieved and to say to Him one by one,*
*"Surely not I?"*

*And He said to them, "It is one of the twelve, one who dips*
*with Me in the bowl."*                                      Mark 14:17-20 NASB

When Jesus chose his twelve disciples three years earlier, he had known that one would be a traitor. It is possible that at that time, the individual in question had not premeditated such a diabolical action, but an ancient prophecy given by King David and recorded

1000 years earlier, revealed the depth of sin to which this man would stoop. David had written from the SAVIOUR's perspective:

> *"Even my close friend in whom I trusted, Who ate my bread, Has lifted up his heel against me."* Psalm 41:9 NASB

## BETRAYED

The traitor was Judas Iscariot. Though he was treasurer for the disciples, he was also a thief. Apparently, he oiled his ambitions and lined his pockets without the disciples being any the wiser. But Jesus knew, and apparently Satan knew it too. He had been watching for a weak link in Jesus' armor, a time and place to crush THE PROMISED SAVIOUR forever. Now Satan saw his opportunity. Judas was willing. As the Passover bread was being served, the Devil made his move.

> *And after Judas took the piece of bread, Satan entered into him.*
> John 13:27 NET

This was satanic possession. Judas was allowing the Devil to use his body to accomplish his satanic will.

> *Jesus said to him, "What you are about to do, do quickly." (Now none of those present at the table understood why Jesus said this to Judas ...)* John 13:27-28 NET

> *And Judas went to the chief priests and the officers of the temple guard and discussed with them how he might betray Jesus. They were delighted and agreed to give him money.* Luke 22:4-5 NIV

## THE BREAD AND THE CUP

This scenario with Judas happened in the middle of the meal. While the traitor went about his diabolical mission, Jesus continued with the supper. It has great significance.

> *While they were eating, [Jesus] took some bread, and after a blessing He broke it, and gave it to [his disciples], and said, "Take it; this is My body."* Mark 14:22 NASB

Obviously, they weren't eating Jesus' flesh, and yet Jesus was saying that the broken Passover loaf—this bread baked without yeast—somehow represented his body. The disciples must have been rather perplexed.

> And when He had taken a cup and given thanks, He gave it to them, and they all drank from it. And He said to them, "This is My blood of the covenant, which is poured out for many."
>
> Mark 14:23-24 NASB

Again the symbolism was similar—Jesus' blood would soon be poured out for many people. We will see the significance of the bread and the cup later on.

> And when they had sung a hymn,* they went out to the Mount of Olives.     Mark 14:26 ESV

*a song praising God

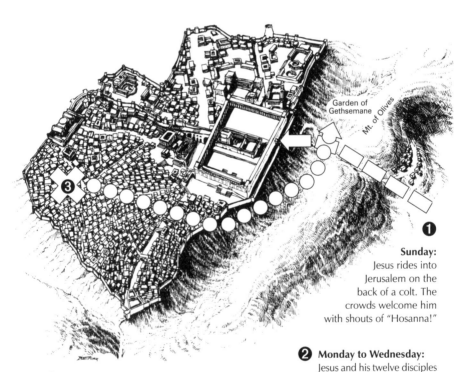

**Sunday:** Jesus rides into Jerusalem on the back of a colt. The crowds welcome him with shouts of "Hosanna!"

❷ **Monday to Wednesday:** Jesus and his twelve disciples spend time in and around Jerusalem and Bethany.

❸ **Thursday Night:** Jesus and his disciples celebrate the Passover together. After singing a hymn they depart for the Garden of Gethsemane, located at the foot of the Mount of Olives.

# CHAPTER THIRTEEN

**1** ARRESTED

**2** TRIED

**3** SCOURGED

**4** CRUCIFIED

**5** RESURRECTED

# 1 ARRESTED

*And they went to a place called Gethsemane. And [Jesus] said to his disciples, "Sit here while I pray." And he took with him Peter and James and John, and began to be greatly distressed and troubled. And he said to them, "My soul is very sorrowful, even to death. Remain here and watch." And going a little farther, he fell on the ground and prayed that, if it were possible, the hour might pass from him. And he said, "Abba,\* Father, all things are possible for you. Remove this cup from me. Yet not what I will, but what you will."*

Mark 14:32–36 ESV

\*a term of endearment similar to Daddy or Papa.

## THE GOD-MAN

Sometimes in emphasizing that Jesus was truly God, it's easy to forget that he was also human. Suffering was not foreign to Jesus—he knew and felt pain. But being God, he also knew the future agony he was about to face. In the intimate language that only a son could have with his dear father, Jesus cried out, *"Abba—Daddy—please find another way."* But then he submitted his human will to his heavenly will and prayed, *"Your will be done."*

*Immediately while He was still speaking, Judas, one of the twelve, came up accompanied by a crowd with swords and clubs, who were from the chief priests and the scribes and the elders.*

*Now he who was betraying Him had given them a signal, saying, "Whomever I kiss, He is the one; seize Him and lead Him away under guard."* Mark 14:43-44 NASB

*Then Jesus, knowing all that would happen to him, came forward and said to them, "Whom do you seek?"*

*They answered him, "Jesus of Nazareth."*

*Jesus said to them, "I am {he}." Judas, who betrayed him, was standing with them.* John 18:4-5 ESV

The word {he} does not appear in the original Greek text. It was supplied to help the English rendering flow better, but in this case it distracts from the significance of what Jesus said. Jesus answered the question with an emphatic *"I AM!"* It could be translated[1] literally, *"I am right now, GOD!"* As we have seen, *I AM* is God's name, and it wasn't just anyone saying it; it was the LORD himself. The effect is worth noting.

*When Jesus said to them, "I am he," they drew back and fell to the ground.* John 18:6 NIV

They didn't simply drop to the ground; they drew back and fell down. Jesus *blew them off their feet* with a mini-burst of his majesty. After the stunned group had clambered to their feet and dusted themselves off…

> …*he asked them again, "Whom do you seek?"*
>
> *And they said, "Jesus of Nazareth."*          John 18:7 ESV

You can almost sense the crowd's respect and fear. Jesus had unsettled the mob. This was not shaping up to be a typical arrest. Their wall of confidence cracked even more when Jesus revealed that he knew the agreed-upon sign of betrayal.

> …*Jesus said to him, "Judas, are you betraying the Son of Man with a kiss?"*          Luke 22:48 NASB
>
> …*Judas immediately went to Him, saying, "Rabbi!" and kissed Him.*          Mark 14:45 NASB

The other eleven disciples were galvanized into action. Simon Peter had a weapon.

> …*one of those who were with Jesus stretched out his hand and drew his sword and struck the servant of the high priest and cut off his ear.*          Matthew 26:51 ESV
>
> *But Jesus said, "No more of this!" And he touched his ear and healed him.*          Luke 22:51 ESV

What can you say? Even in the midst of all the tension, Jesus was thinking of others; he healed the High Priest's servant. It was a short-sighted effort on Peter's part anyway—zeal without knowledge. On a human level, the disciples were greatly outnumbered. You can't help admiring Peter's efforts. At least he tried! But obviously Peter was better with nets than swords. When you aim at the head and get an ear, it tells you something.

### Questions, Questions

Then Jesus asked a question—an uncomfortable question.

> *"Have you come out with swords and clubs to arrest Me, as you would against a robber? Every day I was with you in the temple teaching, and you did not seize Me; but **this has taken place to fulfill the Scriptures**."*          Mark 14:48-49 NASB

God's questions always expose a person's true thoughts, and if the rabble had taken a moment to think, they would have realized the inconsistency of their actions. But they were so fixated in their determination to do away with Christ, even another encounter with the miraculous power of this man did not deter them in the least. Fearing for their lives, the disciples fled into the night.

*And they all left him and fled.* Mark 14:50 ESV

*Then the detachment of troops and the captain and the officers of the Jews arrested Jesus and bound Him.* John 18:12 NKJV

One can hardly read this without feeling some sense of incongruity. Jesus was only one individual. The detachment sent to arrest him would have numbered between 300 and 600 soldiers. In addition, there were Jewish officials, priests, and servants. It was overkill for sure, but you cannot help wondering if deep down inside they felt a poverty of power. They rushed Jesus and bound him. Satan must have been delighted beyond belief.

# 2 TRIED

After the arrest in the garden,

*They led Jesus away to the high priest; and all the chief priests and the elders and the scribes gathered together.*
Mark 14:53 NASB

Temple courts were not held at night. The fact that the Sanhedrin, consisting of seventy-one men, could be assembled so quickly tells you something about the plot. What they were doing was strictly illegal according to their own law.

*Now the chief priests and the whole Council kept trying to obtain testimony against Jesus to put Him to death, and they were not finding any. For many were giving false testimony against Him, but their testimony was not consistent.*

*The high priest stood up and came forward and questioned Jesus, saying, "Do You not answer? What is it that these men are testifying against You?" But He kept silent and did not answer.*

*Again the high priest was questioning Him, and saying to Him, "Are You the Christ, the Son of the Blessed One?"*
Mark 14:55-56,60-61 NASB

## ARE YOU GOD?

The question was black and white: *"Are you the Messiah—THE PROMISED DELIVERER? Are you God or not?"*

> Jesus said, "I am. And you will see the Son of Man sitting at the right hand of the Power, and coming with the clouds of heaven."
> Mark 14:62 NKJV

The High Priest, Caiaphas, knew exactly what Jesus had said. Jesus was claiming to be YAHWEH himself.

> Then the high priest tore his clothes and said, "What further need do we have of witnesses? You have heard the blasphemy! What do you think?"
> Mark 14:63–64 NKJV

Blasphemy was anything that was considered injurious to God's character, and for a mere man to call himself YAHWEH was sacrilege. But Jesus was not a mere man—he was God! However, neither Caiaphas nor the other Jewish leaders believed him, so…

> …they all condemned Him to be deserving of death.
> Mark 14:64 NKJV

But there was a problem. The Sanhedrin did not have the authority to pass a death sentence; only the Romans could do that.

Because night courts were illegal, the Sanhedrin met again just after sunrise to go through the legal motions of trying Jesus. He must have been exhausted. He had not slept all night, and they had given him a severe beating just to make sure he knew who was in control.

> Then the whole body of them got up and brought Him before Pilate.
> Luke 23:1 NASB

## PONTIUS PILATE

Pontius Pilate, governor of Judea, had all the authority of imperial Rome behind him. Since the Jewish courts could not impose the death penalty, they needed Roman sanction. Pilate was their man. The temple leaders knew he was weak-kneed, so a little "persuading" was in order.

> And they began to accuse [Jesus], saying, "We found this man misleading our nation and forbidding to pay taxes to Caesar, and saying that He Himself is Christ, a King." Luke 23:2 NASB

Jesus had never prohibited his followers from paying taxes. In fact, he had said quite the opposite. This was a deliberate lie. On the other hand, it was true that Jesus claimed to be the Messiah!

*So Pilate asked him, "Are you the King of the Jews?"*

*Jesus answered, "My Kingdom is not an earthly kingdom. If it were, my followers would fight to keep me from being handed over to the Jewish leaders. But my Kingdom is not of this world."*
*Luke 23:3; John 18:36 NLT*

Jesus' reign began in the heart. He had no political ambitions.

*"You are a king, then!" said Pilate.*

*Jesus answered, "You are right in saying I am a king. In fact, for this reason I was born, and for this I came into the world, to testify to the truth. Everyone on the side of truth listens to me."*

*"What is truth?" Pilate asked.*
*John 18:37-38 NIV*

Pilate asked the right question, but he was in no mood for listening; he didn't even wait for the answer.

## NOT GUILTY

*With this he went out again to the Jews and said, "I find no basis for a charge against him."*
*John 18:38 NIV*

Pilate mistrusted the priests. As Roman governor, he knew he was hated by the Jews, and he had reason to believe that the priests did not have Caesar's best interests in mind. The Sanhedrin must have some other motive for wanting Jesus dead.

*Then Pilate announced to the chief priests and the crowd, "I find no basis for a charge against this man."*

*But they insisted, "He stirs up the people all over Judea by his teaching. He started in Galilee and has come all the way here."*

*On hearing this, Pilate asked if the man was a Galilean. When he learned that Jesus was under Herod's jurisdiction, he sent him to Herod, who was also in Jerusalem at that time.*
*Luke 23:4–7 NIV*

Pilate had the authority to hear Jesus' case, but the situation was getting uncomfortable. Jesus was being accused of inciting the people to insurrection. How would he explain to his superiors in Rome if Jesus did provoke a riot? It would be easier to dump the whole sorry mess in Herod's lap. Besides, Herod was no friend of his, so Pilate passed the buck.

## HEROD ANTIPAS

Herod Antipas was a son of Herod the Great. As a puppet of Rome, he had been given jurisdiction over Jesus' home province of Galilee. He had travelled to Jerusalem for the yearly Passover festivities. Doctor Luke wrote that...

> *Herod was delighted at the opportunity to see Jesus, because he had heard about him and had been hoping for a long time to see him perform a miracle. He asked Jesus question after question, but Jesus refused to answer.* Luke 23:8-9 NLT

Jesus knew that Herod had no interest in determining the truth. He only wished to be entertained by a miracle, showing his flagrant disrespect for Jesus' character. Jesus did not indulge Herod. Instead, he remained silent.

> *The chief priests and the teachers of the law were standing there, vehemently accusing him. Then Herod and his soldiers ridiculed and mocked him. Dressing him in an elegant robe, they sent him back to Pilate. That day Herod and Pilate became friends—before this they had been enemies.* Luke 23:10–12 NIV

**❸** **Friday Morning Early:**
**❹** Jesus taken to Roman Fortress to appear before Pontius Pilate.

**❹** **Friday Morning:**
**❺** Pilate sends Jesus to
**❹** Herod who returns him to Pilate.

**Thursday Night Late:**
Jesus arrested in the Garden of Gethsemane and taken to the house of the High Priest. It is thought they travelled around the northern wall to avoid Temple traffic.

**Friday Sunrise:**
After appearing before Annas, Caiaphas the High Priest, and the Sanhedrin in a middle-of-the-night session, Jesus is taken to the Temple for a quick court before the Sanhedrin, to formalize accusations.

# 3 SCOURGED

Since his arrest Jesus had been in five court sessions: three Jewish and two Roman. This sixth trial—before Pilate—would be his last. By this time word had spread throughout the city. No longer were the High Priest and Sanhedrin the only ones accusing Jesus. They had been joined by a fickle multitude who only a few days before had shouted, *"Blessed is the King,"* but now vehemently roared, *"Crucify him!"* Pilate was in a dilemma. The more he dealt with Jesus, the more convinced he was that there was something uncommon about this man!

> *Pilate then called together the chief priests and the rulers and the people, and said to them, "You brought me this man as one who was misleading the people. And after examining him before you, behold, I did not find this man guilty of any of your charges against him. Neither did Herod, for he sent him back to us. Look, nothing deserving death has been done by him. I will therefore **punish** and **release him**."*     Luke 23:13-16 ESV

Neither Herod nor Pilate could find Jesus guilty of anything deserving the death penalty. Indeed, it seemed no one could accuse him of any crime. Hoping to appease the crowd, Pilate offered a weak-kneed compromise. It had two parts:

**1. He would whip Jesus:**
This was no ordinary beating. The whip was comprised of a stick with leather thongs affixed to one end. Each thong had a sliver of bone or metal attached to it. The condemned man would have his arms bound and tied above his head to a pole which fully exposed his back to the scourge. As the whip came down, the bone and metal would sink into the flesh. Pulling the whip away virtually stripped the flesh off the back. This type of beating was so severe that often the victim died.

By law a scourging could only be given to a convicted prisoner. Pilate himself had just said that Jesus was innocent. Because a Roman flogging was such a horrible ordeal, it can be assumed that Pilate hoped the whipping would appease Jesus' accusers so that they would accept his next offer.

**2. He would release Jesus:**
It was the local Roman custom to release one convicted criminal during the Passover feast as a gesture of goodwill. Pilate suggested that Jesus be released—after he had been beaten. The crowd was unanimous in their response:

> *But they cried out all together, saying, "Away with this man, and release for us Barabbas!" (He was one who had been thrown into prison for an insurrection made in the city, and for murder.)*
> *Luke 23:18-19 NASB*

Barabbas was legitimately guilty of leading a rebellion and murder. He was on death row awaiting execution. But now the people were calling out for the innocent Jesus to be killed and the guilty Barabbas to be freed.

> *Pilate addressed them once more, desiring to release Jesus, but they kept shouting, "Crucify, crucify him!"*
>
> *A third time he said to them, "Why, what evil has he done? I have found in him no guilt deserving death. I will therefore punish and release him."*
> *Luke 23:20–22 ESV*
>
> *Then Pilate took Jesus and flogged him.*
> *John 19:1 ESV*
>
> *And the soldiers twisted together a crown of thorns and put it on His head, and put a purple robe on Him; and they began to come up to Him and say, "Hail, King of the Jews!" and to give Him slaps in the face.*
> *John 19:2-3 NASB*

 Humiliation was not part of Pilate's sentence. A purple robe was normally worn by royalty. The thorns were a cruel parody of an imperial crown. This was mockery at its worst. Seven hundred years before, the prophet Isaiah had written:

> *He was despised and rejected by men, ... and we esteemed him not.*
> *Isaiah 53:3 NIV*

Pilate went out to the crowd again and said to them,

> *"See, I am bringing him out to you that you may know that I find no guilt in him." So Jesus came out, wearing the crown of thorns and the purple robe. Pilate said to them, "Behold the man!"*
> *John 19:4-5 ESV*

Deep in his heart, Pilate must have known that he was setting aside all justice. No doubt, he had hopes that this lacerated, thorn-crowned, bleeding man might evoke some pity.

> When the chief priests and the officers saw him, they cried out, "Crucify him, crucify him!"
>
> Pilate said to them, "Take him yourselves and crucify him, for I find no guilt in him." John 19:6 ESV

Pilate knew very well that they could do no such thing. The Jewish courts could not impose the death sentence.

> The Jewish leaders replied, "We have a law, and according to our law he ought to die, because he claimed to be the Son of God!"
>
> When Pilate heard what they said, he was more afraid than ever, and he went back into the governor's residence and said to Jesus, "Where do you come from?" John 19:7–9 NET

Pilate had heard earlier that Jesus was from Galilee, thus the reason for having sent him to Herod. Now again, he was asking Jesus where he was from. No doubt, he was feeling a little nervous about someone who claimed to be God! The Greeks believed the gods came down from Mount Olympus to fraternize with man. Perhaps Pilate was wondering if Jesus fit that category. Certainly this was no ordinary criminal. Just the way he handled himself in court demonstrated a peace and confidence that was disconcerting. *Jesus, where are you really from?* But…

> … Jesus gave him no answer. So Pilate said to him, "You will not speak to me? Do you not know that I have authority to release you and authority to crucify you?"
>
> Jesus answered him, "You would have no authority over me at all unless it had been given you from above…"
>
> From then on Pilate sought to release him, but the Jews cried out, "If you release this man, you are not Caesar's friend. Everyone who makes himself a king opposes Caesar."
>
> So when Pilate heard these words, he brought Jesus out and sat down on the judgment seat at a place called The Stone Pavement, and in Aramaic Gabbatha. Now it was the day of Preparation of the Passover. John 19:9–14 ESV

The day of Preparation was when the Passover lamb was killed.

*[Pilate] said to the Jews, "Behold your King!"*

*They cried out, "Away with him, away with him, crucify him!"*

*Pilate said to them, "Shall I crucify your King?" The chief priests answered, "We have no king but Caesar."* John 19:14-15 ESV

This was Israel's final rejection of Jesus as their King. They had chosen the Roman Caesar in place of God.

*…they were insistent, with loud voices asking that He be crucified. And their voices began to prevail. And Pilate pronounced sentence that their demand be granted. And he released the man they were asking for who had been thrown into prison for insurrection and murder, but he delivered Jesus to their will.* Luke 23:23-25 NASB

Barabbas was freed, but Jesus was handed…

*…over to them to be crucified.* John 19:16 NASB

# 4 CRUCIFIED

*So the soldiers took charge of Jesus. Carrying his own cross, he went out to the place of the Skull (which in Aramaic is called Golgotha).[2] Here they crucified him, and with him two others— one on each side and Jesus in the middle.* John 19:16–18 NIV

Crucifixion was a Roman form of capital punishment used only for slaves and criminals. It was a common method of execution, and secular history records hundreds being crucified at one time. Research indicates that there were several different forms:

 **Standing tree:** The victim was backed up to a tree and nailed to it, in whatever shape the branches flowed. Josephus, the first century Jewish historian, records that the Roman soldiers entertained themselves by crucifying captives in unusual positions.[3]

**I-shaped:** A simple post in the ground. Hands were nailed over the head.

**X-shaped:** Two logs planted at angles. The body was splayed out with the hands and feet fixed at four corners.

 **T-shaped:** A pole with a cross bar on the top. This was probably the most common, next to the tree. The arms were stretched out along the top bar.

 **t-shaped:** Usually reserved for criminals of some notoriety. A certificate disclosing one's crime would be tacked to the topmost part of the cross. This was the type on which Jesus was crucified.

The victim was usually stretched out naked. Hands and feet were held in place by nails driven through the wrist and ankle bones. One thousand years earlier, YAHWEH had instructed King David to write a complete Psalm about the way Jesus would die. In it David records God as saying...

> ...they have pierced my hands and my feet.    *Psalm 22:16 NIV*

This was written long before the Romans had come to power, and about 800 years before the Romans adopted crucifixion as one of their official forms of capital punishment.

To this day crucifixion is considered to be the most brutal form of execution. Hanging on out-stretched arms, the pressure on the diaphragm made it impossible for one to breathe. One could inhale only by lifting oneself up, by pulling on the arms, and pushing with the feet to allow room for the diaphragm to work. Of course, this pulling and pushing was done against the excruciating restraint of the nails. Death came by asphyxiation when exhaustion left one unable to lift the body.

> *Pilate also had a notice written and fastened to the cross, which read: "Jesus the Nazarene, the king of the Jews." Thus many of the Jewish residents of Jerusalem read this notice, because the place where Jesus was crucified was near the city, and the notice was written in Aramaic, Latin, and Greek.*
>
> *John 19:19–20 NET*

### GAMBLING

> *When the soldiers had crucified Jesus, they divided his clothes among the four of them. They also took his robe, but it was seamless, woven in one piece from top to bottom. So they said, "Rather than tearing it apart, let's throw dice for it."*
>
> *John 19:23-24 NLT*

Gambling was a distraction from a gory task. As the soldiers sat beneath Jesus' cross, perhaps rolling dice in a helmet, they had no way of knowing they were fulfilling an ancient prophecy.

> This was **to fulfill the Scripture** which says, "They divided my garments among them, and for my clothing they cast lots."
>
> John 19:24 compare Psalm 22:18 ESV

### RIDICULE

As the hours dragged on…

> …the people stood by, watching, but the rulers scoffed at him, saying, "He saved others; let him save himself, if he is the Christ of God, his Chosen One!"
>
> The soldiers also mocked him, coming up and offering him sour wine and saying, "If you are the King of the Jews, save yourself!"
>
> Luke 23:35-37 ESV

In the Psalm that King David wrote about the Messiah's death, he prophetically recorded this very form of ridicule.

> "He trusted in the LORD, let Him rescue Him; Let Him deliver Him, since He delights in Him!"          Psalm 22:8 NKJV

David recorded the Messiah as saying…

> But I am a worm, not a man; people insult me and despise me. All who see me taunt me; they mock me and shake their heads.
>
> Psalm 22:6-7 NET

As Jesus hung on the cross, prophecy after prophecy was fulfilled in detail.

### TWO VIEWS

The two thieves who had been crucified with Jesus also gave their opinion as to his true identity. Doctor Luke wrote:

> One of the criminals who hung there hurled insults at him: "Aren't you the Christ? Save yourself and us!"
>
> But the other criminal rebuked him. "Don't you fear God," he said, "since you are under the same sentence? We are punished justly, for we are getting what our deeds deserve. But this man has done nothing wrong."
>
> Then he said, "Jesus, remember me when you come into your kingdom."
>
> Jesus answered him, "I tell you the truth, today you will be with me in paradise."          Luke 23:39–43 NIV

Jesus assured the thief that as soon as they both died, their spirits would meet each other in paradise. Jesus could say this because he knew that this man was trusting in Him as Saviour.

*It was now about the sixth hour, and darkness fell over the whole land until the ninth hour ...*      Luke 23:44 NASB

*At the ninth hour Jesus cried out with a loud voice, "Eloi, Eloi, lama sabachthani?" which is translated, "My God, My God, why have You forsaken Me?"*      Mark 15:34 NASB

Once again, 1000 years before, King David had written that the Messiah would say just those words.

*"My God, my God, why have you forsaken me?"* Psalm 22:1 NIV

It wasn't without reason that Jesus cried this out loud. We will look at its meaning in a following chapter.

The significance of Jesus' final moments on the cross cannot be emphasized enough. The Bible says,

*And Jesus, crying out with a loud voice, said; "It is finished!" ... Father, into Your hands I commit My spirit."*

*Having said this, He breathed His last…And He bowed His head and gave up His spirit.*
Luke 23:46 combined with John 19:30 NASB

*And the veil of the temple was torn in two from top to bottom.*
Mark 15:38 NASB

Jesus was dead. It's not hard to imagine the whole realm of evil being ecstatic. Satan and his demons had succeeded beyond their wildest dreams. From their perspective, they had killed YAHWEH. THE PROMISED DELIVERER was dead! Satan and his demons had escaped the Lake of Fire! Or had they?!

There were two events that happened in those final moments on the cross that should have left Satan feeling unsettled. Why had the Temple curtain torn—from top to bottom? And why had Jesus shouted *"It is finished!"* with such intensity?

### THE TORN CURTAIN

Remember, the Temple was a permanent replica of the original Tabernacle. The curtain in question separated the *Holy Place* from the sacred *Holy of Holies*. It was no small matter for this veil to be torn.

First of all, the Bible says that the curtain shielded the *Holy of Holies* from man's view. To look behind the curtain was to die.

Second, to tear the curtain in any way would have been a monumental task. It is said that the curtain was 18 metres (60 feet) in height, 9 metres (30 feet) in width, and being the thickness of a man's hand—about 10 centimetres (4 inches).[4]

Third, to be split from the top to the bottom could only mean one thing: *God* had torn the curtain, not man.

By Jewish reckoning, Jesus died at the ninth hour which would have been 3:00 p.m. The temple would have been full of priests performing their sacred duties. This was the time of the evening sacrifice, when a lamb was killed. It was also the Passover. News of the torn curtain could not have been concealed. Too many people were present, and the event was too staggering to be forgotten.

The significance of this whole incident will be explained shortly.

### IT IS FINISHED!

Jesus' final words are also important to note. The phrase *"It is finished"* is translated from a single Greek word: *tetelestai*. *Tetelestai* had many different usages, but the following three have significance to the story:[5]

1.  *Tetelestai* was used by a servant reporting to his master upon completing a task: *"The job you gave me is finished."*

2.  *Tetelestai* was also a familiar term in Greek commercial life. It signified the completion of a transaction when a debt was paid in full. When the final payment was made, one could say *"tetelestai,"* that is, *"The debt is finished."* Ancient receipts have been found with *tetelestai—paid in full*—written across them.

3.  The selection of a lamb for sacrifice in the temple was always an important time. The flock would be searched and, upon finding an unblemished lamb, one would say *"tetelestai"*—*"The job is finished."*

In a sense, Jesus cried out: *"The work is completed, the debt is paid, the sacrificial lamb is found."* The Scripture says Jesus cried out in a **loud** voice, *"It is finished."* Doctor Luke wrote that...

> ...*when the centurion saw what had happened, he glorified God, saying, "Certainly this was a righteous Man!"*
>
> *Luke 23:47 NKJV*

It is noteworthy that it was the centurion, an officer in charge of 100 soldiers, who immediately commented upon Jesus' cry. Surely he, a military man, knew the difference between a gasp of defeat and a shout of victory.

> Then, because it was the day of preparation, so that the bodies should not stay on the crosses on the Sabbath … the Jewish leaders asked Pilate to have the victims' legs broken and the bodies taken down.
> John 19:31 NET

### BREAK THE LEGS

It was Passover week and this day was the climax, when the lamb was to be killed. The chief priests wanted this crucifixion business over and done with, so as not to contaminate the feast. They asked that Jesus' legs be broken. This would mean that the one being crucified could no longer lift himself up to breathe, resulting in quick asphyxiation.

> So the soldiers came and broke the legs of the two men who had been crucified with Jesus, first the one and then the other. But when they came to Jesus and saw that he was already dead, **they did not break his legs**. But one of the soldiers pierced his side with a spear, and blood and water flowed out immediately.
> John 19:32-34 NET

A Roman soldier trained in the art of killing thrust a spear into Jesus' heart. To bungle a public execution was unthinkable. The soldier knew exactly *where* to thrust that instrument of death to make sure not a wisp of life could linger. The Scripture says water and blood flowed out. Medical experts tell us that such an event was a sure sign that death had already occurred. Jesus was definitely dead.

> And the person who saw it has testified (and his testimony is true, and he knows that he is telling the truth), so that you also may believe.

> For **these things happened so that the scripture would be fulfilled**, "Not a bone of his will be broken." And again another scripture says, "They will look on the one whom they have pierced."
> John 19:35–37 NET

We will soon learn the significance of this event.

# 5 RESURRECTED

## FRIDAY: LATE AFTERNOON

*After these things Joseph of Arimathea, who was a disciple of Jesus, but secretly for fear of the Jews, asked Pilate that he might take away the body of Jesus, and Pilate gave him permission. So he came and took away his body. Nicodemus also, who earlier had come to Jesus by night, came bringing a mixture of myrrh and aloes, about seventy-five pounds in weight. So they took the body of Jesus and bound it in linen cloths with the spices, as is the burial custom of the Jews. Now in the place where he was crucified there was a garden, and in the garden a new tomb in which no one had yet been laid. So because of the Jewish day of Preparation, since the tomb was close at hand, they laid Jesus there.* John 19:38–42 ESV

*The women who had come with Jesus from Galilee followed Joseph and saw the tomb and how his body was laid in it. Then they went home and prepared spices and perfumes. But they rested on the Sabbath in obedience to the commandment.* Luke 23:55-56 NIV

Although Joseph and Nicodemus were part of the Sanhedrin, it seems they did not reject the evidence that Jesus was truly YAHWEH. According to their traditional custom, they wrapped Jesus in long burial cloths, intermingled with 34 kilograms (75 pounds) of spices and laid him in a tomb. A large wheel-like stone, weighing as much as 1.8 tonnes (2 tons), was rolled across the front of the sepulcher. The women watched and then went home to prepare additional spices for the final burial. It was Friday night.

## SATURDAY

*Now on the next day, the day after the preparation, the chief priests and the Pharisees gathered together with Pilate, and said, "Sir, we remember that when He was still alive that deceiver said, 'After three days I am to rise again.' Therefore, give orders for the grave to be made secure until the third day, otherwise His disciples may come and steal Him away and say to the people, 'He has risen from the dead,' and the last deception will be worse than the first."*

*Pilate said to them, "You have a guard; go, make it as secure as you know how." And they went and made the grave secure, and along with the guard they set a seal on the stone.* Matthew 27:62–66 NASB

This was no rag-tag band of soldiery that was sent to guard the tomb. A Roman guard consisted of four to sixteen men, each man trained to protect 2 metres (6 feet) of ground. Together they were capable of defending themselves against an entire battalion.[6]

Pilate instructed the chief priests and Pharisees to seal the tomb. Ropes would have been stretched across the large stone door and fixed in place with moist clay. The clay would then be imprinted with a signet ring. Any tampering with the rock would be immediately apparent.

## SUNDAY

The guard was set in place on Saturday, the Jewish Sabbath. On Sunday while it was still dark,

> Suddenly there was a great earthquake! For an angel of the Lord came down from heaven, rolled aside the stone, and sat on it. His face shone like lightning, and his clothing was as white as snow. The guards shook with fear when they saw him, and they fell into a dead faint. *Matthew 28:2–4 NLT*

It took only a glance for these rough and rugged soldiers to know they were no match for this one angel. They passed out from fear!

But they weren't the only ones shaking. The whole realm of evil must have been in chaos. It's not hard to imagine what it was like—Satan in confusion, shouting jumbled orders as demons scrambled in disarray. What a shock! Who would have dreamed that the tomb could be empty? Jesus had obviously come back to life. Impossible!

In the meantime,

> … Mary Magdalene, and Mary the mother of James, and Salome, bought spices, so that they might come and anoint Him. Very early on the first day of the week, they came to the tomb when the sun had risen. They were saying to one another, "Who will roll away the stone for us from the entrance of the tomb?"
>
> Looking up, they saw that the stone had been rolled away, although it was extremely large. Mark 16:1–4 NASB

Mary Magdalene apparently turned away in shock and dismay at the initial sight of the open tomb. She probably assumed the obvious—Jesus' body had been vandalized. Sobbing, she turned and ran to tell the disciples. But Mary and Salome pushed forward …

> And entering the tomb, they saw a young man clothed in a long white robe sitting on the right side; and they were alarmed.
>
> But he said to them, "Do not be alarmed. You seek Jesus of Nazareth, who was crucified. He is risen! He is not here. See the place where they laid Him. But go, tell His disciples—and Peter—that He is going before you into Galilee; there you will see Him, as He said to you." Mark 16:5-7 NKJV
>
> So they departed quickly from the tomb with fear and great joy, and ran to tell his disciples.
>
> And behold, Jesus met them and said, "Greetings!" And they came up and took hold of his feet and worshiped him. Then Jesus said to them, "Do not be afraid; go and tell my brothers to go to Galilee, and there they will see me." Matthew 28:8–10 ESV

## He has Risen

Reading the record,[7] you can sense the confusion and excitement of the early morning news. For those who had seen Jesus die, the report from the elated women was met with a great deal of skepticism. Doctor Luke wrote that, initially,

> … these words appeared to them as nonsense, and they would not believe them. Luke 24:11 NASB

Peter ran to check out the tomb. John ran too, passing Peter on the way, but then waited outside the entrance.

> Then Simon Peter came, following him, and went into the tomb. He saw the linen cloths lying there, and the face cloth, which had been on Jesus' head, not lying with the linen cloths but folded up in a place by itself. John 20:6-7 ESV

This was not the scene of a plundered grave. The strips of cloth used to shroud the body were still wrapped as though around a corpse, but they were collapsed—empty! The body had passed right through them. The head napkin was folded too, as if someone had tidied up before leaving. The Bible says Peter saw, but John saw and believed. For John there was no doubt that Jesus was alive! But Peter's head was spinning. He needed time to think.

It still must have been early morning when Mary Magdalene returned and ...

> ... stood outside by the tomb weeping, and as she wept she stooped down and looked into the tomb. And she saw two angels in white sitting, one at the head and the other at the feet, where the body of Jesus had lain.
>
> Then they said to her, "Woman, why are you weeping?"
>
> She said to them, "Because they have taken away my Lord, and I do not know where they have laid Him." John 20:11–13 NKJV

The tomb was located in a garden so perhaps she supposed these angels were gardeners. Mary was so distressed that she did not think to identify the men. We must remember that Mary was grieving intensely and that the entire conversation was carried on through her sobbing.

> When she had said this, she turned around and saw Jesus standing there, but she did not know that it was Jesus.
>
> Jesus said to her, "Woman, why are you weeping? Who are you looking for?"
>
> Because she thought he was the gardener, she said to him, "Sir, if you have carried him away, tell me where you have put him, and I will take him."
>
> Jesus said to her, "Mary." John 20:14–16 NET

If one can say a name in such a way that it brings back all the memories of every previous encounter with a loved one, then Jesus did just that. Mary recognized the voice immediately.

*She turned and said to him in Aramaic, "Rabboni!" (which means Teacher).*
                                                    *John 20:16 ESV*

Now she had a different reason to weep. She must have flung her arms around him, perhaps embracing his feet in keeping with the custom of that day.

*"Don't cling to me," Jesus said, "for I haven't yet ascended to the Father. But go find my brothers and tell them that I am ascending to my Father and your Father, my God and your God."*

*Mary Magdalene found the disciples and told them, "I have seen the Lord!"*
                                                    *John 20:17-18 NLT*

### THE GUARDS

While all this was happening the guards were hunting down the chief priests. There was no way they were going back to face Pontius Pilate.

*… some of the guard came into the city and reported to the chief priests all that had happened. And when they had assembled with the elders and consulted together, they gave a large sum of money to the soldiers and said, "You are to say, 'His disciples*

> *came by night and stole Him away while we were asleep.' And*
> *if this should come to the governor's ears, we will win him over*
> *and keep you out of trouble." And they took the money and did*
> *as they had been instructed; and this story was widely spread*
> *among the Jews, and is to this day.*  Matthew 28:11–15 NASB

It took an immense sum of money to persuade these proud soldiers to say that they had been asleep. To be caught sleeping while on guard duty carried the death penalty. Of course, the story wasn't true. Once again you can see the hand of Satan behind it all, rushing around doing damage control. After all, he is the *father of lies*. It was an anemic effort to save face. No doubt, Satan realized that he was defeated. Jesus, The Anointed One, had crushed Satan's head, just as God had promised way back in the Garden of Eden.

### Alive

As to the tomb, there was no doubt that it was empty. Even Jesus' enemies agreed on that fact. The reality of the situation was that Jesus had come back to life. He was truly alive—physically! This was not a reincarnation. It was a resurrection. For three days his body had laid lifeless in the tomb, separated from his spirit. But then in a dramatic demonstration of supernatural power, Jesus had been resurrected with a new body. It was just as Jesus had foretold in his teaching.

> *"The reason my Father loves me is that I lay down my life—only*
> *to take it up again. No one takes it from me, but I lay it down*
> *of my own accord. I have authority to lay it down and authority*
> *to take it up again…"*  John 10:17-18 NIV

### Why did Jesus have to Die?

Jesus' death had not been an ordinary one. For mankind, death is a consequence of sin. But Jesus was sinless so he did not need to die. According to *the law of sin and death*, Jesus could have lived on this earth forever. So why did he die? Satan had not killed Jesus against His will, nor had the Jews or the Romans. Jesus had chosen to die, willingly. But why? The next chapter will answer that question.

# 72 HOURS THAT CHANGED HISTORY

**THU** Disciples prepare Passover
Passover Supper
Walk to Garden of Gethsemane
☾ Jesus arrested in Garden; disciples flee

**FRI** 1st Trial — before Chief Priest's father-in-law, Annas
2nd Trial — before Chief Priest and Sanhedrin
3rd Trial — before Sanhedrin (to make it legal)
**6:30 am** 4th Trial — before Pilate
5th Trial — before Herod (Jesus mocked)
6th Trial — before Pilate (Jesus scourged)

**9:00 am** Crucifixion

**NOON**

**3:00 pm** Jesus cries, "It is finished;" Temple curtain torn
Legs of two thieves broken; Jesus' side pierced
Joseph of Arimathea requests Jesus' body for burial
Jesus buried in tomb

☾

**SAT**

Roman guard requested and placed at tomb

Tomb sealed

☾

**SUN** Earthquake - stone rolled away by angels; guards flee
Women go to tomb
Jesus appears to Mary and Salome
Jesus appears to Mary Magdalene
Jesus appears to Peter

*Jewish Friday *Jewish Saturday Jewish Sunday* (side labels)

*Jewish days begin at sundown, continue through the night into the next day until the following sundown.

# Chapter Fourteen

**1** The Stranger

**2** The Emmaus Road Message
*—From Creation to Babel—*

**3** The Emmaus Road Message
*—From Abraham to the Passover—*

**4** The Emmaus Road Message
*—From the Law to the Tabernacle—*

**5** The Emmaus Road Message
*—From Nicodemus to the Resurrection—*

**6** The Court Room

**7** The Person, the Provision, the Promise

# 1 THE STRANGER

*That very day two of them were going to a village named Emmaus, about seven miles from Jerusalem, and they were talking with each other about all these things that had happened. While they were talking and discussing together, Jesus himself drew near and went with them. But their eyes were kept from recognizing him.*

*And he said to them, "What is this conversation that you are holding with each other as you walk?"*

*And they stood still, looking sad.* Luke 24:13–17 ESV

These two were not part of the inner circle of disciples, but they were followers of Jesus nonetheless.

*Then one of them, named Cleopas, answered him, "Are you the only visitor to Jerusalem who does not know the things that have happened there in these days?"*

*And he said to them, "What things?"*

*And they said to him, "Concerning Jesus of Nazareth, a man who was a prophet mighty in deed and word before God and all the people, and how our chief priests and rulers delivered him up to be condemned to death, and crucified him. But we had hoped that he was the one to redeem [set free] Israel. Yes, and besides all this, it is now the third day since these things happened. Moreover, some women of our company amazed us. They were at the tomb early in the morning, and when they did not find his body, they came back saying that they had even seen a vision of angels, who said that he was alive. Some of those who were with us went to the tomb and found it just as the women had said, but him they did not see."*

Luke 24:18-24 ESV

The two disciples gave a brief synopsis of the day. Of course, all of this was not news to Jesus, but he quietly waited for them to finish. He had news for them too.

*And he said to them, "O foolish ones, and slow of heart to believe all that the prophets have spoken! Was it not necessary that the Christ should suffer these things and enter into his glory?" And beginning with Moses and all the Prophets, he interpreted to them in all the Scriptures the things concerning himself.*

*Luke 24:25-27 ESV*

Jesus told them that the Messiah had to suffer, die, and then come back to life. He said it was necessary—it had been foretold by the ancient prophets. You can be sure this raised some eyebrows. But Jesus didn't stop there. He went back into the Jewish Scriptures and taught them about himself, starting at the very beginning. He then progressed step-by-step, story-by-story, through the entire Bible. It must have been quite a lesson.

*And they approached the village where they were going, and He acted as though He were going farther. But they urged Him, saying, "Stay with us, for it is getting toward evening, and the day is now nearly over." So He went in to stay with them. When He had reclined at the table with them, He took the bread and blessed it, and breaking it, He began giving it to them. Then their eyes were opened and they recognized Him; and He vanished from their sight.*

*They said to one another, "Were not our hearts burning within us while He was speaking to us on the road, while He was explaining the Scriptures to us?"* Luke 24:28-32 NASB

God himself had lit a fire of understanding in their minds. They were excited!

*And they got up that very hour and returned to Jerusalem.*

*Luke 24:33 NASB*

You can imagine the trip back to the city as these two elated followers of Jesus discussed what they would say to the eleven* disciples. The journey was all uphill, but they must have pushed themselves. They had good news!

*Judas Iscariot had committed suicide.

*There they found the Eleven and those with them, assembled together and saying, "It is true! The Lord has risen and has appeared to Simon."*

*Then the two told what had happened on the way, and how Jesus was recognized by them when he broke the bread.*

*While they were still talking about this, Jesus himself stood among them and said to them, "Peace be with you."*

*They were startled and frightened, thinking they saw a ghost. He said to them, "Why are you troubled, and why do doubts rise in your minds? Look at my hands and my feet. It is I myself! Touch me and see; a ghost does not have flesh and bones, as you see I have."*

*When he had said this, he showed them his hands and feet. And while they still did not believe it because of joy and amazement, he asked them, "Do you have anything here to eat?" They gave him a piece of broiled fish, and he took it and ate it in their presence.*

*He said to them, "This is what I told you while I was still with you: Everything must be fulfilled that is written about me in the Law of Moses, the Prophets and the Psalms."* Luke 24:33-44 NIV

The Jews divide the Scriptures into three sections—the Law, the Writings (or Psalms), and the Prophets. Jesus took each of those segments and showed the disciples how it all applied to him.

*Then he opened their minds so they could understand the Scriptures. He told them, "This is what is written: The Christ will suffer and rise from the dead on the third day, and repentance and forgiveness of sins will be preached in his name to all nations, beginning at Jerusalem. You are witnesses of these things."* Luke 24:45-48 NIV

Jesus said his death and resurrection was such good news that it would be told everywhere, beginning at Jerusalem.

Before we go on with the story we want to stop and go back to the beginning, just as Jesus did with his disciples. We want to see what Jesus revealed about himself—those things written in the Law, the Prophets, and the Psalms.

Exactly why did Jesus come to earth, and why did he have to suffer and die when all along he planned to come back to life?

Why did he not simply tell people to believe in him and skip the entire crucifixion?

What was this death and resurrection all about?

The last piece of the puzzle is about to be put in place. When you understand this part, you will have the whole picture.

# 2 THE EMMAUS ROAD MESSAGE
## —FROM CREATION TO BABEL—

To answer the question … *Why did Jesus have to die?* … we start at the very beginning, just like Jesus did on the road to Emmaus.

### A HOLY GOD

Remember how our story began with Moses at the burning bush? It was here that the Supreme Being revealed his personal name—Y*AHWEH*—*the self-existent one.*

We also learned at the burning bush that the word *holy* means *unique, one-of-a-kind.* This was important, as the Scriptures tell us over and over again that Y*AHWEH* is a holy God. As we progressed further, we saw many things about this unique, one-of-a-kind God. We learned that:

❖ Y*AHWEH* is an **eternal spirit**.

❖ The L*ORD* is a **person** or **being**, with personality and character, not a universal force or abstract Divine Mind.

❖ Y*AHWEH* is a **king**, the *Most High*, the Sovereign Ruler of all.

❖ The L*ORD* Y*AHWEH* is **all-knowing**, **all-powerful**, and **everywhere present at one time**.

❖ The L*ORD* is a God of **order**; he established both physical and spiritual laws that he faithfully maintains.

❖ Y*AHWEH* is a **perfect** God, morally pure without any sin.

❖ The L*ORD* is a **just** God, absolutely fair in all his dealings. He is the Judge before whom everyone will give account.

❖ The L*ORD* Y*AHWEH* is a **caring** God, one who loves even those who do not deserve it.

❖ Y*AHWEH* is a **faithful** God—a God with a dependable history. He makes promises and keeps them.

❖ The L*ORD* is **great**, yet he **communicates** with man.

❖ The L*ORD* is **one God**, yet **three persons**—the Father, the Son, and the Holy Spirit.

We saw that it was this matchless combination of Y*AHWEH*'s attributes that made for one unique God. The Bible says,

> *"No one is holy like the L*ORD*, For there is none besides You…"*
> 1 Samuel 2:2 NKJV

It is critical that we understand the character of God, for we need to know the identity of the one who was nailed to the cross. The Scripture says it was YAHWEH himself! But why? Why would he choose to become a man and suffer a horrible death?

## A SIN-FILLED AGE

You will remember that soon after creation, Satan led one-third of the angelic spirits in a rebellion against God. We saw that this rebellion started an evil era where Satan and sin dominate the world. To help us understand the nature of sin, the Bible makes some interesting comparisons:

❖ **Moral:** Sin is the opposite of what is morally right. It is that which is "wrong." It is **unrighteousness**.

❖ **Social:** Sin is to disregard authority because one thinks he knows *better-than-God*. It is **disobedience** and **rebellion**.

❖ **Medical:** Sin is compared to a disease. It is a fatal *condition* of the spirit. Acts of sin are *symptoms* of that condition.

❖ **Agriculture:** Sin is compared to "good" that has been **corrupted** (literally "spoiled" or "rotten").

❖ **Military:** Sin is like an archer **missing the target**. Any thought or conduct that falls short of perfection (the bull's-eye) is sin.

❖ **Legal:** Sin is lawlessness. God set the rules, even the least of them. Sin is **breaking the law**.

We learned that this sinful age would not last forever but would be brought to an end by the LORD himself, because…

> …He is coming to judge the earth. He shall judge the world with righteousness, and the peoples with His truth.
>
> *Psalm 96:13 NKJV*

## ADAM AND EVE

As we continued our story, we saw that immediately after creation there was a unique friendship between YAHWEH and man. The LORD had made man not as a robot, but with a will, so that by the obedient choices he made he would honour God, just as an obedient son honours his father.

You will recall that Adam and Eve enjoyed many benefits from this close friendship, for their Creator-Owner was committed to their well-being. As sinless people created in the image of God, they lived as friends in the presence of the perfect God.

But then Adam and Eve sinned. Since the events surrounding this incident contain critical elements of the puzzle, the Scripture uses powerful word pictures to help us understand what happened.

The Bible says man chose to trust Satan instead of YAHWEH. Man joined Satan's rebellious ranks, thus becoming an **ENEMY** of God.

ENEMY

That choice destroyed the unique friendship between God and man. Man was now **ESTRANGED** from God. The LORD seemed remote and distant.

ESTRANGED

Satan was not the benevolent friend YAHWEH had been. The Devil manipulated man with lies to do his satanic will. Man had become a **SLAVE** to Satan and sin.

SLAVE

Man had chosen a path that led into a spiritual wilderness. Though he would try many religions, none would lead him back to the LORD YAHWEH. Man was **LOST**.

LOST

In choosing his own way, man disobeyed the one command God had given him. We saw that whenever you break a law, you also face a consequence. So it was in this case.

YAHWEH took off his mantle of friendship and donned a magistrate's cloak. As a judge, the LORD found man **GUILTY** of breaking his law, of sinning against a righteous God.

GUILTY

In essence, God wrote out a verdict, a *Certificate of Debt*. Man was now a **DEBTOR** with a price to pay. **The penalty for sin was death.**

DEBTOR

Because the stench of sin corrupted man's total being, the LORD **SEPARATED** himself from mankind. Man's close relationship with God was over—it was **dead**.

SEPARATED

Every human being now faced a physical **DEATH**. The spirit would be **separated** from the body; the life **separated** from family and friends.

DEAD

After the body died, there would be a **SECOND DEATH**. Man would be **separated** forever from YAHWEH and His expressions of love. He would be confined in the Lake of Fire, the place prepared for Satan and his demons.

ETERNAL
JUDGMENT

Death in its three aspects now ruled man's life, and he could do nothing about it. It was a bitter, potent reality that all faced, that all shared, that all who thought soberly, feared. With absolute, utter finality, the Scripture clearly states that…

> …*a person shall die for his own sin.*      2 Chronicles 25:4 NKJV

These word pictures helped us understand just how far removed from God mankind had become as a result of Adam and Eve's sin. We summarized with three age-old questions:

❖ How can we escape the consequences of sin—our sin-penalty?

❖ How do we obtain a righteousness that is *equal* to God's righteousness so we can be accepted back into his presence?

❖ How do we get our names written in the *Lamb's Book of Life?*

## A DESPERATE ATTEMPT

Though man had been created in God's image, that image was now marred by sin. Remember how Adam and Eve tried to cover their sin by clothing themselves in fig leaves? We saw that, although YAHWEH rejected their efforts, he did not leave them without hope.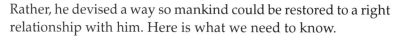
Rather, he devised a way so mankind could be restored to a right relationship with him. Here is what we need to know.

## THE WAY TO ACCEPTANCE

Just as Adam and Eve could not make themselves acceptable to God by fixing up their outward appearance, neither are we accepted based on our externals. We may impress others with what we are on the outside, but God knows what we are really like. He knows our private thoughts—the very things we think and imagine.

Adam and Eve knew they needed a covering, but the fig leaf solution was the wrong idea. They needed "right clothes"—a covering provided by the LORD. The Bible says:

> The LORD God made garments of skin for Adam and his wife, and clothed them.                    Genesis 3:21 NASB

We saw that these physical coverings illustrated spiritual clothing. The fig leaves were like *filthy rags*—they were mankind's self-righteous efforts to cover hearts dirty with sin. On the other hand, the garments of skin were *clean clothes* provided by the LORD, and pictured man as pure—acceptable to God.

But how does this affect us now? Very simply: Just as an animal died to provide an acceptable covering for Adam and Eve, so Jesus died so we could be accepted by the LORD.

As the disciples struggled to comprehend what Jesus was saying, there must have been a torrent of questions. *Why would YAHWEH require an animal to die for Adam and Eve? Why didn't God simply clothe them with his choice of leaves? And why would Jesus have to die for us? Was there not another way?*

Perhaps Jesus continued with the story of Cain and Abel.

Remember how Cain and Abel brought sacrifices to God? Cain brought **vegetables** but Abel brought an **animal**. God rejected Cain's sacrifice, but he accepted Abel's. Why?

## CAIN

The Bible says Cain did not believe God. He had his own ideas about how to get rid of sin and be made right with the LORD. In the same way, our world is full of people who have their own notions about God and how to please him—a custom-designed god is in vogue.

Based on his thinking, Cain did his own thing. But the sacrifice he brought did *not* illustrate God's way of dealing with sin. *Vegetables do not shed blood.* Cain ignored the fact that...

> ...without the shedding of blood there is no forgiveness.
> Hebrews 9:22 NASB

His sacrifice did not picture what Jesus was to do on the cross. The Bible tells us…

> Do not be like Cain, who belonged to the evil one… his own actions were evil and his brother's were righteous.
>
> 1 John 3:12 NIV

The broken relationship could *not* be restored based on the way devised by Cain.

### ABEL

On the other hand, Abel trusted the LORD to be his Saviour, and God accepted his sacrifice because it illustrated what Jesus would accomplish on the cross.

❖ **It pictured atonement:** Just as an animal died to <u>picture</u> how God would provide *right clothing* for sinful mankind, so Jesus died to <u>actually</u> make us clean. Jesus did more than <u>cover</u> sin, his death <u>removed</u> our filthy rags.

> As far as the east is from the west, so far hath he removed our transgressions from us.          Psalm 103:12 KJV

❖ **It pictured substitution:** Just as an animal *died in Abel's place* to <u>illustrate</u> how the sin-debt would be paid, so *Jesus died in our place*, the <u>actual payment</u> for sin.

> For Christ also suffered once for sins, the righteous for the unrighteous, that he might bring us to God…          1 Peter 3:18 ESV

The friendship that was broken by sin is now restored through Jesus' death on the cross.

> Once you were alienated from God and were enemies…
>
> …but now he has reconciled you by Christ's physical body through death…
>
> Colossians 1:21-22 NIV

As children of Adam and Eve, we were born into this world as **ENEMIES** of God…

ENEMY

…but now because of Jesus' physical death on the cross, we are **RECONCILED**. We can be friends again. The broken relationship has been restored.

RECONCILED

| The Way of Cain | The Way of Abel | Jesus |
|---|---|---|
| Offered vegetables | Offered an animal | Offered himself |
| No blood shed | Blood was shed | Blood was shed |
| No forgiveness of sin | Forgiveness of sin[1] | Forgiveness of sin |
| Trusted his own ideas | Abel trusted God. | We must trust God. |
| God rejected Cain. His offering confused the illustration. | God accepted Abel. His offering illustrated what Jesus would do on the cross. | God will accept us. The death of Jesus completes the prophetic picture. |

## NOAH

In the days of Noah, the people ignored the LORD. But YAHWEH did not withhold judgment just because they had the wrong view on life. The Bible says they perished.

In the same way, God says he will judge all mankind, regardless of what they think.

> The fool says in his heart, "There is no God." Psalm 14:1; 53:1 ESV

> He who trusts in his own heart is a fool… Proverbs 28:26 NKJV

YAHWEH will let us ignore him and even reject his way of escape for a time, but eventually we must face the inescapable conclusion: we must pay our sin-penalty with our own eternal death.

Remember how Noah and his family were kept safe in the ark? There was **only one boat**, and **only one door** to enter and gain refuge from the flood. There was no other option.

In the same way, Jesus is the only way to eternal life. Just as safety could only be found inside the ark, so only in trusting Jesus can we find safety from everlasting punishment. Jesus said,

> "I am the way and the truth and the life. No one comes to the Father except through me." John 14:6 ESV

There is only one way to escape judgment. Those who ignore that way face the same fate as those who did not heed Noah's warnings of the coming flood—eternal death with all its implications. The Bible is clear: Jesus is the only way to God.

## BABEL

Remember the people of Babel? We saw that in their ego-driven enthusiasm to devise a way to Heaven, they said ...

> "Come, let us build ourselves a city, and a tower whose top is in the heavens; **let us make a name for ourselves** ..."
> *Genesis 11:4 NKJV*

In contrast the Bible says that Jesus ...

> Who, being in very nature God ... [took] the very nature of a servant, being made in human likeness. And being found in appearance as a man, he humbled himself and became obedient to death—even death on a cross!
>
> Therefore God exalted him to the highest place and gave him the name that is above every name, that **at the name of Jesus** every knee should bow, in heaven and on earth and under the earth, and every tongue confess that Jesus Christ is Lord [YAHWEH], to the glory of God the Father. *Philippians 2:6-11 NIV*

The Bible says all mankind must make a choice:

1. We can be proud like the people of Babel, determined to make a name for ourselves, and devise our own way to God, or ...

2. We can humble ourselves, and acknowledge the name of Jesus as the only way to be accepted by YAHWEH.[2]

There are only two choices. Those who make the first choice will *not* have their names written in *Lamb's Book of Life*. Nonetheless, the Bible says that after death they will be forced to bow the knee and confess that Jesus is YAHWEH.

## RELIGION

Remember how Babel was the first incident of organized religion in the Bible? We said that a definition for the word *religion* is this: **man's efforts to reach a deity with the hopes of gaining favour or removing misfortune**.

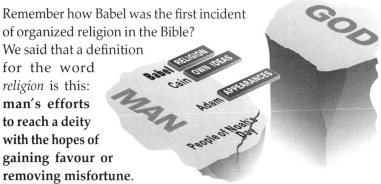

The people of Babel slaved away with brick and tar to build a *Gate to God*. In the same way, religion is a taskmaster that requires constant struggle. It demands ever-increasing efforts to please God, gods, spirits, or idols. But the Scripture tells us that all this effort will not bridge the chasm caused by sin.

In contrast to religion, the Bible says that the only true *gate to God* was opened by the LORD YAHWEH himself when in his mercy, God reached down to man in the person of Jesus Christ. All the work needed to restore the broken relationship was completed by Jesus on the cross.

Though religion supposedly offers many gates to God, Jesus says there are only two paths in life.

> Enter through the narrow gate; for the gate is wide and the way is broad that leads to destruction, and there are many who enter through it. For the gate is small and the way is narrow that leads to life, and there are few who find it.     Matthew 7:13-14 NASB

Every man and woman is born into the world walking the *broad path* that leads to destruction. It is a popular way with many people on it, but the LORD invites us to step off that crowded road and enter a *narrow gate*, to walk the path that leads to eternal life. One prophet wrote of his choice:

> For all the people walk each in the name of his god, But we will walk in the name of the LORD our God Forever and ever.
>
> Micah 4:5 NKJV

| The Way of Babel | The Way of Religion | The Way of Noah | The Way of Jesus |
|---|---|---|---|
| | The broad path | | The narrow gate |
| Made a name for themselves | Many names and many ways to these gods | Only one door and one boat to safety | Only one Saviour, Jesus the Messiah |
| Devised first religion | Many people try this gate | Few people entered | Few people enter this gate |
| Trusted in religious effort | Trusted in religious effort | Noah trusted YAHWEH | Must trust the SAVIOUR |
| People dispersed | Rejected | Noah saved | Safe from judgment |
| | Do's and don'ts | | It is finished! |

# 3 THE EMMAUS ROAD MESSAGE
## —FROM ABRAHAM TO THE PASSOVER—

As Jesus explained to his disciples how he fulfilled the Scriptures, there must have been a glimmer of excitement in the disciples' eyes. It was all making sense. Jesus continued.

### SODOM AND GOMORRAH

Remember when Abraham and Lot first arrived in Canaan, they divided the land between the two of them? In his greed, Lot chose the most fertile region of the country, but his choice led him to settle in the sinful city of Sodom. The Bible says that God…

> …condemned the cities of Sodom and Gomorrah by burning them to ashes, and made them **an example** of what is going to happen to the ungodly…          2 Peter 2:6 NIV

The Bible defines *"the ungodly"* as those who will not trust in Jesus.[3]

> In a similar way, Sodom and Gomorrah and the surrounding towns gave themselves up to sexual immorality and perversion. They serve as **an example** of those who suffer the punishment of eternal fire.          Jude 7 NIV

The LORD said that his judgment on these cities should remind the *Global Classroom* that he must punish all sin. This is not a popular subject, but this is what the Bible clearly teaches.[4] Man is facing eternal separation from God in the Lake of Fire.

### ABRAHAM AND ISAAC

Remember how God instructed Abraham to sacrifice his son? The Bible says Isaac was bound and placed on an altar—helpless.

Just as Isaac was helpless and could not save himself, so all of us are bound by sin and cannot save ourselves from its eternal consequences. And just as the knife hovered over Isaac, ready to bring death, so we all have the penalty of sin hovering over our lives—we are only one heartbeat away from the *Second Death*.

### A SUFFICIENT SUBSTITUTE

The Bible says Abraham trusted in God's goodness to provide a solution to his predicament. And YAHWEH did intervene. At the last moment the LORD spoke from Heaven and stopped the knife.

In the same way, God intervened on our behalf. Just as the LORD provided Isaac with the ram, so we have been provided with the Lord Jesus. And just as the ram died in Isaac's place, so Jesus died in our place. We should have died and been punished for our sin, but Jesus died and took our punishment on the cross. He is our substitute.

If the ram had not died, then Isaac would have perished. If Jesus had not died, then we would have faced the *Second Death*.

DEBTOR

Down through history, every person carried a *Certificate of Debt*, a massive sin-debt that each one was accountable to pay. The only way that debt could be paid was with one's own eternal death. Man was a **DEBTOR**.

CANCELLED
DEBT

But then Jesus came. His death completely paid man's sin-debt—past, present, and future. That is why Jesus cried, *"It is finished." Tetelestai!* The debt is **PAID**!

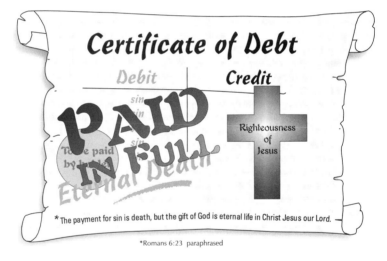

### Certificate of Debt

| Debit | Credit |
| --- | --- |

sin
sin
To be paid
by death
Eternal Death

Righteousness
of
Jesus

\* The payment for sin is death, but the gift of God is eternal life in Christ Jesus our Lord.

*Romans 6:23 paraphrased

### THE MOUNTAINS OF MORIAH

God had instructed Abraham to offer Isaac on the mountains of Moriah. After Isaac was <u>saved</u> from death, Abraham named the mountain, *"The LORD* **Will** *Provide."* One would have thought Abraham would have named it, *"The LORD* **Has** *Provided."* But no, he named it, *"The LORD* **Will** *Provide."* It was as if Abraham was looking forward to a time in history when another sacrifice would be made—one which would *provide* <u>salvation</u> from the *Second Death*. Two thousand years later, in the same location, on the mountains of Moriah, Jesus the Messiah fulfilled Abraham's prophecy and laid down his life as the perfect substitute.

All of this would have been good news to the disciples. It should be good news to us as well. The Bible says:

> …everything that was written in the past was written to teach us, so that through endurance and the encouragement of the Scriptures we might have hope. *Romans 15:4 NIV*

## THE PASSOVER

Remember when the children of Israel were slaves in Egypt? God delivered them from Pharaoh with great plagues. The last plague was the *death of the first-born child.* God had said that if the Israelites followed his Word, they would be safe from this tragedy.

Do you recall how the Israelites were to sacrifice a lamb? *Well, the Bible tells us that Jesus is our Lamb.*

It is hardly a coincidence that from the time of Jesus' birth, he was identified with these harmless creatures. It seems he was born in a stable, a place where lambs could be sheltered. His first visitors were shepherds, men who cared for lambs and made sure no harm came to them. We are told that Bethlehem, his birth city, was commissioned by the high priests as a place to raise lamb sacrifices for use in the Temple. John the Baptist said of Jesus…

> "Look, the Lamb of God, who takes away the sin of the world!" *John 1:29 NET*

So when we find Jesus identified with the Passover lamb, we shouldn't be surprised. The parallels are stunning.

Remember how the Passover lamb could have no defect? *Jesus was sinless.*

The lamb had to be a male. *Jesus was a man.*

The Passover lamb was killed, dying in the place of the firstborn. *Jesus died in our place—as our substitute.*

The blood was applied to the door posts and lintel of the house. *Jesus shed his blood on a wooden cross.*

The Israelites were to go inside the house and remain there until morning. Only in the house was safety to be found. *In the same way, only by trusting in what Jesus did on the cross do we find safety from eternal death.*

The Bible says that when the LORD came in judgment, wherever he saw the blood applied, he passed over that house. Why? It was because death had already come to a substitute lamb.

*In the same way, God provided a way for his judgment on sin to pass over us, and in so doing, all the judgment we deserved came to rest upon Jesus, our substitute Lamb.*

God had specifically told the Israelites that they must not break any bones when they ate the Passover lamb. This was because the lamb was a picture, a foreshadow of Jesus. Jesus' bones were not broken either. When the Roman soldiers…

> …came to Jesus and saw that he was already dead, they did not break his legs.                                    John 19:33 ESV

As the disciples sat there hanging onto every word, listening to Jesus explain the significance of the Passover, they could not help but think of what time of year it was. Jesus had been crucified on the very day the Passover lamb died! They had no way of knowing that the priests had hoped to kill him after the feast was over, but they did know that God's plan had triumphed. Jesus not only died on the right day, but he died at the ninth hour (3:00 p.m.), the very hour the temple lamb was offered—the hour of the evening sacrifice. He died right on schedule, just as the Bible said he would.[5] The Scripture says,

> …Christ, our Passover lamb, has been sacrificed.
> 1 Corinthians 5:7 ESV

## THE FEAST OF UNLEAVENED BREAD

In preparation for the first Passover, the LORD YAHWEH had told the Israelites...

> *That same night they must...eat...bread made without yeast.* Exodus 12:8 NLT

This meal, celebrated during the Passover, was called the *Feast of the Unleavened Bread*. In the Bible yeast is used as a picture of the permeating effects of sin. On the night before Jesus was crucified, he ate this feast with his disciples.

> *...He took bread, gave thanks and **broke it**, and gave it to them, saying, "This is My body which is given for you; do this in remembrance of Me."* Luke 22:19 NKJV

The loaf *without yeast* pictured Jesus *without sin*. Just as the unleavened bread was broken for the disciples, so the sinless Jesus was broken for us on the cross.

> *...He also took the cup after supper, saying, "This cup is the new covenant in My blood, which is shed for you."* Luke 22:20 NKJV

Just as the lamb shed his blood in place of the firstborn, so the wine in the cup symbolized Jesus shedding his blood in our place. The cup was the symbol of a new covenant or new promise—a promise of eternal life for those who have their names written in...

> *...the Lamb's Book of Life.* Revelation 21:27 NKJV

## A SUBSTITUTE

Remember the ice hockey game? We saw that when a player broke a rule, he was penalized. The offender had to sit in a "penalty box" for a set period of time. But the game has an interesting twist. If the goalkeeper broke a rule, another player would *take his place* in the box and *pay the penalty for him!* The goalkeeper was provided with a **substitute**.

In the same way, we humans have broken God's rules. We are faced with an eternity sitting in the penalty box of Hell. But then Jesus *took our place*. He paid our penalty for us. We have been provided with a **substitute**.

# 4 The Emmaus Road Message
## —From the Law to the Tabernacle—

Remember the Ten Commandments? The Israelites thought that it would be easy to obey them. But we saw that trying to follow a list of "do's and don'ts" does not restore the broken friendship with God.

> *Therefore no one will be declared righteous in his sight by observing the law; rather, through the law we become conscious of sin.*
> *Roman 3:20 NIV*

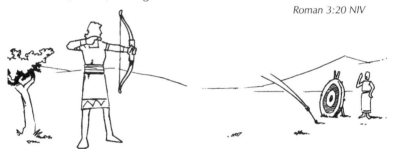

Today many people believe that they can please God by keeping a list of do's and don'ts. But we saw from our study that God expects nothing less than a faultless life. If we just once fall short of the bull's-eye of God's perfection, we are no longer perfect.

No earthly being has ever kept God's laws perfectly—that is, no one except the Lord Jesus Christ. Never did he avoid the Law or create exceptions for himself.

1. For the 30 plus years he lived life on earth, he flawlessly obeyed the Law—he was sinless.

2. And when he did take the sin of the world upon himself, he obeyed the demands of the Law in full. He paid the required penalty—death.

God could not overlook sin and pretend it had never happened. Sin must be punished—there had to be death. Up to the time of Jesus, man sacrificed animals as a death payment, but they only provided a temporary covering for sin. In light of eternity it was…

> *…impossible for the blood of bulls and goats to take away sins.*
> *Hebrews 10:4 NASB*

For man's sin-penalty to be paid, it would take another man—someone who had God's image.

But there was a problem. Remember the story of the two men struggling in the darkness at the bottom of the pit? They could not rescue each other. They needed a saviour from outside the pit.

> Truly no man can ransom another, or give to God the price of his life, for the ransom of their life is costly and can never suffice, that he should live on forever and never see the pit.
> Psalm 49:7-9 ESV

We needed someone from outside the pit to rescue us—someone who had no sin—someone not clothed in filthy rags.

Only Jesus qualified. He had more than the image of God—he was God himself! He was also a human—a perfect human. Not only was he eligible in every way to be our Saviour, he was also willing to save us. In one remarkable act of selfless love,

> God presented him as a sacrifice of atonement, through faith in his blood. He did this to demonstrate his justice, because in his forbearance he had left the sins committed beforehand unpunished... Romans 3:25 NIV

God left the sins *committed beforehand* unpunished because he knew one day Jesus would die for all sin—past, present, and future— paying the sin-debt in full.

## LOVE AND JUSTICE

On the road to Emmaus Jesus told the disciples he *had to die*. Why did he say that? His death was necessary in this sense:

❖ If the LORD YAHWEH had exclusively allowed the **just** side of his nature to rule, then we would have died for our own sin. That would have been fair, but his **love** would not allow that.

❖ On the other hand, if only **love** had ruled his character, he would have ignored sin for eternity. But that was not an option because of his **just** nature. Sin had to be dealt with.

It was on the cross that we find the complete and perfectly balanced expression of both attributes—boundless love shown and infinite justice satisfied. From God's point of view, **love** and **justice** made the cross necessary.

> Greater love has no one than this, that one lay down his life for his friends. John 15:13 NASB

> But God demonstrates His own love toward us, in that while we were still sinners, Christ died for us. Romans 5:8 NKJV

| The Law | Jesus |
|---|---|
| Impossible for man to keep perfectly | Kept the Law perfectly |
| Condemned us as sinners | Loved us even though we were sinners |
| Showed us God's righteous standard—perfection | Lived God's righteous standard—was sinless |
| Could not save us from the sin-penalty | Saved us from the sin-penalty |

### THE TABERNACLE

Recall how God instructed Moses to build the Tabernacle. It was an elaborate visual aid to help us understand what the LORD was doing to mend our broken relationship with him. Remember how God showed his presence among the Israelites with a pillar of cloud by day and a column of fire by night? That pillar hovered over the *Ark of the Covenant* in the *Holy of Holies*.

### ONE ENTRANCE

As man approached God in the Tabernacle, the first thing he saw was the wall around the courtyard which had only one entrance. As we've just seen, there is only one way to God. Jesus said,

*"No one can come to the Father except through me."*

John 14:6 NLT

### THE BRAZEN ALTAR

As a person entered the Tabernacle, the first piece of furniture he saw was the *Bronze Altar,* a reminder that a right relationship with God is only possible through the blood sacrifice. It's the same way with us. A right relationship with God is only possible through Jesus, who sacrificed his life in our place.

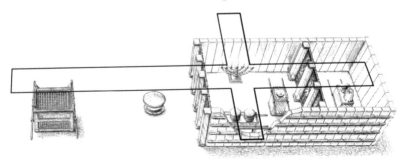

When Israelites thought of the altar, they thought of it as a *place of death*. In the same way, when the people of Jesus' day thought of the cross, they thought of it as an official means of execution—it was a *place of death*.

Even a very brief comparison of these two *places of death*—the *Bronze Altar* and the *Cross*—show how Jesus completely fulfilled the graphic picture illustrated in the Tabernacle offerings.

| The Bronze Altar | The Cross |
|---|---|
| The sacrifice was... | Jesus ... |
| ... *from either the herd or the flock* ... *a male* ... *without defect* ... *[to] be accepted on his behalf* ... *to make atonement [or a sin-covering] for him* ... *[a] blood [sacrifice].* <br> *Leviticus 1:2–5 NIV* | ... *is the Lamb of God* ... *is a male* ... *is sinless* ... *died in our place* ... *provided forgiveness of sin for us* ... *was the blood sacrifice made for us.* |

Just as the **altar** was a visual aid to remind the Israelites of *what it would* take to have our sin-debt removed, so the **cross** reminds us that Jesus paid the sin-penalty for us.

### THE LAMPSTAND

Remember how God told Moses to make a lampstand of pure gold to light the *Holy Place?* This is a picture of Jesus who said,

> *"I am the Light of the world; he who follows Me will not walk in the darkness, but will have the Light of life."* John 8:12 NASB

Jesus is the Light of life, and he wants to deliver people out of the darkness of sin into the light of eternal life.

### THE TABLE WITH THE BREAD

Remember how God told Moses to make a table and place on it twelve loaves of bread, each representing one of the twelve tribes of Israel? Again, this is a picture of Jesus who said,

> *"I am the bread of life."* John 6:35 NKJV

Just as the twelve loaves spoke of a sufficient provision for everyone in Israel, so Jesus, as the bread of life, offers us eternal life.

> *"Truly...I say to you, he who believes has eternal life. I am the bread of life."* John 6:47-48 NASB

## The Curtain

Think again about how God instructed Moses to hang a thick curtain between the *Holy Place* and the *Holy of Holies*. Sinful man was barred from entering God's holy presence.

In the same way, the Scripture tells us we are separated from God—we are **ESTRANGED** from the Lord and his love.

But then Jesus came. When he died on the cross, the curtain was ripped in two. No man could have torn the veil, but God tore it to illustrate Jesus' body being "torn" for you and me. When we put our trust in him, our sin is forgiven and we can enter boldly into God's presence. The relationship has been restored.

> *Therefore, brothers, since we have confidence to enter the Most Holy Place by the blood of Jesus, by a new and living way opened for us through the curtain, that is, his body … let us draw near to God with a sincere heart in full assurance …*
> Hebrews 10:19–20,22 NIV

> *But now in Christ Jesus you who used to be far away have been brought near by the blood of Christ.* Ephesians 2:13 NET

We are not accepted back simply as friends. The Scripture tells us that we are placed into God's family as full-fledged members—it says we are **adopted**.

In the Roman world of Jesus' day, *adoption* was the legal rite of *investing sonship*. In our modern society, a child born into a family is automatically recognized as having all the rights and privileges of that family—a bona fide heir. But in a world where men had wives, concubines, and mistresses, as well as children by their slaves, a child was not a legal heir until invested with that sonship in a special ceremony.

So it is with us. We, who once were **ESTRANGED** from God's love, have now become members of God's family—**ADOPTED** as sons. We are heirs of Heaven; we belong entirely to the Lord.

> *Because you are sons, God sent the Spirit of his Son into our hearts, the Spirit who calls out, "Abba [Daddy], Father." So you are no longer a slave [to sin and Satan], but a son; and since you are a son, God has made you also an heir.*
> Galatians 4:6-7 NIV

## THE ATONEMENT COVER

The *Atonement Cover* was that special lid on the *Ark of the Covenant* which was located in the *Holy of Holies*. It was here that the High Priest brought the blood once a year on the *Day of Atonement*. God gave the Israelites a way to escape judgment of their sin through the shed blood of an innocent lamb.

In the same way, Jesus is now our *Atonement Cover* and, through his blood, God has provided a way for us to escape eternal death. For those who trust him, the LORD says,

> *"Their sins and lawless acts I will remember no more."* And where these have been forgiven, there is no longer any sacrifice for sin.
> Hebrews 10:17-18 NIV

With Jesus' death on the cross, the last Lamb had died. Now it was no longer necessary to offer any kind of sacrifice, because …

> … we have been made holy through the sacrifice of the body of Jesus Christ **once for all**.

> Day after day every priest stands and performs his religious duties; again and again he offers the same sacrifices, which can never take away sins. But when this priest [Jesus] had offered for all time one sacrifice for sins, he sat down at the right hand of God.
> Hebrew 10:10–12 NIV

God accepted the animals because he was looking forward in history to the time when Jesus would die as the final sacrifice. As we saw before, when Jesus died he did more than cover sin for a year. He blotted it out from God's sight forever. On the cross he cried, *"It is finished!" Tetelestai! —the final Lamb is found.*

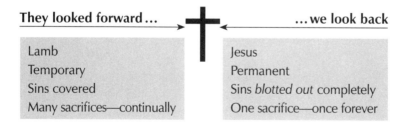

| They looked forward… | …we look back |
|---|---|
| Lamb | Jesus |
| Temporary | Permanent |
| Sins covered | Sins *blotted out* completely |
| Many sacrifices—continually | One sacrifice—once forever |

## PROPHECY

We saw earlier the remarkable accuracy of prophecy in the Bible. Jesus himself said,

> *"Do not think that I came to destroy the Law or the Prophets."*
> Matthew 5:17 NKJV

The phrase, *"the law or the Prophets"* is a biblical way of referring to the entire Old Testament. The verse continues with Jesus saying,

> *"I did not come to destroy but to fulfill. For assuredly, I say to you, till heaven and earth pass away, one jot or one tittle will by no means pass from the law till all is fulfilled."*
>
> Matthew 5:17-18 NKJV

A jot or tittle was either a small letter or mark in the alphabet. What Jesus said was that his fulfillment of Scripture would be completed down to the last detail; in alphabetical terms, to the smallest letter—even the smallest part of a letter.

I remember talking to a surgeon who had participated in an overview of the Bible similar to what you are now reading. He told me that at the beginning he had viewed the stories about creation, Adam and Eve, Noah, etc., as being no more than myths. But as the overview progressed, and he saw how the Bible stories were fulfilled in Jesus, he said he came to the point when he recognized that *"all this could not have happened just by chance."* He told me how, in his mind, he went back and accepted as true all those stories he had previously questioned.

We said earlier that fulfilled prophecy was God's way of astounding us, so that we would listen to the whole message of the Bible, the part that has to do with deliverance from death.

# 5 The Emmaus Road Message
## — From Nicodemus to the Resurrection —

During his earthly ministry, Jesus made it clear that mankind is in trouble and needs a Saviour. The Bible says,

> *All of us like sheep have gone astray, Each of us has turned to his own way…*
>
> Isaiah 53:6 NASB

LOST

We saw that at the beginning of time man chose to go his own way, taking a path that led him into a spiritual wilderness. The Bible says that man is **LOST**.

FOUND

But then the Lord Jesus came looking for us. While on earth, he told a parable that describes God's concern.

*"Suppose one of you has a hundred sheep and loses one of them. Does he not leave the ninety-nine in the open country and go after the lost sheep until he finds it?*

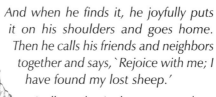

*And when he finds it, he joyfully puts it on his shoulders and goes home. Then he calls his friends and neighbors together and says, `Rejoice with me; I have found my lost sheep.'*

*I tell you that in the same way there will be more rejoicing in heaven over one sinner who **repents** than over ninety-nine righteous persons who do not need to **repent**."*
Luke 15:4–7 NIV

We saw that the word repent means to have *a change of mind.* The term is quite broad and is often confused with penance or sorrow.[6] Neither is in question here. The issue at stake involves *a change in thinking:*

❖ Will a person admit to being a *helpless sinner?*

❖ Will he stop trusting in himself, his own ideas and wisdom, and trust in the Lord Jesus?

❖ Will he transfer faith from his own religion and idols to faith in YAHWEH alone?

A positive answer to any of these questions will have involved *a change of mind.* Repentance is linked to faith. When a person believes, he repents. He has gone from unbelief to belief, from trusting in himself to trusting in the Lord Jesus, from faith in religion to faith in Christ. He has had a *change of mind.* The Bible says that…

*…there is joy in the presence of the angels of God over one sinner who repents.*
Luke 15:10 NASB

### REPENTANCE AND JOY

The reason for this joy is obvious. Think of the cost. Jesus said,

*"I am the good shepherd. The good shepherd lays down his life for the sheep."*
John 10:11 ESV

His death on our behalf involved an immeasurable sacrifice. When Jesus was on the cross he cried out,

*"My God, my God, why have You forsaken Me?"* Mark 15:34 NKJV

Jesus did not just die a physical death, there was also a spiritual dimension. *Sin demands separation.* In those desperate hours on the cross, God the Father turned his back on his Son. It must have wrenched his loving heart, but consistent with his holy nature, God could not look upon Jesus as he took our sin upon himself. The Bible says that the sky grew dark although it was midday. It seems as though the Father did not want the world to see the agony that the Son went through, as Jesus willingly took our sin on himself, became our substitute Lamb, and died. God allowed it; indeed, he planned it. It was motivated by love.

When a sinner repents he is responding to that love. When you think of what Jesus went through to provide for our salvation, it's not hard to see why that brings joy in Heaven!

## NICODEMUS

Jesus spoke of this great love in his conversation with Nicodemus. Nicodemus needed to have a *change of mind.* He thought he was righteous but Jesus made it clear that he was a sinner. He needed to stop trusting in his own righteousness and instead trust in Christ. Jesus told Nicodemus,

> *"For God so loved the world that he gave his one and only Son, that whoever believes in him shall not perish but have eternal life. For God did not send his Son into the world to condemn the world, but to save the world through him."*
>
> *John 3:16–17 NIV*

God promised eternal life not only to Nicodemus, but to whoever believes in him. As we know, the LORD has a long history of keeping his promises. He was not about to ruin his reputation on Nicodemus—or on one of us for that matter. Jesus continued,

> *"Whoever believes in him is not condemned, but whoever does not believe is condemned already, because he has not believed in the name of the only Son of God."*     *John 3:18 ESV*

ETERNAL
JUDGMENT

Jesus said man is born into this world "condemned already." We have no relationship with God; our bodies will eventually die and, after physical death, we will partake of the *Second Death*, an **ETERNAL JUDGMENT** in the Lake of Fire.

ETERNAL
LIFE

But then Jesus paid the sin-penalty with his own death. However, Jesus did not remain dead—he came back to life. When we trust him, we too become spiritually alive with **ETERNAL LIFE**. The Bible speaks of this as being *born again.* It is at this point the LORD YAHWEH records a new believer's name in the *Lamb's Book of Life.*

*When you were dead in your sins … God **made you alive** with Christ. He forgave us all our sins …*        *Colossians 2:13 NIV*

*But because of his great love for us, God, who is rich in mercy, **made us alive** with Christ even when we were dead in transgressions [or sin] …*        *Ephesians 2:4-5 NIV*

## REDEEMED

SLAVE

For centuries man had been a **SLAVE** to Satan's will. Through blatant lies, imitation of the truth, even the denial of his own existence, Satan had manipulated mankind for his own purposes. But even without Satan's influence, man could not live a perfect life. Man was a **SLAVE** to sin.

SET-FREE
REDEEMED

But then Jesus came and **REDEEMED** us. It is difficult for us to grasp the rich significance of this word if we do not understand its association with ancient slavery. Let me explain.

A wealthy man would go to the slave market to buy a slave. There he would see the captives chained, humbled, and broken, each being sold for a given sum. The man would pay the asking price, and the slave would become his. So far this was nothing unusual, but now the story takes an interesting twist. On rare occasions the new owner would then take his new slave out of the slave market, break off the chains and set him free. When this happened it was said that the slave had been **REDEEMED**.

That is what Jesus Christ did for us. We were bound by the chains of sin and Satan in the slave market of life. We were helpless to deliver ourselves. But then Jesus came and purchased us, paying the price with his own blood. He took us out of the market, broke off the chains, and set us free.

*For you know that it was not with perishable things such as silver or gold that you were **redeemed** from the empty way of life …, but with the precious blood of Christ, a lamb without blemish or defect.*        *1 Peter 1:18-19 NIV*

*Christ **redeemed** us [or set us free] from the curse of the law by becoming a curse for us—for it is written, "Cursed is everyone who is hanged on a tree."* Galatians 3:13 ESV

*In him we have **redemption** through his blood, the forgiveness of sins, in accordance with the riches of God's grace.* Ephesians 1:7 NIV

### VOLUNTARY

The Romans have been blamed for executing Jesus, and the religious leaders for pressuring them to do it. Over the centuries the Jews have faced immense persecution on the premise that the whole sorry affair was their fault. Such perceptions are completely false. The truth of the matter is that the sins of the whole world were responsible for nailing Jesus to the cross. Furthermore, the Bible states clearly that it was Jesus who voluntarily laid down his life.

### THE RESURRECTION

Jesus died, yes, but he did not remain dead—he came back to life after three days.

*"The reason my Father loves me is that I lay down my life—only to take it up again. No one takes it from me, but I lay it down of my own accord. I have authority to lay it down and authority to take it up again."* John 10:17–18 NIV

The resurrection was a powerful display that God's just nature was satisfied by Jesus' death on our behalf. The payment had been made and it had been accepted as sufficient! The grave could not hold him in its clutches. He had victory over death! Jesus had broken sin's grip, defeated Satan's power and removed death's terrible finality.

*Therefore, since the children share in flesh and blood, he likewise shared in their humanity, so that through death he could destroy the one who holds the power of death (that is, the devil), and set free those who were held in slavery all their lives by their fear of death.* Hebrews 2:14-15 NET

An overwhelming sense of defeat must have swept over Satan when Jesus was resurrected. Satan thought that when he enticed Judas Iscariot to betray Jesus, he was the winner. Now he had been defeated at his own game. His most powerful tool—death—had lost its sting.

## FINAL JUDGMENT

Though Satan is still a power to be reckoned with during this evil age, a day is coming when the LORD YAHWEH will seize him and cast him into *Gehenna*, the "garbage dump" of the universe.

> *The devil, who deceived them, was cast into the lake of fire and brimstone where . . . [he] will be tormented day and night forever and ever.*                    Revelation 20:10 NKJV

Satan and his demons will be confined in the . . .

> *. . . eternal fire prepared for the devil and his angels.*
>                             Matthew 25:41 ESV

Then those who have rejected Jesus as Saviour will stand in God's courtroom.

> *Then I saw a **great white throne** and Him who sat on it, from whose face the earth and the heaven fled away. And there was found no place for them.*
>
> *And I saw the dead, small and great, standing before God, and books were opened. And another book was opened, which is the **Book of Life.** And the dead were judged according to their works, by the things which were written in the books. . . . This is the second death. **And anyone not found written in the Book of Life was cast into the lake of fire.***      Revelation 20:11-15 NKJV

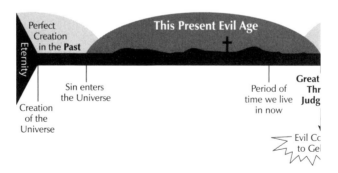

When the *Great White Throne Judgment* is completed, a new age will dawn when all the redeemed of the LORD shall live with YAHWEH forever.

> *. . . according to his promise we are waiting for new heavens and a new earth in which righteousness dwells.*      2 Peter 3:13 ESV

## A New Age

One of the 40 prophets who was given a foretaste of the age to come, wrote:

*Now I saw a new heaven and a new earth, for the first heaven and the first earth had passed away…*

*And I heard a loud voice from heaven saying, "Behold, the tabernacle of God is with men, and He will dwell with them, and they shall be His people. God Himself will be with them and be their God. And God will wipe away every tear from their eyes; there shall be no more death, nor sorrow, nor crying. There shall be no more pain, for the former things have passed away."*

*Then He who sat on the throne said, "Behold, I make all things new."*                                                    *Revelation 21:1,3-5 NKJV*

He wrote that he saw a large city,

*But I saw no temple in it, for the Lord God Almighty and the Lamb are its temple. The city had no need of the sun or of the moon to shine in it, for the glory of God illuminated it. The Lamb is its light…*

*But there shall by no means enter it anything that defiles, or causes an abomination or a lie, but only those who are written in the Lamb's Book of Life."*                          *Revelation 21:22-23,27 NKJV*

Until that day, Jesus—the Lamb of God—says,

*"…I am the gate. Those who come in through me will be saved."*
                                                                                   *John 10:9 NLT*

Jesus is the only door to Heaven. There is no other way. Just as there was only one way in which Abel could approach God, just as there was only one door to safety in Noah's boat, just as there was only one door to the Tabernacle, and just as there is only one door to a sheep pen, so Jesus is the only way to God.

Some people believe you can come to God by another religion, perhaps by some combination of many religions, but the Bible allows no room for other ways to God. This may be viewed as discriminatory in our politically correct age, but repeatedly, the Bible echoes this theme: Jesus is the only way.

*There is salvation in no one else, for there is no other name under heaven given among men by which we must be saved…*
                                                                                   *Acts 4:12 ESV*

Some may call this narrow-mindedness, however, to be true to the text, I must say that this is what the Bible clearly teaches. It also says that God allows us the freedom to reject his chosen way, but then we must also pay our sin-penalty with eternal death. Of course, one can deny the existence of God and ignore the Bible's message entirely, though it is a hazardous option.

---

### TOLERANCE

Though Jesus made it clear that there was no other way to God, he did not advocate violent suppression of other belief systems. His approach was to teach truth. Truth exposes error and people are then free to make their own choice.

---

As the disciples listened to Jesus teach from the Law and the Prophets, they must have had premonitions of the consequences of his message. They lived in the Roman Empire. The Romans were tolerant of other religions up to a point, but they had also come to believe that Caesar was a god. The Romans would not object to Jesus being presented as *another* way to God, but to teach what Jesus taught—that He is the only way—would jeopardize their lives. According to non-biblical sources, all but one of the eleven original disciples were put to death for this message. They died for what they knew to be true. The eleventh was exiled. Doctor Luke wrote that one disciple said,

> *"He commanded us to preach to the people and to testify that he is the one whom God appointed as judge of the living and the dead. All the prophets testify about him that everyone who believes in him receives forgiveness of sins through his name."*
> Acts 10:42-43 NIV

The Bible is full of illustrations of who Jesus Christ is and what he has done. We can only speculate as to which of those illustrations Jesus used as he taught the disciples. He may have used most or all of the ones we have touched on. When he had finished teaching the room must have been silent. The questions which remained for Jesus' disciples are the same questions which remain for us. In whom are you placing your faith—in yourself, your religion, your ideas, your good works, or in the fact that Jesus died in your place to pay your sin-debt?

# 6 The Court Room

We have now answered two of the three age-old questions:

1. **Question:** How can we escape paying the penalty for our sin?

   **Answer:** Jesus paid the penalty for us. He died in our place.

2. **Question:** How do we get our names recorded in the *Lamb's Book of Life?*

   **Answer:** At the point we trust in Jesus, our names are written in the *Book of Life.*

We will now focus on the third ancient question:

3. **Question:** How do we, as sinners, obtain a righteousness that is *equal* to God's righteousness so we can live in Heaven? How do we obtain "clean clothes?"

   Even with our sin-debt paid we are still not perfect. We need to know how a righteous God makes a sinner fit to live in his presence. To answer that question, we need to learn a concept called *justification.*

### JUSTIFIED

We saw that God did not break his own Law—he kept the rules. By the death of Jesus, God was able to...

> ...demonstrate his justice at the present time, so as to be just and the one who **justifies** those who have faith in Jesus.
>
> *Romans 3:26 NIV*

The word *justifies* was a judicial term used in the courtrooms of Jesus' day. We don't use the word in common speech today, but once explained, it is not hard to understand. To begin with, we need to establish the setting.

When the LORD first created Adam and Eve, mankind was innocent of all sin. Because they were sinless, YAHWEH was able to walk and talk with them as a friend. But then man cast off his innocence and followed Satan. As a result, man took on a different nature—a sin nature. Separated by sin, God set aside his friendship and donned the cloak of a magistrate. Man was summoned to the courtroom bench to face the LORD, no longer as a friend but as a Judge.

This is the setting for a passage of Scripture that the prophet Zechariah recorded 500 years before the time of Christ. It is a story that illustrates the concept of justification. Zechariah wrote,

> *Then he showed me Joshua the high priest standing before...*
> *the L*ORD*, and Satan standing at his right hand to accuse him.*[7]
> *Zechariah 3:1 NASB*

Imagine with me for a moment. Visualize Joshua standing in God's courtroom, exhausted, his face flushed. As a religious man, Joshua has lived an upright life. Nonetheless, Satan[8] stands at his side accusing him of all sorts of sins—even private ones that Joshua entertained only in his mind. The courtroom is hushed as the litany of sin goes on and on. To make matters worse, no lawyer rises to defend Joshua. None can. Joshua knows that much of what Satan is saying is true—though granted, it is being said with an ugly twist.

But then, reaching out to Joshua with the same compassion that caused him to touch a leper,

> *...the L*ORD *said to Satan, "I, the L*ORD*, reject your accusations,*
> *Satan."... This man is like a burning stick that has been snatched*
> *from the fire."*                                    *Zechariah 3:2 NLT*

The LORD is looking upon Joshua with compassion—but it is a love that faces an obstacle. You see, the Bible says,

> *Joshua was clothed with filthy garments...*    *Zechariah 3:3 NASB*

Joshua is a sinner as represented by his filthy rags. He is **GUILTY** of breaking God's perfect law.

GUILTY

❖ The LORD cannot excuse Joshua as if he had never committed a sin. That would not be right.

❖ The demands of the law must be met. Joshua must be punished for his sin. That is only fair and just.

Joshua is in an awful dilemma. But God isn't stuck. He has a plan.

The Lord rises from his judgment bench and without taking off his judicial cloak, he puts on the mantle of a friend. He leaves the lofty heights of Heaven, and descends as the righteous Jesus to stand with Joshua in front of the bench. He has only one purpose—to take Joshua's sentence upon himself and pay it for him. Then the Lord…

> …said to those who were standing before him, "Take off his filthy clothes." 
> Zechariah 3:4 NIV

Since Jesus has no sin of his own to die for, he takes responsibility for Joshua's filthy rags of sin and dies in Joshua's place, paying the death penalty for him.

> Then he said to Joshua, "See, I have taken away your sin…" 
> Zechariah 3:4 NIV

Joshua's sin-debt is gone!

### IMPLORING

We will continue the story of Joshua in a moment but let me stress the significance of what we just read.

Let us suppose for a moment that you have been caught in a criminal offense. The judge fines you with the full penalty of the law—a huge sum of money. It will take your lifetime to pay it off! But then the judge steps down from his bench, and at great cost to himself, writes out a cheque for the entire amount. He pays the fine for you! Obviously, those watching the trial are astonished—but they are also satisfied. The fine has been paid! The *demands of the law* have been fully met. Nothing more is expected.

One question remains: *Will you accept the Judge's provision?* If you accept the payment, you are free to go. But if you reject his generosity, then you will have to pay the fine yourself. *Are you willing to humble yourself to accept the payment?* By the way, you need to know that the judge has a personal concern for you—he is not only your judge, but he is also your father! In his love, he wants you to accept the payment, but he will not force it on you. You must accept it of your own free will.

In the same way, the Bible speaks of the Lord "imploring" people to accept his payment on their behalf, but because he is gracious, he will not force them against their will.

We will now return to the story of Joshua.

**RIGHTEOUSNESS**

Though Joshua's sin-debt had been paid, he still could not live in God's presence. Joshua was not perfect. Righteous clothing was needed. To provide that purity, something more had to happen in God's courtroom. Here it is.

Jesus not only took responsibility for Joshua's putrid rags of sin, but then—wonder of wonders—the LORD took his own robe of righteousness and wrapped it around Joshua. Joshua was clothed in God's perfection!

> Then he said to Joshua, "See, I have taken away your sin, and I will put rich garments on you."
>
> Then I said, "Put a clean turban on his head." So they put a clean turban on his head and clothed him, while...the LORD stood by.                                      Zechariah 3:4-5 NIV

Joshua could now say with the prophet Isaiah,

> "I will greatly rejoice in the LORD, My soul shall be joyful in my God; For He has clothed me with the garments of salvation, He has covered me with the robe of righteousness..."
>
> Isaiah 61:10 NKJV

Once again the LORD dons the magistrate's cloak and takes his place behind the courtroom bench. As he looks down and sees Joshua clothed in God's righteousness, the LORD can honestly and justly say, "*In my heavenly courtroom, Joshua, you stand before me perfect.*"

The Almighty Judge of Heaven raises his gavel and with a crash declares Joshua, "*Righteous!*" At this point Joshua's name is recorded in the *Lamb's Book of Life*.

Joshua can now live with the perfect God in his perfect Heaven. Never again will he stand in God's courtroom—he will not face the *Great White Throne Judgment* at the end of this evil age.

DECLARED RIGHTEOUS

With that we conclude the story of Joshua. We now know the meaning of the word **JUSTIFIED**—*to be declared righteous* in the sight of God.[9] The Bible says...

> ...a man is justified by faith...                    Romans 3:28 NKJV

Those who trust in Jesus can be confident that when the LORD looks at them, he no longer sees their sin but rather he sees them clothed in his perfect righteousness.

### Life Priority

One of the 40 writers testified that the ultimate priority in life is to …

> … be found [clothed] in him, not having a righteousness of my own that comes from the law, but that which is through faith in Christ—the righteousness that comes **from God** and is **by faith.** Philippians 3:9 NIV

It is not our righteousness that counts, but His. All our good works, our prayers, our special promises, our performance of religious ritual, our keeping of the Ten Commandments cannot make us righteous, for …

> … a man is not declared righteous by works of law …
> Galatians 2:16 YLT

In YAHWEH's courtroom, none of us can declare ourselves, *"Pure, pure, pure, pure!"* No matter how good our life—like an arrow aiming for the bull's-eye—we miss the mark of perfection …

> … for all have sinned and fall short of the glory of God …
> Romans 3:23 NASB

But in Jesus we have what the prophet Jeremiah foretold 600 years before Christ. He wrote that the MESSIAH …

> … shall be called, The LORD our Righteousness. Jeremiah 23:6 KJV

### In Summary

The story of Joshua can be summed up as a *great exchange*. It involves both an empty cross and an empty tomb.

**The Empty Cross:** The Bible says that …

> God made him who had no sin to be sin for us …
> 2 Corinthians 5:21 NIV

This verse is not saying that Jesus became a sinner. The word *sin* has the idea of a sin-offering. *"God made Jesus, who had no sin, to be a **sin-offering** for us …"* When Jesus took our sin-penalty upon himself, God poured out on him all the fury of his rightful anger towards sin. Then Jesus was able to do something we could not do. He said, *"It is finished."* If we had paid our own sin-debt, we would have gone on and on, paying for eternity. We could never have said, *"It is finished."* But Jesus paid it all.

**The Empty Tomb:** The rest of the verse reads,

> ...*so that in him we might become the righteousness of God.*
> 2 Corinthians 5:21 NIV

It is in Jesus that we find righteousness! It is not ours. When we trust him, we are clothed in his righteousness! We are equipped to live in God's presence in his perfect Heaven.

This is the greatest of all exchanges. Jesus takes our rags of sin and offers us his cloak of righteousness. The answer to that age-old, *two-sides-of-the-same-coin* question is found in this one verse. Read it again.

> *God made him who had no sin to be [a] sin [offering] for us,*
> *so that in him we might become the righteousness of God.*
> 2 Corinthians 5:21 NIV

The death of Jesus as our substitute, and the clothing of us in his righteousness, constitute the message of the *empty cross* and *empty tomb*.

> *He was delivered over to death for our sins **[the empty cross]***
> *and was raised to life for our justification **[the empty tomb]**.*
> Romans 4:25 NIV

This is what the Bible calls the gospel—literally, *the good news*.

# 7 The Person, the Provision, the Promise

Before we complete this chapter we need to clarify one more point. It has to do with the subject of faith. Remember how...

> *Abraham believed God, and it was credited to him as*
> *righteousness.* Romans 4:3 NET

God advanced righteousness to Abraham because the LORD was looking ahead to what Jesus would do on the cross. The same principle applies to us too, only instead of looking forward to the cross, we now look back in time.

> *The words "it was credited to him" were written not for*
> *[Abraham] alone, but also for us, to whom God will credit*
> *righteousness—for us who believe in him who raised Jesus our*
> *Lord from the dead.* Romans 4:23-24 NIV

We too, can have a cloak of righteousness *if* we believe in him.

## BELIEVE, TRUST

Remember that the word *believe,* as used in the Bible, has a fuller meaning than we sometimes give it.

❖ We said that the terms *faith, belief, trust,* and *confidence* all mean essentially the same thing. Faith is believing something to be true—to be trustworthy.

❖ We saw that the warning to *"never trust a stranger"* applies to faith. Before you trust someone, you need to know:

1. **His Identity:** What is his name, where is he from, and who does he claim to be?

2. **His History:** What is his reputation? Is he reliable?

We said that Scripture was written so mankind could become acquainted with YAHWEH. In many ways, you probably now know more about the LORD than you know about many of your friends. If so, that is exactly what Scripture intended.

## BELIEVE WHAT?

This brings us to the question, *"To know forgiveness of sin and gain this righteousness offered by God, just what must one believe?"* The answer brings us back to these two points:

1. **What is the identity of the one whom we are to trust?** As we have seen, the Bible clearly reveals a unique God—the LORD YAHWEH—who is the Supreme Being, Creator, and Owner of all. It is this God who came to earth in the person of the Lord Jesus Christ. It is in him we must trust to the exclusion of all other gods, goddesses, spirits, ancestors, or idols. Only he is worthy of our trust, no others.

It is important to keep in mind that this is not just a matter of believing historical data, but rather trusting in a living being, the "person" of YAHWEH—in whom there is love, guidance, and protection. It is a relationship that has a starting point, but can then grow deeper every day, here on earth and forever in Heaven.

2. **Does YAHWEH have a reliable history?** To answer this question, we will look at two areas:

   a. **YAHWEH's provision:** At a point in time in history, Jesus died on a cross for our sin. Three days later he was resurrected. We must believe both.

b. *YAHWEH*'s promise: The LORD has a long history of keeping promises. He is now promising to save us from sin's death-penalty, clothe us in righteousness and write our names in the *Book of Life*. Do we believe him? Do we trust him? The Bible says we need to simply take him at his word.

We need to reverse what happened in the Garden of Eden. Instead of trusting in yourself or in Satan, you need to...

*Believe on the **Lord Jesus Christ**, and you will be saved...*
Acts 16:31 NKJV

To believe on the Lord Jesus Christ is to believe in *who he is* and *what he has done*—his identity and history.

1. We can trust in our own ideas like Cain—perhaps worship our own man-made gods like the people of Babel, or...

2. We can trust the LORD like Abraham and believe what he has promised.

We have to decide one way or the other. To make no choice is to decide against him. But if we do choose to trust him, the LORD has promised that...

*...God will credit righteousness—for us who believe in him who raised Jesus our Lord from the dead.* Romans 4:24 NIV

There is nothing left for us to do, but to believe.

## GOOD WORKS

Over the centuries man has attempted to bridge the chasm caused by sin. Every method tried has involved some sort of *effort* or *work* on man's part.

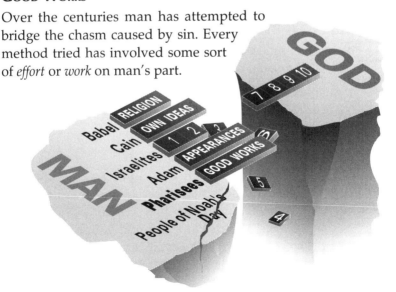

## But Now

> *But now a righteousness from God, apart from law, has been made known, to which the Law and the Prophets testify. This righteousness from God comes through faith in Jesus Christ to all who believe.*
> *Romans 3:21-22 NIV*

The Bible says that salvation is "not from ourselves, it is the gift of God" and is only available to those who believe.

> *For it is by grace you have been saved, through faith—and this not from yourselves, it is the gift of God—not by works, so that no one can boast.*
> *Ephesians 2:8-9 NIV*

The *gift of God* is eternal life.

> *For the wages of sin is death, but the free gift of God is eternal life in Christ Jesus our Lord.*
> *Romans 6:23 ESV*

Notice that the gift is free. If we work for a gift, it is no longer a gift. If we feel we have earned it in any way, then it ceases to be a gift and becomes an award. But the Bible says the gift of eternal life is free—available to those who believe certain facts to be true.

*We believe* Jesus Christ is Yahweh himself.

*We believe* that Jesus died in our place, paying our sin-debt.

We believe that God's justice was satisfied by that death—that when he looks at us, he no longer views our sin, but he sees us clothed in Jesus' righteousness.

*We believe* that God gives us the gift of eternal life.

*We believe* God keeps his promises.

*We believe* that God has written our names in the Lamb's Book of eternal life.

It is all faith, but it is not blind faith. It is faith resulting from knowing Yahweh's long and reliable history.

Some people add a spiritual aura to faith. It becomes quantified. You either have a lot of faith or just a little. But that thinking confuses the issue. Putting faith in Jesus is similar to a drowning man nodding to his rescuer when the lifesaver says, *"Will you trust me to save you?"* The size of the nod is immaterial. The point is not the nod at all. The point is that the drowning man is acknowledging his predicament and trusting in the lifeguard to rescue him. For the drowning man to later claim that his big nod saved his life would be ludicrous.

So it is with us. We need to acknowledge that we are helpless sinners and then trust in Jesus to save us from our sin. It is not the size of our trust that saves us. It is Jesus who does the saving. It is all of him and none of us.

> For in the gospel a **righteousness from God** is revealed, a righteousness that is **by faith from first to last** ...
>
> *Romans 1:17 NIV*

As I write this chapter, an eleven year-old boy has just been found after being lost four days in the wilderness. During that time he often saw people who were looking for him, but in keeping with his parents' training, he did not trust the strangers and hid himself from his rescuers.

The Bible tells us that ...

> ... the Son of Man has come to seek and to save that which was lost.
>
> *Luke 19:10 NKJV*

We hide from the LORD to our own hurt. No longer is he a stranger. We know his history—it is long and reliable. We can trust him.

# CHAPTER FIFTEEN

# 1 WHAT DO YOU WANT ME TO DO?

In the days immediately following Jesus' resurrection, he spent time with his disciples and…

> …showed himself to these men and gave many convincing proofs that he was alive. He appeared to them over a period of forty days and spoke about the kingdom of God.     Acts 1:3 NIV

In the end Jesus took them back to familiar ground, just three kilometres (two miles) from Jerusalem.

> When he had led them out to the vicinity of Bethany, he lifted up his hands and blessed them. While he was blessing them, he left them and was taken up into heaven.     Luke 24:50-51 NIV

> They were looking intently up into the sky as he was going, when suddenly two men dressed in white stood beside them. "Men of Galilee," they said, "why do you stand here looking into the sky? This same Jesus, who has been taken from you into heaven, will come back in the same way you have seen him go into heaven."     Acts 1:10-11 NIV

The angels said Jesus would come again. If we were to study the Bible further, we would see that it has a lot to say about that future event.[1] Just as God kept his promise related to prophecies about his first coming, we can be assured that he will keep his word regarding his second coming. He always does.

The rest of the Bible records the events surrounding the lives of the disciples who became known as *apostles*. These followers of Jesus told multitudes of people about him.

> So the word of God spread. The number of disciples in Jerusalem increased rapidly, and a large number of [temple] priests became obedient to the faith.     Acts 6:7 NIV

But not everyone was convinced and, just as the disciples must have anticipated, there was resistance. One particularly ardent *Jesus-hater* was a young Pharisee named *Saul*, who murdered and imprisoned followers of Jesus.

> Meanwhile, Saul was still breathing out murderous threats against the Lord's disciples. He went to the high priest and asked him for letters to the synagogues in Damascus, so that if he found any there who belonged to the Way, whether men or women, he might take them as prisoners to Jerusalem.

*As he neared Damascus on his journey, suddenly a light from heaven flashed around him. He fell to the ground and heard a voice say to him, "Saul, Saul, why do you persecute me?"*

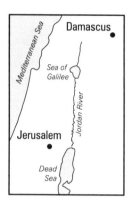

*"Who are you, Lord?" Saul asked.*

*"I am Jesus, whom you are persecuting,"* he replied.                Acts 9:1–5 NIV

This was the beginning of a remarkable life. Saul changed radically. He stopped killing believers and became one himself. The tables turned and the persecutor became the persecuted. On one occasion he was stoned with rocks and left for dead. Three times he was beaten with rods; five times whipped; three times shipwrecked (during one of which he floated on the sea for twenty-four hours). All of this occurred as Saul tried to tell others about his own belief that Jesus was THE PROMISED SAVIOUR. This Saul was none other than the man we know as *Paul the Apostle,* the one who wrote a significant part of the Bible.

Over and over again, we have seen throughout the Scriptures that God asked thought-provoking questions. These queries were designed to expose and clarify a person's innermost thoughts so that the one being addressed would have to grapple with reality. Saul, too, was confronted by God and asked a question:

*"Saul, Saul, why do you persecute me?"*                Acts 9:4 NIV

In a way, God was saying, "Saul, why are you my enemy when you could be my friend?" Saul's reply revealed that he knew exactly who was quizzing him. He said, *"Lord."*

If we were to be so fortunate as to encounter YAHWEH in person, I can not help but feel that he would begin the conversation with a question. The likelihood of being confronted in the same way as Saul is very remote; in all of Scripture it happened to only a few. Even though we may not be confronted in person, we are still faced with what God has recorded in the Bible. Through it he asks us a question. *"Will you trust Jesus as your own personal Saviour—the one and only God-man who paid your sin-debt?"*

Don't answer without thought. Maybe you have been thinking it through. On the other hand, maybe you need to take some time to ponder the question.

If you answer, *"No, I don't trust Jesus,"* then the rest of this chapter will have little relevance for you. You are welcome to read it, but I would suggest you skip this section and finish with the next section titled, *A CONVENIENT TIME* (page 359). The Bible says that if we reject the message of the cross, then the rest of the Scripture will not be understood correctly because …

> … *it is veiled to those who are perishing.*
>
> *The god of this age [Satan] has blinded the minds of unbelievers, so that they cannot see the light of the gospel [the good news] of the glory of Christ, who is the image of God.*
>
> 2 Corinthians 4:3-4 NIV

On the other hand, if you answer, *"Yes, I would like to trust Jesus,"* or *"Yes, I believe He has paid my sin-debt,"* then read on. The rest of the Bible is written for people like you.

If in all sincerity you trust the Lord Jesus, believing that he is YAHWEH, that he died for your sin and rose again, then based on what the Bible says, you can rest assured that your sins are forgiven and that your friendship with God has been restored. You can have complete confidence that your *Certificate of Debt* has been paid in full.

> … *when you were dead in your transgressions²… He made you alive together with Him, having forgiven us all our transgressions, having **canceled out the certificate of debt consisting of decrees against us** and which was hostile to us; and He has taken it out of the way, having nailed it to the cross.*
>
> Colossians 2:13-14 NASB

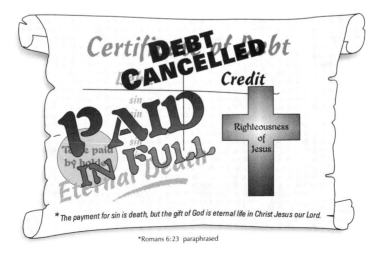

*\* The payment for sin is death, but the gift of God is eternal life in Christ Jesus our Lord.*

\*Romans 6:23 paraphrased

Your sin-debt was nailed to the cross two thousand years ago. Because of your trust in him, God now says that your...

> "...sins and lawless acts I will remember no more."
>
> Hebrews 10:17 NIV

YAHWEH's forgiveness is total. Your filthy rags of sin are gone.

> For as high as the heavens are above the earth, so great is his love for those who fear [or respect] him; as far as the east is from the west, so far has he removed our transgressions[2] from us.
>
> Psalm 103:11,12 NIV

> Therefore, if anyone is in Christ, he is a new creation; old things have passed away; behold, all things have become new.
>
> 2 Corinthians 5:17 NKJV

Now instead of Eternal Death in the Lake of Fire, Jesus says,

> "Let not your heart be troubled; you believe in God, believe also in Me. In My Father's house are many mansions; if it were not so, I would have told you.
>
> I go to prepare a place for you. And if I go and prepare a place for you, I will come again and receive you to Myself; that where I am, there you may be also. And where I go you know, and the way you know."
>
> John 14:1–4 NKJV

### RELATIONSHIP

As a believer, life still goes on, but now you are assured of a future destiny in Heaven. Jesus says he is preparing a dwelling place for you. With confidence you can now say that you are a citizen of Heaven. Your **relationship** with God is now restored.

Just as you were once born into an earthly family, the Bible says you have now been born into God's family. And just as your earthly parents will always be your parents regardless of what happens, so it is that once you are born into God's family, you cannot be *un-born*. It is important to understand that when it comes to your

**relationship** with God, your eternal destiny is settled once for all. You belong to God's family for eternity.[3]

> I write these things to you who believe in the name of the Son of God **so that you may know that you have**[4] **eternal life**.
>
> 1 John 5:13 NIV

> For I am convinced that neither death nor life, neither angels nor demons, neither the present nor the future, nor any powers, neither height nor depth, nor anything else in all creation, will be able to separate us from the love of God that is in Christ Jesus our Lord.
>
> Romans 8:38-39 NIV

Even though you are now part of God's family **(relationship)**, the Bible says that you will still sin. When that happens there is a break in your family **fellowship**.

## FELLOWSHIP

**Fellowship** is different than **relationship**. For instance, if a son is asked by his dad to tidy up his bedroom but instead he goes out with his friends, things will not be right when Dad arrives home. There will be a barrier between father and son, and you would probably sense it if you were there. It is true that the son and dad are still related—their **relationship** has not changed—but the family **fellowship** has gone sour.

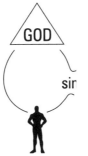

**RELATIONSHIP
unbreakable**
You have been born into God's family. You are eternally His child.

GOD

sin

**FELLOWSHIP
breakable**
Your sin breaks the pleasant harmony you have with your Heavenly Father.

However, the Bible has a solution for broken **fellowship**. When we sin we are told to acknowledge that fact to God, and if we have wronged our fellow man, then we must seek to be reconciled to him as well. God has promised that ...

> If we confess our sins, he is faithful and just and will forgive us our sins and purify us from all unrighteousness. 1 John 1:9 NIV

Our **fellowship** with God will be immediately restored when we acknowledge our sin.

# The Facts
# Without Jesus Christ

"In Adam"

**GUILTY**

I am accused and found guilty of breaking God's perfect law.

**DEBTOR**

To break God's law is to sin, and my sin incurs a sin-debt, a consequence I must pay.

**ETERNAL JUDGMENT**

The debt can only be paid by my death, a payment that is made for eternity in the Lake of Fire.

**SLAVE**

It is impossible to keep God's law perfectly. Even when I try hard, I still find myself failing. In addition, Satan manipulates me to do his will. I am a slave.

**ESTRANGED**

My sin has estranged me from God and his love. God seems distant and remote.

## Born an Unbeliever ...

> **I Do Not Believe ...**
> I believe that there may be many ways to be accepted by God—if there is a God. Jesus may be one way. If I live a good life and do my best, then God will not reject me.

**ENEMY**

When I was born into this world, I joined forces with Satan who also sinned against God.

**LOST**

Having chosen my own way, I find myself in a spiritual wilderness, groping for truth. I am like a lost sheep.

## "IN CHRIST"

# THE FACTS
# BECAUSE OF JESUS CHRIST

God, as the perfect judge, declares me right with him—justified. He now looks upon me as righteous.

**DECLARED RIGHTEOUS**

My sin-debt was taken care of on the cross. The debt is gone—paid in full—erased.

**CANCELLED DEBT**

God gives me a new life, both now here on earth and for all eternity in Heaven.

**ETERNAL LIFE**

## ... IT'S A CHOICE
## TO BELIEVE

Once enslaved, I have now been bought with Jesus' blood and set free. I am no longer a slave to Satan's purposes.

**SET-FREE REDEEMED**

### ...I DO BELIEVE

I believe that Jesus is YAHWEH himself and that he died on the cross in my place, paying my sin-debt. As the resurrected Saviour, I trust in him alone to save me from sin's consequences.

Not only have I been born into God's family, but God has given me the full rights of a son.

**ADOPTED**

Jesus' death and resurrection defeated Satan. I no longer belong to the Devil. I have peace with God.

**RECONCILED**

Jesus, as the Good Shepherd, has found me and given me new life, eternal life, forgiveness, purpose for living, freedom from guilt, and so much more.

**FOUND**

## Conformed to His image

As you have read this book, you may have found yourself captivated by YAHWEH and, hardly without knowing it, found yourself trusting him as one would trust a true friend.

Or perhaps the truthfulness of the Bible hit you like a ton of bricks, and you made a conscious decision to place your trust in the LORD. Either way, you may have found a peace flooding your soul, a deep joy taking hold, perhaps a release from guilt and shame. Or, you may have felt nothing at all. Whatever the case, it is important to know that feelings are not what is significant. What is *important* to know is that when you placed your faith in Jesus, he not only delivered you from sin's penalty but also started a process in your innermost being called *sanctification*. It means *to be set apart.*

Remember how the LORD YAHWEH first created man in his image? We saw that when Adam and Eve rebelled against God, that "image" was marred. You can still see in mankind some of what the LORD created, but it is desperately flawed. However, the moment you trust in Jesus, God begins to conform you back into his image. And he will continue that process until you enter his presence in Heaven. This is so certain, God says that all believers have been …

> … predestined to be conformed to the image of His Son …
>
> Romans 8:29 NKJV

When you put your trust in Christ, you were instantly saved from the **penalty** of sin—but you still remained a sinner. Now the LORD begins to work in your life, this time with the goal of saving you from the daily **power** of sin over your life.

But how does he save us from the constant grip of sin?

Just as we had to come to a point of seeing ourselves as helpless sinners, so we need to see ourselves as spiritual babies needing to grow—to be conformed to his image. We need to see His righteousness lived out in our lives.

This *rules out* the believer being a spiritual couch potato, a blob of humanity waiting for the winds of life to blow favourably. Instead, it obligates us to make wise choices in life. But before we look at that issue, I want to make sure these distinctions are clear.

| Justification | Sanctification |
|---|---|
| Happens at the moment one trusts in Christ, never to reoccur. | Starts when one believes and is ongoing throughout life. |
| The point in time when one is saved from the **penalty** of sin and *declared righteous* in God's eyes. | The process of being saved from the daily **power** of sin. A moment by moment moving from self-centered living to righteous living. |
| A **judicial act** of God occurring in his heavenly courtroom. | A **daily work** of God in one's life here on earth. |
| One cannot be "more" saved, or "more" justified. | One is increasingly *sanctified* or *set apart* for God's use. |
| The point in time when one becomes a child of God—**sonship**. | The process of learning to live as a believer—**discipleship**. |
| Permanent: an official standing before God that never changes. | Changes: growth is small or great. Expect set backs, ups and downs. |
| A new **identity**: God views believers as His—fully accepted children. This is referred to as our **position** in *Christ*—what we are "in Him." (See page 349) The Bible speaks of it as a one-time clothing in His righteousness. | A new **authority**: *What or who reigns in my life? Will I live to indulge in sin or seek to live for Christ?* It is my **condition**—how I am doing as a follower of Christ. The Bible speaks of it as a daily "washing" from sinful living. |
| **Free:** Salvation is based on faith in Christ alone. Being a good person does not earn it. | **Can be costly:** I may be mocked, cast out of my home, or even killed for following Jesus. |
| *Gospel of John, Romans 1 to 4, Galatians* | *Romans 5 to 8, 12 to 16, Ephesians,1 John, James* |

## A RESPONSIBILITY

One time after finishing this study with a couple, the husband said, "John, I know that I am a helpless sinner." He then gave a brief overview of Scripture to assure me that he knew his good living did not earn acceptance with God. He summarized it with a clear statement of his faith in Jesus. Finally he said, "John, you have a son. Just as I didn't have to do anything to become a member of God's family, neither did your son do anything to become a member of your family. But now that he is a member, he has responsibilities. *"As part of God's family, what are my responsibilities?"*

His question was very perceptive, a question which the rest of the Bible answers. The Scripture says that the life a person lives is determined by the **focus** he maintains, on *whom* he fixes his attention. If you focus on yourself, you will become very self-centered. If you focus on the LORD, you will find your life bringing him honour. Therefore to be a responsible believer:

1. You need to **focus** on what you *now have* because of Jesus, which includes all the things you see listed on page 349. God wants you to rejoice in the fact that your sin is forgiven, that you have a new life and the promise of Heaven.

2. You need to **focus** on *getting acquainted* with Jesus. Paul the Apostle wrote that his life ambition was to…

   *… count all things to be loss in view of the surpassing value of knowing Christ Jesus my Lord, for whom I have suffered the loss of all things, and count them but rubbish so that I may gain Christ, and may be found in Him, not having a righteousness of my own derived from the Law, but that which is through faith in Christ, the righteousness which comes from God on the basis of faith, **that I may know Him**…*  Philippians 3:8-10 NASB

   When you fix your attention on the LORD, you take your eyes off yourself. You become captivated with pleasing him and serving others.

3. You need to **focus** on *trusting* Him daily, in all of life's situations, for you can have confidence that he is fully able to handle all your worries and concerns. Jesus said…

   *"Come to me, all you who are weary and burdened, and I will give you rest."*  Matthew 11:28 NIV

As you apply these truths, you will be growing from a spiritual baby into a spiritually mature adult—God will be conforming you to his image. Should you begin to think that this all happens as a result of some sort of super-discipline you conjure up yourself, it is important to understand that…

*… He who has begun a good work in you will complete it until the day of Jesus Christ…*  Philippians 1:6 NKJV

Just as it is not normal for an infant to remain a baby, so it is not right for a newborn *child of God* to remain a spiritual infant. Unfortunately, this is all too common. But it does not need to be that way. Keep your focus on the LORD and he will do the rest.

## RESOURCES

The Bible gives multiple resources to help us maintain our focus:

**1. God Himself:** When you trusted in Jesus, the Bible says the Holy Spirit came to live in you. Now he is constantly accessible—to encourage you when you are downhearted, to urge you to live for him, to rebuke you when you drift into sin. The *Holy Spirit* is such a faithful companion that he is called *the Comforter, the Helper, the Counsellor*—all of which are God's names.

> *"But the Helper, the Holy Spirit, whom the Father will send in My name, He will teach you all things, and bring to your remembrance all things that I said to you."*     John 14:26 NKJV

As parents, we are delighted when our children behave themselves in a pleasing manner. As God's children, it is important that we conduct ourselves in a way that will bring honour and not disgrace to our heavenly Father's name.

Our obedience should be motivated by our love for him, based on the principle that *"he that is forgiven much, loves much."* We have been forgiven much—we should love him much.

(See Luke 7:36-50; John 14 &15; 2 John 6).

**2. Faith:** The process of growing spiritually occurs one step at a time. That is why it is called *walking with God*. Just as we became members of God's family *by faith*, so we are to walk with God *by faith*.

> As you have therefore received Christ Jesus the Lord, [you received him by faith] **so walk in Him**, rooted and built up in Him and established in the faith, as you have been taught, abounding in it with thanksgiving.     Colossians 2:6,7 NKJV

Remember, *faith* is built on the *facts* that are found in the Bible. It is important not to walk with God based on the way you *feel*. You may get up in the morning feeling congested and running a fever. That does not mean you are no longer part of your parents' family or, for that matter, a part of God's family.

Some days you may not *feel* very spiritual, but that does not determine how well you are walking with God. Our walk each day is determined by the choices we make. If we make wise choices, the LORD will be conforming us into his image. If we make foolish ones, we will remain spiritual babies.

**3. The Bible:** It is a source of daily strength, our guide book. I have a friend who calls it *our owner's manual.* The choices we make in life are guided by YAHWEH as we read the Bible.

> *All Scripture is God-breathed and is useful for teaching, rebuking, correcting and training in righteousness, so that the man of God may be thoroughly equipped for every good work.*
>
> 2 Timothy 3:16-17 NIV

The Bible compares itself to spiritual food. The more you study it, the stronger you will become spiritually. God will *speak* to you through the Bible—not audibly, but in your mind. Reading the Scripture is how you get to *know* Him. Without its constant nourishment, you will remain a spiritual baby.

If you do not personally own a Bible, purchase one. (See the Appendix for suggestions.) Begin by reading the entire book of the Gospel of John. It reads like a story. Then re-read this book, BY THIS NAME, and look up every reference in your Bible. It will be slow-going at first, but you will be surprised at how quickly you will catch on. Using a coloured pencil, underline the verses. You may be ready for the books of Acts and Romans after reading BY THIS NAME for the second time. If you do not understand something, mark it down and keep reading. It will slowly come together.

**4. Prayer:** Prayer is simply talking to YAHWEH. You do not need to bow your head and close your eyes, although that is appropriate if it helps you avoid distractions. Because God knows your thoughts, you can silently voice your prayer to him at any time and he will hear it. It is not necessary to pray audibly.

> *Do not be anxious about anything, but in everything, by prayer and petition, with thanksgiving, present your requests to God. And the peace of God, which transcends all understanding, will guard your hearts and your minds in Christ Jesus.*
>
> Philippians 4:6-7 NIV

**5. Other Believers:** When you put your trust in Jesus, some will identify you as being a Christian. The word *Christian* implies *Christ-one* or *belonging to the household of Christ.*

> *And the disciples were first called Christians in Antioch.*
>
> Acts 11:26 NKJV

The biblical meaning of the word has been distorted beyond belief. Those who claim to have been born a Christian are not accurate. Being born in a "Christian" home no more makes you a Christian than being born in a hospital makes you a doctor. Physical birth has nothing to do with our relationship with God.

Although the term *Christian* is used of entire nations, some supposedly Christian nations have perpetrated terrible crimes in the name of Christ. Others are morally corrupt. Rightly understood, the word can only apply to individuals who have made a conscious choice to trust the Lord Jesus Christ.

The Bible tells us that we gain spiritual maturity through friendship with "Christians" who truly believe the Scriptures. This is vital.

> *And let us consider how we may spur one another on toward love and good deeds.*
>
> *Let us not give up meeting together, as some are in the habit of doing, but let us encourage one another—and all the more as you see the Day [of Jesus' return] approaching.*
>
> *Hebrews 10:24-25 NIV*

Most of your friendships with other believers will be built within the context of a church. However, a few cautions are in order.

Remember, Satan comes as an *angel of light*. He loves religion. Just because people talk about God does not mean they are true Christians. Churches range from good to bad in their understanding and practice of the truth. The Bible says true and false teachers will exist until Jesus returns a second time, when he will sort it all out. Until then, be discerning. Ask these questions:

- Does the church believe that the Bible is the true, inspired Word of God, without error in its original writings? Watch out for those who say it only *contains* God's Word.

- Does the church believe the Bible literally, or does it teach that some accounts are fables? (e.g. The Bible tells us there is a literal Hell, a literal Devil, a literal Heaven, etc.)

- Does the church believe such events as Jesus' birth by a *virgin* woman? Be alert for those who say it meant only a *young woman*, that Mary was not a virgin.

- Does the church believe that Jesus is fully God as well as a man? Be on guard for those who say Jesus was just another god, and that we are gods as well.

- Does the church have a good reputation? Are the meetings bizarre or disorderly? Does it hold high moral standards? Are its business dealings of a dubious nature?

- Does the church teach that Jesus died in our place for our sin-debt? If the church is *fuzzy* on this—beware. Some believe that you also need to be baptized, do good works, or participate in special rites to be saved. Avoid such groups.

- Does the church believe in the Trinity?

If the church is questionable in just **one** of these areas, then there is a great likelihood that it will be off-base in other teachings as well. These questions are targeted to reveal symptoms of deeper problems. Do not be caught up in how nice the preacher is, or how persuasively he communicates. Remember, many so-called "Christians" and churches are **not** following the Bible. There is no such thing as a perfect church, but these questions will help you find a group of genuine like-minded believers.

The whole notion of attending a *church* may be a difficult, humbling experience. Just remember, the idea of getting together for mutual strength was God's idea. Let me assure you, it is important for your growth. Fellow believers can be a tremendous help in encouraging you in your spiritual journey.

**6. Music:** King David wrote some of the first songs or *Psalms* for the purpose of encouraging our hearts. Since then other believers have written excellent lyrics about God. Once again, beware—there is both good and bad music. Use the same discernment you would apply in choosing a church. Based on what you have studied, determine whether the words being sung are *true* or *false*. God will help you.

**7. Tell Others:** The disciples went everywhere telling others about this *good news*. You can too. It is encouraging to see friends come to the same understanding. But remember, God has given people the freedom to choose, so respect it. Be patient in your approach and sensitive in what you say. Do not cram it down their throats. The Bible tells us to be *witnesses*, not *lawyers*. A witness explains something; a lawyer argues and tries to convince. Simply passing this book on to friends may help them understand.

**8. Future Hope:** The Bible says that one day Jesus will return to the earth. It is prophesied over and over again.

> *Brothers, we do not want you to be ignorant about those who fall asleep [or have died], or to grieve like the rest of men, who have no hope. We believe that Jesus died and rose again and so we believe that God will bring with Jesus those who have fallen*

*asleep in him. According to the Lord's own word, we tell you that we who are still alive, who are left till the coming of the Lord, will certainly not precede those who have fallen asleep.*

*For the Lord himself will come down from heaven, with a loud command, with the voice of the archangel and with the trumpet call of God, and the dead in Christ will rise first. After that, we who are still alive and are left will be caught up together with them in the clouds to meet the Lord in the air. And so we will be with the Lord forever. Therefore encourage each other with these words.* 1 Thessalonians 4:13–18 NIV

## OBSTACLES

There are obstacles that will destroy your focus and hinder your spiritual growth.

**1. Our human nature:**[5] If there ever was a case of being one's own worst enemy, this is it. The Bible says that our sinful human nature is never satisfied. It always desires more money, more attention, better looks, nicer this, greater that, ad infinitum it goes. It may be satisfied momentarily, but then it will desire something more. Our human nature has one focus—our **SELF**. The Scriptures say,

*…live by the Spirit, and you will not gratify the **desires of the sinful nature**.* Galatians 5:16 NIV

So how do we *live by the Spirit?* It comes back to this matter of focus. As we focus on the things of God, the *desires of the sinful nature* are replaced with a stronger desire to please our LORD. We are told to …

*Put to death, therefore, whatever belongs to your earthly nature [or the sin nature]…* Colossians 3:5 NIV

Before I was married I had girlfriends. They were genuine relationships. But when I got married those former relationships were over. Dead. Now I am caught up in a new relationship—I desire to please my wife. She has become my focus. It would be wrong for me to allow my thoughts to dwell on a former girlfriend. In the same way, before you believed you only had your sinful nature to satisfy—with all its demands and desires. But now as a believer, God wants you to put that behind you and be caught up in pleasing Him and in serving others.

*…let us throw off everything that hinders and the sin that so easily entangles, and let us run with perseverance the race marked out for us. Let us **fix our eyes** [or focus] on Jesus…* Hebrews 12:1-2 NIV

Nowadays we are told to delve into our past to search for the answers to our problems. Every wrong must be righted, and if we have been hurt, we are to be pitied as victims. The end result of all this advice is that we become self-obsessed. By contrast, the Bible tells us to forget about ourselves, including our past. If we have been wronged, we are to forgive, as difficult as that may seem.

> And be kind to one another, tenderhearted, forgiving one another, just as God in Christ forgave you.            *Ephesians 4:32 NKJV*

It may seem strange, but in the process of forgiving others, we experience healing in our own lives.

**2. The world system:** The Bible says that the temptations put before us by the world system shift our focus from Jesus to those things that are fleeting. We are responsible to discern what tends to drag us back into old, sinful patterns and avoid those things that destroy our focus.

> For the grace of God…teaches us to say "No" to ungodliness and worldly passions, and to live self-controlled, upright and godly lives in this present age, while we wait for the blessed hope—the glorious appearing of our great God and Savior, Jesus Christ…            *Titus 2:11–13 NIV*

**3. The Devil:** Even though Satan has been defeated, he still actively tries to influence us. From the very beginning he has tried to destroy us, to "dirty up" the image of God. Satan wants us to be conformed to him, not into the image of YAHWEH.

God did not obliterate the Devil when we became believers. Rather, we are responsible to resist his temptations and seek strength from God alone.

> Submit yourselves, then, to God. Resist the devil, and he will flee from you.            *James 4:7 NIV*

Satan cleverly uses the influence of the world and our self-centered human nature to tempt us, to shift our focus. You can expect him to plant doubt in your mind, even about the choice you have made to trust Jesus. He will say your faith was not big enough or question whether you really understood. Remember, he did that with Adam and Eve too. Resist him and do what Jesus did. Go to the Bible for help.

## SUMMARY

As we combat these three enemies of spiritual growth, and as we maintain our focus, we will grow strong spiritual roots—the LORD will be conforming us into his image.

Well, there is so much more that could be written. But if you are one of those who has put your trust in Christ, then it is good to know that the Bible says God will lead you, step by step. You have started a spiritual pilgrimage. Keep your eyes on him; let him be your focus. Study your map, the Bible, regularly. The road will not always be smooth, but God will be with you—he has given you his promise. May you journey well.

> *May the God of peace, who through the blood of the eternal covenant brought back from the dead our Lord Jesus, that great Shepherd of the sheep, equip you with everything good for doing his will, and may he work in us what is pleasing to him, through Jesus Christ, to whom be glory for ever and ever. Amen.*
>
> *Hebrews 13:20-21 NIV*

# 2 A CONVENIENT TIME

There are those who, after reading the Bible and understanding what it has to say, decide to take a risk. They decide not to believe it. They choose to:

- Ignore its message.
- Reject it outright.
- Get busy with life, and thereby forget it.
- Change its message.
    …and they hope that the Bible is wrong.

Herod Agrippa took such a risk. As the grandson of Herod the Great and nephew of Herod Antipas, he must have been privy to the gossip about Jesus in the royal household. No doubt, spies had reported every word the prophet from Nazareth spoke. But Herod had status; he was an important man. Rather than humble himself before the King of Kings, he continued to live his life for himself. He even gained an element of popularity by beheading one of Jesus' disciples. But then,

> *On the appointed day Herod, wearing his royal robes, sat on his throne and delivered a public address to the people. They shouted, "This is the voice of a god, not of a man."*

> *Immediately, because Herod did not give praise to God, an angel of the Lord struck him down, and he was eaten by worms and died.* Acts 12:21–23 NIV

God in his grace will tolerate sin for awhile, but then in his justice he will judge it. Judgment may come in this life or it may be withheld until after death, but it will happen. Herod died[6] and faced an eternity in the Lake of Fire. The next verse is noteworthy:

> *But the word of God continued to increase and spread.* Acts 12:24 NIV

Do not be casual about the Bible's message or too busy to properly investigate it. It would be a tragedy to not have taken the time to really discover all you needed to know about life and death.

Another contemporary of Jesus was Herod Agrippa II. As the great grandson of Herod the Great, and son of Herod Agrippa, he would also have known about Jesus. The Bible says King Agrippa was *well versed* in all the things concerning Jesus. The apostle Paul[7] was arrested and testified before him. In his defense before Agrippa, Paul told him about Jesus. He said,

> *"For the king, before whom I also speak freely, knows these things; for I am convinced that none of these things escapes his attention, since this thing was not done in a corner. King Agrippa, do you believe the prophets? I know that you do believe."*
>
> *Then Agrippa said to Paul, "You almost persuade me to become a Christian."* Acts 26:26–28 NKJV

King Agrippa seemed to understand Paul quite well, so much so that he even admitted that Paul had almost persuaded him to believe. But Agrippa took the risk. He didn't believe. He sidestepped the question in an effort to avoid making a decision. As far as we know, Agrippa never did believe. He went to his grave *understanding* the gospel but not believing it. It was his choice.

Paul also defended himself before a Roman governor named Felix. In these situations he always took the opportunity to give a lengthy explanation of who Jesus was and what He had done.

> *Several days later Felix came with his wife Drusilla, who was a Jewess. He sent for Paul and listened to him as he spoke about faith in Christ Jesus. As Paul discoursed on righteousness, self-control and the judgment to come, Felix was afraid and said, "That's enough for now! You may leave. When I find it convenient, I will send for you."* Acts 24:24-25 NIV

Felix put off his decision. He was waiting for a more convenient time. It is easy to do that, but the Bible reminds us that now is the time to decide.

> ... now is the accepted time; ... now is the day of salvation.
>
> 2 Corinthians 6:2 NKJV

We never know what the future holds, or how quickly our lives can be taken. We need to decide *now*. Of course, Felix was afraid, and sometimes we become fearful too. We wonder what others may think. It really doesn't matter. What does matter is what God thinks. Neither biblical nor secular history records what happened to Felix but, to the best of our knowledge, he never did find a convenient time to believe.

Felix also had other hopes:

> ... he was hoping that Paul would offer him a bribe, so he sent for him frequently and talked with him.          Acts 24:26 NIV

Felix had ulterior motives. His professed interest in Jesus was distorted by a desire for monetary gain. Nevertheless, he did speak *often* with Paul about Jesus. Many could have interpreted these conversations as Felix having *gotten religion*. Some people are like Felix. They talk a lot about the Bible, but then they use its message for their own profit. Most people recognize the inconsistency, but some are deceived. Because of such hypocrites, some people claim they will never believe the Bible. But hey, wait a minute! Did the Bible's message change? No, not one bit. It still says the same thing no matter how people distort it for their own ends. If you are one who would be tempted to reject the Bible because of guys like Felix, then think again.

If you find yourself vacillating, not understanding, or just outright rejecting what you have read, then might I suggest that you investigate the Bible a little more before you close the case. As we said at the beginning, the Scripture does have a lot to say about life ... and death.

Do not stop your investigation now.

Your life—and your life after death—is at stake.

# APPENDIX

# Glossary

**Abba:** (Aramaic) equivalent to the English words *"daddy"* or *"papa"*

**Adoption:** the rite of investing legal sonship, complete with its obligations and privileges

**Altar:** a platform made of earth or rocks upon which sacrifices were offered to God or gods

**Amen:** (Hebrew/Greek) a word of affirmation; a form of agreement, *"That's right!"* or *"I agree!"*

**Angel:** (Greek) messenger; a created heavenly spirit being

**Anoint:** to pour oil upon the person's head or on an object for the purpose of setting apart for God's use. The word came to mean or refer to anything chosen for the LORD's service.

**Apostle:** (Greek) a *sent one*; used most often in reference to the twelve disciples and Paul

**Ark:** a container; either large (boat) or small (box)

**Blessing:** the receiving or giving of God's favour

**Centurion:** (Greek/Latin) a Roman army officer responsible for 100 men

**Christ:** (Greek) *"the anointed one,"* translated *Messiah* (Hebrew) in the Old Testament

**Confess:** to *agree with* or *acknowledge*

**Covenant:** a promise, agreement

**Curse:** to incur or bestow displeasure

**Demon**: a created evil spirit being giving allegiance to Satan

**Devil:** (derived from Greek) false accuser, slanderer; another name for Satan, the most powerful of all evil spirit beings

**Disciple:** a follower

**Faith:** to *trust* or *put confidence in* (see pages 118-119)

**Genesis:** (Greek) *beginnings* or *origins*

**Glory:** literally *"to have weight,"* as in the sense of worth

**Gospel:** good news

**Grace:** God's kindness to undeserving sinners

**Holy Spirit:** Not an angel or a man, but the very Spirit of God Himself

**I AM:** a name of God, meaning *"the self-existent one"* or *"the one who exists by His own power."*

**Immanuel:** (Hebrew/Greek) *"God with us"*

**Jesus:** (Greek—derived from Hebrew) means *Saviour, Deliverer*

**Justified:** a judicial act whereby God declares a person righteous in His sight

**Mercy:** God's love demonstrated towards undeserving sinners, pity

**Messiah:** (Hebrew) *"the anointed one,"* translated *"Christ"* (Greek) in the New Testament

**Parable:** a short story with a lesson

**Pharisee:** a Jew who followed God's law meticulously to the point of creating additional laws so as not to break God's laws

**Priest:** a man who performed assigned duties in the Tabernacle or Temple

**Prophet:** a messenger who spoke for God

**Psalm:** (Greek) a song

**Rabbi:** (Greek) teacher, master

**Redeem:** *to buy*, as in the sense of purchasing a slave in a market

**Repent:** to have a *change of mind* (see page 187)

**Righteous:** to be viewed as right with God. This does not mean that a person is sinless. Can also be used in the sense of how one lives; of having a good or right sort of lifestyle.

**Sabbath:** the seventh day of the week; Saturday

**Sanhedrin:** (Greek) a Jewish court comprised of seventy-one men

**Satan:** (Hebrew/Greek) adversary; the supreme enemy of God

**Saviour:** someone who delivers or rescues another

**Scribe:** one who made copies of the Scriptures in ancient times

**Sin:** has the idea of shooting an arrow and missing the mark, in this case aiming for God's holiness, but falling short; to despise God and his Word; refusing to live as God intended

**Sin Nature:** sometimes referred to as the *human nature* or *Adam's nature*; a condition

**Son of God:** an idiomatic term, having no physical implications, designating the same attributes as God (see pages 216-218)

**Son of man:** a phrase used by Jesus in reference to himself to emphasize His humanity, also understood by ancient scholars to be a term referring to Messiah (see pages 218)

**Synagogue:** (Greek) assemblies; commonly used in reference to the building

**Transgression:** see sin

**Worship:** to declare God's worth

## Choosing a Bible

The Bible was written in the common language of each generation—Hebrew, Aramaic or Greek. God intended it to be accessible to every person regardless of their background or social status. Since the age of Greek civilization, translations were made in other languages.

During the Dark Ages, the Bible was commonly available only in Latin and only the clergy had access to the limited, handwritten copies. It was considered a sin for the man on the street to read or try to understand it for himself. Satan had seemingly succeeded in hiding God's Word behind a clergyman's robe.

Then in the early 1500's, William Tyndale committed himself to putting the Bible into the everyday language of the English-speaking people. It is said that at one time he told a clergyman,

*"If God spare my life, ere many years pass, I will cause a boy that driveth
the plough to know more of the Scripture than thou doest."*

Tyndale was harshly opposed in his task by both the clergy and the
political powers of that day. Suffering shipwreck, loss of manuscripts,
pursuit by secret agents, and betrayal by friends, he succeeded in
translating the Bible into English at the expense of his own life.
Captured, imprisoned, sentenced, then strangled and burned—his
last words were, *"Lord, open the King of England's eyes."*

Today, the English language offers a plethora of translations—many
with varying degrees of supplementary Bible helps. In choosing a
Bible, remember two things:

1.   Whatever English Bible you buy, it is a translation of the original
     languages. Any time you translate a message from one language to
     another, the accuracy, the readability—the entire production—will
     have its strengths and weaknesses. Fortunately, the translation of
     the Bible into English has usually been done with meticulous care,
     so that what we have today is very accurate. There are, however,
     both good and not-so-good translations of the Bible. I strongly
     suggest you aim to get the most precise translation you can, but in
     so doing, still remember it is a translation. I say this, not depreciating
     one iota the power of the Bible's message in another tongue.

2.   Get a translation that is simple for you to read. Remember,
     Tyndale gave his life to make the Bible readable to the common
     man. He wanted people to understand it easily, and not feel like
     they were reading a foreign language.

In light of the above two points, the following translations are efforts
at maintaining accuracy and readability:

| Translation | School grade level [1] |
|---|---|
| New International Version | 7.8 |
| New King James Version | 9.1 |
| New American Standard Version | 11.3 |
| King James Version (old English) | 14.0 |

To help explain the Bible in greater detail, many versions come with
cross-references, notes on customs, maps, etc.—all listed under the
category as Bible helps. These can indeed be helpful, but remember,
they are nothing more than man's comments on the Bible text, and
are not the Scriptures themselves.

In obtaining a Bible, you may wish to have a small one that can be
carried with you, and a larger one that you can leave at home for
greater in-depth study.

# RESOURCES

Due to the range of issues covered in any list of books, DVD's, web sites, or magazines, by policy, GOODSEED does not issue specific endorsements. Nonetheless, the following resources contained helpful information on creation/evolution and other Bible/science issues. The following list is representative:

**Web Sites:** AnswersInGenesis.org    CreationOnTheWeb.com    icr.org

**Magazines:** *Creation Magazine*—for adults, sections for children; *Journal of Creation*—for advanced studies. Both are available from www.CreationOnTheWeb.com.

## Books:

*Bones of Contention: A Creationist Assessment of Human Fossils* – Marvin L. Lubenow, *Darwin's Black Box* – Michael J. Behe

*Dismantling the Big Bang: God's Universe Rediscovered* – Alex Williams and John Hartnett

*Evolution: A Theory in Crisis, New Developments in Science are Challenging Orthodox Darwinism*—by Michael Denton

*Genetic Entropy & The Mystery of the Genome* – Dr. John C. Sanford

*In the Beginning Was Information: A Scientist Explains the Incredible Design in Nature* – Dr. Werner Gitt

*Not by Chance! Shattering the Modern Theory of Evolution* – Dr. Lee Spetner

*Refuting Compromise* – Dr. Jonathan Sarfati

*Refuting Evolution: A Response to the National Acad. of Sciences' Teaching About Evolution & the Nature of Sciences* – Dr. Jonathan Sarfati

*The Biotic Message: Evolution Versus Message Theory* – Walter James ReMine

*The Creation Answers Book* – ed. Dr. Don Batten

*Unwrapping the Pharaohs: How Egyptian Archaeology Confirms the Biblical Timeline* – John Ashton and David Down

## DVDs:

*Apemen, Missing Links & the Bible* – Philip Bell

*Chemicals to Living Cell: Fantasy or Science?* – Dr Jonathan Sarfati

*Creation Astronomy: Viewing the Universe though Biblical Glasses* – Dr. Jason Lisle

*Creation/Evolution: The Controversy* – Dr. Carl Wieland

*Dinosaurs and the Most Asked Questions – Answered!* – Dr. Carl Wieland

*Dynamic Life: Changes in Living Things* – Dr. Carl Wieland

*Fearfully & Wonderfully Made* – Dr. David Menton

*Geology & Cave Formation: A Post-Flood Story* – Dr. Emil Silvestru

*Hubble, Bubble, the Big Bang in Trouble* – Dr. John Hartnett

*In the Beginning Was Information* – Dr. Werner Gitt

*"Junk" DNA Is Not "Junk"* – Dr. David DeWitt

*Millions of Years: Where Did the Idea Come From?* – Dr. Terry Mortenson

*Origins in the Modern World: Why it Matters* – Dr. Carl Wieland

*Putting the Puzzle Pieces Together* – Dr. John Baumgardner

*Rocks Around the Clock* – Dr. Emil Silvestru

*Starlight, Time and the New Physics* – Dr. John Hartnett

*The Age of the Earth* – Dr. Tas Walker

*The Bible Explains Dinosaurs* – Ken Ham

*The Fossil Record* – Mike Riddle

*The Grand Canyon: Monument to the Flood* – ICR

*The Origin of Old-Earth Geology & Christian Compromise* – Dr. Terry Mortenson

*The Riddle of Origins Series* – Mike Riddle

*Thousands ... Not Billions* – Dr. Don DeYoung

*Unlocking the Mystery of Life* – Illustra Media

# END NOTES

**CHAPTER ONE**

1. Norman L. Geisler and William E. Nix, *From God To Us, How We Got The Bible*, Moody Press, Chicago, 1974, p. 7.
2. Barbara Watterson, *Gods of Ancient Egypt*, Sutton Publishing, 1984, 1996, p. 5. *"Two great French Egyptologists, Jean-Francois Champollion (1790-1832) and Emmanuel de Rouge (1811-72)... read Egyptian texts and came to the conclusion that the Egyptian religion was a pure monotheism which 'manifested itself externally by a symbolic polytheism'."*
3. Ibid., p. 19. *"There were, for instance, several variations on the theme of the creation of the world, for the great creator gods such as Atu, Re, Ptah and Neit each had his or her own version.*
4. We will learn the content of that faith as we progress in the story.
5. This part of the Bible was written in ancient Hebrew, a language that had no written vowels. Thus YAHWEH (written YHVH) could never have been pronounced correctly by someone who had not heard it directly. Centuries ago, to facilitate the pronunciation of this word, it was supplied with vowels and spelled YAHVEH , YAHWEH or JEHOVAH. I have used YAHWEH as it has the most common usage, though probably YAHVEH is closer to the original.
6. The one exception was Greek by birth. We will meet him later in the book.
7. Some English Bibles translate *"God-breathed"* as *"inspired."* *"God-breathed"* is the more literal translation.
8. *Illustrated Bible Dictionary*, Pt 3, IVP The Universities and Colleges Christian Fellowship, 1980, p. 1538.
9. Philip W. Comfort, *The Origin of the Bible*, Mark R. Norton, Texts & Mscripts of the Old Testament, Tyndale House Pub. Inc., 1992, p. 151ff.
10. Translated by William Whiston, *The Works of Josephus*, Hendrickson Publishers, Inc., 1987, p. 776.

**CHAPTER TWO**

1. Barbara Watterson, *Gods of Ancient Egypt*, Sutton Publishing, 1984, 1996, p. 40. *"Re was the self-engendered Eternal Spirit who first appeared on the waters of the Nun as a beautiful child floating on a great blue lotus."* To call Re or Ra eternal and then say he was self-created does create a problem with logic. Probably both were believed.
2. The Galaxy pictured here is not the Milky Way, as it is impossible to photograph. A similar one, the Andromeda, has been substituted.
3. www.imagine.gsfc.nasa.gov/docs/ask_astro/answers/021127a.html; www.answers.com/topic/galaxy
4. Jude 6
5. Luke 20:36 Death in the physical sense. Angels never cease to exist.
6. Mark 12:25

**CHAPTER THREE**

1. The word *expanse* is synonymous with space, and can be used in reference to either earth's atmosphere or deep space. The Scripture says the Creator took some of the water and placed it high in the heavens. Though some commentators have suggested that this refers simply to the clouds, others have theorized the existence of a transparent canopy of water vapor surrounding the globe. Whether the waters above suggest

a canopy or not, there is evidence that the climate was substantially different from what we now know. It seems to have been uniformly tropical. It is known that an atmosphere containing more water vapor would have achieved some sort of greenhouse effect.

2.  If it seems strange to us that God would create light before He created the sun, we must remember that it is just as easy for God to create the light as it is for him to create the light-givers.

3.  If it were possible to fire a bullet while travelling on another bullet, and then hit a third bullet while you watched from the first bullet, that is exactly what happened on July 4th, 2005, when Deep Impact, a NASA Discovery Mission, succeeded in flying a spacecraft to Comet Tempel 1 and hitting it with a 370 kg "impactor." The exact time of collision was forecast to within a few minutes. This was possible because the entire universe functions with the precision of a cosmic clock.

4.  Literally a "channel."

5.  If you are wondering who God was talking to when he said *"Let us make man in our image..."* we will cover that later on in the book.

6.  God did not create mankind because he needed a friend. God is completely independent of any need. He is the self-existent one.

7.  This speaks of moral perfection in contrast to being perfect in attributes (i.e. knowledge, power, etc.) See Matthew 5:48.

8.  By definition, the universe is all the mass/energy there is, so it is an isolated system.

9.  In his 1981, 1984 book *Evolution from Space* (co-authored with Chandra Wickramasinghe), he calculated that the chance of obtaining the required set of enzymes for even the simplest living cell was one in $10^{40,000}$. Since the number of atoms in the known universe is infinitesimally tiny by comparison ($10^{80}$), he argued that even a whole universe full of primordial soup wouldn't have a chance." http://www.answers.com/topic/fred-hoyle He also compared the likelihood of just one protein evolving—life depends on many—to the solar system packed with blind people randomly shuffling Rubik's cubes and arriving at the solution simultaneously. Hoyle, F., The big bang in astronomy, New Scientist 92(1280):527, November 19, 1981.

10. http://pages.britishlibrary.net/charles.darwin/texts/variation/variation01.html; http://www.answersingenesis.org/creation/v18/i2/dogs.asp

11. *Evolution: A Theory in Crisis* (1986) by Michael Denton; *Darwin's Black Box* (1996) by Micheal Behe; DVD - *Unlocking the Mystery of Life* (2002) produced by Illustra Media

12. Geochronology is a vast area of study. A search on the WEB brings up numerous papers on different clock models.

## CHAPTER FOUR

1.  Obedience and worship are indivisible in the scripture. The Bible says God is looking for "true worshipers." John 4:23-24

2.  The Bible contains no hint of a possibility for angelic beings to change their final destiny.

3.  Revelation 12:3–9; Verses 3 & 4 are generally considered to refer to the fall of Satan. Verses 7–9 are viewed by many scholars as having to do with a yet future event. I have quoted the entire passage as the latter verses explain the portion we are concerned about—verses 3 & 4—the who that is in question.

4. This passage reflects the choices Adam and Eve made.
5. See Romans 5:12–14 for more details. Also see Chapter Ten, end note 6. Adam was the father—the head—of the entire human race. We were *in him* when he sinned.
6. *Newsweek*, January 11, 1988, pp. 46–52.
7. *Time*, December 4, 1995, USA Edition, p. 29.

## CHAPTER FIVE

1. The Greenfield Papyrus is 41 metres in length, one of the longest known.
2. Luke 17:27; Matthew 24:38
3. Romans 1:21–32; Though this passage does not make direct reference to the people of Noah's day, it does reflect the choices they made at the time with the attending ramifications.
4. Probably made from pine-tree resin boiled with charcoal. Bituminous tar would have come into being after the Flood.
5. 2 Peter 2:5
6. A number of scholars have calculated the room on the Ark. One helpful resource is: *Noah's Ark: A Feasibility Study*—by John Woodmorappe, ICR, El Cajon, CA.
7. Dr. John Baumgardner, geophysicist at the Los Alamos National Laboratories in New Mexico, proposes a model known as Catastrophic Plate Tectonics. He is one of several scientists to advance theories on how the Flood could have occurred.
8. Job 40:15-24; 41:1-34
9. Akkadian *Bab-ili*, 'Gate of God'
10. Akkadian *ziqqurratu*, 'temple-tower'
11. *"The Lord came down…"* If God is everywhere present at one time, why did he have to "come down"? The Bible often uses terms in relationship to God that enhance our understanding of the passage. For example, God is spoken of as "seeing" even though, as a Spirit, he does not have physical eyes.
12. Archer, G. L. (1998, c1994). *A Survey of Old Testament Introduction* ([3rd. ed.].) (Page 226). Chicago: Moody Press quotes, *"Jastrow's Dictionary of Talmudic Hebrew,* p. 173, lists the pilpel stem *balbel* as an intensive with the same meaning of *confusion, 'mix up, confuse.'* Needless to say, there is a significant similarity between *Babel* and *balbel."* Babylon is the Greek form of the name.

## CHAPTER SIX

1. Acts 7:2-4 (NKJV) *"The God of glory appeared to our father Abraham when he was in Mesopotamia, before he dwelt in Haran, and said to him, 'Get out of your country and from your relatives, and come to a land that I will show you.' Then he came out of the land of the Chaldeans and dwelt in Haran. And from there, when his father was dead, He moved him to this land in which you now dwell."* Joshua 24:2-3 (NKJV) *"And Joshua said to all the people, 'Thus says the LORD God of Israel: "Your fathers, including Terah, the father of Abraham and the father of Nahor, dwelt on the other side of the River in old times; and they served other gods. Then I took your father Abraham from the other side of the River …"'"*
2. Notice how life spans decreased dramatically after the flood. Abraham was considered old at the age of seventy-five.
3. God commended Abram for his faith, an action that would not make sense if God had given Abram the faith in the first place.
4. Abram became a great nation: the father of both the Jewish and Arab nations.

5. Abram's name did become great; he is revered by Jew and Arab alike. It is important to note that it was God who made Abram's name great, whereas at Babel, the desire was self-motivated.
6. When God blesses, he bestows favour and well-being. When God curses, he brings misfortune.
7. John 8:56
8. Matthew 17:20
9. *"For the wages of sin is death…"* Romans 6:23. See Ch 4, Death, p. 74.

**Chapter Seven**

1. The twelve tribes of Israel are the twelve sons of Jacob. Exceptions: There was no tribe of Levi since they became the nation's religious leaders. There was also no tribe of Joseph—his two sons Ephraim and Manasseh made up the difference.
2. *"Included in the account of the move to Egypt is a listing of Jacob's descendants. In verse 26 the number of descendants is said to be 66, whereas the number in verse 27 is 70. The first number represents those who traveled with Jacob to Egypt, and the second number includes the children and grandchildren already in Egypt."* Walvoord, J. F., Zuck, R. B., & Dallas Theological Seminary. (1983-c1985). *The Bible Knowledge Commentary : An exposition of the scriptures.* Wheaton, IL: Victor Books. When you add in women and children the number would have been somewhat larger. I have used the biblical figure found in Genesis 46:26.
3. Mathematicians generally consider any event with a probability of less than 1 chance in 10 to the 50th power as having a zero probability. In other words, it is impossible. In his "single law of chance" the French expert on probability, Emile Borel, defined 1 chance in $10^{50}$ as beyond which things never occur, and carrying *"…with it a certainty of another nature than mathematical certainty…it is comparable even to the certainty with which we attribute to the existence of the external world."*
4. This word can be translated "lice."

**Chapter Eight**

1. Dutch Egyptologist Adriaan A.deBuck
2. R.O. Faulkner, *Book of The Dead*, University of Texas Press, Austin, Spell 125, p. 31.
3. Both Hebrew and Greek use "missing the mark" as a word for *sin*. Many sources state that this transferred into medieval history, but I was unable to independently verify it. Since this book is not about medieval history and the illustration serves well to make the point existing in the Hebrew and Greek, I have used the story.

**Chapter Nine**

1. ❶ The Bronze Altar: Exodus 27:1,2
   ❷ The Basin: Exodus 30:18
   ❸ The Lampstand: Exodus 25:31
   ❹ The Golden Altar or The Altar of Incense: Exodus 30:1,3
   ❺ The Table with the Bread of the Presence: Exodus 25:23,30
   ❻ The Ark of the Covenant: Exodus 25:10,11
   ❼ The Atonement Cover or Mercy Seat: Exodus 25:17–21
2. The weight was given as *one talent*, equaling 30 to 40 kgs, or 65 to 85 lbs.

3. The priests could not enter the sanctuary when the pillar of cloud hovered over the Holy of Holies. It signified God's presence. When the cloud moved to lead them on the journey, then they would have been free to pack up the entire Tabernacle and follow.

4. God only overlooks sin for a period of time. He does judge all sin. Compare Acts 17: 30

5. *"The image of Dagon is a debated issue. The notion that Dagon was a god whose upper body was that of a man and the lower body that of a fish has been prevalent for decades. …Whatever the image, a varying perception of Dagon developed around the Mediterranean."* http://ancienthistory.about.com/od/godsmyth/a/Dagon.htm

6. 2 Samuel 7:12–17

7. *And they came, bringing to Him a paralytic, carried by four men.* Mark 2:3 NASB

8. Some attribute this question to Frederick the Great, King of Prussia. Perhaps it was both. I quote Pascal as he left no doubt as to what he thought about the prophecies. (See *Pensees* by Blaise Pascal pt. 620)

9. See Deuteronomy 28:45-68, compare with *Josephus*, Book 5 and 6, a secular historian, writing during the destruction of Jerusalem. Josephus, F., & Whiston, W. (1996, c1987). *The works of Josephus: Complete and unabridged.* Peabody: Hendrickson.

10. The Jewish history of persecution would fill volumes.

11. The miracle surrounding the survival of the Jews has been commented on by many of the world's "greats." Mark Twain (Samuel Clemens) wrote: *"The Egyptian, the Babylonian, and the Persian rose, filled the planet with sound and splendor, then faded to dream-stuff and passed away. The Greek and Roman followed, made a vast noise and they are gone. Other peoples have sprung up, and held their torch high for a time, but it burned out and they sit in twilight now or have vanished. The Jew saw them all, beat them all, and is now what he always was…All things are mortal, but the Jew. All other forces pass, but he remains. What is the secret of his immortality?"* (1899 Harper's Magazine)

12. The return of the Jews to their ancient homeland is foretold by many of the prophets. (Ezekiel 37:1-14; Isaiah. 11:11-12 ) It would seem that the return occurs in two stages, with the first stage being a return in unbelief (what we are seeing now), and then a later return accompanied by a sincere worship of YAHWEH.

13. Scholars differ somewhat on the exact dates associated with Creation, the Noahic Flood, and Babel. Taking the Bible at face value does rule out periods of time involving millions or billions of years. All three of these events had to have happened in a period of time of not more than a few thousand years.

**CHAPTER TEN**

1. Peter W. Stoner, *Science Speaks.* Chicago: Moody Press, 1963.

2. See Chapter Seven, end note-3

3. Or 1 in $10^{17}$

4. 2 Corinthians 11:14

5. From this point on, the personal name of YAHWEH is substituted with "Lord" (upper and lower case), instead of "LORD" (all capital letters). The reason for this is that we have progressed from the Old Testament part of the Bible, which was largely written in Hebrew, to the New Testament

which was written in Greek. To the reader of that day, depending on the context, Lord and Lᴏʀᴅ usually referred to the same person—Yᴀʜᴡᴇʜ. To avoid confusion, I will continue to use Lᴏʀᴅ in my commentary.

6.  This should not be thought of as being some sort of genetic link—that the sin nature can be found in a string of DNA. The association is purely spiritual. God held man responsible for the rebellion in the Garden of Eden, and because of that *"...just as sin entered the world through one man, and death through sin, and in this way death came to all men, because all sin..."* (Romans 5:12 NIV) We all have a human father, therefore we are all sinful. Jesus' father was God, the Holy Spirit, so He had God's nature.

7.  Mary had other children but by Joseph. Jesus had four half-brothers and at least two sisters. Matthew 12:46-47; 13:55-56; Mark 6:2-3; John 7:5; Acts 1:14

8.  A fragrant perfume

9.  Arnold G. Fruchtenbaum, *Messianic Christology,* Ariel Ministries, 1998, p. 108.

10. The word "person" is not the best word, but language fails us at this point. "Person" is the most common word used in reference to the Trinity in spite of its known lack.

11. For more information on the Trinity see: http://www.bible.org/page. asp?page_id=215

## Chapter Eleven

1.  John was imprisoned by Herod Antipas, son of Herod the Great. John had spoken against Herod's sin, that of living with his half-brother's wife.

## Chapter Twelve

## Chapter Thirteen

1.  Emphatic personal pronoun "I" followed by present indicative active (*"...at this present time while I am speaking, I Am."*)

2.  I have not included all the details of the trial and crucifixion. Of some significance, at this point, is this event: *"As they led him away, they seized Simon from Cyrene, who was on his way in from the country, and put the cross on him and made him carry it behind Jesus."* Luke 23:26 NIV

3.  Whiston, *The Works of Josephus,* p. 720.

4.  J. W. Shepard, *The Christ of the Gospels,* Eerdmans, Grand Rapids, 1964 p. 604 as quoted by Pentecost, *The Words and Works of Jesus Christ,* p. 487

5.  John F. Walvoord, Roy B. Zuck, *The Bible Knowledge Commentary,* 1983, SP Publications, Inc. p. 340.
    Pentecost, *The Words and Works of Jesus Christ,* p. 487.
    Warren W. Wiersbe, *The Bible Exposition Commentary,* Vol. 1, 1989, SP Publications, Inc. p. 384.

6.  A battalion is an army unit consisting of 300 to 1000 men.

7.  The exact sequence of the resurrection morning events is not recorded. I have given one of the more likely scenarios.

## Chapter Fourteen

1.  Forgiveness based on atonement is more complex than a simple *covering* for sin. Atonement also includes God's wrath on sin and propitiation, concepts I touch on under other headings.

2.  Compare Romans 10:9-13

3. *For while we were still helpless, at the right time Christ died for the ungodly.* Romans 5:6 (NASB)

4. We readily agree that someone who is really bad should be punished—Hitler, Stalin and Pol Pot all deserve Hell. It is those who are just a "little bad" that cause us questions. The Bible does clearly teach that great sinners will be punished severely, and lesser sinners will be punished less severely—but all will be punished. To only punish some sinners would not be just. Hell is a matter of God's justice. Love is not in the picture.

   Some struggle with the length of the punishment, the fact that it is eternal. There are several different ways of looking at this:

   Hell is the consequence for sin, not its cure. Gehenna is not a reformatory. No amount of time spent in Hell makes a person fit for Heaven. Since any sin is an eternal offense against an infinite God, the rightful consequence must also be eternal.

   Since the concept of time is hard to grasp let's compare it to money. Let's suppose that the condemned sinner has an **unlimited supply of wealth**. If God's punishment was a fine how much would he have to fine the sinner for it to be a just punishment? If the fine was $10,000 the sinner would have thousands more of his own. A $10,000 fine would be no punishment at all. The same could be said for any other amount of money. If the fine was $1 billion, the sinner would still have billions of his own. It is only if the sinner is fined everything he has that it amounts to any consequence. For God to be just, the sinner must be punished, and it is only when the sinner loses all, that he has lost anything. When you replace wealth with time you see why the punishment is eternal.

5. According to Temple custom, the time of the morning sacrifice was 9:00 AM (the time when Christ was placed on the cross according to Mark 15:25). Jesus died at the time of the evening sacrifice, 3:00 p.m. See Luke 23:44-46.

6. http://www.bible.org/qa.asp?topic_id=13&qa_id=305; and http://www.bible.org/page.asp?page_id=2505

7. For simplicity of understanding, I have reduced the phrase, *"the angel of the LORD,"* to simply *"the LORD,"* a synonym for YAHWEH.

8. The word *Satan* means *accuser*.

9. In the book of Romans, *justification* is used in reference to God declaring the sinner righteous. In the book of James, the same word is used in reference to man declaring the deeds of a believer to be good deeds, or righteous deeds. The context reveals the direction of the word usage.

## CHAPTER FIFTEEN

1. Approx. 27% of the Bible is prophecy, either completed or yet to be fulfilled.

2. Another word for "sin"

3. This is often referred to as your position in Christ.

4. The word "have" is present tense, signifying that eternal life is a present possession.

5. Some English Bibles use the term *flesh* in reference to our human nature.

6. Josephus, the first-century historian, also records this man's death.

7. Saul's name was changed to Paul.

## APPENDIX

1. Based on computer analysis

GOODSEED® International is a not-for-profit organization that exists for the purpose of clearly communicating the contents of this book in this language and others. We invite you to contact us if you are interested in ongoing projects or translations.

## GOODSEED® International

P. O. Box 3704
Olds, Alberta T4H 1P5
CANADA

Bus: 403 556 9959
Fax: 403 556 9950
info@goodseed.com

| | |
|---|---|
| GOODSEED Australia | 1800 89 7333 |
| | info.au@goodseed.com |
| GOODSEED Canada | 800 442 7333 |
| | info.ca@goodseed.com |
| BONNESEMENCE Canada | 888 314 3623 |
| Service en français | info.qc@goodseed.com |
| GOODSEED UK | 0800 073 6340 |
| | info.uk@goodseed.com |
| GOODSEED USA | 888 654 7333 |
| | info.us@goodseed.com |

**goodseed**
see·hear·understand

**www.goodseed.com**